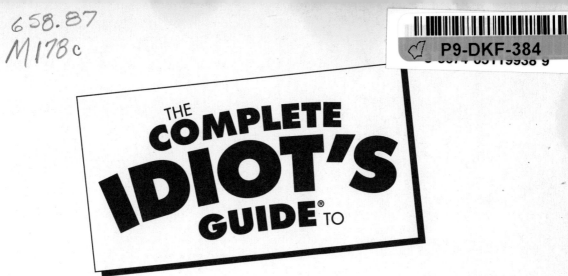

eBay®

Second Edition

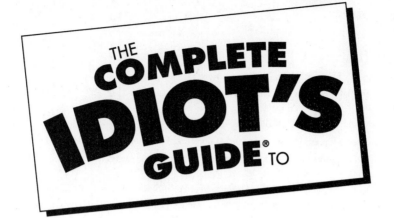

eBay®

Second Edition

by Lissa McGrath and Skip McGrath

ALPHA

A member of Penguin Group (USA) Inc.

ALPHA BOOKS

Published by the Penguin Group

Penguin Group (USA) Inc., 375 Hudson Street, New York, New York 10014, USA

Penguin Group (Canada), 90 Eglinton Avenue East, Suite 700, Toronto, Ontario M4P 2Y3, Canada (a division of Pearson Penguin Canada Inc.)

Penguin Books Ltd., 80 Strand, London WC2R 0RL, England

Penguin Ireland, 25 St. Stephen's Green, Dublin 2, Ireland (a division of Penguin Books Ltd.)

Penguin Group (Australia), 250 Camberwell Road, Camberwell, Victoria 3124, Australia (a division of Pearson Australia Group Pty. Ltd.)

Penguin Books India Pvt. Ltd., 11 Community Centre, Panchsheel Park, New Delhi—110 017, India

Penguin Group (NZ), 67 Apollo Drive, Rosedale, North Shore, Auckland 1311, New Zealand (a division of Pearson New Zealand Ltd.)

Penguin Books (South Africa) (Pty.) Ltd., 24 Sturdee Avenue, Rosebank, Johannesburg 2196, South Africa

Penguin Books Ltd., Registered Offices: 80 Strand, London WC2R 0RL, England

Publisher: *Marie Butler-Knight*
Editorial Director: *Mike Sanders*
Senior Managing Editor: *Billy Fields*
Acquisitions Editor: *Tom Stevens*
Development Editor: *Nancy D. Lewis*
Senior Production Editor: *Janette Lynn*
Copy Editor: *Krista Hansing Editorial Services, Inc.*

Cartoonist: *Steve Barr*
Cover Designer: *Rebecca Batchelor*
Book Designer: *Trina Wurst*
Indexer: *Brad Herriman*
Layout: *Ayanna Lacey*
Proofreader: *Laura Caddell*

Contents at a Glance

Part 1:   **Getting Started**   1

1 How It Works   3
   *How to register, what to do if you forget your user ID/
   password, basic eBay security, and how to spot fake e-mails.*

2 It's All About the Money!   19
   *Paying for items you've won, and how PayPal compares to
   your other options.*

3 Navigating Without a Compass   29
   *Exploring the eBay home page—and using the site map if
   you get lost—and browsing auctions by category.*

4 My eBay   37
   *Everything you need to know about My eBay, My Messages,
   favorites, and account options, and ways to customize what
   you see.*

Part 2:   **Buying on eBay**   55

5 Finding What You Want to Buy   57
   How to search effectively and narrow your results.

6 The Listing Page   75
   *Exploring the listing page and looking for the right
   information.*

7 Advanced Research   87
   *Researching the item and seller to make sure you're getting
   a good deal from a trustworthy seller.*

8 Bidding to Win   103
   *The best days, times, and sniping techniques for getting
   good deals. How to get a Buy It Now price when one wasn't
   listed.*

9 Rules and Retractions   113
   Rules for eBay buyers, when and how you can retract a bid.

10 Once You've Won   121
   *Contacting your seller, and what to do if you can't reach
   him. Leaving feedback and Detailed Seller Ratings.*

11 Avoiding Fraud and Fakes   135
*Identifying and avoiding the various types of fraud, and
spotting fake or counterfeit merchandise. How to use eBay's
Resolution Center if something goes wrong and you have a
dispute with the seller.*

Part 3:   Getting Ready to Sell on eBay   149

12 Getting Started as a Seller   151
*Getting your eBay and PayPal accounts geared up for
selling. Rules for eBay sellers and items that cannot be
sold on eBay.*

13 What Can I Sell on eBay and Where Do I Find It?   169
*Locating new and used items, and the quick, easy research
to see if it's worth selling them on eBay.*

14 What It Will Cost You   179
*All the basic fees and optional upgrades for eBay.com, and
where to find the information for eBay's international sites.*

15 Pictures That Sell Products   199
*Making the most of your items with good auction
photography. How eBay's VeRO copyright program
affects you.*

Part 4:   Creating Your Listing   217

16 Describing Your Item   219
*How to write a keyword-rich listing title, select the best
category, and upload photographs to your auction.*

17 Writing Your Listing Description   239
*What to say to get the bids, and how to make your listing
look more appealing to buyers.*

18 Choosing Your Listing Type   249
*The types of listings you'll find on eBay and when you
should use each of them.*

19 Choosing the Listing Details   257
*The final Sell Your Item form details, including the start-
ing price, duration, shipping rates, returns policy, and sales
tax.*

20 Optional Listing Upgrades   281
*What you get for your money and when it is worth using
upgrades (Bold, Listing Designer, Scheduled Listing, and so on).*

Part 5:   **During and After the Auction**   **293**

21   Tracking and Revising Your Item   295
My eBay for sellers, plus how to fix mistakes, change your starting price, or cancel a bid/listing.

22   Post-Sale Customer Service and Shipping Tips   307
How to print a shipping label through eBay. Plus, customer service, packaging, and shipping techniques that will get you positive feedback.

23   The What-Ifs   325
Answers to common questions, such as "What if my item didn't sell?" and "What if the buyer doesn't pay?" Includes a look at the Resolution Center from the seller's perspective.

24   Building and Monitoring Your Seller Reputation   343
Using eBay tools to build a good reputation and make buyers more comfortable purchasing from you. How to monitor your seller performance using the Seller Dashboard.

25   Taking the Next Step   359
Learn how to take your eBay hobby to the next level and start a part-time or even full-time eBay business.

Appendixes

A   Glossary   375

B   Where Do I Go from Here?   381

C   Quick Reference Tips   385

Index   391

Contents

Part 1: Getting Started   **1**

1 How It Works   **3**

What Is eBay?..4
    What eBay Is Not..4
    Introduction to eBay Terms..4
Setting Up Your Free eBay Account 6
    Registering as a Buyer 7
    Why Is a Secure Password Important?..............................9
    Secret Questions...10
    Logging On 12
    What If I Forget My User ID or Password? 13
How Secure Is eBay?..14
Phishing for E-Mails 15

2 It's All About the Money!   **19**

What Is PayPal?..20
Setting Up Your PayPal Account......................................20
Adding Your Bank Account and Getting PayPal Verified 23
Adding Your Credit Card and Getting a Confirmed Address....25
Instant Transfers...26
Buying from Overseas 26
Personal vs. Premier PayPal Accounts 27
Other Payment Options..28

3 Navigating Without a Compass   **29**

The eBay Home Page 29
    Signing In 30
The Navigation Tabs...30
    Buy 31
    Sell...32
    My eBay 32
    Community 33
    Help 34
The Site Map...35

4 My eBay   37

Activity 38
   Items You're Watching *38*
   Adding a Note to an Item You're Watching *40*
   Bidding *41*
   Won *41*
   Didn't Win *45*
   Customizing Your Summary *46*
   Summary Links *47*
Messages 49
Account 50
   Personal Information *51*
   Addresses *52*
   Notification Preferences *52*
   Site Preferences *53*
   Other Account Options *53*

Part 2: Buying on eBay   55

5 Finding What You Want to Buy   57

The Search Results Page 58
   Changing the Display Order *59*
   Customizing the Search Results Page *60*
   Adjusting the Listing Types *61*
   Why Do So Many Listings Offer Free Shipping? *61*
   Featured Items *62*
   Why Do Some Listing Titles Look Different? *62*
   Gallery Plus *62*
Browsing by Picture 63
Using Keywords in Your Search 64
   Common Acronyms and Abbreviations *65*
   Misspellings Can Equal Major Bargains *66*
Advanced Use of the eBay Search Engine 66
   Exact Phrase *67*
   Either/Or Words *67*
   Excluding Words *67*
   Alternative Endings *68*
   Putting It All Together *68*
   Saved Searches *68*
Refining Your Search 69

Selecting Your Preferences...71
Product Pages 72

6 The Listing Page   **75**

Listing Summary 76
   Seller Information *78*
   What Do Icons After User IDs Mean? *78*
Listing Tabs 80
   Description *80*
   Shipping and Payments *81*
Types of Listing 81
   Buy It Now Auction *82*
   Fixed-Price Listings *83*
   Best Offer *84*
   eBay Store Inventory *85*
   Restricted Access *86*

7 Advanced Research   **87**

How Much Is Too Much? 88
Comparing Items..90
What About Shipping Costs? 92
   Maximum Shipping Cost *94*
Overseas Sellers 94
Seller Feedback...96
   Recent Feedback Ratings *97*
   Detailed Seller Ratings (DSRs) *99*
   Detailed Item Information *100*
It's All About Me 101
Buying on eBay Motors 101

8 Bidding to Win   **103**

When and How Much to Bid 103
Reserve-Price Auctions 105
   Second Chance Offers for Reserve-Price Auctions *105*
Placing Your Bid..106
   Spotting an International Seller *108*
   I Need It Now, but There Is No Buy It Now Price *108*
   Sniping Techniques *109*
   How Much Do I Bid? *111*
   Why Was I Outbid? *111*

9 Rules and Retractions **113**

eBay Rules for Buyers 113
Can I Retract a Bid I've Placed? 115
Time Restrictions for Bid Retractions 117
How to Report Listing Violations 118
Report This Item 118

10 Once You've Won **121**

Contacting Your Seller 121
Requesting an Invoice 122
What If I Can't Reach My Seller? 123
eBay Checkout 124
Paying Using PayPal 125
International Transactions 128
Giving and Receiving Feedback 128
What to Write in Your Feedback Comment 129
When a Negative Feedback Comment Is Appropriate 129
Detailed Seller Ratings 130
How to Leave Feedback 130
Can Feedback Be Removed? 132
Follow-Up Feedback Comments 132
Reply to Feedback Comments 133
When Is It Okay to Purchase from an eBay Seller Off
eBay? 133

11 Avoiding Fraud and Fakes **135**

Types of Fraud and How to Avoid Them 136
Seller Impersonation 136
Account Takeover 137
Inaccurate Descriptions and Photos 138
Fake or Counterfeit Merchandise 138
Nonexistent Products 139
Escrow Fraud 140
What If I Didn't Get My Item or It Wasn't What I Was
Expecting? 141
eBay Resolution Center 142
PayPal Buyer Protection 144
Card Chargeback and Insurance Programs 144
buySAFE 145
Square Trade Warranty Services 146

Part 3:   Getting Ready to Sell on eBay   149

12   Getting Started as a Seller   151

Registering as a Seller 152
The Abridged Version of How to List an Auction 152
eBay Rules for Sellers..154
    Selling Practices Policy *154*
    The Short List of Banned Items.....................................*155*
    Shill Bidding *156*
    Fee Avoidance *157*
    Solicitation of an Off-eBay Sale....................................*158*
    Seller Nonperformance *159*
PayPal for Sellers...160
    Remove the Withdrawal Limit Using Your Social Security
      Number.. *161*
    Upgrade Your Account *161*
    Customized PayPal Tools for eBay Sellers *162*
    PayPal Preferred *163*
    End of Auction Email *164*
    Refunds *165*

13   What Can I Sell on eBay and Where Do I Find It?   169

Where to Find Items to Sell..170
    Items from Your Home...*170*
    Yard Sales...*171*
    Making Sure Your Effort Is Worthwhile *172*
    Trading Assistant Consignment Program *173*
    Closeout Section of Outlet Stores..................................*174*
    Thrift Stores..*174*
How Do I Know What Will Sell?......................................175
    Third-Party Research Tools *176*
When Should I Sell? 177

14   What It Will Cost You   179

eBay Auction Fees 180
    Insertion and Final Value Fees *180*
    Listing Upgrades *183*
    International Site Visibility *183*
    Buy It Now...*184*
    Reserve-Price Auction *184*

Fixed-Price Listings 185
  Fixed-Price Listing Insertion Fees 185
  Fixed-Price Listing Final Value Fees 185
  Fixed-Price Listing Optional Listing Upgrades 187
  Listings With Variations 188
eBay Stores Fees 189
  Monthly Subscription 189
  Insertion and Final Value Fees 189
  Optional Listing Upgrades for eBay Store Inventory 191
Comparing the Fees for Auctions, Fixed-Price Listings,
  and eBay Store Inventory 191
  eBay Picture Hosting 193
eBay Motors Fees 194
  Insertion and Successful Listing Fees 194
PayPal Seller Fees 196

15 Pictures That Sell Products   199

Camera Specifics 200
How to Set Up Your Shots 200
  Lighting 201
  White Balance 202
  Tripod 203
  Optical Zoom vs. Digital Zoom 203
  Photograph Composition 204
Common Photography Errors and How to Fix Them 205
  Photography Tools That Make Your Life Easier 213
Editing Your Photos 213
  File Sizes for Uploading to eBay 214
Stock Photography, Copyright, and VeRO 215
  Minimizing the eBay Picture Hosting Fees 216

Part 4: Creating Your Listing   217

16 Describing Your Item   219

eBay's Sell Your Item Form.. 219
  Category Selection 220
  Product Details 222
  Customizing the Sell Your Item Form to Show Other Options ... 224
Writing Your Listing Title.. 225
  Incorrect Spellings Can Increase Sales 229

When and How to Use a Subtitle 231
Item Specifics...232
Uploading Pictures...233
Basic and Standard Uploaders 236

17 Writing Your Listing Description   239

Writing the Description..240
All About the HTML Editor 241
But I'm No Shakespeare! 242
Features and Benefits 244
Listing Designer 247
Tracking Your Traffic..248

18 Choosing Your Listing Type   249

Types of Listing...249
Lot Auction...250
Buy It Now 252
Fixed-Price Listing...253
Best Offer..254
Multiple-Item Fixed-Price Listing 255

19 Choosing the Listing Details   257

Selling Format...258
Reserve Price 261
Buy It Now Price 262
Fixed-Price Listing..263
More Selling Specifics 263
Duration 264
Scheduled Start...264
Best and Worst Days to End Your Auction............................265
eBay Giving Works 266
Payment Methods...267
Shipping Information 268
Flat-Rate vs. Calculated Shipping 269
Flat-Rate Shipping 269
Calculated Shipping 271
Insurance and Tracking..271
Free Shipping 273
International Shipping and Customs 274

Combined Shipping Discounts 275
Handling Time 275
Item Location 275
Buyer Requirements and Return Policy 276
Return Policy 277
Paying Taxes 278

20 Optional Listing Upgrades **281**

Title Upgrades 282
Gallery Plus (35¢/$1) 282
Subtitle (50¢/$1.50) 283
Bold ($2/$4) 284
Featured First 285
Upgrade Packages 286
Value Pack (65¢/$2) 286
Free Alternatives to the Sell Your Item Form 286
Auctiva 288
Using the Free Auctiva Scrolling Gallery to Increase
*   Multiple Sales* 289

Part 5: During and After the Auction **293**

21 Tracking and Revising Your Item **295**

My eBay for Sellers 296
Active Selling 296
Items I've Sold 298
Unsold 300
Fixing Mistakes During the Auction 300
Before the First Bid 300
Revising Your Item After the First Bid or Within 12 Hours
*   of Auction End* 301
Raising or Lowering the Starting Price 301
When a Buyer Asks for a Buy It Now Price 302
Cancelling a Bid 302
Cancelling an Auction 303
Managing Your Blocked Buyers 305

22 Post-Sale Customer Service and Shipping Tips   **307**

Customer Service 308
  E-Mail Example for PayPal eCheck Payment............................ *309*
  E-Mail Example for When Payment Clears and Item Ships...... *310*
  Make It Personal *310*
Packing Your Item..311
  Shipping Supplies.. *312*
  Safe Shipments *313*
  Extras to Include in the Package..................................... *314*
Create a Shipping Label Through eBay...............................314
  Insurance *317*
  Shipping to International Destinations *317*
  USPS International Services... *318*
  Free USPS Pickup from Your Door.................................. *319*
Leave Feedback 319
Enticing Buyers to Purchase More....................................320
  Combined/Free Shipping.. *320*
  Add-On Selling Strategies *321*
  Offers for Repeat Buyers *321*
  Information Products *322*

23 The What-Ifs   **325**

What If My Item Doesn't Sell? 325
  Relisting Options... *327*
  Insertion Fee Credit.. *327*
What If the Buyer Doesn't Respond to My End of Auction
  Email? 328
  Sending an Invoice.. *329*
  Follow-Up E-Mails.. *330*
  Find the Buyer's Telephone Number *331*
What If the Buyer Still Doesn't Pay? 333
  Report Unpaid Item.. *333*
  Cancel Transaction... *334*
  Filing an Unpaid Item Claim *336*
  Unpaid Item Assistant *337*
  Second Chance Offer... *338*
What If I Have Another Similar Item to Sell?.....................340

24   Building and Monitoring Your Seller Reputation   343

Self-Promotion Pages...344
  About Me *344*
  My World..*345*
  Reviews and Guides *346*
Feedback Profile 348
  Negative Feedback *348*
  Replying to Feedback Received *349*
  Revising Negative Feedback *350*
  Requesting a Feedback Revision *351*
buySAFE and ID Verify 352
  Becoming ID Verified...*352*
Tracking Your Performance with the Seller Dashboard...........353
  How Important Are Detailed Seller Ratings? *355*
  PowerSeller Discounts...*355*
Search Visibility Analysis Tool...356

25   Taking the Next Step   359

Can I Really Make a Steady Income from eBay?.....................360
What to Sell..360
Organizing Your Business 362
  Business Licensing, Taxes, and Insurance *363*
  Insurance...*365*
  Equipment and Software..*365*
Automating Your Auctions..366
Wholesale Product Sourcing 367
  Drop-Shipping on eBay...*368*
  Trade Shows and Gift/Merchandise Marts *369*
Consignment Selling for Others...370
Beyond eBay 372
  Getting Your Own Website...*373*
  Selling Up River..*373*
  Etsy..*373*

Appendixes

A   Glossary   375

B   Where Do I Go from Here?   381

C   Quick Reference Tips   385

    Index   391

Introduction

In my opinion, eBay is one of the greatest marketplaces in the world. Where else can you find the girl next door competing with—and succeeding against—big corporations? Or find rare antiquities for sale right next to the latest video game? Or do all your holiday shopping from the comfort of your own home, avoiding the crowds, getting better prices, and having far more fun doing it?

When eBay started, people scoffed at the basic premise that you could create an online platform where complete strangers would buy from and sell to each other based on nothing but trust.

Before eBay, could you imagine reading a classified ad for something expensive, mailing your money to someone in a distant city (or country), and waiting for the item to arrive in the exact condition it was described?

Friends would have called you crazy and sworn that you'd never see your money again. But that is exactly the business model eBay was founded on. When the dot-com bubble burst, eBay survived, and it is now one of the largest shopping sites on the Internet.

It doesn't matter whether you're a student in college, you've been retired for a decade, or you're anywhere in between. Anyone can be a successful eBay buyer and, with a little instruction, a successful seller, too.

How This Book Is Organized

This book is broken up into five parts, two for buying and three for selling. The topics covered in each part are chronological based on the order in which you will need the information.

In **Part 1, "Getting Started,"** the first few chapters are for true beginners. They cover getting registered, understanding eBay security, and setting up payment methods (including setting up your PayPal account). If you've already done all this, you can skip those chapters and move on to more interesting topics. Also in this section, we talk about navigating eBay and using eBay's powerful search engine to search for items.

In **Part 2, "Buying on eBay,"** you learn how to actually buy the item you've found. I know that sounds like a simple process, but there is a lot to consider, such as when to bid, what amount to bid, what to do if you accidentally add an extra zero to your bid ($100 instead of $10), and how to use advanced buying techniques to get the best price possible. We take you through researching the item and seller to help ensure that you know who you are buying from and what exactly you are buying. We also talk about fraud-prevention techniques, as well as what to do when things go wrong.

Part 3, "Getting Ready to Sell on eBay," is the first of the selling sections. As with Part 1, the first chapter in this section covers registration (this time as a seller), eBay rules for sellers, and other basics. Also in this part, we cover how to find items to sell on eBay, which items are restricted or prohibited, what it will cost you to sell your item, and how to take professional-looking photographs and fix common photography problems.

In **Part 4, "Creating Your Listing,"** we show you, step by step, how to list an item using eBay's Sell Your Item form. We show you how to write a title that gets buyers clicking on your listing and craft an item description to close the sale. You have a lot of choices to make, but we guide you through them and show you which of the fee-based optional listing upgrades are worthwhile and which you can usually ignore so you don't end up overpaying in eBay fees. You'll learn what to do after your item is listed and how to upsell your buyers to purchase more from you now and in the future.

Part 5, "During and After the Auction," covers how to track and revise your listings as needed. We talk about My eBay for sellers, including how to track your seller performance with the Seller Dashboard. We cover all the final post-auction steps, including packing, shipping, and leaving feedback. We also preempt your "what if?" questions in Chapter 24. The final chapter of the book gives you an introduction to taking your hobby further, if you want to.

In the appendixes, you'll find a glossary of terms used throughout the book. This is a handy reference for when your mind goes blank on a specific term. You'll also find a list of top buyer and seller quick reference tips, as well as resources for how to take the next steps.

Extras

Throughout the book, you will see boxes set aside from the main text with extra tidbits of information to help you navigate eBay with ease and keep you from making typical "newbie" mistakes.

Tips

These are exactly what the name suggests: short, practical tips of things I have discovered during my years as an eBay buyer and seller.

def•i•ni•tion

These explain eBay terms (and there are a lot of them). You'll find all the definitions in this book in Appendix A.

Did You Know?

These give extra information that's not critical to the topic at hand but that's interesting nonetheless.

I Remember When ...

These boxes are anecdotes of my experiences on eBay and those of my friends. They show real-world examples to make concepts easier to understand.

Shark in the Water

Don't ignore these boxes: they're warnings about legalities and ways to prevent problems and protect yourself while enjoying your eBay experiences.

We take you through all aspects of buying and selling on eBay right from the beginning, in the order you will need the information. However, I do have to make a few assumptions:

1. You are over 18 years old.

2. You have access to a computer and an Internet connection.

3. You have access to one of the approved browser programs. Minimum requirements (newer versions also work) for Windows users: Internet Explorer 6, Mozilla Firefox 1.5, AOL. For Mac users: Mozilla Firefox 1.5, Apple Safari 2.

4. You want to either buy or sell on eBay, or both.

That said, welcome to eBay—and let's get started!

Acknowledgments

Both Skip and I would like to acknowledge Marilyn Allen, our agent, who has been wonderful as always. Also, a big thank-you to Tom Stevens, Nancy Lewis, Janette Lynn, and all the other people at Alpha who helped produce this second edition. Each of you has brought something different to this book and made it so much better because of your input.

The biggest thank-you has to go to our spouses, who kept us sane, brought us copious amounts of coffee when we needed it instead of complaining about the long hours, and forced us to eat when we hadn't surfaced from the computer in a few days. We couldn't have done it without you!

Special Thanks to the Technical Reviewer

The Complete Idiot's Guide to eBay®, Second Edition, was reviewed by an expert who double-checked the accuracy of what you'll learn here, to help us ensure that this book gives you everything you need to know about eBay. Special thanks are extended to Kevin W. Boyd.

Kevin W. Boyd, M.B.A., M.S., is a multi award-winning eBay Education Specialist and published author of the books *eBay® Business at Your Fingertips, eBay® Rescue Problem Solver,* and *eBay® Rescue Profit Maker.* As a professional online marketing consultant, he has appeared on various TV and radio programs including eBay radio. Reporters have interviewed him for his insights to online entrepreneurship with published articles appearing in *Bloomberg News, Inventor's Digest, Antique Trader, The Seattle Times,* and several other newspapers and magazines. Kevin teaches beginner to advanced entrepreneurial courses at several colleges around the Pacific Northwest. The primary objective for his writing, teaching, and consulting, is to educate online sellers at all levels and equip them with the skills necessary for online entrepreneurial success. His website is www.trainingu4auctions.com.

Trademarks

All terms mentioned in this book that are known to be or are suspected of being trademarks or service marks have been appropriately capitalized. Alpha Books and Penguin Group (USA) Inc. cannot attest to the accuracy of this information. Use of a term in this book should not be regarded as affecting the validity of any trademark or service mark.

Part 1

Getting Started

Welcome to eBay! Your journey is just getting started, and it's going to be a lot of fun!

In this first part, we cover all the basics to prepare you for buying on eBay. In addition to registering with eBay and PayPal, you'll learn how to navigate the eBay site. We show you how to use eBay's new search engine, Refine Search, and set Preferences to find the items you really want. You'll learn about different types of listings (no, eBay is not all auctions), get a crash course in My eBay, learn how to customize the search results page, and much more.

Sure, you could muddle through on your own, but why bother when you have two experts here to show you how to do it properly right from the beginning?

How It Works

In This Chapter

- ◆ What eBay is and isn't
- ◆ Getting registered the right way
- ◆ Security and protecting your account
- ◆ Spotting a scam e-mail instantly
- ◆ Getting to know the eBay Toolbar

Buying and selling on eBay isn't as hard as many people think. No doubt you will experience a steep learning curve as you go through this book, but learning how to find bargains and sell profitably on eBay is quite simple if you follow the steps.

You don't need to know every little detail about eBay before you get started. In this first chapter, I show you the basics you *do* need to know. As you read through the rest of the book, I introduce other critical elements that will affect your success on eBay—whether as a buyer, seller, or both.

What Is eBay?

eBay is an immense online marketplace where you can find virtually any item, in any condition, quickly and easily.

Think of eBay as the biggest outlet mall in the world, filled with stores for every type of product you can think of. One entire floor of the mall is a garage sale full of used items, while other sections are dedicated to electronics, antiques, clothing, toys, home and garden items, and more.

eBay itself does not sell products. It simply provides a marketplace where buyers and sellers can connect to conduct transactions. eBay is essentially a broker facilitating the sale—or, if you prefer, the landlord of the outlet mall. Sellers pay fees to eBay to "rent" space for their listings, but it is completely free for buyers.

What eBay Is Not

eBay is not solely a place for weird and wacky items. A few years back, crazy items were selling on eBay for thousands of dollars. The grilled cheese sandwich with the image of the Virgin Mary on it (sold for $28,000), and William Shatner's kidney stone (sold for $25,000) are just two examples. Typically, these types of items were bought by casinos or other businesses using them as PR gimmicks. The tightening economy and eBay's repositioning of itself in the marketplace has slowed this trend of wacky items. They're still out there if you search for them, but the vast majority of the items you'll find on eBay now are products of interest to the general population at competitive prices.

Selling on eBay is not a get-rich-quick scheme. If you think you're going to become a millionaire within the first few weeks you start selling, you're sorely mistaken. Sure, it's possible to make a fortune from selling on eBay (and it has been done), but it takes work, time, and the skills I'm going to teach you.

eBay is also not solely for used items. You will find a variety of items in new, used, and refurbished condition.

Introduction to eBay Terms

In the next few chapters, you'll come across a few technical terms that I cover in detail in later chapters. I've listed the most important terms here, but you'll also find them in the glossary.

Buy It Now   A way of purchasing an item immediately, without waiting for the auction to end. This is an option the seller chooses, so not all auctions have a Buy It Now price.

My eBay	The hub of all your eBay activity. You can see the items you've won, lost, bid on, or watched here, along with items that you currently have listed, have sold, or did not sell.
My Messages	Located inside My eBay. All e-mails sent to you by other eBay members, or by eBay, are displayed here. Most of these messages are also sent to the e-mail address you registered with eBay.
PayPal	The preferred payment service for eBay. It allows sellers to accept credit cards without having an expensive merchant credit card account and prevents the seller from ever seeing the buyer's credit card details. You must use PayPal to be eligible for fraud protection for eBay transactions.
PowerSeller	Sellers who sell at least $1,000 worth of products (not including shipping costs) per month for an average of three months and continue to reach that amount each month. To be a PowerSeller, the eBay seller must also maintain a 98 percent positive feedback rating and Detailed Seller Ratings (DSR) of 4.5 or higher in all four rating categories.
Top-Rated Seller	This is part of the PowerSeller program, but has more of an emphasis on customer service than quantity of sales. Sellers only need to sell 100 items totaling $3,000 per year to qualify financially. However, they must maintain very strict Detailed Seller Ratings. Rather than an average, they may only have a certain percentage of 1 or 2 star ratings overall. The percentage changes based on the seller's volume.
Feedback	The system eBay created to allow buyers and sellers involved in a transaction to leave a comment about the other trading partner and assign a rating for each specific aspect of the transaction. Potential buyers and sellers can view this in the member's Feedback Profile so they can be better informed about how this particular person conducts business on eBay.
Detailed Seller Ratings	Anonymous ratings the buyer can leave for the seller. This is a five-star rating system for each of the four aspects of the transaction: item as described, communication, shipping time, and shipping and handling charges. DSRs do not impact the member's feedback score and only remain for

12 months, but they are an integral part of the Best Match algorithm, and the qualification for the Top-Rated Seller program.

Setting Up Your Free eBay Account

You can make up to 15 purchases on eBay as a guest without registering. Most people who buy as a guest later come back and set up an account, so you may as well start out as you intend to go on. It's much easier to use eBay once you are properly registered, and it doesn't cost anything—just a few minutes of your time.

Shark in the Water

Unless you have a burning desire to get scammed, don't use your actual name as your user ID. Your full name is something only members involved in a transaction with you should know—not just any guy with an Internet connection.

Picking your user ID (or username) is probably the most time consuming part of getting registered, simply because of the volume of existing eBay users.

If you want to sell on eBay as well as buy, you'll want a fairly "normal" user ID, maybe a childhood nickname or something that represents who you are. You might choose a name that is related to your products if you already know what you intend to sell. For instance, if you sell only Starbucks collectibles, you might have a user ID like I_Sell_Starbucks or addictedtocoffee. You cannot use spaces, but you can use underscores, as in the first example.

eBay has some fairly specific rules about characters you can and cannot use in your eBay user ID:

 ◆ It must be six characters or more.

 ◆ You can use letters or numbers (abc123).

 ◆ You can use a single underscore (_), dash (-), or period (.) between letters or numbers.

 ◆ You cannot use two underscores (__) in a row.

 ◆ You cannot use underscores, dashes, or periods at the beginning of your user ID.

 ◆ You cannot use spaces or tabs.

 ◆ You cannot use the word *eBay* in your user ID. This is reserved for eBay employees only.

 ◆ You cannot use URLs (www.skipmcgrath.com or skipmcgrath_dot_com).

- You cannot use these symbols: @ & ' < > ! # $ %

- You cannot use profane or explicit language.

- You cannot start the user ID with *e* followed by numbers.

- You cannot use the username of another member, a trademarked name, or the name similar to another member's eBay store.

Your eBay account could be cancelled if you violate any of these rules, so be sure to read this again once you've decided on a user ID, to make sure it's acceptable.

Remember, there are over 88 million active users worldwide (as well as hundreds of millions of registered users who aren't currently active buyers or sellers), so you may find that your first choice is already taken.

Tips

> You can confirm that a user ID is available on the registration form, but if you're planning to sell on eBay more than just occasionally, it's wise to check what user IDs are already out there. As you build your reputation and attract repeat buyers, you don't want someone with a similar user ID (and products) either benefiting from or ruining your hard-earned reputation.

To check if a user ID is already taken, go to the eBay home page and click the **Community** tab. Enter the user ID in the box and click **Find A Member.** (You'll have to enter a six-digit verification code shown in an image [called a Captcha] to verify that you are a real person, not a computer program searching for user IDs.) Now it will show you if an eBay member already has that user ID, and the closest matches that are not exactly what you searched for.

You can change your user ID later, but as a seller it's better to build your brand from day one rather than change your name when you've been established for a while and risk confusing or losing your repeat buyers.

Registering as a Buyer

Now that you've chosen a user ID, it's time to register. Go to the eBay home page (www.eBay.com) and click on **Register.**

Begin by completing the personal information boxes shown in Figure 1.1.

Now scroll down to the section titled **Choose your user ID and password.** Click on the **Check your user ID** button to confirm that your choice is available (see Figure 1.2).

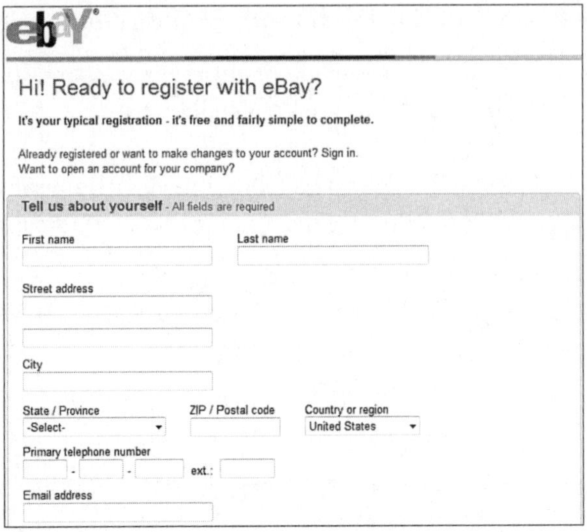

Figure 1.1

You must include your correct telephone number in case eBay or your seller needs to get hold of you. It does not set you up for telemarketing calls.

Next, you need to select a password. Your choice will go a long way toward protecting your account. If you choose something obvious or is easy to guess, you are leaving yourself open to problems.

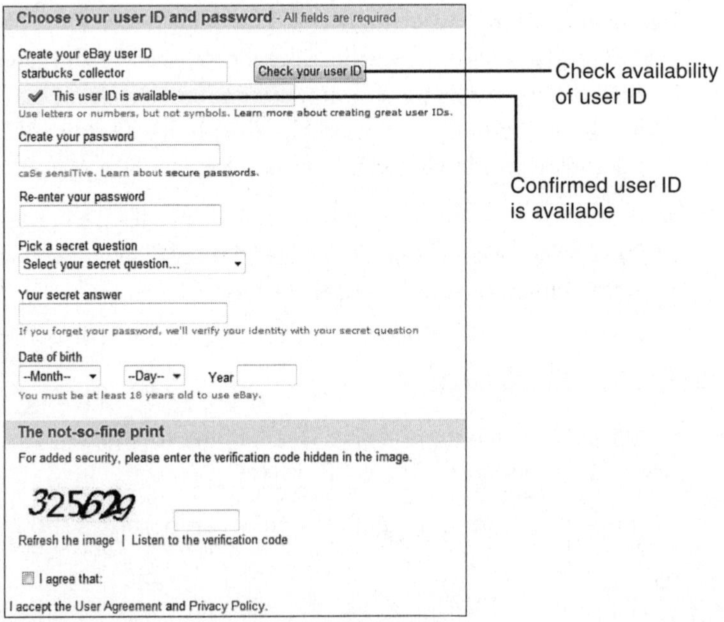

Figure 1.2

Remember to use a memorable, easy-to-spell user ID that isn't too similar to the user ID of another eBay user.

Why Is a Secure Password Important?

You might not think your eBay password is particularly important, but consider this scenario: a hacker gains access to your account while you're on vacation. The first thing he does is change the e-mail address and password so you can't log in to the account. Then he lists expensive items on short-duration fixed-price listings and undercuts all the competition's prices.

Because of your good feedback, buyers are happy to purchase and think they're getting a great deal. You don't receive any of the notifications because the e-mail address was changed. He convinces the buyer to pay him via a nonelectronic method (generally a money order), even though this is against eBay policies, and has it sent to a post office box (which he later closes). He has the money but never delivers the goods, and you come back from vacation to furious buyers who did not receive their items, threats of seller fraud, and possibly a temporary account suspension until eBay sorts it out.

Even if you're not a seller, a hacker could use your account to buy expensive items, pay using a stolen credit card, and then leave you to take the heat when the seller finds out the payment was fraudulent.

Now, as bad as these situations are, imagine how much worse it would be if your eBay and PayPal passwords were the same. This scammer would have access to all the funds you have in your PayPal account, plus your bank and credit card funds because he can purchase from anywhere that accepts PayPal using your backup funding sources.

It's important to have significantly different passwords for eBay and PayPal, and also other websites you may have registered on. In the past, hackers have obtained e-mail addresses and passwords through another company's security breach and then used them to gain access to eBay and PayPal accounts that used the same e-mail address and password. Avoiding this scam is simple—have a password dedicated only for PayPal and another only for eBay. It's just that easy.

You can see why secure passwords are important. Here are a few tips for creating a secure password:

- ◆ Use a combination of numbers, uppercase and lowercase letters, and symbols.
- ◆ Use a password of at least six to eight characters (the more, the better).
- ◆ Use random combinations of letters and numbers—not words.
- ◆ Never tell anyone your password.
- ◆ Don't set your computer to automatically remember your password.

◆ Don't use your e-mail address or anything else obvious relating to yourself (child's name, pet's name, street address, and so on).

◆ Don't use any universally obvious passwords (1234, ABCD, and so on).

Computer hackers have software that can try thousands of common password combinations, so the stronger the password (that is, harder to guess or figure out), the better.

You can change your password later if someone does discover it or you forget it, but you should do everything you can to prevent that from happening.

Above all, never write your password on a sticky note next to your computer. It may be convenient for you, but not just hackers can get into your account—think of the number of people who come in and out of your home or office space. Do you really want your clients and colleagues, the evening cleaners, your teenagers, and their friends knowing the login information for your accounts?

Kids don't always understand the "legal binding contract" part when they bid on that new $500 video game console that you refused to buy for their birthday. Or maybe it's lower-priced items and you'll hear "But Mom, it's only $80, and that's a really good price for True Religion jeans!"

You are still responsible for the purchases if your kids get into your eBay account and start buying things. Most sellers will be nice about it and cancel the bid, but they are not required to do so.

Just think, if your PayPal password were on that sticky note, too, the first you might know of your kid's new purchase could be when it shows up at your door.

Secret Questions

You may not think of the secret question as a security risk, but it could be. What do you do when you forget a password for a website? You get a new one using your secret question. So if you use obvious answers for your secret question (maybe a pet's name that is on your Facebook account, or your mother's maiden name available in the public records), you're just handing this information to a hacker.

Give some thought to the secret question and answer you choose. Your options are listed here:

1. What street did you grow up on?

2. What is your mother's maiden name?

3. What is the name of your first school?

4. What is your pet's name?

5. What is your father's middle name?

6. What is your school mascot?

I like options 1, 3, and 6 best because most people won't know that information or have easy access to finding it. Even your kids probably don't know the answers (which is a comforting thought).

Obviously, if you're still living in the same town you grew up in, options 3 and 6 might not be as secure as if you've moved across the country. Use your common sense on which answer will be hardest for someone to figure out.

Now you have to enter your date of birth and then the Captcha verification code, which ensures that you're a real person signing up, not a computer program.

When you check the **I Agree** box, you're acknowledging that you have read the terms and conditions, and agree to all eBay policies. Checking that box is legally the same as signing your name on a document stating that you have read it. So take a few minutes and read it before you "sign."

Now check your e-mail: eBay has sent you a confirmation message to the address you provided (see Figure 1.3). You have the option to change it if you can't access that e-mail account.

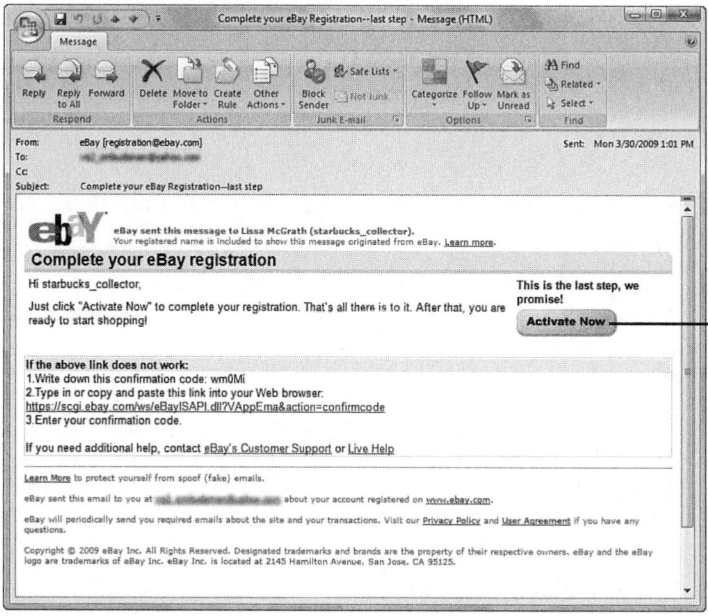

Figure 1.3

Verify that the gray text at the top of the e-mail has your full name in it and the user ID you registered with before you click on the link.

Activate your account

Just click on **Activate Now** (see Figure 1.3), and the link will take you to eBay.

Congratulations! You are now ready to start buying. We will talk about the extra steps needed to become a seller in Chapter 12.

Logging On

You can browse for items on eBay without being logged in, but if you want to watch, bid on, or buy an item, you will need to be signed in to your account. You can watch and buy items using a Guest account, but it's very limited and can get confusing when you also have a registered account. It's much better to log in and save yourself the hassle.

If you're doing some shopping around, you might want to check the **Keep me signed in for today** button (see Figure 1.4). This will keep you from having to sign in again each time you want to add an item to your watch list, go to **My eBay,** place a bid, and so on. That can save some time and frustration.

Figure 1.4

Sign In page.

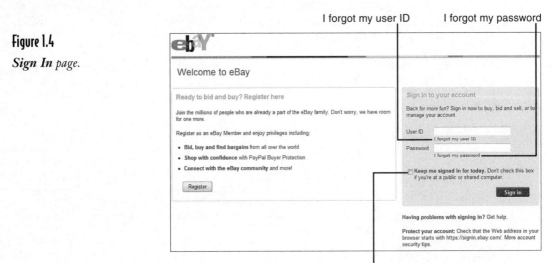

I forgot my user ID   I forgot my password

Keep me signed in for today

Shark in the Water

If you are on a public computer (such as at work, an Internet cafe, a friend's house, or the library), do not check the box to remain signed in for the day. Even if you are at work, I recommend that you just sign in as needed. It's safer to deal with the little hassle of repeated sign-ins than to enable someone to get into your account. When you're done, make sure you sign out of eBay.

Your Internet browser may offer to save the password and remember it each time. I strongly advise that you say no to this. Think about it: what is the point of having a password if you don't need to know it to gain access to the account?

What If I Forget My User ID or Password?

Don't panic! It's not the end of the world, or even your eBay account. This happens all the time, and it's a relatively simple process to get a user ID reminder or to reset your password.

If you have forgotten your user ID, follow these steps to recover it:

1. From the Sign In page, click the link marked **I forgot my user ID** (see Figure 1.4).

2. Enter the e-mail address that you used to register the account.

3. You should receive an e-mail from eBay within a minute or so with your user ID. You can then go back to the **Sign In** page and sign in (provided that you can remember your password).

If you have forgotten your password, follow these steps to create a new one:

1. From the Sign In page, click the **I forgot my password** link beneath the **Password** box.

2. Enter your eBay user ID. If you can't remember it, follow the earlier steps to have eBay e-mail it to you.

3. You will be asked to provide one of four pieces of information: the secret question that you set up at registration, your postal code (zip code), your telephone number, or your date of birth. You need to answer only one of these correctly.

4. Check your e-mail for a message from eBay and click on the link to reset your password.

5. You will be asked to enter your eBay user ID again; then click **Continue.**

6. Enter a new password. Keep in mind my earlier tips about choosing a secure password. A secure replacement password is just as important as your original one. Click **Submit Changes** when you are done.

Did You Know?

You cannot set your new password to be the same as a password you used in the past for your eBay account (eBay will prompt you if this is the case). Each time you change your eBay password, you must create an entirely new password.

How Secure Is eBay?

You have two main security issues to consider. The first is fraud, and I deal with that in Chapter 11. The other is account hijacking—someone gets into your eBay account, changes your password, and freezes you out while they perform fraudulent transactions using your user ID and hard-earned reputation.

First let me assure you that the eBay and PayPal servers are very secure. Both companies work hard to maintain the integrity of their servers and keep hackers out. It's a lot easier to trick someone into giving out their user ID and password than it is to hack into eBay or PayPal and get it.

Once you start using eBay, you will notice that you are prompted to sign in again when you go to certain areas of the site—for example, when using discussion boards, forums, and chat; searching for another user's ID; starting the listing process; or placing a bid. This is because there may be other people around your computer (particularly if you check eBay at work during your lunch break, use an Internet cafe, or have kids). It doesn't take much to view or modify your account because you didn't sign out before you went to get that cup of coffee.

If you have set up your account to stay signed in for one day, and you don't sign out of eBay when you are finished, anyone with access to your computer can go to My eBay and see your personal information. Another person cannot make any changes to your account details, but she can see your home address, the items you are selling, how much you made in the last month, what you've purchased, your bank account routing number (it hides all but the last four digits of the account number), e-mails that have been sent to you, and so on. So if you are using a public computer, make sure you sign out when you are done. If you don't want your colleagues, kids, and kids' friends knowing precisely how much you are making on eBay, you should always make it a habit to sign out when you are finished on your home and work computers, too.

Phishing for E-Mails

You would never give your user ID and password to anyone other than eBay, right? Well, what if the site looked like eBay? What if you got there by clicking a link in an e-mail that appeared to come from eBay or PayPal?

The most common way an unauthorized person gains access to an eBay user's account details is through *phishing* e-mails.

def•i•ni•tion

Phishing, or fake, e-mails look like they are sent from eBay or PayPal. They usually tell you that your account has been suspended, that you need to verify your account details, or that you haven't paid your eBay fees; they can also look like a message from another eBay member. When you click on the link, you're sent to a page that looks just like the eBay **Sign In** page. You enter your eBay user ID and password, and presto, you just gave your account information to the person who set up the scam.

Okay, so what can you do to prevent this from happening to you? Well, first look at the e-mail. Figures 1.5 and 1.6 show two e-mails I received recently. One is a genuine e-mail from eBay. The other is a phishing e-mail. Without looking at the figure captions, can you tell the difference and work out which is the genuine eBay e-mail?

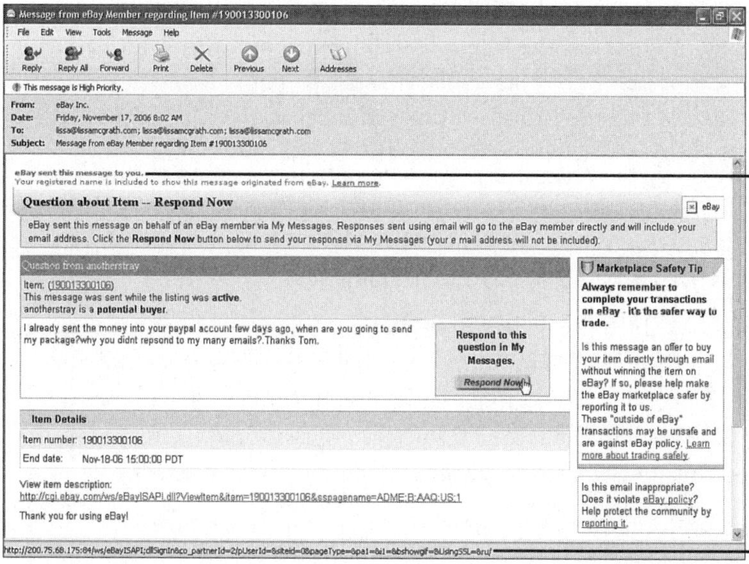

Figure 1.5

Example of a phishing e-mail.

— eBay sent this message to you

— IP address

Figure 1.6

A genuine e-mail received from eBay.

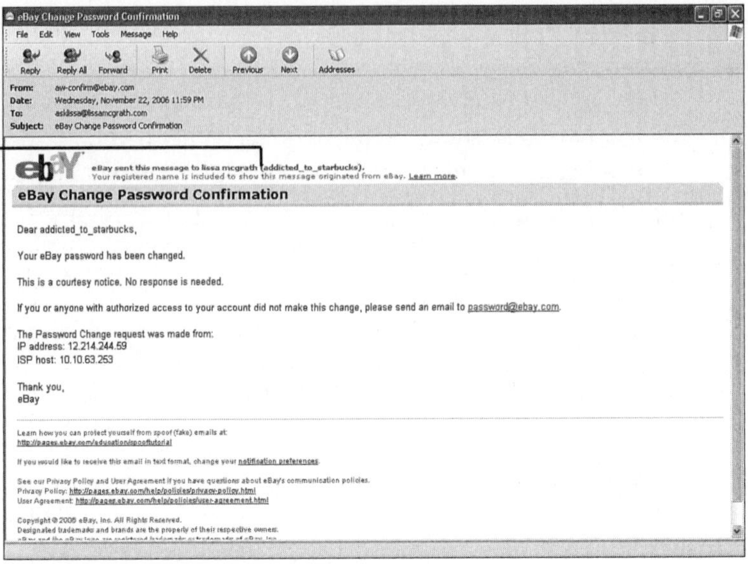

Your full name and registered eBay user ID

It's very important to learn the tricks to spotting fakes. You don't want to ignore all e-mails that look like they came from eBay because you will get genuine e-mails with special offers and important information in them that you won't want to miss.

If you spotted the fake straight away, good for you! But do you know the universal way to spot all phishing e-mails pretending to come from eBay?

Look at the gray text at the very top of each e-mail. First if an e-mail says it's from eBay and doesn't have any grey text at the top, it is definitely a fake. Now let's actually read the text. In Figure 1.5, it says "eBay sent this message to you." Beneath that, it says, "Your registered name is included to show this message originated from eBay." But it doesn't say your registered name or your user ID. It just says "you."

Now look at Figure 1.6. The bottom line is the same, but the top line is very different. It says "eBay sent this message to Lissa McGrath (addicted_to_starbucks)." Only eBay would know your actual name, user ID, and e-mail address.

Yes, a seller you have purchased from will also have this information, but these phishing e-mails are sent out in mass quantities. The scammers do not have the facility to add in each personal sentence. Hence, they try to fool you by saying "eBay sent this message to you," by using another person's name and user ID where yours should be displayed, or by saying "eBay sent you this message from <another eBay member's user ID>."

By reading this gray text, you can instantly see whether an e-mail is a fake.

Another option, if you're still unsure, is to look at the link before you click on it. In Figure 1.5, the link the scammers want me to click on is the yellow **Respond Now** button. By hovering your mouse over that link (but not actually clicking on it), you can see where that link will take you in the bottom status bar of the e-mail window. You can see that Figure 1.5 shows a string of numbers (actually, an IP address), which is obviously not eBay. The eBay **Sign In** page should always begin https://signin.ebay.com. (Note the *s* after http. That means it's a secure page.) If it doesn't start exactly this way, the site is a fake.

If you're still unsure, open a new browser window (do not click on the link in the e-mail) and go to www.eBay.com. Click the **My eBay** tab and then **Messages.** This takes you to your eBay e-mail inbox. If the message is not here, it's a fake.

The eBay Toolbar

You can take security one step further, and I suggest you do. Every step you take toward protecting your account makes you less of an easy target.

The eBay Toolbar is, in my opinion, one of eBay's best inventions (see Figure 1.7).

Account Guard

Figure 1.7

The eBay Toolbar offers many features that you can customize for exactly how you use eBay.

The toolbar is a free feature that you can download from the eBay home page, as follows:

1. Scroll to the bottom of the home page, where you'll see a line of links in bold.

2. Click on **eBay Toolbar.**

3. On the next page, click **Download Now.**

4. Follow the prompts for download and installation.

During the installation process, you are asked for your eBay and PayPal passwords. You do not have to enter this information, but I recommend that you do. This activates the Account Guard feature, which I think is the most important part of the eBay Toolbar.

Account Guard prevents you from inadvertently putting your eBay user ID and password into a fake site that looks like eBay or PayPal.

When Account Guard is on, if you attempt to enter your eBay or PayPal passwords into a site that is not either eBay or PayPal, the eBay Account Guard Alert warning box will appear telling you that you are trying to send a password to a non-eBay site (see Figure 1.8).

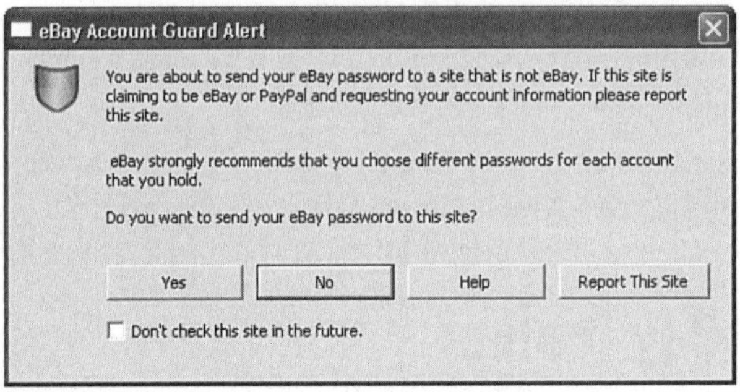

Figure 1.8

If the site is pretending to be eBay or PayPal, click the box for Report This Site.

If you have the same password for another site (which you shouldn't, but I'm sure you do), you can check the box marked **Don't check this site in the future** and then click **Yes** to send the password to the site. This prevents Account Guard from flagging that site again.

Even before you get as far as signing in, you can tell if the site is a legitimate eBay site by looking at the Account Guard button on the toolbar. If it is green, the site is verified as an eBay or PayPal site. If it is gray, it is not an official eBay or PayPal site. I strongly recommend that you download the eBay Toolbar for the Account Guard feature (you can turn off all the other features if you want).

The Least You Need to Know

♦ Choose an easy-to-remember and easy-to-type user ID.

♦ Make your password secure with letters and numbers, and never write it down near your computer.

♦ Look for your registered name and user ID in the gray text at the top of every eBay e-mail, to confirm that it is really from eBay.

♦ Download the eBay Toolbar and enter your passwords to get Account Guard protection.

It's All About the Money!

In This Chapter

- ◆ Using eBay's online payment company, PayPal
- ◆ Why and how should you get PayPal verified?
- ◆ Comparing PayPal's Personal and Premier accounts
- ◆ Using payment options other than PayPal

eBay requires you to use an electronic form of payment, such as a credit card or its own payment processor, PayPal. eBay also authorizes a few other online payment processors, but you can only get eBay's own fraud protection if you use PayPal (which I talk about in a moment).

The reason for using "paperless payments" is that it significantly cuts down on fraud. Cashier's check and money order fraud were the two biggest problems on eBay. Neither is viable now unless the seller convinces the buyer to send one of these unauthorized payments (don't do it!).

> **Tips** _____
>
> I will repeat this advice ad nauseam: *never* pay for an auction using a money order, cashier's check, Western Union, MoneyGram, or other similar payment services. If a seller won't accept anything else, look for the item you want elsewhere.

What Is PayPal?

PayPal is, in my opinion, one of the greatest inventions since, well, eBay.

I was a PayPal user years before eBay purchased the company in 2002. For me, it was an easy, cheap way to transfer money between my British bank account and my American one while I was in the process of immigrating and had bills in both countries.

Now, of course, I use PayPal for eBay. And I'm not the only one: over 90 percent of eBay buyers prefer PayPal. What's not to love? You can send an instant payment to your sellers so they can ship your items sooner, and it costs you nothing as a buyer to send a payment—not even a stamp.

You can send payments using your existing PayPal account balance, your credit card, or your bank account.

If you plan to buy frequently or to sell any items, you'll find a PayPal account indispensable. It will save you time, and you may find that you use it for non-eBay items, too. Currently, 55 percent of PayPal's revenue comes from non-eBay sources. Most websites are now setting up a PayPal checkout option, so it's becoming more widespread.

def•i•ni•tion _____

PayPal, www.PayPal.com, is an online payment company. As the go-between for buyers and sellers, it allows individuals to accept credit card payments without having a merchant credit card account, and without actually seeing the buyer's credit card details.

Setting Up Your PayPal Account

Remember, PayPal is a type of bank account. It may not have ATMs and service centers, but the same rules apply to PayPal as to any other financial institution. That's why you will be asked for quite a bit of personal information during the registration process.

Only nine steps are involved to setting up your PayPal account, and it's a quick and painless process:

1. Go to www.PayPal.com and click **Sign Up** at the top of the page (see Figure 2.1).

Figure 2.1

The look of this page changes to reflect seasonal promotions, but don't worry—the main links are always in the same place, just like on eBay.

2. Select your country and language of choice, and then click on the account type you want. I recommend that you start with a Personal account unless you know you will want to be an eBay seller. PayPal requires eBay sellers to have a Premier or Business account. You can upgrade at any time, so there's no reason to make that decision just yet.

3. On the next page, enter your personal information. The e-mail address you enter will be what your sellers and buyers see instead of an account number. Use the same e-mail address for your eBay and PayPal accounts, to make it easier for sellers to reconcile records and find your transaction if you have a question. This is also what you will use as your login.

4. Choose a secure password. Do not use the same password you used for your eBay account (particularly if your e-mail addresses are the same). Refer back to Chapter 1 for information about creating secure passwords.

5. I know, few people actually do this, but read the User Agreement and Privacy Policies before signing up. If you don't read it, you have no idea what you are agreeing to.

6. Decide whether you want to add your credit card or bank account at this point. You will want to do both eventually, but you can do this from your account page later on. If you do want to add either here, click whichever you want and follow the instructions. I cover this in more detail in a moment.

7. Now go to your e-mail account and look for an e-mail from PayPal. Click **Activate** (see Figure 2.2).

8. A new browser window opens to a page for you to enter your password and click **Confirm.**

9. You are prompted to enter two security questions. As I mentioned when we covered eBay registration in Chapter 1, don't pick answers that are obvious. The fewer people who can figure out the answer, the better.

Figure 2.2

*If you're concerned about the validity of the e-mail, hover your mouse over the **Activate** link. Look at the bottom of the e-mail box. If it shows https://www.paypal.com/, you know it is genuine. Make sure there is a slash (/) directly after the .com.*

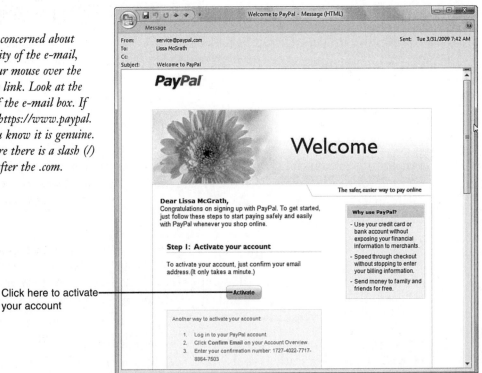

Click here to activate your account

See, that wasn't so painful, was it? Now you have a PayPal account, and you can receive up to $500 a month from other people. However, you must add either a credit card or a bank account to be able to send any money.

I recommend adding both a credit card and a bank account: a bank account will make you *PayPal Verified,* and a credit card will give you a *Confirmed address.* Both are preferred by buyers and sellers.

def•i•ni•tion

Being **PayPal Verified** simply means that PayPal has verified your identity and has removed the spending limits on your account. A **Confirmed address** is the billing address for your credit card that PayPal has confirmed as accurate. PayPal used to require sellers to ship only to a Confirmed address to receive fraud protection, but this requirement has been lifted. Even so, many sellers still state they will ship only to Confirmed addresses.

Adding Your Bank Account and Getting PayPal Verified

Figure 2.3 shows what you will see each time you log in to your PayPal account. In the **Notifications** box, you will see **Add Your Bank Account.** Grab your checkbook and click on this link.

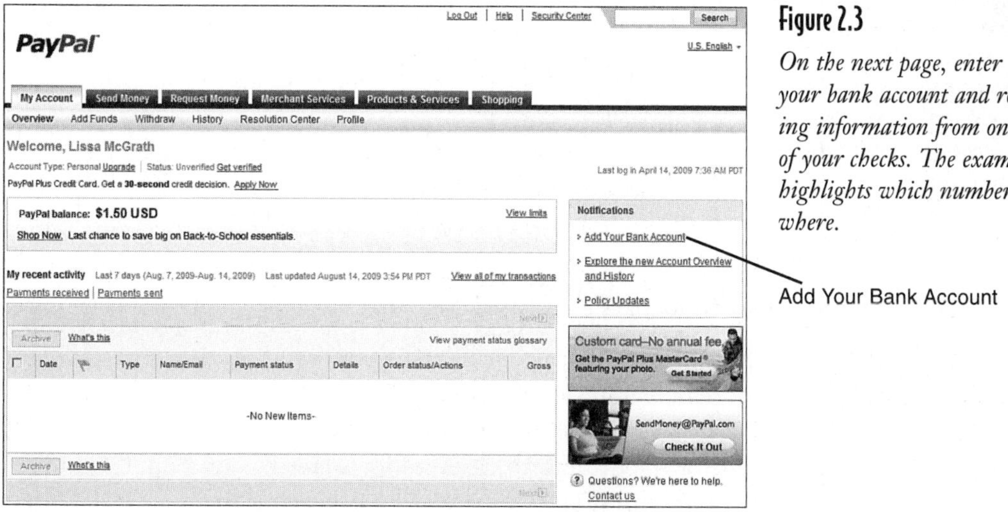

Figure 2.3

On the next page, enter your bank account and routing information from one of your checks. The example highlights which numbers go where.

Add Your Bank Account

Now you have to confirm your bank account. This proves that you have access to this account and aren't just adding it from a check you received from someone else. You have two options: you can instantly confirm it by entering your online banking login details, or you can have PayPal deposit a couple of very small amounts into your account, which you then verify to PayPal after they show up in your account.

Tips

You are allowed only one PayPal account per bank account. So if you want to have a second PayPal account and you don't have two checking accounts, you can use your savings account number.

Personally, I don't like the idea of giving out my banking login information to anyone. If you do decide to go this route, I recommend that you change the password for your online banking when confirmation is complete. PayPal doesn't save that information after the confirmation, but I like to be overcautious regarding my banking security.

The alternative takes two or three days. When you see the deposits show up in your account, write them down and go back to PayPal and sign in. Now, you'll see a link in the **Notifications** box to **Confirm bank account** (see Figure 2.4). Click on this link, enter the deposit amounts, and click **Submit.**

Figure 2.4

*The **Notifications** box reminds you of account specific tasks that you still have outstanding as well as new changes from PayPal.*

View limits

| My Account | Send Money | Request Money | Merchant Services | Products & Services | Shopping |

Overview   Add Funds   Withdraw   History   Resolution Center   Profile

Welcome, Lissa McGrath

Account Type: Personal Upgrade | Status: Unverified Get verified
PayPal Plus Credit Card. Get a **36-second** credit decision. Apply Now

Last log in August 14, 2009 3:52 PM PDT

PayPal balance: $1.50 USD   View limits

Shop Now. Last chance to save big on Back-to-School essentials.

Notifications

› Explore the new Account Overview and History

My recent activity   Last 7 days (Aug. 7, 2009–Aug. 14, 2009)   Last updated August 14, 2009 4:17 PM PDT   View all of my transactions
Payments received | Payments sent

› Confirm bank account

› Policy Updates

Confirm bank account

Congratulations, you are now PayPal Verified. See, that wasn't so painful, was it?

If you choose to stop here and just have your bank account funding all your transactions, each payment you send will be an eCheck. This takes four to five days to clear. Sellers do not like eChecks because they disrupt their flow of selling and shipping items. They have to wait for the eCheck to clear before sending your item. Of course, this also means you will wait almost an extra week to receive your item.

Your alternative is to transfer money from your bank account into your PayPal account before you need it. Now, providing that you have enough money sitting in your PayPal account to cover the payment you're sending, the transfer from your account to the seller's is instant.

Adding Your Credit Card and Getting a Confirmed Address

Although you don't have to add a credit card, you should because it opens up instant transfers (which I talk about in a moment), it gives you an additional funding source option, and it is required for PayPal to remove the $500 a month withdrawal limit on your account (very important if you plan to be a seller).

You can add your credit card while you are waiting for your bank account deposits to show up, so at least you can get started buying and selling.

Click **View limits** on your PayPal account page (see Figure 2.4). On the next page, click **Lift limits** next to **Withdrawal limit.** Now you will see three options:

1. Confirm a bank account.

2. Confirm your Social Security number.

3. Link and confirm your credit or debit card.

Click on the third option, **Link and confirm your credit or debit card** and then enter your credit card information, ensure the billing address is correct, and then click **Save and Continue.** You are now prompted to confirm your card. You don't have to do this, but you can't remove the withdrawal limit on your account until you do. However, you do now have access to instant transfers. I recommend you do confirm your card. If you go back to your **My Account** page, you will see a link in the **Notifications** box for **Confirm my debit or credit card.** Clicking this link will authorize PayPal to charge $1.95 to your card. (Don't worry, it gets refunded to your PayPal account as soon as the card is confirmed.)

Tips

If possible, add a credit card rather than a debit card. Credit cards have one extra layer of fraud protection that debit cards do not have.

You will see a four-digit code next to the charge on your credit card statement (if you have online banking you should be able to see this within a day or two). Once you have the code, come back to this page to enter it and click **Submit.** Now your card and address is confirmed, the $1.95 fee is refunded to your PayPal account, and your withdrawal limit is removed.

Instant Transfers

I mentioned earlier that your payment is sent as an eCheck if you only have a bank account on file. The alternative is to keep a balance in your PayPal account, but who likes to do that? What about impulse buys? What if you don't quite have enough to cover the sale price?

def•i•ni•tion _____

With **instant transfers**, PayPal credits the seller's account immediately even when you don't have the funds to cover the transaction sitting in your PayPal account.

Here's the cool thing about PayPal: if you have both a bank account and credit or debit card on file, PayPal treats your bank account–funded transaction as if the money was already cleared and sitting in your PayPal account. This is called an *instant transfer.*

The funds come out of your bank account as usual, but the money clears in the seller's account instantly—there's no waiting period for the transaction to process through your bank. The seller can ship the item right away, and you get your item much more quickly.

PayPal can do this because you have a back-up funding source on file. If the bank account transfer doesn't clear, PayPal just charges the amount to your credit card.

Having both a credit card and a bank account confirmed on my PayPal account gives me the convenience of paying through my bank account for most transactions using an instant transfer. However, I like to pay for high-ticket items using my credit card as the funding source because that gives me one extra level of protection if the transaction goes sour. (I can contact my credit card provider and have them charge back the transaction.)

Buying from Overseas

I like a particular UK clothing brand for my daughter called NEXT. Unfortunately, NEXT clothing is not available in the United States, so I purchase most of her clothes on eBay UK.

PayPal makes it easy for me to buy from international sellers. Since PayPal accepts so many different currencies (currently 18 of them), it's easy to pay sellers in a different country in their local currency. There's no waiting time for payment to arrive or clear and there are no hefty fees like your bank would likely charge you.

When I check out, PayPal automatically knows that I am paying a seller in British pounds instead of U.S. dollars. It shows me the winning bid plus shipping in eBay Checkout in British pounds. Then when I log in to my PayPal account to pay, it shows me the U.S. dollar amount that will be withdrawn from my account and the currency conversion I am getting. I've found PayPal to be quite good on currency conversions (it's a 2.5 percent spread). For me, this makes international buying a breeze.

You can find many items cheaper on eBay sites in other countries either because the item originates there (like the NEXT clothes) or because eBay is not as big and well-known in that country as it is in the United States. Just keep the shipping costs in mind; never bid without knowing the shipping cost. Don't assume that "flat-rate" means it is the same rate for international shipping—99 percent of the time, it won't be.

Personal vs. Premier PayPal Accounts

While you are solely a buyer, you do not need a Premier account. However, if you decide to sell, you'll have to upgrade your Personal account to a Premier one. This is a requirement of the PayPal terms and conditions.

You are charged a transaction fee on all "purchase" payments you receive, whatever account type you may have. Payments you receive for eBay items are automatically marked as purchases.

Did You Know?

Even if you have a Premier PayPal account, you can send and receive money to friends and family within the United States without incurring fees to either of you, provided you use your bank account or existing balance to fund the transaction. If you use a credit card, a small fee applies, but you can decide who pays it (the sender or recipient). This can be a great way to transfer money to your kids at college, or even split a check with friends (yes, you can send the money via your cell phone while you're still at the restaurant).

Stick with a Personal account unless you need to upgrade. You can see the fees in Chapter 14 if you want to upgrade, and we talk about setting your PayPal account up for selling in Chapter 12.

Other Payment Options

eBay restricts the payment methods it allows sellers to offer. Money orders, personal checks, cashier's checks, Western Union, MoneyGram, and cash in the mail are no longer allowed on eBay. The reason is simple: electronic payments can be tracked. The majority of fraudulent transactions on eBay were using these untraceable payment methods, so eBay put a stop to it.

PayPal is the preferred payment method for the vast majority of buyers and sellers, and has been for long before the paperless payments policy came into effect. However, other online services are also approved. eBay is still adding to this list, so it may be longer now. Currently, ProPay, MoneyBookers, and PayMate are the approved alternative payment methods. Sellers may also process credit card transactions using their own merchant credit card account. For high-ticket items, escrow is also approved (eBay recommends www.escrow.com).

PayPal offers both buyer and seller fraud protections. I talk about these later, but generally your transaction is covered for the full amount (including shipping) when you purchase using PayPal. As of this writing, none of the other approved payment processors offer fraud protection other than what you automatically receive from your credit card company. For me, that's a good enough reason to stick with PayPal, and I recommend that you do the same.

The Least You Need to Know

- Get PayPal Verified by adding a bank account, and get your address confirmed by adding a credit card.

- You must have a Premier PayPal account to register as an eBay seller, so get signed up and verified to stay ahead of the game.

- When you have both a credit card and a bank account on file, you get access to instant transfers, which gets you your items much quicker.

- Always pay using one of eBay's approved electronic payment methods. Do not send checks, money orders, Western Union, cash in the mail, or any other untraceable payment.

- PayPal can be used to pay sellers in other countries in their local currency.

- PayPal is currently the only approved payment processor that offers fraud protection to both buyers and sellers.

Navigating Without a Compass

In This Chapter

♦ Exploring eBay, one click at a time

♦ Using the navigation tabs and what you'll find there

♦ Finding your way when you're completely lost

Do you remember the first time you went to an amusement park as a kid? There was so much to see, you didn't know where to start. The first time you go to eBay can be a bit like that. Hang in there—it's not as daunting as it first seems.

The eBay Home Page

Your adventure begins at eBay's home page. Figure 3.1 shows you what you will see when you go to www.eBay.com. If it doesn't look quite like this, don't panic. eBay changes the theme of the home page quite frequently to keep it interesting and to promote specific items or categories based on your browsing history. But you will always see the five navigation tabs on the top right, the search box beneath the eBay logo, and the tabs beneath the search box to navigate to specific Categories, eBay Stores, eBay Motors, and the Daily Deal. When you are signed in, you will see a snapshot of your current transaction information on the right side as well.

If you ever get lost and want to get back to the home page, click on the eBay logo on the top left of whatever page you're on. This takes you straight back to the home page.

Signing In

Right above the search box at the top of the page (see Figure 3.1), you will see **Welcome! Sign In** or **Register.** If you have already registered, just click **Sign In.** In Chapter 1, I talked about the option to sign in for a full day and when it is and is not appropriate.

Figure 3.1

Scroll down to see all the information on the home page.

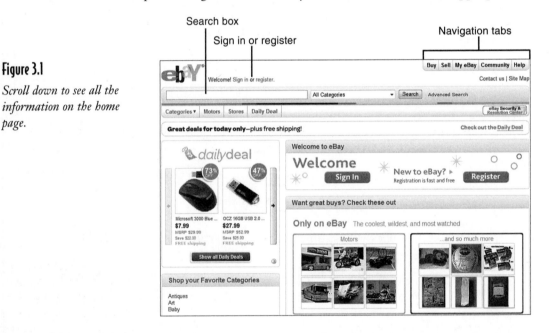

The Navigation Tabs

You'll see five navigation tabs on the top right of the home page. They take you to the five major areas of eBay: Buy, Sell, My eBay, Community, and Help. You will see them at the top of virtually all eBay pages. Each of the tabs also has a drop-down menu of shortcuts to common areas within that section. Let's look at where each tab takes you, one at a time.

Buy

Clicking on the first tab, **Buy,** takes you to the buying hub (see Figure 3.2).

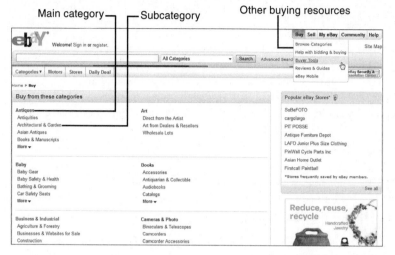

Main category — Subcategory   Other buying resources

Figure 3.2

*Hovering your mouse over the **Buy** tab displays a number of other buying resource pages you can go to.*

Clicking on any of the main categories (shown in bold) opens a page displaying all of that category's subcategories. For example, if you click on **Cameras & Photo,** you will see product categories for Binoculars & Telescopes, Camcorders, Film Cameras, and so on. (See Figure 3.3.) Each of these categories also has subcategories.

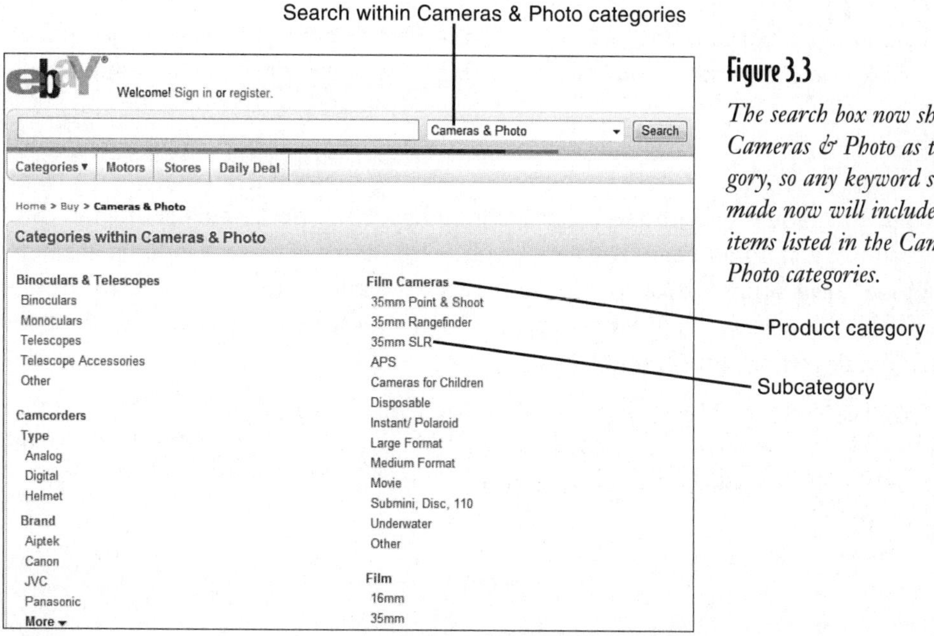

Search within Cameras & Photo categories

Figure 3.3

The search box now shows Cameras & Photo as the category, so any keyword searches made now will include only items listed in the Cameras & Photo categories.

Product category

Subcategory

Tips _____

If you have time to browse, you can find some amazing deals from sellers who don't know how to write an auction title. If the keywords are not there (or are misspelled), they won't show up in a search. But they will show up if you are just browsing in the category.

I recently bought a gorgeous summer dress from an inexperienced seller who didn't put the designer's name in the auction title. The exact same dress had sold three times on eBay in the previous week (from different sellers) with an average price of $63. My maximum bid was $60, but I was one of only two bidders (and I think the first bidder forgot about the auction). I won the dress for $2.25. So if you have the time, browsing can really pay off.

From here, you can search for items within the Cameras & Photo categories, or you can continue to browse and select one of the subcategories. Once you choose a subcategory, eBay takes you to the search results page.

I find browsing too time-consuming, but if you're not sure exactly what you want, it can be a good way to kill some time. I prefer to search and then narrow my categories afterward, rather than the other way around. I show you my strategies for searching, browsing, and finding bargains in Chapter 5.

Sell

The Sell tab is not relevant to you as a buyer. But if you decide to become a seller, this is where you go to create your auction listing. We cover this in detail in Chapter 16.

My eBay

Imagine a "Home sweet home" sign hanging inside My eBay. This is the hub of everything you do on eBay. You can see all of the items you are watching, are bidding on, have bought, have sold, or have listed for sale. E-mails you receive from eBay and other eBay users are located here, too. This is also where you can view and make changes to your eBay account.

There's so much to My eBay that we have an entire chapter about it (Chapter 4). You have to be signed in to eBay before you can access your My eBay page because all of the information displayed is personal to you.

Community

Many people rarely access the community pages because they are just not interested in eBay beyond it being a place where they can find good deals. It's true that a lot of the community pages are social networking (neighborhoods, groups, chat rooms, and so on) that have very little to do with eBay, but you really need to be aware of a few sections.

Feedback Forum	This is where you leave feedback for your buyers or sellers, leave a follow-up comment to a feedback comment you have already left, leave a response on a feedback comment you have received, and look up your own or someone else's feedback profile.
Discussion Boards	This is where members get together to discuss eBay-related topics. The discussion includes questions, answers, and comments among members about a variety of topics.
	You can see when eBay employees post on the discussion boards because their user IDs always appear in a nice shade of magenta. Because of this, eBay members refer to them as "pinks."
Answer Center	This section is a wonderful resource for anyone new to eBay because users can get answers to specific questions from other eBay members. There are 21 answer boards on topics including Bidding, My eBay, International Transactions, PayPal, and more.
Announcements	Many announcements are seller specific, but they can also be useful to buyers. For instance, let's say you're looking for a camera and see that eBay is running a listing fee special for sellers who begin their listing next Wednesday. You now know there will be more items to choose from during the following week. It might be a better idea to wait until the special, so you have more items to choose from and bidding may not go as high.
	You will also get advance warning of changes to the eBay site through the announcements, which is always useful whether you're a buyer or a seller.

Workshops

You'll see free workshops for various aspects of buying and selling on eBay. Usually when eBay introduces a major new feature, you will see a workshop covering it within a month of the launch. Workshops are live and interactive, so you post your questions while the workshop is happening and the host will answer them. Workshops also are archived so you can read the questions and answers later if you miss the live session.

Resolution Center

This is where you report problems, such as if you paid for an item and never received it. I cover this in detail in Chapter 6.

Help

If you're unsure about an eBay policy, take a look in the Help pages. You'll find clear explanations with examples, which makes it much easier to understand.

You can search using keywords (like "eBay fees"), but I find that I often get too many irrelevant results. My preferred method is to use the **Browse help** links below the **search** box (see Figure 3.4) to go directly to the main topic. From there, you'll find additional links to relevant subtopics.

Figure 3.4

You can use the links at the bottom for a quick reference to eBay acronyms and terms.

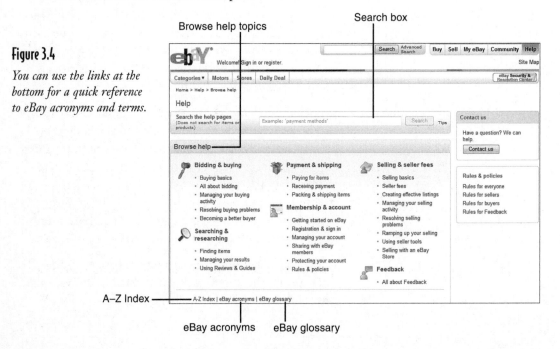

Browse help topics

Search box

A–Z Index

eBay acronyms   eBay glossary

The A–Z Index is very comprehensive but far too long for me, so if you search for a topic and it doesn't come up on your first couple of attempts, try the Site Map instead.

The Site Map

This is the road map to eBay. If you can't find a particular section, check the Site Map (see Figure 3.5). The Site Map link is at the top right of the home page, below the navigation tabs.

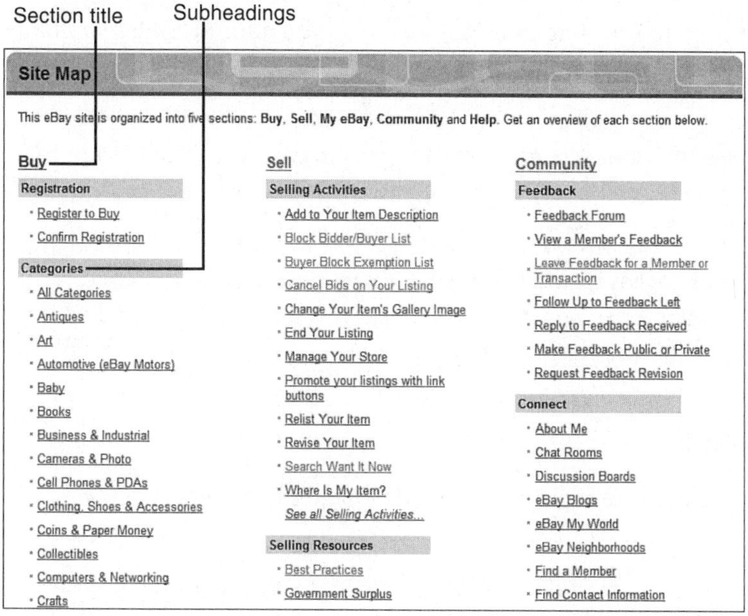

Section title   Subheadings

Figure 3.5

You need to scroll down to see all the topics.

I find it much easier to use the Site Map when I'm looking for a section or topic that isn't linked from the main eBay navigation pages. The Site Map links instantly take you to the page you need.

The section titles are the same as the navigation tabs on the home page (Buy, Sell, Community, My eBay, Help), but they also have subheadings, which makes it much easier to locate the information or place you are looking for. These are the subheadings you will see:

Buy   Registration, Categories, More Ways to Find Items, Buying
                   Resources

Sell	Selling Activities, Selling Resources, Selling Tools, Web Stores
My eBay	My Account, My Selling Account
Community	Feedback, Connect, News, Marketplace Safety, More Community Programs
Help	Resources, Help Topics

When you've used it a couple of times, you will instinctively know which sections to look in for specific topics or pages. The Site Map can save you a lot of time searching around the site.

If you still can't find what you're looking for, try Google. Yes, I know that sounds counterintuitive, but eBay pages rank highly on Google searches, so if you search for a specific tool or question, you will likely see the correct eBay page in the first few results of a Google search.

We've looked at the main sections of the site except searching. This is deliberate because it takes an entire chapter to cover. In Chapter 5, we look at finding items and narrowing your results. But before that, we look at another area of the site: My eBay.

The Least You Need to Know

◆ Click on the eBay logo at the top left of any eBay page to get back to the home page.

◆ eBay is organized into five sections—the navigation tabs Buy, Sell, Community, My eBay, and Help. You'll find most of the resources related to each of these areas linked from the main page for each of the tabs.

◆ If you can't find something on a navigation page, look in the Site Map or Help files.

◆ If you have a question, go to the Answer Center or Discussion Boards.

◆ Keep an eye on the Announcements boards and attend online workshops to increase your eBay knowledge and understanding.

Chapter 4

My eBay

In This Chapter

- ◆ What is available in My eBay, and how do I use it?
- ◆ Sending and receiving e-mail through My Messages
- ◆ Changing eBay to suit yourself

Think of My eBay as your eBay daytimer or personal digital assistant (PDA). It tracks all of your activities on eBay: buying, selling, feedback, e-mail messages, and account details. It also serves as a doorway to many other services, features, and frequently accessed areas of eBay.

To enter My eBay, click on the **My eBay** navigation tab at the top of the eBay home page. If you are not already signed in to eBay, you will be prompted to sign in to your account.

This chapter focuses on the features of My eBay relevant to a buyer. We go into more detail on the selling aspects in Chapter 21.

My eBay has three tabs: Activity, Messages, and Account (see Figure 4.1). We look at each one and explore what you'll find in each of these sections.

Activity

When you go to **My eBay,** you land on the **Summary** page within the **Activity** tab. This is a snapshot of your current transactions and important information (see Figure 4.1).

Figure 4.1

*You can customize the look of this first page to display only the features you want by clicking **Page options** and adding or removing sections.*

General settings

Messages   Account   Buying Reminders   Page options

Items I'm watching

The Buying Reminders section lets you know when you need to leave feedback, when an item you're watching is ending soon, when you have items that you need to pay for, if you have an important e-mail from eBay (called an Alert), or if you have a pending *Second Chance Offer* that needs a response.

def•i•ni•tion

If you don't win an auction, you may still be offered a **Second Chance Offer.** This means the seller is offering you the item (or another exactly like it) for your highest bid. It is optional, so you are not obligated to accept the Second Chance Offer.

Items You're Watching

For people who like to shop around and compare items, there is a prominent link to **Watch this item** at the top of each item listing page. This tracks the auction in the **Watching** section of My eBay (see Figure 4.2).

From left to right, each line shows a thumbnail photograph of the item, the title, the number of bids, the current price, the shipping cost, and the time remaining on the listing. Beneath the title, you'll also see the seller's user ID and feedback score/rating.

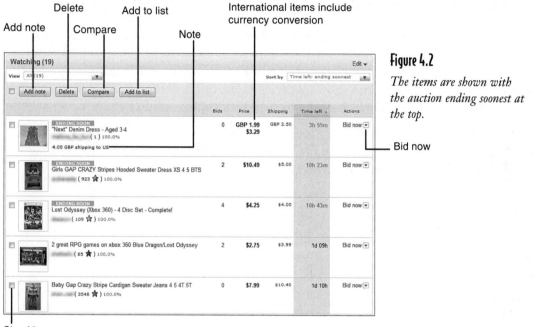

Figure 4.2

The items are shown with the auction ending soonest at the top.

The column to the far right of each line is a link for the most common action related to that item. For auctions that you have not bid on (or have been outbid on), it reads **Bid now.** For those you are the high bidder on, it reads **View seller's other items,** in the hope of selling you other items from the same seller. For fixed-price listings, it reads **Buy It Now.** An arrow next to the text opens a drop-down menu of additional options. These include **Contact Seller, View Seller's Other Items, Visit Seller's Store, Add Note,** and more.

When you are the high bidder for an item in this list, the price appears in green and bold. If you have been outbid, it appears in red without bold. If you have not bid on the item, the price appears black.

Adding a Note to an Item You're Watching

It's easy to forget why you're watching a particular item. Invariably, you'll remember just moments after the listing ends (without you bidding). I've done this many times and, believe me, it can get very frustrating.

A better option is to add a note to remind yourself: "Gift for Aunt Sally," or whatever the case may be. Adding notes is also useful when you asked the seller a question. I use it to remind me of the international shipping costs for eBay UK items I'm watching. Usually the shipping price shown is the domestic price, so this saves me from searching through my e-mails looking for the correct shipping cost before I bid.

To add a note, simply click the checkbox to the left of the item thumbnail, then click the **Add note** button at the top of the Watching section (see Figure 4.2). Now just type the note and click **Save.** Done!

Tips

Sometimes you will see the Add note, Delete, Compare, and Add to list buttons at the bottom of the Watching section instead of at the top. I'm not sure why this changes, but if you don't see them at the top, scroll to the bottom of the section and you'll see them there.

Your note is now added to the listing and shows up below the item title, as you can see in the first item on Figure 4.2.

At the top of the Watching section are three other buttons—**Delete, Compare,** and **Add to list.** To use any of these buttons, you must first click the checkbox(es) to the left of the appropriate listing(s) (as you did for adding a note), then click the button for the option you require.

Delete is obvious (and you'll use it a lot once items have ended). Compare is a great feature that compares the selected listings side by side (I talk more about this in Chapter 7).

Add to list is a useful feature if you're watching several different types of items and want to organize them into groups and view just one group of items at a time.

Let's say you're looking for shoes for your daughter, jeans for your son, and a new cell phone for yourself. Rather than having all the items jumbled together in your Watching list, you can make lists for each of them and then just view one list at a time.

When you add an item to a list, you get the option to create a new list by typing a new title, or select from a list you've previously made to add this item to the others already in that list.

Bidding

Below the Watching section is, quite logically, the Bidding section (see Figure 4.3). This screenshot only shows two items, but if you're bidding on more items, they will all show up here.

Outbid notice

Figure 4.3

Each section only shows up on your Summary page if you have eBay activity that fits into that section. So if you haven't bid on anything, the Bidding section will not display here.

Your current maximum bid   Current selling price

Did You Know?

When you bid on an item, it automatically shows up in the Bidding section, but it won't be copied to the Watching section unless you specifically click Watch this item on the listing page.

So always monitor your active bids from the Bidding section, or make sure you always add items you're bidding on to your Watching list.

It's a good idea to keep checking the current price even if you are the high bidder because it will show you how close the bidding is coming to your maximum bid. If it is getting very close, you need to decide whether you're prepared to pay more; if so, you should place a higher bid before your current one gets outbid. It won't increase your actual current bid unless someone else places a bid.

Once an auction ends, it moves from the Bidding section to either the Won or Didn't Win sections.

Won

I love the thrill of winning an auction and seeing it show up in the Won section. This is the reality check that, yes, you really did win those tickets to that sold-out

Tim McGraw concert, or you won that Nintendo Wii console your kids so desperately wanted. Every item you have won during the last 60 days shows up in this section unless you remove it.

The Won section on the Summary page is a little different from the Watching and Bidding sections because it only displays a snapshot of the few most recent purchases and their details. These are shown on the left side of the screen. The neat part about this is that you can immediately see which items you've won. Hover your mouse over the thumbnail photo, and it will show you the date you won the item, the seller's user ID, the sale price, and whether you have paid (see Figure 4.4).

Figure 4.4

The sale price on the snapshot does not including the shipping cost.

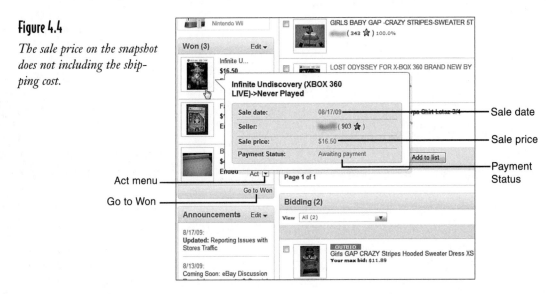

To the right of the thumbnail photo, you'll see the word **Act** with a down arrow next to it. This is a drop-down menu that lists common activities you can do related to this item. The first option is always the most likely. For example, until you pay, it will have **Pay now** at the top of the list. Once you have paid, the first three options (**Pay now, Request total,** and **Mark payment as sent**) disappear and your first option is **Leave feedback.** Other options include **View seller's other items, Contact seller, Resolve a problem,** and **View similar items**.

At the bottom of the Won snapshot section is a link to **Go to Won** (see Figure 4.4). This takes you to a page similar to the Watching and Bidding views. Here you'll see all the details about the transaction, including tracking information for your shipment.

Most of the information is the same as you'll see on the Bidding page. The only additions are the Sale date beneath the item title, the icons to the right, and the tracking number (see Figure 4.5).

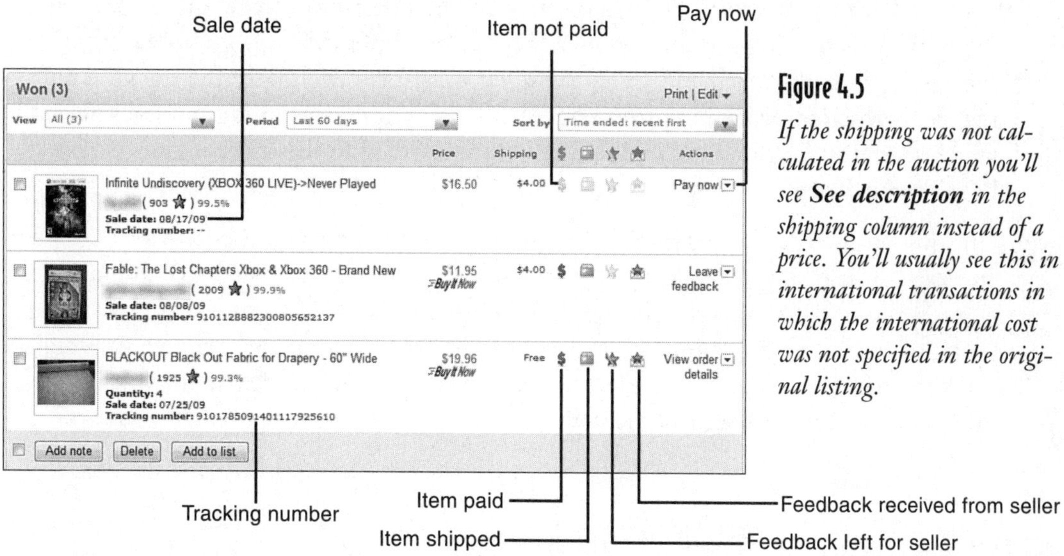

Figure 4.5

*If the shipping was not calculated in the auction you'll see **See description** in the shipping column instead of a price. You'll usually see this in international transactions in which the international cost was not specified in the original listing.*

The icons are a clear indicator of where you are in the post-auction process for each item. The first icon (dollar sign) indicates when you have sent the payment to the seller. The second icon (package) shows whether the seller has identified that they have shipped the package. The third icon (star with a pencil in front) shows when you have left feedback for your seller. The fourth icon (star inside an envelope) identifies when the seller has left feedback for you.

The icons are grayed out until that part of the process has been completed. They turn bold automatically as you complete each task. So in Figure 4.5, you can see that the first item has not been paid for and that neither the buyer nor the seller has left feedback yet (all icons are grayed out). The second item has been paid for, shipped, and the seller has left feedback, but the buyer has not yet left feedback (the first, second, and fourth icons are bold). The third item has been paid for, shipped, and both the buyer and the seller have left feedback for the transaction (all icons are bold). This shows that the third item's transaction is complete.

Tips

Once all four icons are bold, I usually delete the item from my Won list because the transaction is now complete.

Beneath the item title, you will often see a tracking number (see Figure 4.5). If there are just dashes (as in the first listing) either the item hasn't been shipped (as in this case), or the seller did not enter a tracking number.

If the seller uses eBay's shipping center to pay for and print postage online, the tracking number will automatically be entered (and the parcel icon will go bold as soon as the seller prints the postage). If not, the seller must manually enter the tracking number. Not all sellers are willing to do this as it can be time consuming. Still, it's always worth checking for the tracking number before contacting the seller if your parcel hasn't arrived yet.

Clicking on the tracking number brings up a box showing when the item was shipped, and extra in-transit tracking information if available (see Figure 4.6). I've found there is often a long delay between the carrier's website updating the status, and it showing up on eBay. So you may find it more accurate to note the tracking number and then track the parcel through the carrier's website. You can copy and paste the tracking number so you don't have to type it all out.

Figure 4.6

The tracking is usually delayed. You may find more up-to-date tracking by using this number on the shipping carrier's own website.

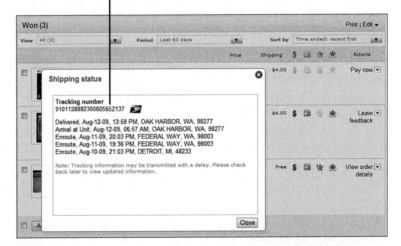

Did You Know?

USPS delivery confirmation is not "in-transit" package tracking. This only confirms when the package was delivered. So you will be able to see when the shipping label was printed, where it was scanned (if at all), and then when it was delivered. You cannot guarantee to track the parcel all the way from the seller's location to your door. The only way you'll get this is if the seller uses a carrier such as UPS or FedEx, or USPS's overnight service: Express Mail.

Didn't Win

It's not much fun, but many times you will bid on an item without winning it. eBay can be very addictive, and it's important to set your limits and stick to them. Still, it's never easy to see an item you really wanted in your **Didn't Win** section. But don't get too depressed. First, it's only an auction. Second, the seller may have a duplicate item for sale (so check the seller's other items). Third, there's always the possibility of a Second Chance Offer.

Second Chance Offers are usually sent when the high bidder doesn't pay or backs out of the sale, or when the seller has more identical items for sale than he has listed.

The seller sets how long a Second Chance Offer is good for, so keep checking back. It could be as short as 24 hours. If you accept the offer, you are sent to a Buy It Now page unique for you so that you can purchase the item immediately for the highest bid you made during the auction.

You can easily see if you have a Second Chance Offer in the **Buying Reminders** section at the top of your Summary page.

Sometimes the most depressing part of the Didn't Win section is comparing the **Sale price** to **Your max bid** (see Figure 4.7). If it's only 50¢ different, that can really feel like a kick in the gut. But if you were outbid at the last second, the selling price will only ever be one bid higher than your maximum, no matter how high a maximum bid the winning bidder actually placed. If the final price is much higher, then more than one person placed a bid higher than your maximum.

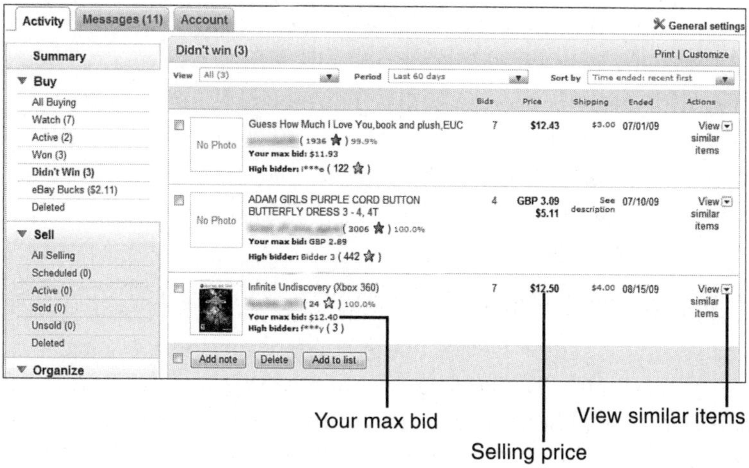

Figure 4.7

*The **View similar items** link searches active listings on eBay that have similar keywords to the one you didn't win.*

Your max bid

Selling price

View similar items

Customizing Your Summary

The screenshots throughout this chapter show the default **Summary** page. But if you want to choose exactly which sections display, click **Page Options** at the top right of the **Summary** page and adjust any of the settings you want.

Figure 4.8 shows all the options available to you. Simply check or uncheck each section you want (or don't want) to display.

Figure 4.8

If you change your mind about your customized display, you can always return to the default display by clicking **Restore Defaults.**

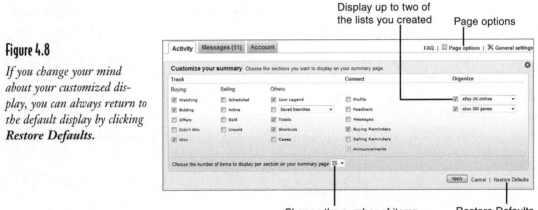

Display up to two of the lists you created

Page options

Change the number of items to display per section

Restore Defaults

Many people get frustrated at having to view multiple pages when they have more than 10 items in their Watching list. The answer is simple: change the default.

Few people know they can do this, but one of the check boxes in **Page options** is to change the number of items to display per section on your **Summary** page. Your options are 5, 10, 15, 20, or 25. Mine is now set to 25. This makes it much easier to compare items I'm watching and see what's coming up in the next few days. If you have a slow Internet connection, this option could be a real timesaver for you because it means far fewer page loads to see the same details.

You can even change the order and location the sections display on your Summary page by clicking **Edit** at the top-right corner of that section (see Figure 4.9).

You can change the color scheme to color-code sections if you want, but I've never really bothered with this. You can also "collapse" the section so that just the section title displays on the Summary page. Then when you want to view the full section, you click **Edit** and then **Expand.**

Figure 4.9

*Move **up** and **Move down** are fairly self-explanatory. **Move left** means to move the section to the left sidebar (where the Won summary is). **Move right** moves it back to the main window (where the **Watching** and **Bidding** sections currently display).*

To change the information that displays within each section, click **Customize** from this menu. The options will be different for each section. Figure 4.10 shows the options for the Watching section. You can choose to use one of the presets (**Just the basics,** or **All the details**), or you can select **Choose your own** and then check or uncheck individual boxes. Always remember to click **Apply** when you're done; otherwise, your changes will not be made.

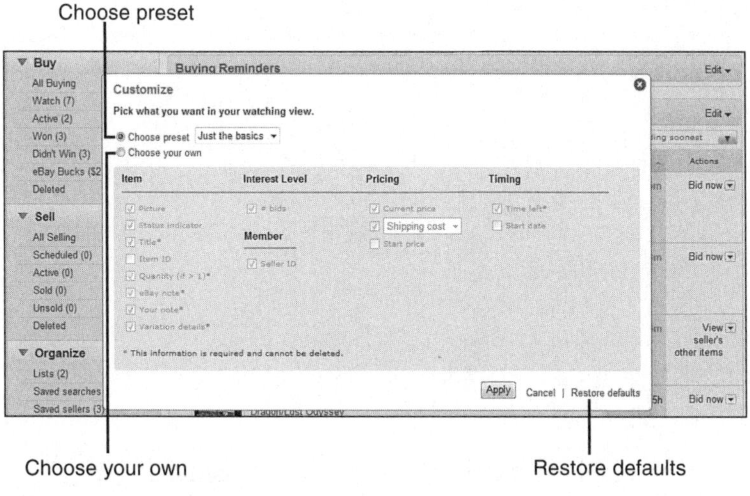

Choose preset

Figure 4.10

Some options are required and cannot be unselected. These are identified with a green asterisk to the side of the label.

Choose your own   Restore defaults

Summary Links

On the left sidebar, above the **Won** summary, you'll see links to various other pages within My eBay (see Figure 4.11). We've already talked about the pages under the **Buy** heading (**Watching, Bidding, Won, Didn't Win,** and so on). If you click one of these links it shows only that section. We'll skip the Sell section for now, since we're primarily talking about buying here.

Did You Know?

You may or may not have a link to eBay Bucks in the Buy headings. eBay Bucks is an opt-in program that is currently invitation only. If you are invited to join, you can earn eBay bucks on each of your purchases (kind of like a rewards card). It works out to 2 percent of the item cost (not including shipping). At the end of the earning period, you then have 30 days to redeem your bucks against eBay purchases during this time. Don't worry if you aren't invited yet: this program will likely go live site-wide soon. I've been an eBay member for 11 years and I only just got my invite last month!

The third heading is **Organize.** Remember those lists we talked about earlier? This is where you access them. Clicking **Lists** brings up a page with the titles of all your lists. From here, you can select whichever one you want to view.

Figure 4.11

The summary shows how many items are shown within each of the pages by putting that number in parentheses after the page title.

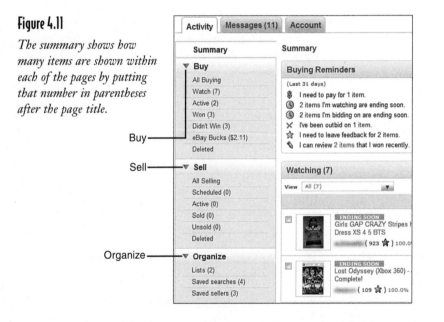

The other two options under Organize are **Saved searches** and **Saved sellers.** In Chapter 5, I show you how to save a search or a favorite seller, but for now, just file away that this is where you access them when you want to perform a saved search, change details or cancel the saved search, or view items from your saved sellers.

Phew! That was a crash course in the options within the **Activities** tab. I promise, the other two tabs are much less involved!

Messages

You can see how many unread messages you have in your eBay e-mail inbox from any of the My eBay pages. The number is shown in parentheses after the word "Messages" on the tab. When you click the **Messages** tab, you are taken to your inbox (see Figure 4.12).

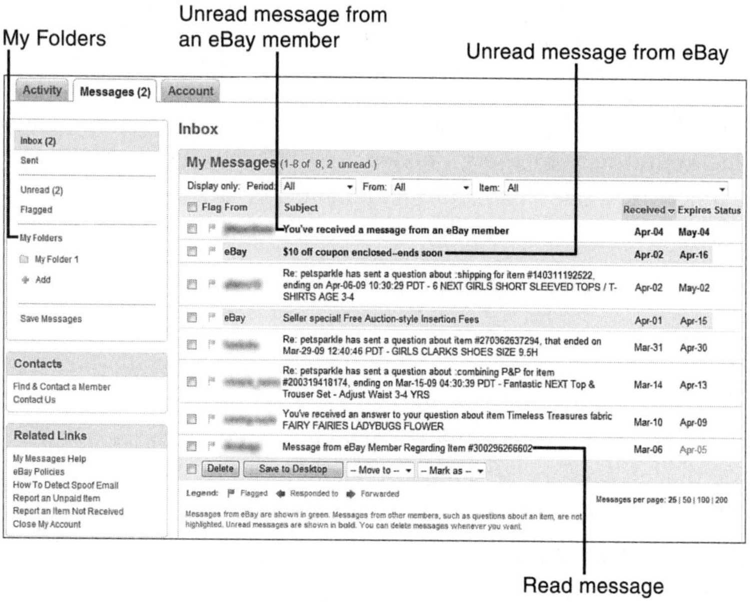

My Folders

Unread message from an eBay member

Unread message from eBay

Read message

Figure 4.12

All messages from eBay have a green highlighted background.

As you can see, I have eight messages. The top two are unread (shown in bold); all of the others have been read (not bold).

Most of the e-mails you receive here, you will also receive in your regular e-mail inbox (for the account you used to register on eBay).

You can respond to e-mails either here in your **Messages** box or through your e-mail program. I recommend using your Messages box because you can guarantee that the seller will receive it. Sometimes e-mails get caught by junk mail filters, and the seller may not be ignoring your question—he may never have seen it! If it is sent through eBay's messaging system, you can guarantee that the seller will get it.

The other advantage is the option to hide your e-mail address from the seller. This is very useful when you're just asking a question about a listing and don't know if you are even going to buy from this seller. Sellers have requirements on what they can and can't do with your e-mail address, but the more people who have it, the more likely you are to be opened up to spam.

I know I've said this a couple of times, but it bears repeating. If you get an account message or a message from another eBay user in your regular e-mail account and it doesn't look right or the topic doesn't sound right, open a new browser window and navigate to your Messages box. If the message is not here, it is not from eBay or another eBay member.

You delete messages by checking the box to the left of the message(s) and clicking **Delete.** A box pops up letting you know that it will permanently delete the message. Click **OK** and you're done. You can't recover e-mail once you have deleted them, so be sure you won't need it again before you get rid of it.

If you want to keep a message, check the corresponding box to the left of it and then use the **Move to** menu at the bottom right to select a folder. The default is **My Folder 1.** I know, that title's a bit clinical. You can rename this folder and add other folders if you want to keep and organize your e-mails in My eBay.

You can return to the My eBay Summary by clicking the **Activities** tab.

Account

Once you click the **Account** tab, you'll see a summary of your account in the center of the page and then links to the left for each account-specific item you may want to access. You can view or modify all of your personal information in this section of My eBay.

If you're new to eBay, you are immediately offered to link your PayPal account to your eBay one (see Figure 4.13). This makes eBay Checkout much smoother. It imports all of your PayPal shipping addresses into your eBay account.

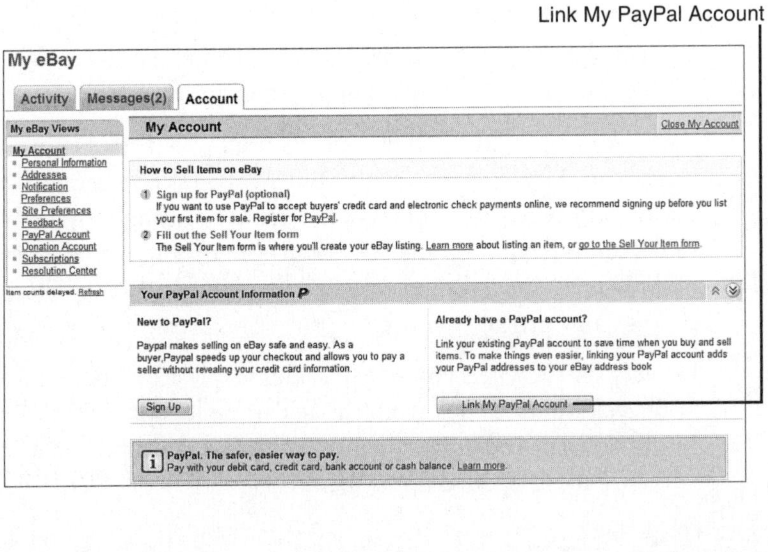

Link My PayPal Account

Figure 4.13

Linking your PayPal account now will save you time later on.

To link your account, just click **Link My PayPal Account,** enter your PayPal e-mail address and password (don't worry, eBay doesn't store your password), and then click **Link Your Account.** That's it, your accounts are linked.

Now let's look at the Account links on the left side of the page. The options are as follows:

- Personal Information
- Addresses
- Notification Preferences
- Site Preferences
- Feedback

- PayPal Account
- Donation Account
- Subscriptions
- Resolution Center

You will also see **Seller Account** if you register as a seller.

Personal Information

The first option, **Personal Information,** allows you to change various personal details about your account:

- Account type (individual/business)
- User ID
- Password
- Secret question (for password/User ID retrieval)
- About Me page
- E-mail address
- Name (if you get married or divorced)
- Street address
- Cellphone/instant messenger information for alerts
- Bank account/credit card information
- Automatic Payment Method (for monthly eBay fees)

Now you can see why your eBay password is so important. Do you really want someone else to have access to all of this information? An unauthorized user with your password could get into your account, change your password, and freeze you out completely. eBay would shut them down when you reported it, but the thought of someone else having access to all of these details (and access to your buyers if you're a seller) is quite distressing. This is why you are always asked to sign in again when you first go to **My eBay,** unless you checked the **Keep me signed in for today** box when you signed in.

To change any of these details, click **Personal Information,** and then click **Edit** to the far right of the item you need to change (see Figure 4.14). You must keep your information, including your phone number, updated to comply with eBay's regulations.

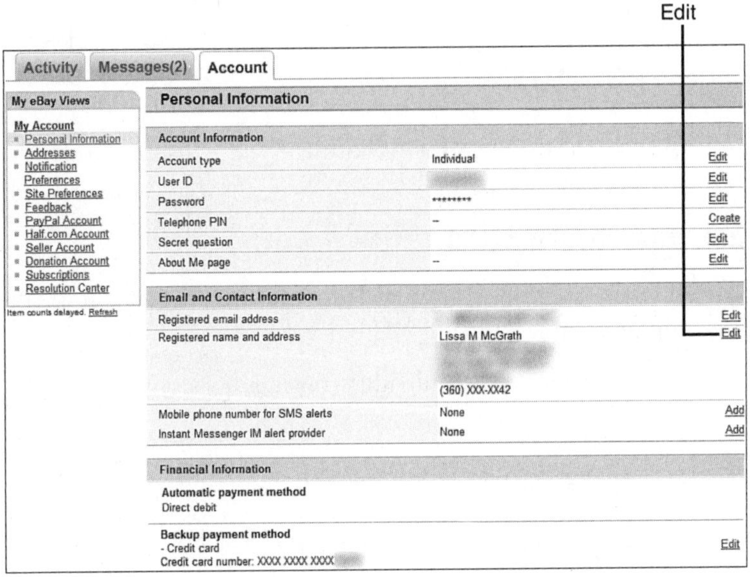

Figure 4.14

Certain aspects of this screen-shot are blurred out to protect personal information, but in your My eBay Account, you'll see all of it clearly.

Addresses

It really shouldn't be this complicated, but there are three types of addresses: Registration Address, Payment Address, and Primary Shipping Address. When you first register, they will all be the same, but if you want to change your shipping address or registration address (if you move), just click **Addresses** on the side bar and then click **Change** next to the address that needs modifying.

Notification Preferences

You can choose how much or how little contact you receive from eBay. Do you want to receive an e-mail notification each time you place a bid, are outbid, win an item, and so on? If not, you can change that here. You can decide whether you want eBay to contact you with special offers and promotions or just leave you alone. It's entirely up to you. You can change your notification preferences whenever you want.

Site Preferences

In this section, you can set your preferences for how things display on the site. Do you want an alert at the top of the page when you have a Second Chance Offer pending? What about changing your preference for seeing related ads from other companies? You can change these preferences here. Many seller preferences are also in this section.

Other Account Options

Let's quickly run down the other options available in the **Account** tab.

Clicking **Feedback** shows you a list of items you have won/sold that you have not yet left feedback for. You will also see a short list of the most recent feedback you have received.

PayPal Account shows you what PayPal account e-mail address is linked with your eBay account. It also gives you some direct links to PayPal for changing account settings or addresses. You'll still have to log in to PayPal after you click on these links.

The **Resolution Center** is where you file a report if you don't receive an item or if what you get is significantly different from the listing description. I talk about this in Chapter 11, but for now, just understand that the Resolution Center is the last resort—not the first step toward getting an issue resolved.

You may also see **Seller Account, Donation Account, Seller's Dashboard, Manage My Tools, Subscriptions,** and so on. These are seller tools and are not relevant to buyers. See Chapter 21 for more detail about these tools.

The Least You Need to Know

◆ My eBay shows you everything you are watching, are bidding on, won, didn't win, and more.

◆ You can track packages sent via USPS or UPS through My eBay (provided that the seller printed postage through PayPal or manually entered the tracking number).

◆ You can customize your My eBay page or individual sections within it.

◆ You can organize your Watching section by creating lists of related products you are watching.

◆ Use eBay Messages when you don't want the seller to have your e-mail address, and always check it if you are not sure of the authenticity of an e-mail that looks like it came from eBay or another eBay member.

◆ Go to My eBay anytime you need to change or update your account information.

Part 2

Buying on eBay

Now that you know the basics, it's time to get into the nitty-gritty of buying on eBay. In this part, you'll learn how to determine whether that "bargain" you've found really is one, and see whether the seller is trustworthy. You'll learn advanced buying techniques, including when and how much to bid, to help you get the best items at the best prices. We also teach you how to spot fakes and protect yourself against seller fraud.

Mistakes happen, so we explain how to fix them when they do. Don't worry, you're not the first person to worry about accidentally adding an extra zero to your bid. We also show you what to do once you've won an item, how to handle any issues with sellers that may arise, and how eBay's Feedback and Detailed Seller Ratings programs work.

Finding What You Want to Buy

In This Chapter

- ◆ Searching for items and navigating the search results page

- ◆ Advanced use of the eBay search engine

- ◆ Refining your search by category and item specifics

- ◆ When words are not enough—searching by picture

You can buy pretty much anything you can think of on eBay, but first you have to find it. You can browse the categories from the eBay home page and keep drilling down through subcategories to find one that interests you, but chances are, you'll still have way too many results to sort through.

A better option is to start with a basic search term and go from there (for example, searching for rain boots and then refining the search by size, brand, color, and so on). This is how the vast majority of eBay buyers (as opposed to "browsers") find their items.

Enter your search keywords in the search box at the top of the eBay home page and click **Search.** This brings up all listings with those matching keywords in the title or the *Item Specifics*.

def•i•ni•tion

Item Specifics are details about the item that sellers can choose to select when they create the listing. This may include an item's size, style, color, brand, and so on.

The Search Results Page

On the search results page, you'll see a list of 50 items per page that match your search terms. Figure 5.1 shows the search results page for a search for "Macbook Pro."

Figure 5.1

As with most eBay pages, you can customize what you see by clicking **Customize view** *at the top right of the page.*

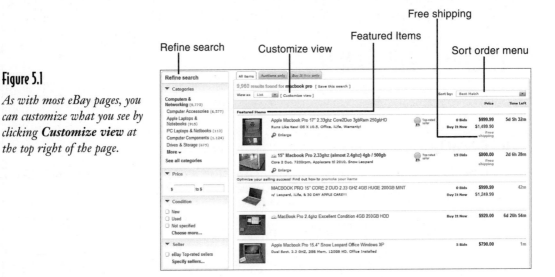

Free shipping

Featured Items

Refine search   Customize view   Sort order menu

From left to right, you can see …

1. A thumbnail picture of the item.

2. The listing title.

3. The subtitle, beneath the item title (if the seller chose to use one).

4. The PayPal icon, to the right of the item title. (If the seller accepts PayPal as a payment method, the icon appears here.)

5. The number of bids. (This can take 15 minutes or so to update, so be sure to check it on the actual auction page.)

6. The all-important current price.

7. Finally, the time left before the auction ends.

Changing the Display Order

The default (as shown in Figure 5.1) is **Best Match.** Personally, this sort order drives me crazy. It is eBay's attempt to show buyers what eBay thinks they are looking for, without giving the buyer the control to go out and find it for themselves. Why would I want a company telling me what I'm looking for, when I'm quite capable of determining that myself?

The idea is that the most relevant items from sellers with the best customer satisfaction will appear at the top. Still, I find it doesn't often work that way. Personally, I just want to see the items listed in the order of when they end and then do the checking myself to make sure the seller is trustworthy. Thankfully, eBay allows you to change this sort order. The other options are as follows:

◆ **Time: ending soonest** (auctions with the least time remaining display at the top)

◆ **Time: newly listed** (auctions most recently listed display at the top)

◆ **Price + Shipping: lowest first** (auctions with the lowest total price, including shipping, display at the top, regardless of when the auction ends)

◆ **Price + Shipping: highest first** (auctions with the highest total price, including shipping, display at the top, regardless of when the auction ends)

◆ **Price: highest first** (all listings with the highest price display at the top, regardless of when the item ends)

◆ **Distance: nearest first** (all relevant listings sorted with the closest to your registered location at the top)

◆ **Payment: PayPal first** (auctions that offer PayPal display at the top)

◆ **Category** (auctions sorted into category headings)

Before Best Match, the default sort order was **Time: ending soonest,** and that is still the option I prefer.

You can change the order in which the items display using the **Sort by** drop-down menu, or you can change the default so that it always uses your preferred sort order; I talk about this in a moment.

Customizing the Search Results Page

A number of options are available to you through the **Customize view** link (see Figure 5.1). They are split up into **Formatting, Item Information, Seller Information,** and **Advanced Options.** You have a lot of options here, so I suggest that you play around with it until you are seeing all the information you want and nothing you don't want. To get you thinking, though, here is what I changed:

On the **Formatting** tab, I added the **Shipping Cost** column so that I always see the shipping cost to my zip code right on the search results page (assuming that I am signed in to eBay). I also changed the default number of items per page in list view from 50 to 100.

> **Tips** _____
>
> If you do add the shipping cost to the search results page, be aware that this is not always the cheapest shipping option the seller offers. Some sellers put the fastest shipping service first (Express Mail, Next Day Air, and so on). If so, that is the price you'll see on the search results page.
>
> Whether or not you add the shipping cost, you will always see a "Free Shipping" logo if that is one of the seller's options (see Figure 5.1).

Under **Item Information,** I added **Watch This Item Link.** This is very useful if I'm comparing a lot of auctions for the same item. I often watch 10 to 15 items right from the search results page and then go back to my Watching list in My eBay and sort through them to find the ones I really do want to consider bidding on.

Under **Seller Information,** I added the **Seller User ID** and **Seller Feedback.** This is great information to have on the search results page. I talk more about feedback later, but suffice it to say that if I see a $500 item I'm looking for and I see that the seller has a feedback score lower than 50 and/or a feedback rating below 98 percent, I know not to even bother clicking on the auction.

Under **Advanced Options,** you can change the default sort order from **Best Match** to any of the other alternatives. You can do this for both **Search** and **Browse** (where you go straight to a category without searching). I have both set to **Time: ending soonest.**

That's it—those are my changes. For comparison's sake, Figure 5.2 has the same search result for "Macbook Pro" so you can see the difference.

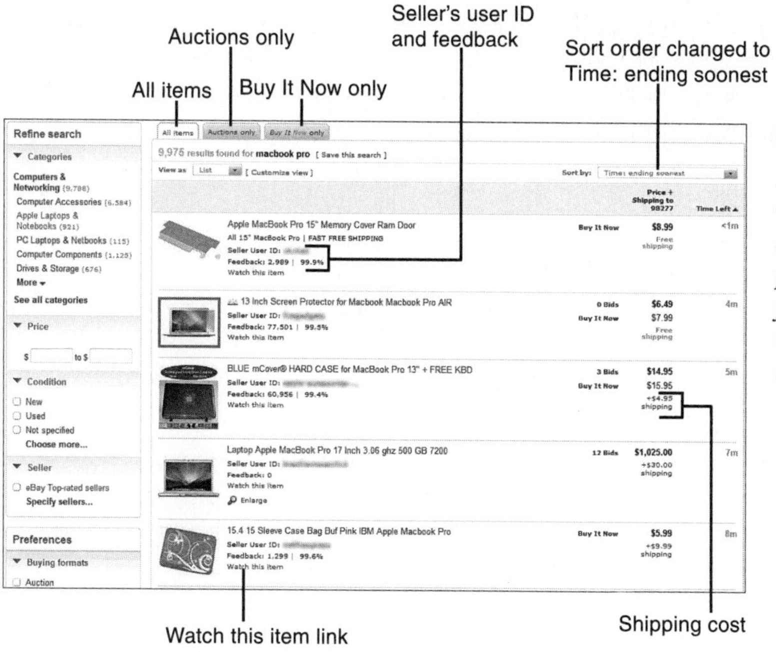

Auctions only

Seller's user ID
and feedback

Sort order changed to
Time: ending soonest

All items   Buy It Now only

Figure 5.2

*Each listing takes more room
with the options I've chosen,
but it also means far fewer
page loads jumping back and
forth from the search results
to the listing descriptions and
back again.*

Watch this item link

Shipping cost

Adjusting the Listing Types

Sometimes you will only want to see listings for items you can purchase immediately.
Other times you might only want auctions. eBay makes it easy to change using the
tabs at the top of the search results (see Figure 5.2). The default is **All items** which
shows all auction and fixed-price listings. Auctions only excludes fixed-price listings. If
you choose Buy It Now only you may see an increase in the number of items in your
results. This is because it not only includes fixed-price listings, but also eBay Store
inventory. No other results include Store inventory. You can exclude those using the
preferences that will appear at the top, but usually you can find some good bargains in
Store inventory.

Why Do So Many Listings Offer Free Shipping?

In years past, sellers have used the shipping cost as a bit of a profit center which
annoys buyers (and eBay, which doesn't get paid fees on the shipping cost). To combat
this, eBay worked free shipping into the Best Match algorithm. So if a seller offers
free shipping for an item, it typically displays higher in the Best Match sort order than
a seller who charges a shipping fee. eBay also offers promotions from time to time for
sellers who choose to offer free shipping.

Of course, sellers work the shipping fee into their item cost, so you usually find the items that offer free shipping and those that don't tend to come out to about the same cost. In one, you're paying a higher item price; in the other, you're paying a lower item price plus the shipping cost.

Featured Items

You may see a section of **Featured Items** at the top of the search results. The sellers of these items have paid extra to get this increased visibility. Only *Top-Rated Sellers* can purchase this option, so you won't always see a lot of Featured items, but if you do see them, you'll know they're from sellers with a proven customer service record.

def•i•ni•tion

Top-Rated Sellers are PowerSellers who have met a strict set of customer service and satisfaction standards. They also have to have sold $3,000 worth of items in the past 12 months and have 100 percent feedback at 98 percent positive.

Why Do Some Listing Titles Look Different?

As well as some listings being placed before others in the featured section, you may also see some listings with titles in bold or with a subtitle beneath the title.

These are listing upgrades that the seller has paid extra for. It does not mean that this item is any better than the others that do not use these upgrades.

Tips

When you think about it, the seller who uses the fancy upgrades has to recoup his cost somewhere (from you, his buyer). He's not going to pay extra fees if he can't make more money than if he didn't use them. So you'll typically find a better price on items that do not use many upgrades because they don't "pop" as much and so tend to get overlooked.

Gallery Plus

Gallery Plus is another listing upgrade you may encounter. This is often used when a seller is offering a bundle of items in one auction (maybe a Nintendo Wii bundled with four games and a Wii Fit) or the item has a high level of intricacy in its details (such as fine jewelry). Gallery Plus enlarges the thumbnail picture to take up most of the screen when you scroll your mouse pointer over the word **Enlarge.** In fact, the fourth item shown in Figure 5.2 is using Gallery Plus. Look back at it in Figure 5.2, and then look at Figure 5.3 to see how the Enlarge link works.

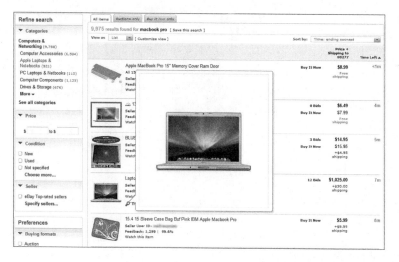

Figure 5.3

*Sellers may have to pay extra for the **Gallery Plus** feature, so not everyone uses it.*

Gallery Plus is free for items listed in the Collectibles, Art, Antiques, or Pottery and Glass categories, so expect to see it there.

Browsing by Picture

In addition to the traditional list view, you can view the search results page in two other ways. These are the **Gallery** and the **Snapshot** view. Both are ways you can browse the results with the focus being on the picture, not the listing title.

The best way to view the search results really depends on the type of item you're looking for. For example, I always view consumer electronic items in list view so that I can see the full title, since that is usually the most important part (because it details the main specifications of the item). Plus, most new electronic items use the same stock image, so the picture isn't all that relevant. However, when I am buying clothing, I always use the snapshot view (see Figure 5.4).

When you hover your mouse over a thumbnail picture in Snapshot view, it enlarges to fill most of the screen, and also gives you a snapshot of the listing details. This includes the item title, current price, shipping cost, time remaining on the listing, and number of bids. Much to my chagrin, there isn't a Watch This Item option yet. I hope this will become available soon, because it would be the icing on the cake for me.

Figure 5.4

*The **Snapshot** view is like having Gallery Plus for every listing in the search results.*

Select your view

The other option is Gallery, which shows only three item pictures across but includes the listing title without hovering your mouse over the picture. The pictures do not enlarge in the Gallery view. For most of my bidding, I use the **Snapshot** view. Sometimes I use the default **List** view, but I haven't used the Gallery view since Snapshot was introduced.

Using Keywords in Your Search

Most buyers look for items by searching keywords, which are simply obvious words that describe the item.

Let's say you're looking for an iPod. You can search just the word "ipod," but it will bring up thousands of results (I tried it and got 123,795 active listings), including accessories, screen protectors, covers, actual iPod units, and more. That is way too many to browse through.

What about "ipod nano"? That removes over two thirds of the listings (40,281 remaining), but that's still too many.

Let's try "green ipod nano." Much better. That gives you 820 listings. That's still a lot, but it's more manageable than the 123,795 listings we started with.

Now let's add the capacity, "16GB." Now there are just 45 results. With the addition of three keywords ("nano," "green," and "16GB"), you've quickly gone from 123,795 listings to 45, and these 45 are highly specific to the item you are looking for. I doubt that any items in that list are not a perfect match for the item you're searching for.

When choosing your keywords, start with a combination of the following options:

- Item name
- Manufacturer (if multiple companies make the same product)
- Color or style
- Condition (only if it is new)

Let's look at a couple of examples in different categories:

Instead of "baby swing" (871 listings), you could search for "fisher price rainforest swing" (14 listings).

Instead of "coffee maker" (2,859 listings), try "delonghi stainless coffee maker" (7 listings).

Putting a little bit of thought into your keywords can make the difference between trawling through hundreds of irrelevant listings to the point that you forget what you were originally looking for, and finding relevant listings quickly and easily so you can get your bid in before the auction ends.

Common Acronyms and Abbreviations

Sellers get only 55 characters in their listing title to entice you to click on their auction. Because of this lack of space, many standard acronyms and abbreviations have developed on the eBay site.

These are just a few of the common ones. To see eBay's full list, click on the eBay **Help** tab and click on the **eBay acronyms** link at the bottom of the **Browse help** box.

Common eBay Acronyms

Acronym	Meaning
BIN	Buy It Now
EUC/GUC	Excellent used condition/Gently used condition
HTF	Hard to find

continues

Common eBay Acronyms   (continued)

Acronym	Meaning
NIB	New in box
NR	No reserve
NWOT	New without tags
NWT	New with tags
RET	Retired

Misspellings Can Equal Major Bargains

Make sure you check misspellings. The eBay search engine catches a lot of them, but others still get through. Try international spellings (jewellery, flavour, colour, aluminium, and so on) because often international sellers list on eBay.com but don't modify their spellings.

If the item doesn't show up in the search results for the correct spelling, fewer people will see it, so you're more likely to get a good bargain. For example, a search for "Sony Vaio Laptop" brought up 12,932 listings, but changing the second word to "Viao" displayed just 27 items. Only one of them had any bids.

Sometimes the item name is completely different in other countries. I'm at an advantage when shopping on eBay UK because I am familiar with the different words in British English versus American English. For example, in England, the accessory a lady puts her wallet, keys, and cell phone into is called a "handbag" no matter what size it is. If you asked for a "purse," you would be directed to the ladies' wallets section.

Advanced Use of the eBay Search Engine

If you're feeling particularly adventurous, you can use certain symbols to narrow results directly from the search box. You can make it as simple or as complicated as you like, so don't worry if you see examples that you're not comfortable trying; just stick with the simpler ones for now. In the next section, I show you another way of refining your search results.

This table shows a quick reference if you need to come back and refresh your memory again on this. Remember, these words are only in the auction title, unless you also check the Search Title and Description box below the search box.

Quick Reference for Search Engine Symbols

Example	Result
"formula one"	All auctions where *Formula* comes directly before *One*.
laptop (sony,dell)	All auctions that have the word *laptop* and either *sony* or *dell*.
tanzanite earrings -stud	All auctions that have both the words *tanzanite* and *earrings*, but do not have the word *stud*.

Exact Phrase

Using quotation marks (") returns only listings with the exact phrase inside the quotes (in the order shown). So if you want items relating to Formula One racing, you would type *"formula one"* to display only listings that have the word *one* directly following the word *formula* in its title. This prevents you from getting auctions with titles such as "<u>one</u> can of baby <u>formula</u>" or "<u>one </u>day only new <u>formula</u> weight loss pill."

Either/Or Words

Now, let's say you're looking for a laptop and you want either a Sony or a Dell. You would type *laptop (sony,dell)*. This would show only listings with the word *laptop* and either *sony* or *dell* in the title.

You can also use this when there are many varieties of spelling. Most of the time, eBay will catch common differences and return all results (for example, a search for *t-shirt* automatically brings up listings using the variations *t shirt*, *t-shirts*, and *t shirts* as well). But this works with brand names that are commonly misspelled too, such as *(Skechers,Sketchers)*.

Either/or searches are very useful when there is sometimes a space between two words and sometimes not. Going back to the iPod example, you could have used *(16GB, 16 GB)* instead of *16GB* to catch all listings that used one or the other. Another example would be *(XBOX360,XBOX 360)*.

Excluding Words

If you want a pair of tanzanite earrings but you don't want them to be stud earrings, you would type *tanzanite earrings –stud*.

You can exclude multiple words by putting them in parentheses, such as *tanzanite earrings –(hoop,stud)*. Or you get the same effect by using *tanzanite earrings –hoop –stud*. It's entirely up to you. Note that the minus sign is next to the word you are excluding—there's no space between them. This is important because you won't exclude the word if you don't type it correctly.

Alternative Endings

If you want to search a word but don't want to use the whole word, you can use an asterisk (*). For example, say you're looking for a 1970s Camero car, but don't mind which actual year model it is. You would search *Camero 197**. This will bring up all listings with the word *Camero* and one of *1970, 1971, 1972*, and so on.

This can also be very useful when a word is commonly misspelled a number of different ways. For example, *porcelain* is often spelled incorrectly. Rather than listing all of the variations, you can just put *vase porc** and all the listings with any variation will display. Yes, you may get some irrelevant listings, but you'll catch all the misspellings that other buyers don't see, too.

Putting It All Together

This is not for the faint-hearted, but if you understand all of the examples I used earlier, you should be able to grasp this after the initial "eeek" response wears off.

Let's say you want a pair of white gold or silver tanzanite earrings, but you don't want stud or hoop earrings. You would type *tanzanite earrings ("white gold",silver) –(hoop,stud)*.

I know, this last example feels a little like an algebraic equation, but it shows you what you can do with the search engine. I put quotes around *"white gold"* so the search results do not return yellow or rose gold items.

If this is all a bit too much for you, you can go to **Advanced Search** (beside the search box on the home page) and specify your choices in the appropriate boxes there. eBay will work out the symbols for you. It is more limited, and you would not have been able to do the final example, but you can do all the others.

Saved Searches

If you do a very long, complicated search that you will want to use again, you may want to save it so you won't have to type it out every single time. When you're on the search results page for the search you want to save, simply click **Save this search** (see Figure 5.6).

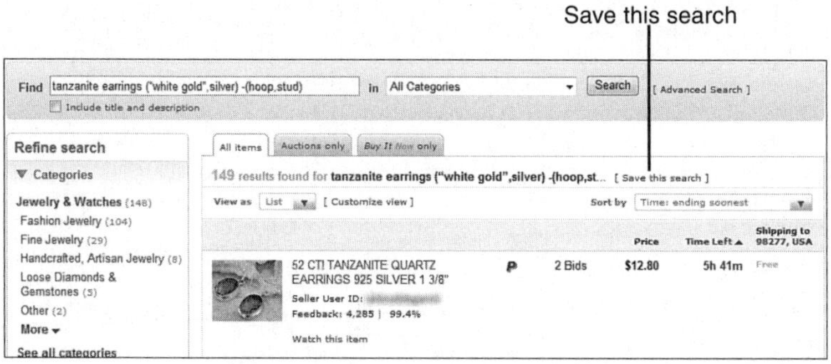

Save this search

Figure 5.6

*You access your saved searches in the **Organize** section on the left bar on the **Activities** tab in My eBay.*

When you select **Save this search,** you will see a pop-up window offering to e-mail you matching results for the foreseeable future. It's entirely up to you whether you want to do this. You can select to have eBay e-mail you for 7 days, all the way up to 12 months. If you don't want daily e-mails from eBay about this saved search, just uncheck the box and click **Save.** This search will now show up in My eBay. You can go to it at any time and perform the search without having to type the whole string again.

Refining Your Search

Think back to the iPod example. We got our results down to 45, which is great. But what if we'd not been able to get that far? Let's say the search was *red ipod nano (16GB,16 GB)*. That would have brought up 68 results—not too many more, but worth looking to narrow, if possible.

Take a look at Figure 5.7. The **Refine search** box on the left shows the categories those 68 items are in. As you would expect, all of them are in the **Electronics** main category. But look at the subcategories. There are two showing: **iPod & MP3 Accessories,** and **iPod & MP3 Players.** Since you're looking for the actual iPod unit, the second subcategory is the one that fits.

Next to the category title, you'll see a number. This is the number of items that match the search terms within that subcategory. In this case, only 10 items match *red ipod nano 16GB* in the iPod & MP3 Players category. Now that's a highly specialized search!

Figure 5.7

The categories display in popularity order (the one with the most items that match the search keywords will be at the top, and so on).

Refine search

Main category

Subcategories

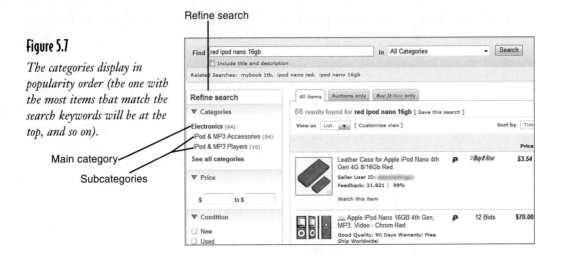

Sometimes you'll have more than one layer of subcategories to go through. For example, if you searched *True Religion jeans*, the first Refine search categories option would include men's clothing, women's clothing, and a bunch of others. So you might select Women's clothing. Now you'd still have 1,863 items, so you get to select another subcategory. Options include Jeans, Juniors, Maternity, Skirts, and more. Selecting Jeans gets us to the lowest subcategory. So we are currently in the *Clothing, Shoes and Accessories—Women's Clothing—Jeans* category.

Now there are additional options in the **Refine search** box (as shown in Figure 5.8). These include the style of jeans, the size type, the size, the condition, the price, and more.

Figure 5.8

You can select as many or as few options as you want.

Choose more ...

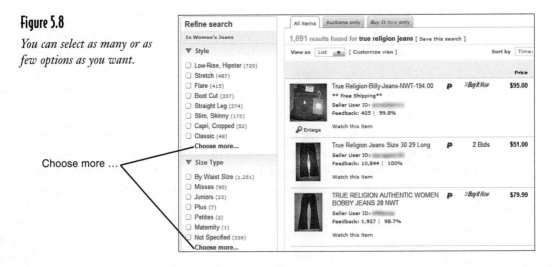

One of my favorite features of Refine search is the **Choose more...** option shown beneath each section. This allows you to make more than one selection.

Let's say that you fit in both size 6 and size 8 jeans. Rather than having to run the search twice (once for each size option), you can select **Choose more** beneath the **Size** section, and check the boxes for both 6 and 8. Now all of the results that match either of these sizes will display for you.

You can also use this to exclude just one option. Let's say you're interested in any style of jeans except straight leg. You could use the **Choose more** option to select all of the other styles (Bootcut, Low Rise, Flare, and so on) and just leave Straight Leg unchecked.

You'll notice that only a few of the listings have all of these selections as keywords in the listing title. The search engine is able to narrow the results because of additional details about the item that the seller added during the listing process. These are called Item Specifics.

If your original search keywords match a selection the seller made in Item Specifics, but the words were not actually in the listing title as well, the seller's item still shows up on your search results page. Let's go back to the red iPods for a moment. Listings that did not have the word *red* in the title, but whose seller had selected **Red** for the color in the Item Specifics section would still show up in the results.

By using descriptive keywords and Refine Search, you can find far more relevant items in your searches.

Selecting Your Preferences

You will find yourself using this feature a lot once you get comfortable searching for items. The Preferences box displays on the left-side bar of the search results page beneath the Refine Search box (see Figure 5.9). It enables you to narrow your results by location, payment method, auction type, free shipping only, and more.

While you are starting out, I suggest that you select **US Only** for the **Location** so that you're not dealing with international sellers. Choosing **North America** will show listings from the United States and Canada only, so that is the next step. Even when you are comfortable buying overseas, you will probably use the **US Only** option when you need something quickly because there is no point in looking overseas when shipping time is critical.

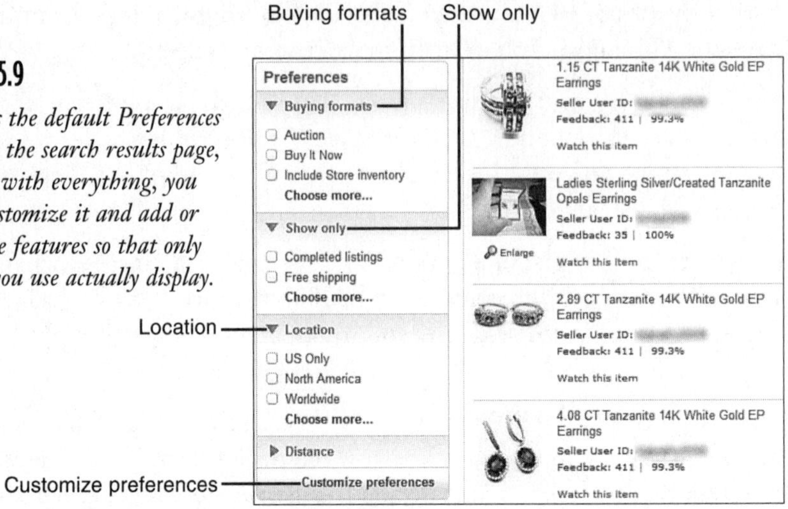

Figure 5.9

This is the default Preferences box on the search results page, but as with everything, you can customize it and add or remove features so that only those you use actually display.

Buying formats   Show only

Location ——

Customize preferences ——

Preferences

▼ Buying formats
☐ Auction
☐ Buy It Now
☐ Include Store inventory
  Choose more...

▼ Show only
☐ Completed listings
☐ Free shipping
  Choose more...

▼ Location
☐ US Only
☐ North America
☐ Worldwide
  Choose more...

▶ Distance

Customize preferences

1.15 CT Tanzanite 14K White Gold EP Earrings
Seller User ID:
Feedback: 411 | 99.3%
Watch this item

Ladies Sterling Silver/Created Tanzanite Opals Earrings
Seller User ID:
Feedback: 35 | 100%
Watch this item

2.89 CT Tanzanite 14K White Gold EP Earrings
Seller User ID:
Feedback: 411 | 99.3%
Watch this item

4.08 CT Tanzanite 14K White Gold EP Earrings
Seller User ID:
Feedback: 411 | 99.3%
Watch this item

The **Buying formats** section is the same as the tabs at the top of the search results. You can select **Auction, Buy It Now, Include Store inventory,** or any combination of the three options.

The **Show only** section offers you two ways to restrict the results: **Free shipping** or **Completed listings.**

Free shipping is nice but is unlikely to actually be "free," as I mentioned earlier. **Completed listings** is a very important option to look at. This shows you only items matching your search terms that have already ended (within the last two weeks). This is the only way you can see what similar items have actually sold for recently. It's very important to always check the Completed listings before you decide on your maximum bid, to keep from overpaying and know what range you should expect to bid in. We talk about this more in Chapter 7.

Product Pages

Some items are easily categorized with ISBN numbers, Model numbers, and so on. For these items, eBay often offers a *product page.* You may see this offered as you type your search terms (see Figure 5.10) or you may just be taken there after you click search.

def•i•ni•tion

A **product page** is like a catalog page for the item. It shows you details of the item, and then lists all the sellers who are offering it for sale and their price. You will only see product pages for easily categorized items.

Figure 5.10

Product pages can be helpful for locating multiple options for the exact same item.

The look of a product page is very different from the search results page, but it can help you find your item much quicker. Let's say you're looking for a video game and end up on the product page for that title. You know that every listing shown is for that specific item on that video game platform.

Figure 5.11 shows the product page for Madden NFL 09 for the Xbox 360. As you can see, it shows the listings titles in the center. To save space, it has the seller's information on the same line to the right of the title. The rest of the information is the same as you see on the search results page.

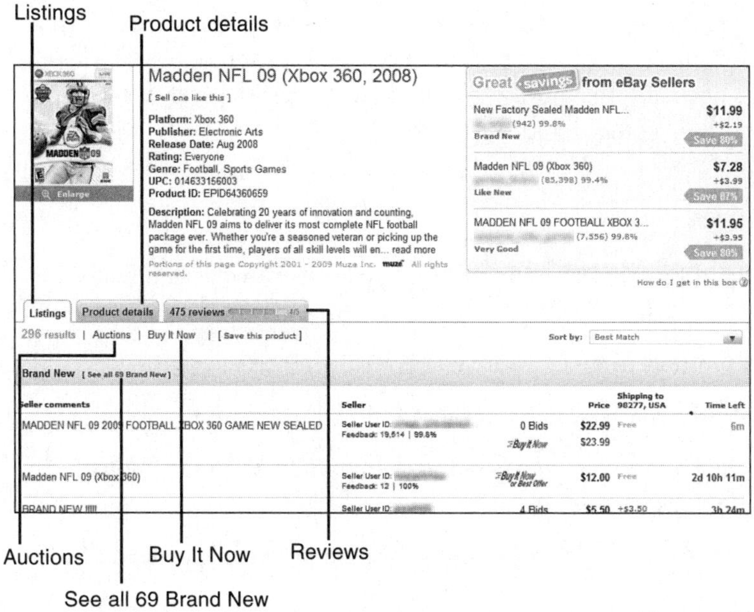

Figure 5.11

Product details pages give you access to more product information, easier ordering based on item condition, and reviews from other eBay members.

One thing I like about product pages are the two additional tabs: **Product details** and **Reviews.** If you're not sure about a product, this will give you far more information, just like you'd see in a catalog. Sometimes sellers don't include this in their listing, so the **Product details** tab can be a real timesaver when searching for more details about the product. The **Reviews** tab shows you reviews made by other eBay members. You can access this from the **Reviews and Guides** page, but this makes it much easier and quicker to find.

On the **Listings** tab you'll notice that the items are sorted by Best Match, but also separated by condition. Brand New is at the top, followed by Like New, then Very Good, Good, and finally Acceptable. Make sure you're in the right section for the item condition you want. You may find a great bargain because something is Like New instead of Brand New. Only a handful of items are shown for each condition. To see all of the listings for that item condition, you need to click **See all 69 Brand New** (see Figure 5.11). This link is available at both the top and bottom of the section.

The only thing I don't like about product pages is the inability to exclude international sellers. I choose to only purchase DVDs and video games from U.S. sellers. I don't get the option to automatically exclude all non-U.S. items on a product page. I have to make sure to check for that within each listing I consider bidding on.

The featured items box on the top right show a selection of sellers who have shown a good track record for customer service, buyer satisfaction rating, and offer free or very low shipping costs. This does not mean these are the best deals. However, it's worth comparing those to the others you consider.

The Least You Need to Know

- ◆ Use Refine search and Preferences to narrow your results to what you really want to see.

- ◆ Use search engine symbols to make your search results more relevant.

- ◆ Try misspellings and alternative spellings to find hidden bargains.

- ◆ Save your searches for more rare items, and have eBay e-mail you if any listings are made that meet your criteria.

- ◆ Switch to the Snapshot view when you want to browse by picture instead of by title.

- ◆ Use product pages to find more product details and reviews of the item.

Chapter 6

The Listing Page

In This Chapter

- ◆ Exploring the listing page sections
- ◆ What to look for in Seller info
- ◆ Types of auctions you will encounter

When you click on a listing title from the search results page, you will be taken to the listing page for that item. It really goes without saying that understanding the listing page is paramount to your success on eBay. There's a lot of information on this page, and it's split up into three main sections:

1. The **listing summary** at the top of the page
2. The **Description** tab
3. The **Shipping and Payments** tab

You need to read *all* of the listing before deciding whether you want to bid. In this chapter, we look at each of these sections.

Listing Summary

At the top of the page (above the tabs), you'll see a summary of the most important details about the listing (see Figure 6.1):

◆ A picture of the item, with an **Enlarge** link to show a bigger picture.

◆ **Item condition** (new, new in package, new with tags, like new, used, and so on).

◆ **Time left** on the listing, shown with a real-time countdown timer, as well as the ending date and time.

◆ **Bid history** showing how many bids have been placed. Click **See History** to see how many unique buyers actually make up those bids.

◆ **Starting bid.** This will read "Current bid" once a bid has been placed on the item.

◆ A box to enter a bid of your own and the **Place bid** button to submit it.

◆ If there is a **Buy It Now** option, this button will also appear beneath the **Place bid** button.

◆ **Watch this item** link. This adds the listing to your Watching list in My eBay. Note: This is at the very top right corner of the page as well as in the gray bidding box.

◆ **Shipping** details, including the price, shipping service (for example, U.S. Postal Service Priority Mail), and estimated delivery time (this includes the seller's handling time before shipping).

◆ **Returns** policy. This shows how long the buyer has to return an item (if at all), who pays return shipping, and how the return is repaid (replacement only, money back, and so on). Sellers must specify a returns policy if only to say "no returns accepted."

◆ Coverage for fraud protection. Most items will say "Pay with PayPal and your full purchase price is covered," but always check for this.

Did You Know?

eBay doesn't display the high bidder on the listing page, and masks all user IDs on the bid history page (click the link labeled History). You will see two random letters taken from the user ID, with three asterisks in between (for example, e***r). The Feedback Score shown after this masked ID is accurate for the bidder, but it is not an active link through to his Feedback Profile.

Countdown timer

Bid history

Item condition

Starting bid

Place bid

Watch this item

Seller info

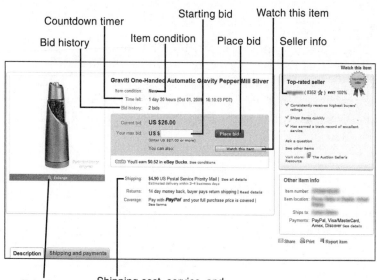

Figure 6.1

*A fixed-price listing will look identical, but the **Place bid** button in the gray box will be replaced with one that says **Buy It Now**.*

Enlarge

Shipping cost, service, and estimated delivery time

Some fixed-price listings (Buy It Now only) offer color, size, or style choices. If you happen to be looking at one of these, the gray center bid area will include drop-down menus for the options you can choose. For example, in Figure 6.2 you can see the options for these sneakers are color and size. You select your options before you buy so you can be certain the seller has what you want in stock.

Color and size choices for the item

Figure 6.2

Sellers can offer very similar items in the same listing using these choice options rather than list a separate auction for every color or size choice they have in stock.

Seller Information

The great thing about eBay is that you get to see relevant information about your seller and her track record right on the listing page, before you ever place a bid. This is the **Seller info** box, displayed to the right of the item summary at the top of the listing page. In the **Seller info** box you'll see a summary of the seller's feedback, as well as links to **Ask a question, See other items** from the same seller, and **Visit store** to go to the seller's eBay Store if she has one.

Tips _____

I talk about feedback in Chapter 7, however it's worth mentioning here that the seller's feedback is vitally important. You get a snapshot of information in the **Seller info** box, which is great, but you should also do further research (as I explain in the next chapter) before bidding or committing to buy.

Beneath this box is an **Other item info** box. This shows the item number, the location, where the seller will ship to, and the payment options.

What Do Icons After User IDs Mean?

The icons you see after the user ID in the **Seller info** box are a quick at-a-glance reference of facts about the seller.

mcgrrrrr (8311 ☆)   **Feedback Score**—This is the net number of positive feedback comments left by other eBay users who have bought from or sold to this user. It is shown in parentheses after the user ID.

    Feedback star—Most sellers have a colored star after the Feedback Score inside the parentheses. This means they have a Feedback Score of 10 or more. The color changes as the Feedback Score increases.

    Shooting star—Some sellers have a colored shooting star instead of a single colored star. This means their Feedback Score is over 10,000. The highest is a silver shooting star, which indicates a Feedback Score of over 100,000.

About Me page—This shows that the user has created an About Me page where other eBay users can read more about the person and the business, and link through to their off-eBay website, if they have one.

 ID Verified—The ID Verify process is optional and costs the eBay user $5. A third-party company verifies the seller's address, as well as information that only that person would know from their credit report. If you see the ID Verified logo, it means that the seller has completed the process and that his identity and address have been confirmed correct.

 Changed User ID—If a seller has changed his user ID in the past 30 days, this icon appears after his name.

 New Member—When you first register on eBay, the New Member icon appears after your user ID for the next 30 days. It disappears automatically after that. If you intend to sell as well as buy, I recommend waiting until after the first 30 days to offer your first item because many buyers are more wary of very new sellers.

eBay Store—This shows that the seller manages an eBay Store, and provides an active link to that store.

Reviewer—If a user writes a review or guide about a product—or, in fact, anything about eBay—he can get a pencil-and-paper icon after his username once 100 people have read the article and voted that they found it helpful.

 Top Reviewer—Once the seller's review or guide is in the top 10,000 most helpful reviews (as voted by readers), the pencil-and-paper icon will show "Top XX Reviewer" after it (with the "XX" indicating how popular the review is). It's not an exact number, as in Top 25, Top 100, or Top 5,000.

 In addition to these icons, you may see a **Top-Rated Seller** badge at the top of the **Seller info** box. When a seller earns a Top-Rated Seller Badge (TRS), she gets this icon after her user ID. Top-Rated Sellers are those who qualify for the PowerSeller program ($3,000 in sales plus 100 transactions per year and 98 percent positive feedback),

but also maintain a high level of customer service. This is measured by the number of low (1 or 2 star) Detailed Seller Ratings (DSRs) this individual receives. The percentage of low DSRs allowed varies by the sellers volume of sales, but you can be certain that if you see this logo, the seller has a good customer service record.

Listing Tabs

There are two listing tabs which hold different information about the item and seller's terms: **Description and Shipping Payments.** This is the remainder of the listing details. Much of it is repeated in the listing summary at the top, but you'll see more options, and more information on each of the tabs.

Description

The first tab, and the default when you get to the listing page, is **Description.** Here you'll find the Item Specifics (if the seller selected any) and the description of the item that the seller has written.

The description will look different depending on which seller listed the item. Many sellers use templates to make their listings look more professional. Some business sellers have their own custom templates to make their listings look more like their website or eBay Store.

Where additional photographs display depends on what service the seller used to upload them. If the seller used eBay's picture services to upload (and therefore paid fees to eBay per picture), small thumbnail images will display beneath the main image in the item summary at the top of the page (see Figure 6.2). However, if the seller used a third-party host for the pictures, you will only see one picture at the top, and any additional pictures will only display as you scroll down on the **Description** tab.

If the seller's photograph is high enough resolution, you may also see a **Zoom** option as well as the usual **Enlarge** one. The zoom feature will let you zoom in on any area of the photograph currently shown in the listing summary. As neat as this is, I think the enlarge is better. You're going to see the biggest image you can get using the **Enlarge** option, so I think it is better to just do that and see the whole image enlarged at once than try to zoom in on certain areas. Still, there may be times that you want to use this function.

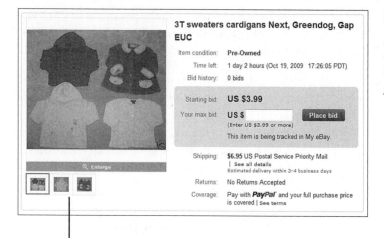

Figure 6.3

Hovering your mouse over a smaller thumbnail image will display it in the main photograph box.

Additional photographs uploaded using eBay's picture hosting service

Shipping and Payments

On this second tab, you'll see all the details about shipping, return policies, and payment options. The listing summary at the top of the page shows only the first listed shipping option. If the seller has alternatives (for example, an overnight service or two-day air service, for a higher price), you can click **see more services** and it will pop up a window showing the alternative, or you can click the **Shipping and Payments** tab and see each option and price here.

Again, on the listing summary at the top of the page, you will see the basic returns policy, but here on the Shipping and Payments tab you'll find the expanded version with all terms and conditions.

Your payment options also show on this tab. Almost every seller offers PayPal, but if the seller offers other payment methods, they will show on this tab.

If the description or shipping options aren't clear, or if you have questions about the item that are not covered in the listing, always use the Ask a question link in the Seller info box and send the seller an e-mail *before* you bid. Don't ever assume details that are not clearly stated.

Types of Listing

So far, we've mainly talked about auctions. The seller lists the item, the buyers bid, and at the end of the specified duration, the highest bidder wins the item. But other

def•i•ni•tion

Buy It Now is simply an instant purchase listing. As soon as the buyer selects the Buy It Now option, the listing ends and the buyer has won the item.

types of listings don't require you to wait until the end of the duration to buy. These are all forms of a *Buy It Now* listing.

Because it is so easy to use **Buy It Now,** you must be extra careful to read the description thoroughly and make sure it really is what you want, at the price you want to pay. You should also look at the shipping and handling times to make sure it will arrive in time for whatever you need it for, and read the seller's return policies in case something goes wrong.

Buy It Now Auction

Buy It Now auctions are a bit of both worlds. They are auctions, with a starting price and regular duration, but they also have a Buy It Now price (see Figure 6.4).

You decide whether you want to pay the Buy It Now price or take a chance on bidding and see how high it goes. In most categories, the Buy It Now price disappears after the first bid is placed, however this is not always the case. Sometimes it remains until a certain dollar value or a percentage of the Buy It Now price is reached, or a certain amount of time is remaining on the auction. This is not something the seller can control.

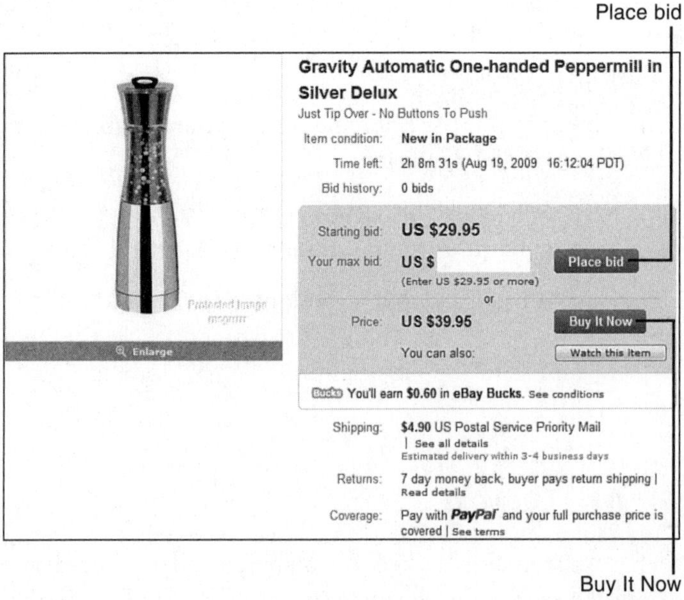

Figure 6.4

*The **Buy It Now** price is always at least 10 percent above the starting bid.*

Place bid

Gravity Automatic One-handed Peppermill in Silver Delux
Just Tip Over - No Buttons To Push

Item condition:	**New in Package**
Time left:	2h 8m 31s (Aug 19, 2009 16:12:04 PDT)
Bid history:	0 bids
Starting bid:	**US $29.95**
Your max bid:	**US $** [ ] Place bid
	(Enter US $29.95 or more)
	or
Price:	**US $39.95** Buy It Now
	You can also: Watch this item

Bucks You'll earn $0.60 in eBay Bucks. See conditions

Shipping:	$4.90 US Postal Service Priority Mail
	| See all details
	Estimated delivery within 3-4 business days
Returns:	7 day money back, buyer pays return shipping | Read details
Coverage:	Pay with **PayPal** and your full purchase price is covered | See terms

⊕ Enlarge

Buy It Now

If the seller put a *reserve price* on the auction, then the Buy It Now price won't disappear until at least that reserve amount is met.

def•i•ni•tion

Items with lower starting prices usually get more bids and higher final prices. For example, if a seller is willing to sell an item for no less than $100, she may set the starting price at $9.99 but set the **reserve price** at $100. Now the bidding starts at $9.99, but if it does not meet or exceed $100, the seller is not obligated to sell the item to the highest bidder.

Once the reserve price is met, the Buy It Now option disappears and the auction runs its course as if that option had never been available.

Fixed-Price Listings

Fixed-price listings do not have a starting price. They only have the Buy It Now price. These listings are much more like online purchases you'd make from any other website. There is no bidding—only purchasing. Figure 6.5 shows a Buy It Now fixed-price auction.

Figure 6.5

Keep an eye on the quantity available so your seller doesn't sell out before you buy!

Every so often, you will see a Buy It Now listing with the words "Immediate Payment Required" beneath the price. This requires the buyer to pay as soon as she confirms her Buy It Now purchase. The buyer is taken straight to PayPal to make the payment, so she doesn't have the option of waiting to pay. The listing doesn't actually end until the buyer completes the payment.

This is an option that the seller selects to prevent buyers from using the Buy It Now option (which otherwise ends the listing) and then not paying. You don't see it on every Buy It Now listing (the listing in Figure 6.5 does not use it), but you'll see it from time to time.

Best Offer

This is an option you may see in addition to the Buy It Now price on a fixed-price listing (see Figure 6.6). **Best Offer** lets you haggle with the seller over the price for the item.

To submit a Best Offer, click **Make Offer** and enter a price lower than the Buy It Now price. The seller will respond one of three ways:

1. Accept the offer (and you win the item).

2. Reject the offer (and you can submit a higher offer, use the Buy It Now option, or move on to find another item).

3. Counter the offer with a price higher than yours but lower than the Buy It Now price.

Figure 6.6

*Always make an offer if that's an option. The seller is expecting to sell the item for less than the Buy It Now price, or he wouldn't have added **Best Offer**.*

You can track items you've made offers on in My eBay. You'll also get an e-mail from eBay when the seller takes action on your offer, but you should always go to your **Messages** box in My eBay to confirm that this is a genuine offer.

If the seller counters your initial offer, you can choose to accept it, counter it yourself, or just move on to another listing if the price the seller is asking is way too high for you.

Best Offer can only be attached to a fixed-price listing. It is not available for auctions (even those with an additional Buy It Now price).

You may find that you get an instant response to your offer. Sellers can set their preferences to automatically accept offers over a certain amount and reject offers below a certain amount. So don't be surprised if you make an offer and immediately see the "Your offer has been accepted" screen.

You'll notice that there is a reduced price for the item in Figure 6.6. Sellers can put their inventory on sale, and many do to increase immediate sales. You see both the original price and the sale price. To the right of the photograph, you'll also see the discount percentage. In the gray box you will also see when the sale is ending. Usually sales only last for a few days up to a week.

eBay Store Inventory

eBay Stores are fixed-price listings, which don't usually show in the main search results. You can view eBay Store inventory items in three ways:

1. Check the **Include Store inventory** option in the **Preferences** box on the search results page. The search results page then displays all listings: auctions, fixed-price listings, and store inventory.

2. Click **Stores** on the eBay tabs at the top of the page and then use the search box on this page. This brings up results only in eBay Stores.

3. Click the **Buy It Now only** tab at the top of the search results page. The search results page then displays fixed-price listings, store inventory, and auctions that have a Buy It Now option, but no traditional auctions.

eBay Stores were originally the only way a seller could list an item at fixed price. There is a monthly fee to the seller for having a store, but the per-item fees tend to be lower. Still, more and more sellers are moving away from store inventory to the fixed-price listing format that displays their items in amongst the main search results.

Restricted Access

Restricted access auctions are for items that may not be sold to minors. There are mature audience categories on eBay that you must have a credit card on file with eBay proving that you are over 18 to access. This is another reason for not letting your teenagers know your eBay password. eBay requires you to sign in again before going to those categories (even if you have checked the **Keep me signed in for today** box).

The Least You Need to Know

- Look at all the details on the listing page, including the **Seller info** before deciding if this item is right for you.

- Some fixed-price listings offer choices (such as size or color) whereas others are strictly for the item listed.

- Watch for items that are on sale. The discount won't last long, but it could save you a bit of money on your purchase.

- Sellers who use the **Best Offer** option are expecting to sell the item for lower than the **Buy It Now** price. To get the best bargains, always make an offer rather than using Buy It Now.

- Click on the **Shipping and Payments** tab to see all the seller's shipping options. Sometimes you'll see a cheaper option than the one shown in the listing snapshot.

- If there is contradictory information in the listing or something isn't clear, make sure to e-mail the seller for clarification *before* you bid.

Chapter 7

Advanced Research

In This Chapter

- ◆ Using eBay tools to find the best deal
- ◆ Comparing items that aren't quite the same
- ◆ Avoiding being overcharged for shipping
- ◆ Putting the seller under a microscope
- ◆ How to read a seller's Feedback Profile

You've found an interesting item, so you're ready to place your bid, right? Wait! The Irish proverb "Don't test the depth of a river with both feet" certainly holds true here.

Before you bid, you need to ask yourself a few questions:

- ◆ Is this item really what I want?
- ◆ What total price (including shipping) am I prepared to pay for it?
- ◆ Am I getting a better deal here than I can get locally or at another online site (such as Amazon.com)?
- ◆ Who am I dealing with?

Most disputes between buyers and sellers stem from misunderstandings. Perhaps the item description was unclear, or maybe the buyer simply didn't read it correctly.

Never assume anything; be extra careful to read everything about the item, the shipping costs, and the seller's terms and conditions. If it looks too good to be true, it probably is.

If in doubt, e-mail the seller and ask. This is the only way you will get a definitive answer. "I assumed it was …" is not a valid reason to complain to eBay if you didn't get what you actually wanted.

How Much Is Too Much?

I'm going to digress a little bit here, but bear with me; it's an important step for deciding if this item is really right for you.

We talked about Completed Listings briefly in Chapter 5. It's very important to use this option when deciding how much you are willing to pay. There's no point bidding if most items are selling for $50 above what you can afford, or if you can find the item cheaper locally or elsewhere online.

Search for your item as I explained in Chapter 5, and use the **Refine Search** options to get you to the exact items you're looking for. Now select **Completed Listings** in the **Preferences** box (on the left sidebar).

The Completed Listings page (Figure 7.1) shows only items matching your original search requirements that have ended in the last two weeks. Items that sold show the price in green with **Sold** in a box beneath the number of bids. All others did not sell.

Sometimes you'll see a listing that has bids but did not sell. These are auctions with reserve prices. You will see **Reserve Not Met** in red next to the listing title to indicate that this was why the item didn't sell.

You are interested only in items that actually sold, so look for the "Sold" tag and the green prices. You're also looking for an average total price, so make sure you add the shipping costs to the selling prices to see what buyers are actually paying. Ignore prices that are wildly high or low because they will skew your average. Also, make sure to compare apples to apples. An electric guitar sold with a strap and case is going to sell for more than the same electric guitar without the additional accessories. So, make sure the listings you compare have the same accessories.

It's usually quite easy to spot the average, but I like to jot down the approximate total prices just so I don't have to use my brain so much. Figure 7.1 shows the Completed Listings page for a new 16GB iPod Touch.

You can use the **Sort by** drop-down menu to change the sort order to **Price + Shipping: highest first** to see the top selling prices, and then **Price + Shipping: lowest first** to see the lowest prices. This can help you find your average price.

Tips _____

You can use the **Price + Shipping** sort orders to see when the item sold for the lowest prices and highest prices. This tells you when is a good time of the week to buy, and when to specifically avoid.

I can see that the average selling price for this item is around $220 to $250, including shipping. So I know I won't likely get it for under $200, but equally I know that $300 is far too much.

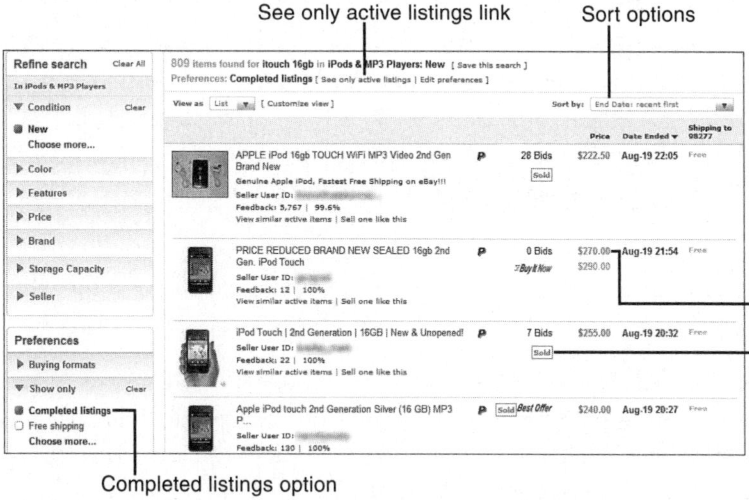

See only active listings link   Sort options

Figure 7.1

To return to the active listings search results page, just click the See Only Active Listings link at the top of the page.

Item did not sell

Item sold

Completed listings option

This information is invaluable when you actually get into the bidding process. You are less likely to get "auction fever" and overbid if you know that you can stop and bid on a different one and get it for less.

But wait. Completed Listings tells you only the price items are selling for *on eBay*. You should always check local and online retailer prices in case there are sales or other specials.

This particular model of iPod retails for $299 direct from the manufacturer (Apple) with free shipping, but when you add sales tax (I'm using Washington's 9 percent here), the cost becomes $325.91. Looking on Amazon.com, which is another competitive website, I can get the iPod for $299 (including tax and shipping).

It pays to shop around, both locally and online. For new items, eBay doesn't always have the best price. In this case, though, it looks like I can get a better deal on eBay as long as I stick to my maximum and avoid sellers from my state (so I don't pay sales tax). In this example, my maximum would be $299 because that's the cheapest I can get it elsewhere.

Now you know not to bid $1 over the $299 price you can get elsewhere (including shipping) unless it comes with extra accessories you want and would pay extra for anyway.

It is very easy to get caught up in the excitement of an auction. It may be difficult at the end of the auction seeing yourself get outbid by 50¢, but you don't know what the other bidder's final bid was. It could have been 50¢ higher, or it could have been $20 higher. You know you can get the item for $299 elsewhere. Other bidders may not, and may overbid.

At the end of the day, I can't tell you how much is too much. That is a decision you have to make. Do the research—check the retail cost locally and elsewhere online, check the average total cost in the Completed Listings, and then decide how much this item is worth to *you*. But please always decide on your maximum before you ever place your first bid.

Comparing Items

To compare items, you first need to add them to your **Watching** list by clicking **Watch this item** from the listing page. Now go to My eBay. Select each of the listings you want to compare by checking the corresponding boxes to the left. Now just click **Compare,** at the bottom of the section (see Figure 7.2).

The default comparison page compares up to four items per page side by side (see Figure 7.3). The auction specifics include the following:

- Item (listing title and thumbnail picture)

- Time left

- Bids

- Seller's user ID and feedback information

- Current price (and/or Buy It Now price)

◆ Shipping cost to your zip code

◆ Country the item ships from

◆ Payment methods accepted

◆ Return policy details

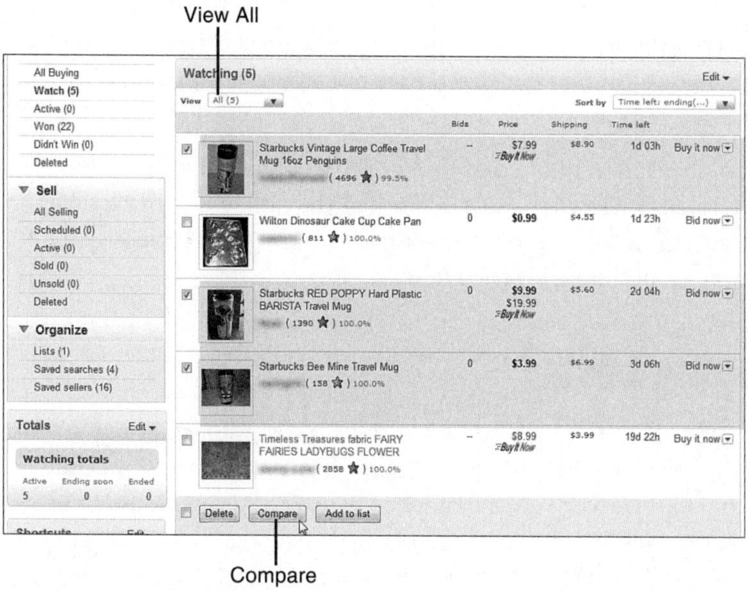

View All

Figure 7.2

*If you want to compare items that are on more than one page, just click **All** in the **View** menu at the top of the **Watching** section.*

Compare

Remove All   Remove Item   Show All Items

Figure 7.3

Comparing items shows a side-by-side snapshot of details from multiple listing.

Sort Order

If you're impatient (like me) and don't want to view multiple pages when comparing more than four items, you can click the **Show All Items** link at the top or bottom right of the page to display all of the items you compare, and just scroll sideways to see the other items.

You can change the order of the items by using the **Sort by** drop-down menu, as shown in Figure 7.3.

If you decide you are no longer interested in an item, click **Remove Item** at the top or bottom of that item's column. If you decide you are not interested in any of the items, click the **Remove All** button.

If the price, shipping, feedback, and item condition are comparable between a few sellers, look to see which sellers allow returns and look at the policy details. A seller who offers a 30 day no questions asked money-back guarantee is preferable over one who doesn't allow returns, or has more restrictive policies.

What About Shipping Costs?

You can end up paying more than the local retail cost because of high shipping. Heavy items are more expensive to ship, but you should always watch out for sellers using shipping as a profit center. Every once in a while, you will see auctions listed for a penny or a dollar for something far more valuable. When you look at the shipping costs, you see that the seller charges $20 or $30 over the actual shipping cost to recoup what they lost on the actual auction price.

This may sound redundant because they end up with the same amount of money, but it's all about eBay fees.

eBay doesn't charge selling fees on the shipping cost—only on the purchase price. So let's say you purchased an item for 99¢ and paid $30 in shipping. You sent the seller $30.99, but he paid the selling fees on only 99¢. The remaining $30 (minus his actual shipping cost) is pure profit for him. This is a type of fee avoidance, and eBay is cracking down on it.

Did You Know?

Excessive shipping is fee avoidance. In Chapter 9, I show you how to report listing violations like this one. Reporting these listings helps maintain eBay as a safe trading environment for everyone. If your sister was looking at this auction, you'd warn her about the shipping gouging, so why not other members of the eBay community?

On the **Shipping and Payments** tab on the auction page, you can see the shipping services that the seller offers and the corresponding costs. Sometimes they are flat-rate costs to all buyers in that country; other times they are calculated based on your zip code. If you are already signed in to eBay, your zip code will be filled in for you. If not, you can enter it in the box provided (see Figure 7.4).

Sometimes you will see a **Quantity** box, as shown in Figure 7.4. This means it is a fixed-price listing and the seller has more than one identical item for sale. If you want to purchase two or more, change the quantity and then click **Get Rates.** Often sellers offer a reduced rate if you purchase more than one item from them, so the total cost now displays next to each shipping service.

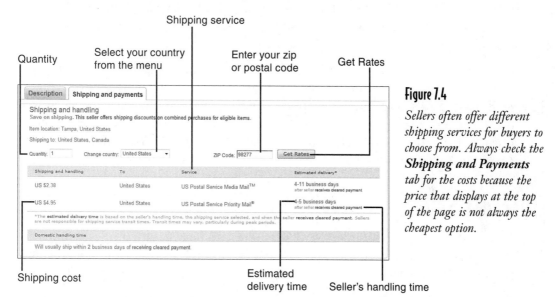

Figure 7.4

*Sellers often offer different shipping services for buyers to choose from. Always check the **Shipping and Payments** tab for the costs because the price that displays at the top of the page is not always the cheapest option.*

Sellers are required to specify the shipping cost in the listing. However, if it is a flat rate (that is, not calculated based on exact postage to your address), they do not have to specify the service they use.

Never assume a shipping service based on the shipping cost. A price of $10.95 may seem logical for Priority Mail, but unless it is specified, there is nothing to stop the seller from shipping Parcel Post or Media Mail and pocketing the difference. So if in doubt, ask.

Maximum Shipping Cost

Some categories have maximum shipping charges. Currently, these categories are Books, DVDs & Movies, Music, and Video Games. http://pages.ebay.com/sell/august2008update/maxshipping/index.html shows the current rates (or you can go to the **Help** tab and search for "maximum shipping"—it should be the second link).

You should assume that all media items from these categories will be mailed via Media Mail because this is the cheapest option for the seller. For example, the maximum shipping for a DVD or Blu-ray is $3. That doesn't give the seller a lot of wiggle room to add a packaging and handling fee, so he will use the cheapest shipping option. He may offer other, more expensive options (for example, Priority Mail shipping for $7). That's okay, as long as he also offers a shipping option for $3 or less.

Many sellers offer free shipping because it gets them benefits from eBay. Often eBay runs promotions specifically for items offering free shipping. If you see free shipping, always assume it is the cheapest service. Listings with free shipping typically have a higher starting price or Buy It Now price than those without (the seller has to recover the shipping cost somehow). I expect we will see additional categories and maximum prices added to the list over the next year or so. Check the eBay **Announcements** board to keep up on new changes like this.

Overseas Sellers

You can see the item location in the **Other item info** box beneath the **Seller info** on the listing page (see Figure 7.5), but this doesn't mean the seller is actually located in that place. You need to click the seller's Feedback Score to visit his Feedback Profile to see what country the seller is registered in.

Be a little more careful when buying from overseas because these sellers are not subject to U.S. laws and can be less scrupulous about shipping times, Customs declarations, fake merchandise, and so on. Until you are an established buyer and have a few transactions under your belt, I recommend limiting yourself to purchasing from sellers in the United States or Canada. You can restrict the search results using the **Preferences** box on the left-side bar of the search results page.

In the **Location** section, select **US Only** (or **North America** if you want to include Canada) as shown in Figure 7.6. This restricts your results to show only items located in the United States, or those in the United States and Canada depending on which selection you made.

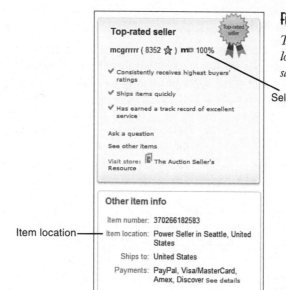

Figure 7.5

The item location and seller location are not always the same.

Seller's Feedback Score

Item location

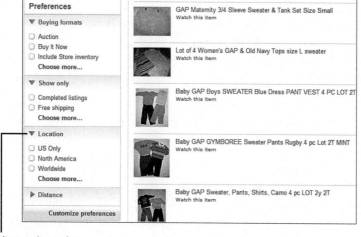

Figure 7.6

Setting your search results to display listings in the United States only is useful when shipping time is critical (such as near to Christmas).

Limit search results
by country

Most international sellers are honest. However, if something goes wrong with an international transaction, it is harder to track down sellers if they don't use PayPal. The chances of something going wrong in transit are higher, too. Breakages, Customs, and so on can be a serious headache new buyers can do without.

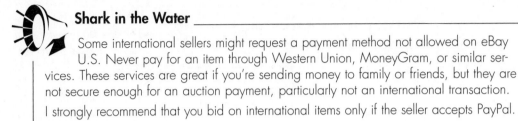

Shark in the Water _____

Some international sellers might request a payment method not allowed on eBay U.S. Never pay for an item through Western Union, MoneyGram, or similar services. These services are great if you're sending money to family or friends, but they are not secure enough for an auction payment, particularly not an international transaction.

I strongly recommend that you bid on international items only if the seller accepts PayPal.

Don't exclude international sellers forever. You can find some things overseas that you just can't get in the United States or that are much cheaper elsewhere.

When you are comfortable with the buying process, you can change the Preferences to **Worldwide.** But be extra vigilant about checking international sellers' feedback comments and Detailed Seller Ratings (we talk about those in a moment).

Seller Feedback

I've mentioned feedback a few times already, but here we look at all the details.

Every website you go to has a testimonials page where previous buyers rave about how good the service and products are from that seller. The difference with eBay is that the sellers can't pick and choose what comments are shown. Every buyer gets to leave a comment about the seller (positive, neutral, or negative), and the seller cannot remove it.

To get to a seller's **Feedback Profile,** just click on the **Feedback Score** (the number in parentheses) next to the seller's user ID.

The Feedback Profile (see Figure 7.7) shows much more detailed information than the snapshot shown in the **Seller info** box.

The seller's Feedback Score (shown next to his user ID at the top) is calculated by adding 1 for every positive comment he receives and deducting 1 for every negative. Neutrals count as 0, so they don't increase or decrease the score.

The **Positive Feedback Percentage,** as the name suggests, shows the percentage of the seller's feedback that is positive. Only feedback comments from the last 12 months count toward this percentage. So a negative comment from two years ago does not affect it.

Recent Feedback Ratings

Positive Feedback Percentage

Feedback Score   Detailed Seller Ratings

Figure 7.7

The user's entire history of transactions (both buying and selling) is shown here. The buyers' user IDs are blurred in this screenshot to protect their privacy, but you will see them displayed on the **Feedback Profile** *page.*

Total Feedback Received

Revised Feedback

Did You Know?

Sellers can leave a response to the buyer's feedback comment. This is often more telling than the feedback comment itself. If a seller admits fault, I am more likely to buy from him than if he blamed the buyer. I once saw a negative comment from a buyer just ripping the seller apart for slow shipping and sending the wrong item. The seller's response was something like "He's right, I messed up. Doesn't happen often. Refunded buyer ASAP." I had no hesitation buying from this guy.

Recent Feedback Ratings

The **Recent Feedback Ratings** box (see Figure 7.7) tells you about the user's recent transactions in the past month, past six months, and past year. This is a very important piece of information. Not only does it tell you how many transactions the seller has been involved in during these time periods, but it also shows quickly and clearly how many recent transactions were positive, neutral, or negative.

If there are negatives within the **1 month** or **6 months** columns, go and look at the actual comment (at the bottom of the page). If not, don't worry about it.

Personally, if I see a lot of recent negatives, I look elsewhere for my item unless it's something I absolutely have to have and no one else is selling it. Even then, I make sure to pay with PayPal so that I'm covered by the Buyer Protection Policy. Sellers cannot leave negative or neutral feedback for buyers, so if you see a negative rating or a low positive feedback percentage, you know this is based solely on the eBay member's selling track record.

There are four tabs for viewing the actual feedback comments, as shown in Figure 7.7:

◆ **Feedback as a seller** shows all comments from people who bought an item from this eBay member.

◆ **Feedback as a buyer** shows all comments from people this eBay member bought an item from.

◆ **All Feedback** shows all comments left for this eBay member from both buyers and sellers.

◆ **Feedback left for others** shows the feedback comments this eBay member has left for other people.

Many eBay members have a high Feedback Score but got most of it from buying items on eBay. You need to know how this person works on the other side of the transaction as a seller. By looking only at the comments listed in the **Feedback as a seller** tab, you can exclude all the transactions in which the member was the buyer.

You should also check out the **Feedback left for others** tab because it can show you how this seller gives feedback. If he's trigger-happy on negatives when he's the buyer, do you really want to do business with him?

When eBay first prevented sellers from leaving negative feedback, many left a positive rating, but the comment was negative. The same has been true from buyers who didn't want to leave a negative rating, but weren't happy with the transaction. This undermines the feedback rating system so eBay now reserves the right to remove feedback where the comment and the rating do not match. So a negative rating with the comment "Wonderful seller, A++++ will do business again!" could be removed. So too could a positive rating with a comment like "Horrible seller. Received 3 weeks late and broken. No refund."

Detailed Seller Ratings (DSRs)

When a buyer leaves feedback for a seller, she is also able to rate the seller on each of four criteria:

1. How accurate was the item description?

2. How satisfied were you with the seller's communication?

3. How quickly did the seller ship the item?

4. How reasonable were the shipping and handling charges?

The rating is from 1 to 5 stars. After 10 buyers have rated a seller, these responses are displayed in the **Detailed Seller Ratings** box (see Figure 7.8).

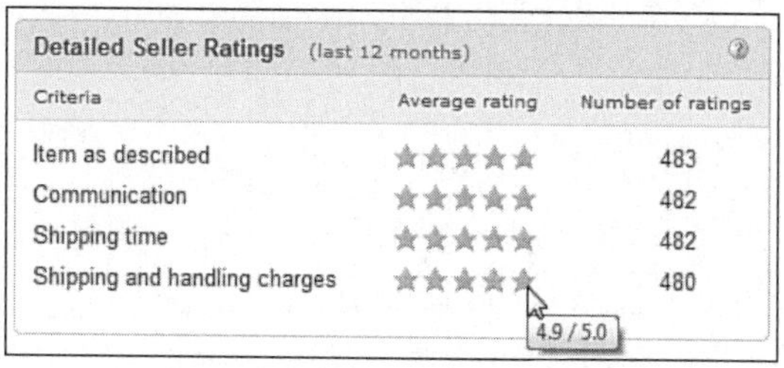

Detailed Seller Ratings (last 12 months)		
Criteria	Average rating	Number of ratings
Item as described	★★★★★	483
Communication	★★★★★	482
Shipping time	★★★★★	482
Shipping and handling charges	★★★★★ 4.9 / 5.0	480

Figure 7.8

Hover your mouse over the stars to see the exact DSR rating (out of 5.0).

Rating the seller is completely optional and cannot be linked to any individual buyer, because eBay delays posting the updated ratings so it's not immediately clear after a buyer posts the feedback comment.

This anonymity used to be important when sellers could leave negative feedback, because it meant buyers would be more honest since the seller wouldn't know who they were and, therefore, couldn't retaliate with negative feedback. The anonymity is less important now because sellers cannot leave negative feedback at all.

Looking at the Detailed Seller Ratings is a great way to get a quick snapshot of how recent buyers rate the seller.

The numbers to the right of the stars tell you how many buyers rated the seller on each of the criteria.

Did You Know?

Detailed Seller Ratings are a rotating score. They are based on the responses of buyers from the last 12 months only. This keeps the ratings current and relevant, just like the Recent Feedback Ratings.

Hover your mouse over the star ratings to see the actual score (as shown in Figure 7.8), because it can be hard to see the difference between 4.6 and 5.0. For an established seller, anything under 4.6 is worrying. For sellers with very few ratings (look to the number to the right of the stars), lower ratings are okay because one low rating will have a higher impact. To continue selling, a member may have only a very few instances of 1 or 2 star ratings. Fee discounts and better Best Match placement are also linked to the seller's DSRs.

Detailed Item Information

In addition to the actual comment left by the buyer, the Feedback Profile shows the item title and the selling price (excluding shipping), as shown in Figure 7.9. Sellers often sell the same items over and over, so this makes it easy for a potential buyer to find a feedback comment from someone who has already purchased the item from the seller.

Figure 7.9

The buyers' user IDs are blurred in this screenshot to protect their privacy.

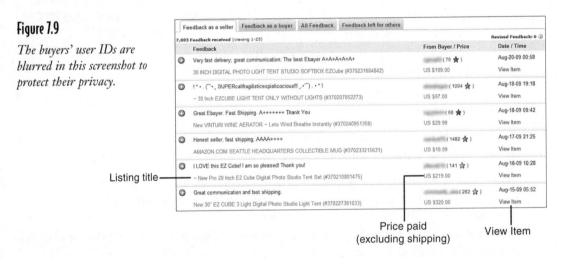

All in all, feedback rewards the sellers who are honest and working to make their buyers happy, and makes it easy for potential buyers to spot the sellers who aren't doing this.

It's All About Me

The **About Me** page is exactly what the title says. It's a page eBay members create to tell other people about them. It can cover anything from your business, to your family, what you buy or sell on eBay, hobbies, interests, pets, whatever.

About Me pages are primarily used by sellers, but as a buyer, you can set one up for yourself if you want.

Click on the **Community** tab and then select **Create an About Me page** in the **More Community Programs** box at the bottom of the page. Alternatively, you can go directly to http://pages.ebay.com/community/aboutme.html.

Follow the template for adding text and pictures. It's quite fun to set up, and you can modify it at any time.

My About Me page talks about what I sell, about my books and articles, and a little about my family.

Shark in the Water

If you do set up an **About Me** page, never list personal information like your last name or your home address, because anyone on the Internet can see it.

Did You Know?

The **About Me** page is the only place sellers can put a link to an off-eBay website.

Skip's talks about his family and his business, and offers a free download for one of his products. The link takes you to a page on his website to start the download.

Buying on eBay Motors

eBay Motors (motors.ebay.com) is the section of eBay dedicated to vehicles, parts, and accessories. I don't go into great detail here because this is such a specific area; however, if you are looking at buying a vehicle, doing your homework is even more important. Here are a few tips for buying on eBay Motors:

♦ Do your research on the sellers; make sure they know what they're doing and have a good feedback record for this type of item.

♦ Always get a vehicle report (CarFax or similar).

♦ Never buy off-eBay, even if the person lives in the same town as you. You lose all of eBay's fraud protection (which is more extensive for eBay Motors).

◆ Know how much the item/vehicle retails for (www.kbb.com and www. nadaguides.com are good resources), and make sure your bid (including shipping) doesn't exceed this amount.

◆ Get a vehicle inspection. If you can't check out the vehicle in person, you can order an inspection from a third-party company and get an online report within 48 hours.

◆ Ensure you know the cost of transporting the vehicle if you are not picking it up locally. This can cost hundreds of dollars and needs to be factored into your total purchase price.

◆ Use a reputable escrow company for the funds transfer (eBay recommends www. escrow.com). Never use a cashier's check, loan check, or other payment unless you're collecting the vehicle in person.

There's much more to eBay Motors, and you can really get some great deals there. But you must be extra wary, considering the amount of money changing hands. I wrote *The Pocket Idiot's Guide to eBay Motors* (Alpha, 2008) specifically for people buying and selling on eBay Motors because it is so different from the rest of eBay. So if buying or selling vehicles or parts and accessories interests you, you might want to read that book, too.

The Least You Need to Know

◆ Look at the total cost, including shipping, and compare it to the cost of purchasing the item locally or at another online website.

◆ If the seller's shipping is marked as "flat-rate," make sure you know what service the seller is using. If it's not clear in the listing, e-mail the seller to find out.

◆ Compare items side by side to decide which is the best one for you.

◆ Read feedback comments from previous buyers and look at the Detailed Seller Ratings and Recent Feedback Ratings to see how the seller has performed in each area over the last 12 months.

◆ Limit initial purchases to U.S. sellers only. Then expand to the international sites after you're comfortable with the buying process. But remember to always pay via PayPal for international purchases.

Chapter 8

Bidding to Win

In This Chapter

- ◆ The best day and time to find the best deals
- ◆ How Reserve-Price Auctions can work in your favor
- ◆ Placing your bid
- ◆ Placing a bid when you're nowhere near your computer

Finally, we're ready to bid! In this chapter, we look at exactly what happens when you place your bid, when you will find the best deals, and what days and times to avoid. We also talk about a technique for winning an auction that ends in the middle of the night while you are tucked up in bed asleep (and your computer doesn't even have to be turned on!).

When and How Much to Bid

A lot has been written about the best day and time to sell on eBay. It makes sense that if a certain time is a good time to sell, it is a bad time to buy (because of the increased competition and higher prices). So my advice is to look at when the highest prices are paid and avoid them. Obviously, this applies only to auctions not to fixed-price listings where it's simply the first bidder wins.

In years past, Sunday evening was considered the prime time of eBay buying, but this has altered somewhat as the eBay clientele has changed. Now it really depends on the item you are buying.

If you're purchasing office equipment or supplies, midweek during the day is probably a time to avoid because that's when all the business professionals will be on. Lunchtime during the week is also a time to avoid because many people check eBay on their lunch break.

As a seller, I have found Monday to be a good day for getting higher prices (because people who find the auction during the weekend haven't yet forgotten about it). So Monday is another day I avoid buying.

In my opinion (and some people will disagree with me) the best time to buy is very late at night or early morning (during commuting hours) in the middle of the week. You'll often find items from overseas sellers ending at weird times (3 A.M. or so) because they got mixed up with the time zones. I even see items ending late at night from U.S. sellers.

The least competition for buying is typically on Tuesdays and Wednesdays. If the item is popular with people in their late teens and early 20s, Friday and Saturday evening are also slow times (because a lot of people will be out for the evening). So as a savvy buyer, those are the times you want the auctions you're watching to end (because you're less likely to have bidding competition and will usually get the item for far less than at peak time).

When you use **Completed Listings** to find the average selling price, change the sort order to **Price + Shipping: lowest first** to see what day and time the lower-priced items ended. This will tell you the best time to buy that specific item.

Of course, if it is a rare or highly desirable item, it doesn't really matter when it ends—it's going to get a lot of bidding activity.

In Chapter 7, we discussed how much is too much. Really, the question has to be, how much is this item worth to *you*? Once you determine that (by using Completed Listings, checking local and other online prices, and deciding how much you really want it), you will know what your maximum bid is.

Reserve-Price Auctions

Reserve-price auctions (also known as RPAs) are auctions on which the seller has set a hidden minimum price (called a reserve). We mentioned this briefly in Chapter 6, but let's expand on it a little.

It is a well-known fact that items with lower starting prices end up with higher final prices because they get more interest from buyers. Once a buyer has placed one bid, he is more likely to bid again if he is outbid by another buyer. Also, the eBay listing fee is calculated on a tiered scale based on the starting price. eBay charges the seller a fee for using a reserve price, but if it's a high-priced item, it is usually worth it to the seller for those "just in case" scenarios.

Reserve-price auctions can be a double-edged sword because some buyers will not bid on them. They want to know exactly how high the reserve is and don't want to waste their time if it is more than they want to pay.

One option many sellers with reserve-price auctions use (and you should look out for) is a **Buy It Now** price, as well as the starting price. You may not know the exact reserve price, but you do know that it is no higher than the Buy It Now price. It's probably close, though.

I expect to see reserve prices on expensive items (electronics, computers, cars, antiques, and so on), but not on cheaper things unless it is a new seller.

You can easily see whether the auction has an unmet reserve price because you will see **Reserve not met** below the price on the listing page (see Figure 8.1).

Once a reserve price has been met, the text disappears so no future bidders know that there was ever a reserve price to start with.

Second Chance Offers for Reserve-Price Auctions

It pays to bid up to your maximum on a reserve-price auction even if it doesn't reach the reserve price. This is because the seller may decide that the closing high bid is actually high enough for him. In this case, you may receive a **Second Chance Offer** to purchase the item for the bid you placed.

Figure 8.1

*This seller has both a **Buy It Now** price and a **Place Bid** option.*

New EZ CUBE TABLE TOP PHOTO STUDIO TENT WITH LIGHTS 20"

FREE Shipping and 3 Free Bonuses

Item condition:	**New**
Time left:	3 days 2 hours (Aug 23, 2009 14:39:04 PDT)
Bid history:	4 bids
Current bid:	**US $10.49**
	Reserve not met
Your max bid:	US $ _____ [Place bid]
	(Enter US $10.99 or more)
	or
Price:	US $219.00 [Buy It Now]
You can also:	[Watch this item]

Bucks You'll earn $0.21 in eBay Bucks See conditions

Buy It Now price | Current bid

Reserve not met

Shark in the Water

Do not buy from a seller if he e-mails you and offers to sell the item to you directly. If there is no corresponding **Buy It Now** page, you are not protected through either eBay or PayPal if the transaction goes south.

If you really want the item and you haven't received a Second Chance Offer within 24 hours, you might try e-mailing the seller and asking whether she plans to relist the item. Ask if she would consider setting a Buy It Now price so you could purchase the item immediately, and ask what price she would be looking for.

You can then decide whether that price is acceptable to you or if it is too much. If it's acceptable, the seller can put up a Buy It Now auction rather than relisting the item as an auction, and you can buy the item immediately without having to go through the auction process again.

Placing Your Bid

To place a bid, simply enter your maximum bid in the box on the listing page and click **Place bid.** You're taken to a page that shows the bid amount and the shipping cost. You need to click **Confirm Bid** to actually place the bid. At this point, you will see one of two versions of the auction page. It will say either …

♦ You are the current high bidder. (See Figure 8.2.)

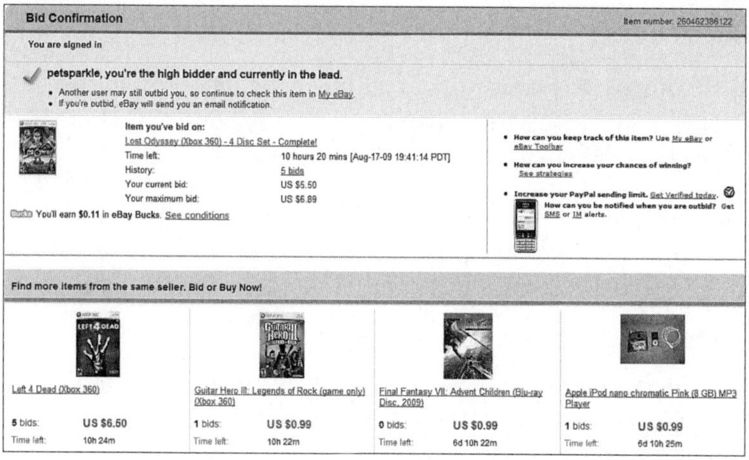

Figure 8.2

eBay will also e-mail you to let you know that you are the high bidder.

♦ You have been outbid by another bidder. (See Figure 8.3.)

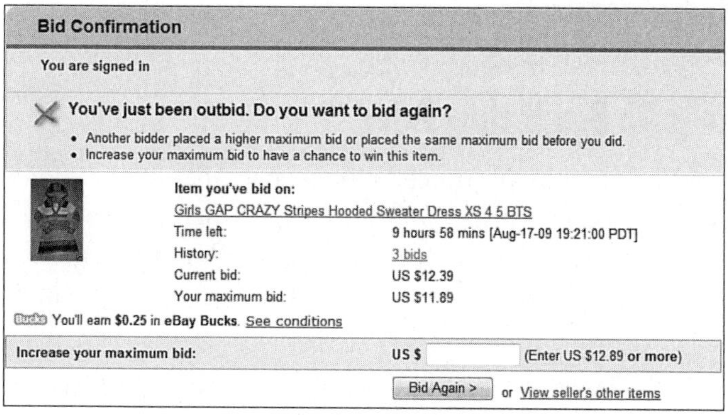

Figure 8.3

*If you use the **eBay Toolbar**, you will get a pop-up message on your desktop telling you that you have been outbid, in addition to getting an e-mail from eBay.*

In Chapter 4, we talked about tracking items in My eBay. Keeping track means you are less likely to be outbid if you are the current high bidder.

If two buyers place the same bid, whichever one came in first gets the high bidder slot. For example, let's say the current bid on an auction is $14.50. You place a maximum bid of $35. The auction displays the next bidding increment ($15) until someone else bids, at which point you automatically outbid him until he bids higher than your maximum bid. Let's say that bidder gives up at $30, but two days after you placed your bid, someone else bids $35—the same as your maximum bid. The current price jumps to $35, but you are still the high bidder because your bid was placed before the other bidder's. (If he had bid $35.01, though, you would have been outbid.)

Spotting an International Seller

In Chapter 7, we talked about why it is safer to start off buying from sellers in the United States and Canada while you are a new eBay buyer, and I showed you how to limit your search results to show only items in those two countries.

But you can spot an international seller in other ways if you choose not to limit the search results:

1. On the **search results** page, the price appears in italics. (This is the price converted to U.S. dollars from the currency the auction is listed in.)

2. On the **listing** page, the item location does not identify a city and state in the United States. (Be careful—I saw "Fast Shipping to United States" as the Item Location for an item located in Australia recently.)

3. If a seller is registered in another country, the seller's **Feedback Profile** reads, "Member since 12-06-06 in China" (or whatever country he is registered in). This does not always match the **Item Location** on the listing page.

I Need It Now, but There Is No Buy It Now Price

If you happen to find a perfect item that you need immediately (before the auction ends) and it doesn't have a Buy It Now price, you can ask the seller if she would be prepared to revise the listing to include a Buy It Now option. eBay allows this when the auction has 12 hours or more remaining before it ends and there are no bids on the auction.

Tips

When I ask a seller to add a Buy It Now price, I ask him to include the Buy It Now fee so that I pay for that. It's only 5¢–25¢ (based on the price set), but that gesture has obtained me a Buy It Now price when I wasn't sure if I'd get one.

If the seller says yes, she can revise her listing to add the Buy It Now price, and you just treat the auction as if it had always had that option. Not all sellers will do this, but it's worth asking. Quite often, professional sellers are happy to do it because it means they are turning their inventory quicker.

If there are already bids on the item, you can ask a seller if she would be prepared to sell the item for your current high bid, but this doesn't work all that often—usually only when the seller is expecting to get just one or two bids.

Sniping Techniques

Placing bids early in an auction's duration drives up the number of bids. You'd think that auctions with low (or no) bids would be more desirable because there is no bidding competition. However, the opposite is actually true. Items with bids get more people looking at them, which gets more bids, and so on.

Experienced buyers avoid placing their bids until near the end of the auction so it looks like the auction has little or no interest. Often they *snipe* the auction placing their maximum bid during the last few seconds to outbid the current bidder (or any other snipers doing the same thing). Sniping is a perfectly acceptable bidding practice, and one that almost all experienced buyers use. Just make sure your spouse isn't also bidding on the same item! Since you can't see who the bidders are, you'll need to check with your family members just in case! (Yes, this has happened to me when my mother and I were bidding against each other on the same pair of shoes for my daughter. Now I always send her links to items I'm watching or bidding on so she knows not to, and vice versa.)

> ## def•i•ni•tion
>
> **Sniping** is when a buyer places a bid within the last few seconds of an auction. By the time the current high bidder knows he has been outbid, the auction has ended and he cannot place another bid.

You can snipe in two ways: the first is manually, and the second is using sniping software.

To manually snipe an auction, you really need to be on a high-speed Internet connection:

1. Open two browser windows and navigate to the auction listing page on both windows.

2. Now place your maximum bid in one window and click **Place bid** so you are at the **Review and Confirm Bid** page. Leave this window open, but don't click the **Confirm Bid** button yet.

3. Go to the other window (still showing the auction listing page) and keep watching the countdown timer until there are only maybe 10 seconds to go.

4. Now click over to the other browser window and click **Confirm Bid.** If your bid is high enough, you will become the high bidder with only two to three seconds to go. That's not enough time for the current high bidder to get another bid in.

If you didn't get the high bid status … well, you put in your maximum bid, so obviously the other person was prepared to pay more than you were.

As you get accustomed to sniping techniques, you can place your bid closer and closer to the end of the auction. The first time you try sniping, you will want to place the bid with 20 or 30 seconds to go, as the speed of your Internet connection determines how long it takes for eBay to register your bid. You don't want to cut it too close and not get your bid in before the auction ends.

The adrenaline rush when you snipe an auction is great, but it's very frustrating to be on the other side of it. So if you are the high bidder on an auction that's about to end, make sure you have submitted the maximum amount you are willing to pay for the item. There is nothing worse than being the high bidder with $50.52 and being outbid at the last second by someone who bid $51.52 when you would happily have paid up to $60 for the item. You don't know how much the other person bid, but it could have been less than you were willing to go.

> **Did You Know?**
>
> Sniping is a very popular technique, so don't be surprised if you're not the only person sniping that same auction.

If you do get sniped at the last second, keep a level head and remember your preset maximum when you're looking at other items.

What if the auction ends at 2:30 A.M.? Not many people want to wait up until then to manually snipe an auction. You have two options:

- ◆ Place your maximum bid right before bed and see if it was high enough when you get up the next morning.

- ◆ Use an online sniping service such as BidSlammer (www.bidslammer.com).

There are many sniping services available now, and they all work approximately the same way. Most are web based, so you log in to their website to give the service authorization to place the bid for you. You then enter the item number and your maximum bid and forget about it. Within the last few seconds of the auction, the sniping service places the bid. If your bid was high enough, you win the item even if you are fast asleep or out at the movies. Web-based sniping services work even when your computer is completely shut down.

> **Tips**
>
> Using a sniping service is like having a dedicated person sitting at your computer waiting for the auction to end while you are out enjoying yourself.

Other sniping software programs reside on your computer so you don't have to log on to their website, but your computer must be switched on at the end of the auction for them to work. This isn't a good solution if you are traveling or just prefer to shut down your computer each night.

Both types of sniping services charge a fee, but it is usually quite low. Most of the services offer a free trial, so try before you buy and find one you like before subscribing to it.

There are so many sniping programs, I don't want to list them all. Just go to your favorite search engine (Google, MSN, Yahoo!, and so on) and type in **auction sniping software;** and the search engine will bring up a bunch of results. I do like BidSlammer, but that is just my personal preference; you might find a different one you prefer.

How Much Do I Bid?

You have determined your maximum bid, but you shouldn't ever use a full dollar amount. This just leaves you open to sniping. Let's say you decided your maximum was $20. You actually want to go slightly above that. Personally, I would bid $20.57. That gets me through the next bid increment plus a little extra. So I would remain high bidder if someone bids $20 or $20.50.

If you're strict about being right at $20, I would bid $20.09. A lot of bidders are getting wise to the trick of bidding a few cents above the whole dollar amount, so this will still outbid a $20.03 or $20.07 previous maximum bid.

Why Was I Outbid?

In this section, I've talked about your "maximum bid." This is actually a "proxy bid." Proxy means "in place of." In this case, eBay is acting as your proxy to place bids only as needed to keep you as the high bidder. If the next bid increment is $5, you could choose to bid only $5, but then the next person to bid would outbid you. If you enter your maximum (proxy) bid, you can let eBay do the bidding for you. Each time someone places a bid, eBay will automatically place the next bid for you up to your maximum. So instead of bidding $5, you could bid $35, or whatever your maximum bid. The current price would still say $5. If someone bids $5.50, eBay would automatically place the next bid for you. You would outbid them automatically and the current bid would then say $6. eBay only ever bids one bid increment above the amount the other person bid.

If you place a bid and are immediately outbid (see Figure 8.3) that means the current high bidder has a proxy bid in place. Technically, you don't know the other person's proxy bid until you exceed it. However, if you place a bid and the next bid is lower than the next increment should be, you know that this is the maximum bid the previous person placed. eBay will always bid in full increments unless there isn't enough left in the high bidder's proxy bid.

For example, if you bid $20.53, the next bid increment is $21.03. If you are automatically outbid and the new current bid is any number between $20.54 and $21.02, you know that this was the high bidder's maximum and only one more bid will put you in the lead.

If I see this towards the end of an auction, I don't immediately outbid the high bidder. If the high bidder is outbid, he will receive an e-mail from eBay, and a pop-up alert if he is also using the eBay Toolbar. Instead I wait and snipe the auction just as if I didn't know where his maximum bid was. Don't forget, there may be other snipers trying to win that auction, too. But by waiting, you have a chance at the original high bidder forgetting about the auction and not getting the outbid alert until too late.

The Least You Need to Know

- Check the **Completed Listings** for your item search to see what day and time the item is selling for the lowest prices. Look for active auctions ending around this time to find the best deals.

- Sniping an auction can get you a great price, but you will invariably get out-sniped sometimes. Don't be discouraged. Just always put in your absolute maximum bid when you snipe.

- Snipe in your sleep using a sniping service, such as BidSlammer.

- If you need it *now* and there are no fixed-price listings for that item, you can ask the seller if she would add a **Buy It Now** price to her auction. She can say no, and there must be no bids on the auction for her to do this.

- Even if an auction ends with the reserve price not met, if you are the high bidder, the seller may offer the item to you for your maximum bid anyway using **Second Chance Offer.**

Chapter 9

Rules and Retractions

In This Chapter

- ◆ When you can and can't retract a bid
- ◆ eBay rules for buyers
- ◆ Reporting seller violations

Buyers must follow a variety of eBay rules. Most are common sense. Some apply specifically to the listing process and specifically to when you can and can't retract a bid you've placed.

In this chapter, we also look at the dispute-resolution process. This applies when something goes wrong in the transaction (for example, you never receive the item, or the item you receive is not as the listing advertised).

eBay Rules for Buyers

It would be nice if everyone always did the right and honest thing, but the world just isn't that way. eBay is no different. eBay has some strict rules for both buyers and sellers, which are designed to help protect all eBay members. We cover only the buying rules here, but you can read the seller rules in Chapter 12 if you're interested.

It seems like a lot, but most of it is common sense. eBay has been around for over a decade, and these rules evolved as they were needed.

Bidding Violations

Violation	Explanation
Transaction interference	E-mailing a user warning him away from an item or seller, or offering to purchase an item currently listed on eBay without using the eBay system.
Invalid bid retraction	Bidding a high amount to discover the current high bidder's maximum bid, or the seller's reserve price, then retracting the bid and using that information to snipe the auction at the last minute.
Unpaid items	Not paying for an item you have won.
Unwelcome buying/bidding	Bidding if you do not meet the seller's requirements (for example, he doesn't ship internationally and you live in Canada), or the seller has cancelled your bid and you bid again without confirming that you are welcome to do so.
Shill bidding	Bidding on an item listed by a friend or colleague to increase the number of bids showing or to drive up the price. You may not bid on any auction listed by a family member or employer/employee, although purchasing using Buy It Now is permitted. Under no circumstances may you bid on any of your own listings using another user ID.
Solicitation of an off-site sale	Accepting an offer from a seller to purchase an item off-eBay that is currently listed on eBay.

Here are some other violations that apply to all eBay users, not just buyers.

General Violations

Violation	Explanation
Feedback extortion	Threatening to leave neutral or negative feedback for the seller if she does not do something you request.

Violation	Explanation
Malicious feedback	Bidding on an item with the intent to leave negative feedback, regardless of how the transaction actually works out.
False or missing contact information	Not keeping your contact information current.
Invalid e-mail address	Not updating your e-mail address if you change it.
Publishing contact information	Publishing any contact information of another eBay member (name, e-mail address, phone number, physical address, and so on) in any public area of eBay (listing page, discussion board, blog, feedback comment, and so on).
Spamming eBay users	E-mails sent without the permission of the receiving eBay member discussing buying or selling of goods.
Use of racist, obscene, or harassing language	This is fairly self-explanatory. If you wouldn't be happy with your mother or boss seeing what you wrote, don't write it. You should always treat everyone else with the respect you would like to receive (even if they don't reciprocate).

If you want to see all of the regulations, go to http://pages.ebay.com/help/policies/index.html, or click on the **Help** tab and then click **Rules & policies** (under the **Membership & account** heading).

Can I Retract a Bid I've Placed?

Yes and no. Sometimes you can retract a bid, but other times you must request that the seller cancel it for you (which sellers are not obligated to do).

The most common reason for retracting a bid is the slip of the mouse, such as bidding $100 when you meant $10. As long as you immediately return and place the bid you had intended, there is no problem with retracting the initial mistake bid.

In two other instances, it is also okay to retract a bid:

1. The seller makes a change to the description that significantly alters the item you are bidding on (you bid on a black iPod for your boyfriend's birthday gift, but the seller later adds that it is actually pink, not black).

2. You cannot reach the seller (this means you've tried his phone number and the number is a nonworking number, and the e-mails you sent are returned as undeliverable).

Here are examples of when you may not retract a bid:

♦ You have bidder's remorse and decide that you didn't actually want to bid that much.

♦ It was an impulse bid and you decide you actually don't want the item at all.

♦ You read the description again and realize it isn't what you want. (You can contact the seller, tell her that you misread the description, and ask if she will cancel your bid, but she is not obligated to do so.)

♦ You decide you can't really afford the item.

♦ You bid on multiple items of the same thing (from different sellers) and don't actually want them all.

Really, this is just common sense. Often sellers will work with you if you accidentally bid on the wrong item or something like that. Frankly, sellers hope that their high bidder actually wants the item so they will pay and leave positive feedback!

If you clicked **Buy It Now** and don't actually want the item, or the listing ended and you didn't correct or cancel your bid, the seller may still work with you. If he offers an unconditional money back guarantee, he'd generally prefer to be told you don't want it now than deal with the hassle of shipping the item, you returning it, and then him refunding you the purchase price.

He does have to file a form with eBay to get his fees back, and then relist the item, so don't expect him to be happy about it, but he'll generally appreciate you contacting him sooner rather than later.

Most sellers will refund you if they haven't shipped the item yet. You'll probably end up on his blocked bidders list for wasting his time, but at least you don't end up with an item you don't want, or paying more than you can afford. Still, remember an auction is a binding contract so if you bid or click **Buy It Now,** you are entering a contract to purchase the item for that price. The seller is well within his rights to tell you to pay up.

Time Restrictions for Bid Retractions

If you do need to retract your bid, some specific restrictions and consequences apply, depending on when you initially placed the bid you are retracting and how close the auction is to ending.

◆ You can cancel a bid up until the final 12 hours of the auction. For example, if the auction ends at 8:30 P.M. Monday night, you have until 8:30 A.M. on that Monday morning to retract any bids placed previous to those last 12 hours. All of your previous bids will be cancelled and you will have to bid again if you still want the item.

◆ You can retract a bid during the last 12 hours of an auction only if the bid you are retracting was also placed during that 12-hour period. If this is the case, you have one hour to retract your bid. This will affect only that one bid, so all other bids you placed before the final 12-hour mark will still be valid. So if the auction ends at 8:30 P.M. and you placed your bid at 4:30 P.M., you have only until 5:30 P.M. to retract the bid.

If you placed your bid before the last 12 hours began and you want to retract the bid within the last 12 hours, you must contact the seller and he must cancel the bid for you (if he agrees to it). If he does not agree, you cannot retract the bid.

Yes, I know this looks a bit confusing. The following table spells it out in simpler terms.

When You Can Retract a Bid

Bid Placed	Retraction Allowed	Bids Cancelled
More than 12 hours from the auction's end.	Until the auction has only 12 hours remaining.	All bids made on this auction.
Within the last 12 hours of the auction.	Up to one hour from when the bid was placed.	Only that one bid. All previous bids still count.

The number of bid retractions you have made in the last six months displays on your **Feedback Profile,** but no one really cares about one or two. Sellers do get worried if you're approaching double figures, though, as does eBay. They thoroughly investigate any buyer who has a high number of bid retractions.

If you need to retract a bid, go to the **Bid Retraction Form** at http://offer.ebay.com/ ws/eBayISAPI.dll?RetractBidShow. That's a bit much to type into the browser, so I've used TinyURL to reduce the size of it. If you just type http://tinyurl.com/y88j3t into your browser, it will take you to the same place as the long link. You can also navigate there by clicking on the **Help** tab and searching for "retract bid." You'll find the link in one of the first results pages.

How to Report Listing Violations

Listing violations are directly linked to the item description. It may be a seller who requires a payment method not allowed on eBay (for example, checks or money orders), or maybe it's excessive shipping charges (charging $30 to ship an item that needs a first-class stamp). Any violations to eBay's listing policies are reported directly from the listing page using the **Report item** link. You do not have to be involved in a transaction with this seller to report his item.

Report This Item

If the item is in violation, you can report it directly from the listing page. Beneath the **Seller info** and **Other item info** boxes, you'll see three links: **Share, Print,** and **Report item** (see Figure 9.1). Click **Report item** and then use the drop-down menus to select the violation. You can also add a comment in the box provided, but your space is very limited.

Figure 9.1

*Reporting a violation from the **listing** page.*

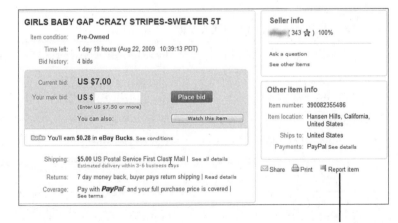

Report item

You're not a snitch for reporting listing violations. Think of it this way: some buyers don't know as much as you do and might not see the excessive shipping or other violation. They think they're getting a great deal. Reporting these types of listing violations keeps eBay as safe as possible for other buyers. Plus, it's not fair to sellers who are following the rules, so you're helping them, too.

It is very easy to report listing violations. These instructions specifically show how to report excessive shipping costs, but you can see the other options:

1. After you click the **Report item** link (see Figure 9.1), you are sent to the **File a report—Report item** page (see Figure 9.2).

2. Listing violations will already be selected in the first box. In the second box (**Reason for Report**), click **Listing policy violations (improper keywords, outside links, excessive shipping, etc.).**

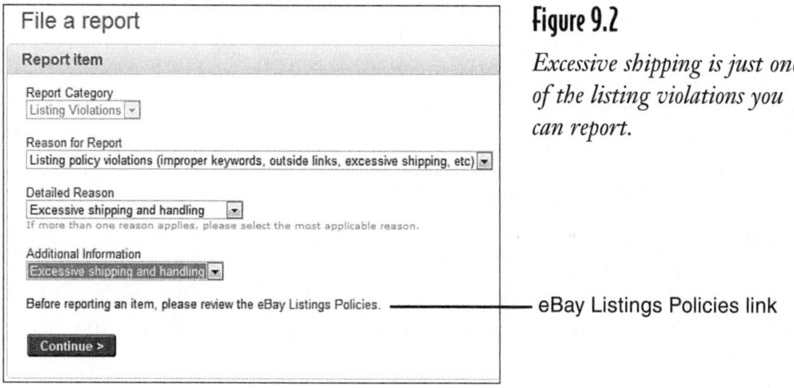

Figure 9.2

Excessive shipping is just one of the listing violations you can report.

3. In the third box (**Detailed Reason**), select **Excessive shipping and handling.**

4. In the final box (**Additional Information**), select **Excessive shipping and handling** again. (It is the only option in this box.)

5. You can confirm that the listing you are reporting really is violating the terms by clicking on the **eBay Listings Policies** link.

6. After you have read the rules and made sure you were right about the listing violation, click **Continue.**

7. The next page (see Figure 9.3) shows the four selections you made, the item number you are reporting, and finally a box where you can enter a brief message—for example, "Seller is charging $30 to ship a postcard via Media Mail that should cost less than $1."

8. Now just click **Send Report.**

Figure 9.3

Keep your message brief and to the point. You have only 100 characters.

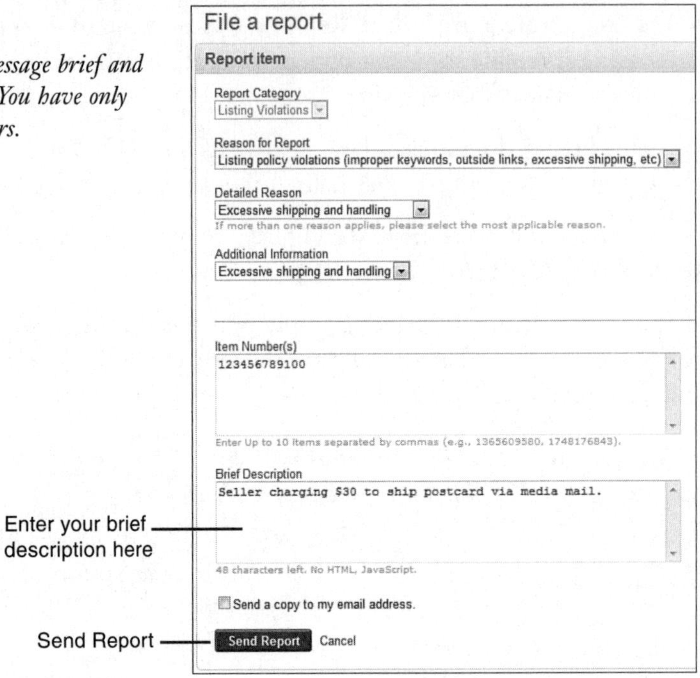

File a report

Report item

Report Category
Listing Violations ▾

Reason for Report
Listing policy violations (improper keywords, outside links, excessive shipping, etc) ▾

Detailed Reason
Excessive shipping and handling ▾
If more than one reason applies, please select the most applicable reason.

Additional Information
Excessive shipping and handling ▾

Item Number(s)
123456789100

Enter Up to 10 items separated by commas (e.g., 1365609580, 1748176843).

Brief Description
Seller charging $30 to ship postcard via media mail.

Enter your brief
description here

48 characters left. No HTML, JavaScript.

☐ Send a copy to my email address.

Send Report ——— Send Report   Cancel

eBay won't inform you of what (if anything) it does about your report, but you will get an acknowledgment through your **Messages** box that it has been received. It's always nice to see the listing often removed a few days later though.

The Least You Need to Know

◆ It's okay to retract a bid if you made a typo mistake or for many other reasons, but be aware of the time remaining on the auction.

◆ A won auction or Buy It Now purchase is a binding contract, however many sellers would prefer to know you don't want the item *before* they ship it—particularly if they offer an unconditional guarantee and will have to take the returned item back anyway.

◆ Reporting listings in violation of eBay's rules helps protect other buyers and is fairer to the sellers who do abide by the rules.

◆ eBay has a number of rules for buyers, but most are common sense.

Once You've Won

In This Chapter

- ◆ When and how to contact the seller
- ◆ Using eBay Checkout
- ◆ Leaving feedback and what to say
- ◆ When it is okay to buy from an eBay seller off eBay

Congratulations, you've won your item! But now what? You need to select a shipping service, figure out how much your total is, pay your seller, and, after you have received your item, leave feedback for the seller.

We look at the different steps you need to take and offer some tips for making it go as smoothly as possible.

Contacting Your Seller

If you had any questions about the item, you should have asked them before bidding. If you need to ask something now (other than requesting an invoice), go to your **Won** summary in My eBay and use the **Act** drop-down menu next to the item to select **Contact Seller** (see Figure 10.1). You could also do this from the main **Won** page rather than the snapshot on the summary page if you prefer. It's in the same menu. Here you can send an e-mail to the seller through eBay's Messages system.

Asking for combined shipping is best done before you bid. However, if you win one item and then look at the seller's other items and see other auctions about to end for items you want, you may not have time to ask in advance. If this is the case, contact the seller, but be prepared to pay the full price for each auction's listed shipping. Some sellers fulfill their orders through multiple warehouses, so they can't combine the shipping cost.

When you click **Contact Seller,** you're presented with a number of questions and answers. These are the seller's frequently asked questions. Some are generated from eBay and pull information directly from the listing, others are specifically added by the seller. You may see "When will my item ship?," "What shipping service do you use?," "How can I track my item?," "What do I do if the item arrives damaged?," and so on. Some sellers don't use these FAQs, but most larger sellers do. If the answer is in the FAQs, don't bug the seller for further details.

Requesting an Invoice

Most of the time, you won't need to request an invoice because you will see the **Pay now** button everywhere. A **Pay now** link appears on the drop-down menu next to the item in the **Won** section of My eBay (see Figure 10.1), on the ended listing page, and in the e-mail eBay sends you. Do you ever get the hint that eBay doesn't want you to forget to pay?

Figure 10.1

*The same options are available on the drop-down menu from the **Won** page as are shown on the **Won snapshot** here.*

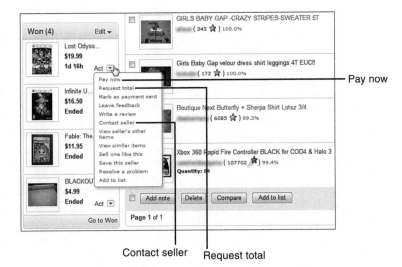

Contact seller   Request total

If you don't see a **Pay now** button, or you are unsure about how much the total will be because of combined shipping, you can request the total from the seller using the **Request total** link in the drop-down menu in My eBay (see Figure 10.1).

You can send a message to the seller through this form, and she will e-mail you an invoice. Now when you click on the invoice or click **Pay now,** the options she selected will be shown in the eBay **Checkout** process.

Most of the time, you can just click on **Pay now** and the shipping and item totals will be completed for you (even if you are purchasing multiple items). So don't waste the seller's time unless the totals showing in checkout don't seem to be correct or you have prearranged shipping options that aren't displayed.

What If I Can't Reach My Seller?

Unfortunately, this occasionally happens. If you are getting no response to your e-mails, you need to get the seller's phone number.

1. Make a note of the seller's user ID and the eBay item number for the listing you won.

2. From the eBay home page, click **Advanced Search** (to the right of the search box at the top of the page).

3. On the left-side bar, click **Find contact information** under the **Members** heading (see Figure 10.2).

4. Enter the seller's user ID and the item number in the corresponding boxes, and click **Search.**

5. Check your e-mail for a message from eBay with the seller's full contact information, including phone number. Your seller will be sent your contact information at the same time.

Information about international sellers is somewhat limited, so this is another reason to do all of your checks about the seller before getting involved in a transaction with him.

If you call the seller and it is a nonworking number, report this to eBay and try again

 Tips _____

Make sure you check your spam box, in case e-mails from your seller are not making it through to your inbox. Services like AOL and MSN are notorious for this.

with the e-mail. If you already paid for the item, you can open an **Item Not Received** claim through the **Resolution Center.** (I cover this in detail in Chapter 11).

Figure 10.2

You can get this information only if you are involved in a transaction with this other eBay member.

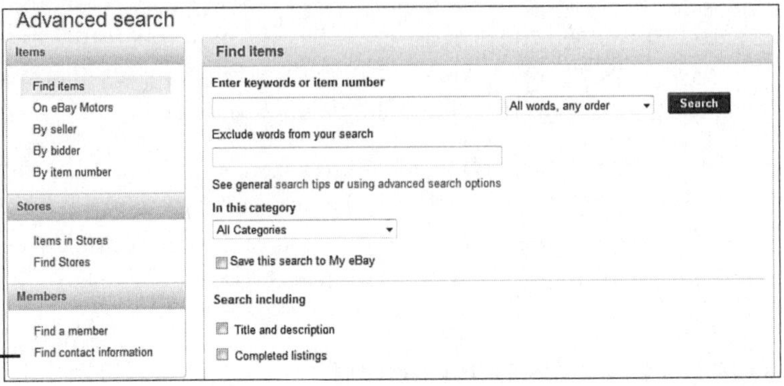

Find contact information ———

Advanced search	
Items	**Find items**
Find items	Enter keywords or item number
On eBay Motors	
By seller	All words, any order ▾ Search
By bidder	Exclude words from your search
By item number	
	See general search tips or using advanced search options
Stores	**In this category**
Items in Stores	All Categories ▾
Find Stores	☐ Save this search to My eBay
Members	**Search including**
Find a member	☐ Title and description
Find contact information	☐ Completed listings

eBay Checkout

Checking out is very easy. Start by clicking on the **Pay now** button in any of the locations we discussed earlier.

The first shipping option shown in the listing displays here (as you can see in Figure 10.3). If the seller offers other shipping options, you'll see a **More options** link. Click this and you can select any of the other options the seller offers. This updates the price for you, too.

If you are purchasing multiple items from the same seller, the title of each item displays at the top and your total includes all items. Ensure that the combined shipping is calculated correctly. Some sellers have their listings set to automatically calculate combined shipping when you check out. Others require you to request an invoice and send you a total with the corrected shipping cost.

Shark in the Water _____

Always check that the invoice totals are what you expected. I once received an invoice from a seller with shipping charges $1.50 higher than listed in the auction. I asked about it and she immediately resent the invoice with the correct amount, but no apology or comment about it. It made me wonder whether it was just a simple mistake. How many buyers would notice a slightly higher shipping charge in their invoice? The seller had sold over 200 items that month. Call me cynical, but that $1.50 per listing could really add up if it wasn't just a one-off mistake.

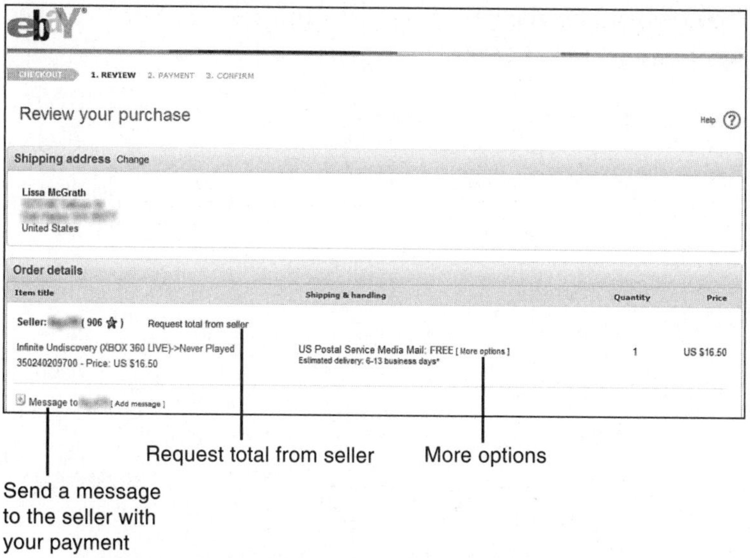

Figure 10.3

You can add a message to the seller by clicking **Add message.** *Just make sure you click* **Save message** *when you're done or it won't save your message.*

Request total from seller   More options

Send a message to the seller with your payment

Did You Know?

Sellers are not allowed to charge buyers for insurance separately from the shipping charge. It can be included in the total (you'll usually see it mentioned in the item description if it is). Sellers are responsible for the item reaching you safely, not just getting it to the carrier, so many have blanket policies with third-party insurers to cover all of their eBay shipments. Still, if something happens en route, it is the seller's responsibility to deal with the claim, not yours.

When you get the total, you need to select the payment method. Scroll to the bottom of the page and select the payment method you want to use (all of the options the seller specified in the auction are available here). Most of the time, this will just be a **Continue with PayPal** button (see Figure 10.4).

Paying Using PayPal

Most, if not all, of your transactions will be with PayPal, so let's look at how that works.

Click **Continue with PayPal** and then log in to your PayPal account when prompted.

Review the transaction (including your shipping address) and, when you are satisfied that it is correct click **Confirm Payment** (see Figure 10.5).

Figure 10.4

If you have a coupon code or gift certificate, you can enter it here to deduct it from the total.

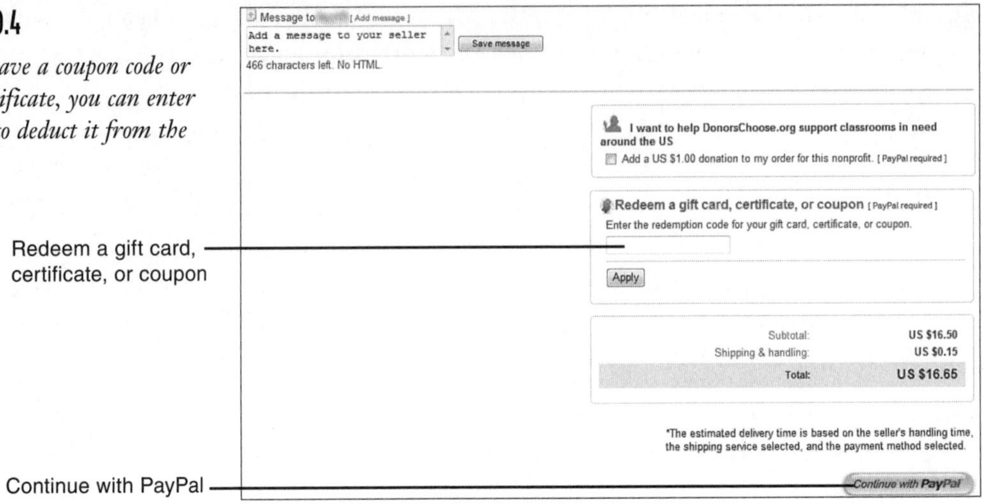

Redeem a gift card, certificate, or coupon

Continue with PayPal

Payment method

More funding options

Figure 10.5

*To change the funding source for the payment, click **More funding options**.*

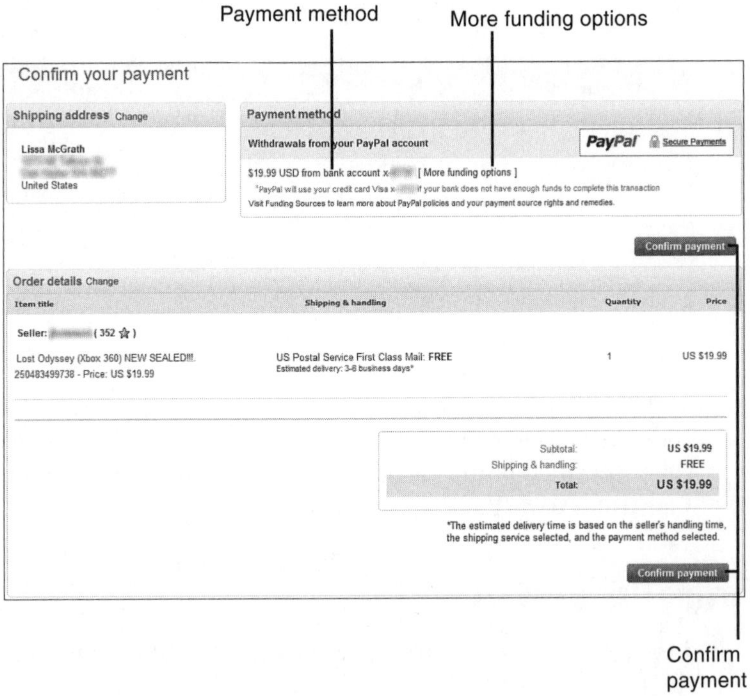

Confirm payment

You will receive an e-mail from PayPal confirming your payment. Sometimes your seller will also acknowledge your payment, but don't worry if he doesn't. You may also receive an e-mail when the item is shipped. Sometimes this comes straight from

PayPal; if that is the case, it means that the seller has printed the shipping label through PayPal. It does not mean that the item was shipped that day. But you can pretty much assume that it will be mailed that day or the next business day.

If the seller printed the shipping label through eBay, the tracking number automatically shows beneath the item title in the **Won** section of My eBay. The seller can also enter the number manually if he didn't use the eBay shipping center. This shows you when the seller printed the label and, if it is scanned, when and where it was scanned. If your seller is using USPS Media Mail, Parcel Post, First Class, or Priority Mail, the next notice will likely be when it is delivered to you. These services do not offer in-transit tracking—only confirmation that the item was delivered.

Even if there is no tracking number, the seller may mark the item as shipped. This makes the parcel icon bold. If you hover your mouse over this icon, it will tell you the date the seller marked it as shipped (see Figure 10.6).

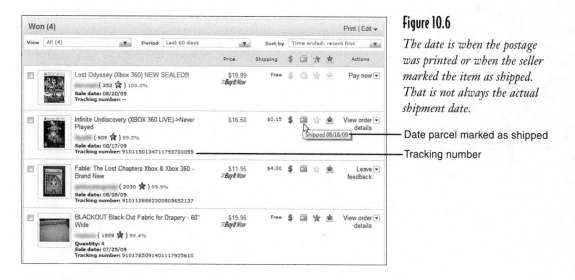

Figure 10.6

The date is when the postage was printed or when the seller marked the item as shipped. That is not always the actual shipment date.

Date parcel marked as shipped

Tracking number

Tips

When e-mailing a seller to follow up on an item shipment, be sure to include your full name, eBay user ID, PayPal e-mail address, date of purchase, date of payment, and eBay item number.

I know that sounds like a lot, but if a seller has sold 200 items in the last couple of weeks, finding your transaction may take a little bit of time. You'll get a much quicker response if you give him all of the information to track down your item.

If you don't see a tracking number and the parcel icon does not illuminate, don't worry. Many sellers don't use these tools. Look at the seller's handling time and the estimated shipping time. Only after that time expires should you contact the seller regarding tracking.

International Transactions

We've talked a lot about the caveats of international transactions, but if you have completed one, the process for paying is pretty much the same as for a domestic transaction. You see the price in the seller's local currency, and PayPal makes the currency conversion for you.

International sellers cannot use Delivery Confirmation or tracking unless they ship with an expensive service such as UPS or FedEx, so don't be surprised if there is no tracking number. Shipping always takes longer from overseas, and the item does have to go through Customs.

Shark in the Water

Never ask an international seller to put "gift" as the item type on the Customs form or to lower the value amount. You would be asking the seller to do something illegal, and both you and he could be fined a lot of money if you were caught. In years past, U.S. Customs didn't check smaller parcels with lower values, but now Customs is getting more vigilant.

It's important that your seller knows how to deal with Customs; otherwise, your item could be sitting at a port instead of on your doorstep. I really can't say this enough—make sure an international seller you deal with has a good amount of feedback and has sold to people in your country numerous times already.

If Customs dues are owed, this is your responsibility. You are importing the item. This amount is usually very little, but it is collected at the time of delivery. Don't confuse this with "extra postage owing," which is entirely different. The seller cannot (and should not try to) do anything about the Customs fees. You may never have to pay a Customs fee, but I mention it because you shouldn't get upset with the seller if you do have to pay it.

Giving and Receiving Feedback

We've talked about reading a seller's feedback, and now you get the opportunity to leave your own. You should never leave feedback until you receive the item and have had a chance to look it over. I usually wait until a day or two after I get it to leave feedback (so I can make sure it works properly and has no defects that I might initially have overlooked).

What to Write in Your Feedback Comment

Most of the time, you will want to leave positive feedback. When you think about what to say, think about what you would tell your best friend if she was considering buying from this seller. "A+ seller" is an okay comment, but "Fast shipping, great communication, will buy from again" is much better. Remember, you are limited in the number of characters you can use, so be concise and to the point.

If the shipping was slow but everything else was good, that doesn't warrant neutral or negative feedback. Maybe say something like "Good communication, shipping a little slow, but love the item!" That way, you are still giving the positives due to the seller, but you're also preparing other buyers that they may have to wait for delivery.

 Tips

Sellers cannot leave negative feedback, so you should be honest in your feedback comment. But still be polite.

You should certainly give the seller a lower score in the Detailed Seller Ratings for shipping time if the time he took to get the parcel in the mail was much slower than indicated in the listing. Look at when you sent the payment versus the postage date on the parcel to determine whether the shipping time was acceptable. You shouldn't factor the date the parcel arrived at your home into the equation. Sometimes the post office is delayed, and it's not fair to hold the seller responsible for the package delivery time after he dropped it off. Still, I would only reduce my rating to 4 stars if it was a day or two later than he said. If it was a week late with no explanation, then I would consider a 3 or possibly even 2 star rating.

When a Negative Feedback Comment Is Appropriate

If you have tried to work out a problem with the seller and she is being uncooperative, she refuses to return your e-mails or phone calls, or she is rude or threatening when you have been very polite throughout to her, negative feedback is warranted—and rather necessary, in my opinion.

Think back to your friend: would you warn her if she were planning to buy from this seller?

If you do need to leave negative feedback (and it is very rare), make sure you are very specific about the problem. "Deadbeat seller" doesn't tell other buyers anything. "Item not as described, no response to e-mails/calls, refused refund" is much more useful to other buyers.

I can't stress this enough: negative feedback should be reserved for when you have tried everything else and it has failed. Jumping in with negative feedback if the seller sent the wrong item makes him less likely to want to help you in a timely manner.

If you open a claim through eBay's Resolution Center (see Chapter 11) the seller has to work with you. However, she doesn't have to be any more accommodating than eBay requires. If you hold off on your negative feedback, she might be more willing to help in more ways than she's required.

Detailed Seller Ratings

In Chapter 7, we talked about how the Detailed Seller Ratings (DSRs) work. I highly recommend that you take the time to rate your seller on each of the four criteria.

Some confusion has arisen over what ratings you should give. If a transaction is good but nothing special, you might think 3 stars would be appropriate (average). However, this is not a good score at all. Most sellers have between 4.6 and 5.0 for their DSR averages. So a 3 star rating is actually quite low.

If the transaction had no issues, I would give the seller 5 stars across the board. Deduct only if you had issues. I wish half-stars were available, but unfortunately, at this time, they are not. A low rating for a newer seller will have much more of an impact than for a seller with hundreds of ratings. Keep that in mind when you select your Detailed Seller Ratings.

A 1 or 2 star rating hurts the seller in a number of ways. His percentage of 1 and 2 star ratings per DSR determines whether he qualifies for the Top-Rated Seller program (if he otherwise meets the criteria), whether his items get promoted or demoted in the Best Match sort order, and even whether he may continue selling. So think very carefully before leaving a 1 or 2 star DSR.

How to Leave Feedback

If you want to leave feedback for just one item, you can select **Leave Feedback** from the drop-down menu next to the item in the **Won** section of My eBay. However, if you want to leave feedback comments for all transactions, go to the **Community** tab and click on **Feedback Forum** (the top link).

When you click **Leave Feedback** on the **Feedback Forum** page, you are taken to a page showing all your recent transactions that you have not yet left feedback for.

You can easily see which transaction is which because of the item picture and title at the top of the box. But you should always make sure you have left the correct comment for the correct seller before you click **Leave Feedback.** The default is **I will leave feedback later,** so you have to select **Positive, Neutral,** or **Negative** for the comment to post.

To save you from having to go back to the closed listing page if you can't remember a detail about the transaction, you can just click the **View Item Summary** link (see Figure 10.7) and it will pop up a window showing you the selling price, the shipping and handling cost you paid, and the seller's location. The transaction date already appears on the main page.

Did You Know?

From the Feedback Forum, you can leave feedback, reply to feedback received, follow up on feedback you have already left for someone else, and find out more about feedback in general.

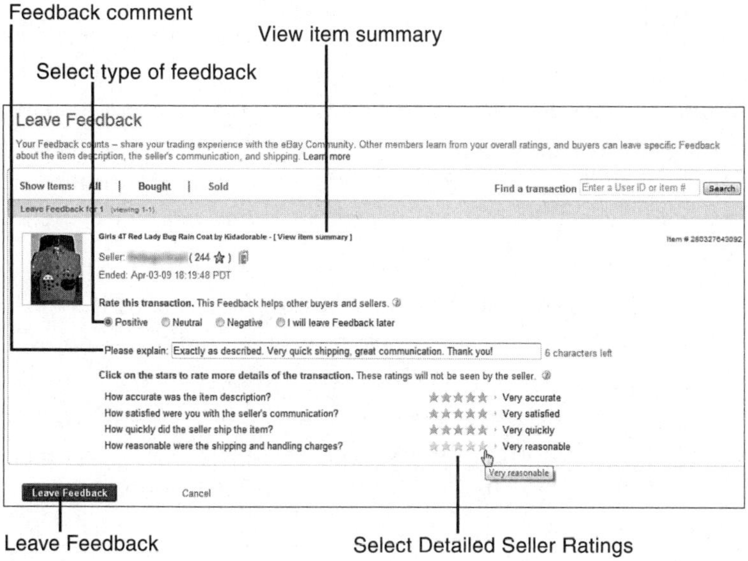

Feedback comment

View item summary

Select type of feedback

Figure 10.7

You are reminded if the seller offered free shipping. That way, you know to automatically give 5 stars for the shipping and handling cost.

Leave Feedback

Select Detailed Seller Ratings

To complete the Detailed Seller Ratings, use your mouse to hover over the stars to select the level you want, and click when it is at the right level. The stars become bold and bright orange when you select the rating. One left-click on the rating lets you adjust it if you made a mistake. Nothing is set in stone until you click **Leave Feedback** at the bottom of the page.

If you have more than one seller to leave feedback for on this page, just type all the comments and select the DSRs for all sellers first before you click **Leave Feedback.**

The ratings take a while to update (to protect the buyer's privacy), so you won't see the effect of your ratings immediately.

Can Feedback Be Removed?

Once you leave feedback, you cannot remove it unless it violates eBay's feedback policy (it gives some personal contact information about the other eBay user, uses profanity, and so on). However, the seller can initiate a **Revise Feedback** process. The seller gets a limited number of feedback revisions, so don't leave a negative comment thinking that if the seller makes good on the transaction, you can just revise the feedback later.

One example of when revising feedback is appropriate is if you left a negative comment because you didn't receive the item, but then a week later it arrives, and you can see from the postage that the seller did ship it when he said; the post office was simply delayed in delivering the package to you.

If the seller requests a feedback revision, you will get an e-mail through eBay in which you can select **Accept Request** or **Decline Request.** If you accept the request, you're sent to the feedback revision page, where you can enter your new feedback comment and Detailed Seller Ratings. If you decline the request, you're given the opportunity to tell the seller why, but you can select **I don't want to share the reason with the seller,** if you prefer.

If a seller makes good on a transaction (by replacing or refunding an item), or if it becomes clear that the seller just made a mistake (missed your order and then shipped the item quickly to you), it's polite to revise the feedback if the seller requests it. Remember, in most cases, this is the seller's business we're talking about. Sometimes honest mistakes are made, and your neutral or negative comment could have a severe impact. The seller's Feedback Profile shows that the feedback comment was revised, so other buyers will see that.

Follow-Up Feedback Comments

You can place a follow up on comments you've left (you access this from the main Feedback Forum page). You might have left a positive comment that mentioned good things but stated that the shipping was slow, only to take a second look at the parcel and see that the seller took the package to the post office two weeks ago—the post office was slow, not the seller. Since the feedback was positive, there's no reason to use one of the seller's Revise Feedback options. You would simply put a follow-up comment on your original feedback stating that the shipping delay was not the seller's fault and that you can see he shipped it on time.

Follow-up comments can also be used if a seller replies to the feedback comment you made and you feel like you need to add another comment after that. Be careful not to get into a name-calling match—it makes both of you look petty and helps no one.

Reply to Feedback Comments

You can also reply to feedback that has been left for you. If you get a comment that you don't think is fair, you can respond and have your comment shown below. Be careful what you say, because other people will read it and make a lot of assumptions about you based on what you write.

I Remember When ...

I saw one seller a few years back with a whole string of negatives within two weeks, but a perfect record before that. All of the negatives were from buyers saying they had received no communication from the seller after paying.

The seller was able to add a reply to each of these comments explaining that she had been evacuated from her home due to a hurricane and hadn't had power for two weeks.

eBay eventually removed those negatives, but having the replies on the feedback comments helped relieve the concerns of potential buyers who read her Feedback Profile until that time.

When Is It Okay to Purchase from an eBay Seller Off eBay?

I've said it many times—never purchase from an eBay seller who offers you the item off eBay for a lower price, quicker delivery, and so on. If anyone offers to do this, you should report that seller to eBay.

Right. Having said that, there is one exception. If you have already bought something from the seller, she has now established a business relationship with you, and eBay cannot control any private buying and selling that takes place between you. Most large eBay sellers have websites, and it is common practice to direct you to their websites for future purchases. Most sellers prefer that, because then they are not paying eBay fees on your repeat purchases. If they keep sending you e-mails (over and above checking about the item), report this as spam to eBay—that is, unless you added the seller as a favorite and signed up for their newsletter or other communication. You can change that preference at any time if you're getting too many e-mails from the seller.

If I received good service from a seller on eBay, I will usually not hesitate to buy from her website—but remember, you are not eligible for eBay's Fraud Protection (see Chapter 11) if the transaction takes place off eBay.

The Least You Need to Know

- Check your spam filter and junk mail box if you don't receive any response from your seller. Also check your Messages box on eBay because most e-mails from sellers will also be here unless the seller already has your direct e-mail address.

- You can get the seller's phone number if you can't reach him by e-mail (but he will also get your phone number).

- Be specific in your feedback comments (both positive and negative), or there is not much point leaving the comment.

- Feedback comments are permanent, and the feedback you leave is just as much a reflection of you as the feedback you receive.

- It is okay to buy from a seller off eBay once you have already purchased from her on eBay (but understand that you will lose eBay's fraud protection).

Avoiding Fraud and Fakes

In This Chapter

◆ Types of eBay fraud

◆ What to do if you received the wrong item, a counterfeit, or none at all

◆ Using the eBay Resolution Center

◆ Non-eBay (third-party) fraud protection

Internet fraud exists. Statistically, you are unlikely to be affected by it, and you can almost eliminate the risk by always following eBay rules. However, it's a good idea to be alert. The first section of this chapter tells you about some of the things you should watch out for. The second half then explains what redress you might have. Don't let it put you off bidding—just try to be wiser than the villains.

eBay and PayPal each have aggressive and sophisticated antifraud departments working around the clock to prevent fraudulent transactions and to catch and stop cybercriminals.

Nevertheless, it is a never-ending battle, and some of these Internet barbarians still get past the gate. This means that you are the final barrier between them and your money. I don't want to frighten you or make you suspicious about every transaction. After all, a big part of eBay is the fun factor. But you do need to be alert and take sensible precautions.

Types of Fraud and How to Avoid Them

Much of the fraud on eBay originates overseas from countries that don't seem to care whether their citizens are committing crimes outside of their country or can't find a way to prosecute them. These people are beyond the reach of U.S. law enforcement agencies, so it can be hard to hold them accountable for their actions.

You could run into several types of fraud on eBay. We talked about identity theft and account takeover in Chapter 1, but other types include the following:

- Seller impersonation

- Inaccurate descriptions and photos

- Sale of nonexistent products

- Escrow fraud

- Fake or counterfeit merchandise

We take a look at each one, but one general rule to follow is to always check a seller's feedback. The eBay feedback system (which we talked about in Chapters 7 and 10) is your first line of defense and biggest weapon against fraud.

The reason I'm mentioning these types of fraud is not to scare you away from eBay, rather to make sure you're aware of what to look for so you don't get caught by these scams. The likelihood of you actually being scammed on eBay is very slim, particularly if you follow my advice throughout this book.

In almost a decade of buying and selling on eBay, I have encountered only one fraud-related problem as a buyer (a fake DVD). Looking back at it, I should have known better based on the seller's lack of feedback and the "too good to be true" price. Since then I limit my DVD and video game purchases to U.S. sellers only and don't buy this type of item from sellers with less than a 50 Feedback Score. I've never had a problem since. Still, it pays to know the warning signs, so that is what we cover here.

Seller Impersonation

This is a scam also known as *Stealing First Base*. The scammer watches an auction for an expensive item. She waits for the auction to end and then immediately sends you an e-mail through the eBay system that says "Congratulations for winning auction number 123456789, Ladies Gold and Diamond Pendant. Please click here to pay" (or it may ask you to send the payment to a certain PayPal address). The problem is, this person is not the actual seller. She's hoping you are so excited that you pay quickly before realizing you paid the wrong person.

eBay no longer displays the high bidder or winning bidder's user ID on the listing page or the bid history. It is masked like a***r and all you see is that and the Feedback Score. This prevents a scammer from catching U.S. buyers in this scam. However, not all eBay sites mask user IDs the same way as the U.S. site. So it pays to be aware whenever you purchase from an international eBay site. Take a moment to look at the user ID of the seller; make sure you are paying the correct seller, not Mr. Chui in Macau.

> **Shark in the Water**
>
> Some eBay international sites only mask bidders IDs when the bid price goes over a certain amount. If your purchase is below that threshold, you could be open to the seller impersonation scam, so be extra careful and only ever pay using eBay **Checkout**.

Account Takeover

We talked about this in Chapter 1, but to recap, account takeover occurs when someone learns your user ID and password. It usually happens when you have an easy-to-guess password, if you follow a link in an e-mail that you think came from eBay and enter your user ID and password into a fake site, or if you use the same login and password for another website that gets hacked into and the information stolen. This is the most common type of fraud on eBay because it's not something eBay can control or protect against.

Account takeover targets both buyers and sellers. If a thief gets into your account, he will use your eBay identity to purchase dozens of expensive items very quickly. Thieves know that most people work during the day, so they will often make these purchases early in the day and send payment to the sellers using a stolen credit card.

The idea is that the thief gets the items shipped to him, and you get blamed for the fraudulent transactions when they show up as coming from a stolen credit card.

If you ever try to log in to eBay and can't get in with a password you know is correct, check that no family member changed it, and try again to ensure you didn't type it incorrectly. If you still can't get in, you must immediately contact eBay. The **Contact**

Us link at the top of the home page will guide you. Select **I think someone used my account** and eBay will offer you three contact options: **Email us, Chat with us,** or **Call us.** If you choose **Call us** to telephone eBay (my preference), you will be given the phone number and a temporary web pin to get you through the prompts. This expires in one hour so make sure to call soon. The customer service agent will be able to verify it's your account and help you retake control over it.

Inaccurate Descriptions and Photos

A bad description can be fraudulent if the seller deliberately misrepresents an item or its condition, but sometimes it's just the work of a lazy or incompetent seller. In either case, the result is the same. If you relied on the accuracy of the description and then received something that was not what was represented, you have been ripped off.

This type of fraud happens occasionally on eBay, but the good news is that the same sellers don't usually get much opportunity to repeat it. eBay usually shuts down the accounts of obviously fraudulent sellers. If it was just a lazy or incompetent seller, he will certainly earn negative feedback and other buyers will not buy from him. eBay's Resolution Center provides a way to report items that are not as described in the listing. If eBay agrees with you, you will usually receive a refund after you return the item. I cover the Resolution Center in more detail later.

The best way to defend against sellers who distort information (and sometimes photographs) for their own gain is to read the description very carefully. Next check the seller's feedback. Look at the **Detailed Seller Ratings** for **Item As Described** and see how high the rating is. Look at the feedback comments, too. Although eBay will remove comments that don't match the rating at the seller's request, most seller's don't bother. Sometimes you'll see a positive rating with a scathing comment.

If you are at all concerned or suspicious, use the link to **Ask a question** and ask for details. If the seller does not respond or is evasive in any way, just go on to another item, or if you are really suspicious, use the link beneath the **Seller info** and **Other item info** boxes to report the item to eBay.

Fake or Counterfeit Merchandise

Authentic Gucci or Hermes handbags sell for between $500 and $2,000 each. If you were strolling down the sidewalks of New York City and you saw a street vendor selling Gucci or Hermes handbags for $90 each, you would probably be suspicious that they were copies or fakes. And you would be correct. Unfortunately, some of this counterfeit merchandise makes its way onto eBay.

eBay is fighting back hard, but it is a constant battle.

Your best defense against buying counterfeit goods is to buy only from sellers with very high feedback. eBay will shut sellers down if it catches them selling fake or counterfeit goods. Most large sellers won't risk this and will, therefore, deal only in genuine products.

Limiting your search results to U.S. only also helps because you typically see less fake merchandise sold from within the United States. Law enforcement are often involved in counterfeit merchandise claims on eBay and sellers know they can be caught. The United States doesn't have jurisdiction in foreign countries, so that's where the fakes typically come from.

Nonexistent Products

Listing items for sale that the seller doesn't actually possess is an out-and-out scam. This scam works in two ways:

1. A person, usually located overseas, sets up an eBay account, often using a stolen credit card as ID to open the account. Then he makes a few dozen very cheap purchases on eBay just to build up his feedback. Then he lists an auction for a very expensive but nonexistent item such as a diamond ring or a plasma TV. These sellers usually set a Buy It Now price that is significantly lower than the value of the item. You click on the **Buy It Now** price and think to yourself, "Wow, I just bought a $2,000 plasma TV for $1,400." When you go to pay, the seller has some excuse for not taking PayPal or credit cards and insists that you send a certified check or money order, or wire the money through Western Union. You send the payment, and then nothing happens. After a few days, you try contacting the seller and get no replies. You log on to eBay and check up on the seller, only to find out that the seller is NARU (Not A Registered User) and that the account has been closed.

2. A thief gets into the account of a seller with very high feedback and then lists the nonexistent items using the seller's feedback as a shield. As in the first example, he requires payment using nonrefundable methods (cash, money order, Western Union, and so on, all of which are banned from eBay). The buyers send the payments because the seller has such good feedback that they assume it can't be a scam. Of course, they never receive the items. The seller's feedback is ruined, the buyers are out the money they paid, and the thief walks away with the cash.

You can't do much if you get taken in by either of these scams, so prevention is the word of the day.

The thing all these scams have in common is that they want you to bypass eBay's policies and send payment via a method banned from eBay. There's a reason eBay has banned these payment methods, and it's not just to get more people to use PayPal. Even before eBay banned checks and money orders, 80 percent of buyers preferred PayPal.

There's really only one foolproof solution to buying expensive goods (such as vehicles or very expensive antiques) when you can't get the protection of PayPal or your credit card company. That is to use eBay's official *escrow* company, Escrow.com.

def•i•ni•tion

An **escrow** service is a licensed and regulated company that collects, holds, and sends a buyer's money to a seller according to instructions agreed on by both the buyer and seller. (You may have seen it used when purchasing a house.)

Typically, after the buyer receives the item, she must approve it within an agreed-upon period. As soon as the approval is made, the escrow service sends the payment to the seller.

Another type of fraud uses phony escrow companies, and we talk about this next. eBay advises that you use only Escrow.com.

Escrow Fraud

You just learned what an escrow company was. Now imagine if you sent your money to a phony escrow company. This type of fraud is related to selling nonexistent merchandise. The seller writes and says he understands that you are reluctant to send a large cash payment to a stranger, so he gives you a link to an escrow company. You visit the website, create an account (thereby also giving away your credit card number), and follow the instructions to send your money. The address is usually overseas, or if it is in the United States, it's a postal mailbox company address. Once you mail off the cashier's check, the escrow website you signed up with mysteriously disappears.

So if a seller wants to use an escrow company, insist on using Escrow.com and go to the site either by linking from eBay or by going directly to the website. Do not click on an e-mail link to Escrow.com that a seller sent you.

Shark in the Water

It is very easy to create a link that says www.escrow.com but actually sends you to a different, fake site. You can check the link just like I showed you in Chapter 1, but it's much easier to just type www.escrow.com into your browser when you want to go to that site.

What If I Didn't Get My Item or It Wasn't What I Was Expecting?

If you got the item but it wasn't what you thought you should be getting, go back and look at the item description. Did you misinterpret it? Does the seller accept returns?

Whether misinterpretation is or is not a possibility, the next step is to contact the seller. Be nice. If you go in with a confrontational attitude, you're going to get the same attitude reflected back at you. Give her the benefit of the doubt. If you explain what you thought you were getting versus what you got, often sellers who don't actually have a specified return policy will allow you to return the item. Expect to pay the original shipping and the return shipping, though.

Tips

If it's only a minor issue, the seller may offer to refund part of your payment and let you keep the item. This happened to me when I bought a laptop a few years back. The description clearly stated that it included an internal wireless card. When it arrived, the wireless card was missing. I contacted the seller, and she offered to accept a return (but I would pay the return shipping) or give me a refund for the cost of a wireless card. I opted for the refund and used the money to go get the card myself.

If the item was misrepresented and the seller won't do anything about it, you never received the item, or you can't get hold of the seller, the next step is to go to eBay's **Resolution Center.**

eBay Resolution Center

Reporting a seller through the Resolution Center is not your first step when there is a problem. You should *always* contact your seller and try to work it out with him first. But if the seller is not cooperating or is not responding to your e-mails, you should involve eBay.

The Resolution Center on eBay is currently changing. Previously, all claims were filed through PayPal and no other payment methods were covered. This has changed. The Resolution Center is now back on eBay and all eBay-approved payment methods are covered.

Currently, the easiest way to start a claim is to find the item you're disputing in the **Won** section of My eBay. Using the drop-down menu to the right of the item, select **Resolve a problem.**

There are two types of claim:

♦ **Item Not Received** (it never arrived)

♦ **Not as Described** (it arrived but was significantly different from what the seller had advertised in the listing)

Tips _____

You have 45 days from when you paid the seller to file a claim with eBay. You can contact eBay either via web-form or telephone, whichever you prefer.

Did You Know?

eBay does not routinely read e-mails between buyers and sellers. However, if you open a claim, the customer service agent will have access only to the e-mail thread between you and your seller. He won't be able to read any other communications you may have had with other eBay members.

Whichever claim you file, and whether it's via web-form or by calling eBay, you'll get to a Customer Support Agent who will review the case. He will confirm that you have already tried to work with the seller (he will have access to the e-mail conversations you have had going back and forth), and if not, he'll tell you to do so. He will also run a fraud check to make sure you haven't made a lot of claims, and that no seller has appealed that what you returned to them was not what they had originally sent, or was in significantly worse condition when it was returned.

Next, the agent reviews the item description, seller's location, payment, shipping method, and tracking information if available. If you're filing an Item Not Received claim, you may be asked to wait longer to see if it arrives. eBay won't continue the claim until the total of the seller's listed handling time, the maximum of the shipping carrier's estimated delivery time, plus a three day buffer has elapsed. He may ask you to wait longer if extenuating circumstances exist, too (such as a hurricane hit the seller's location).

If your claim qualifies, the customer support agent then contacts the seller. The seller has seven days to respond. For an Item Not Received claim, he can:

◆ Appeal the claim by providing proof of delivery (delivery confirmation or signature confirmation if the item price was over $250) to your address.

◆ Agree to send the item or a replacement to you.

◆ Send you a refund.

If the claim is for an item Not as Described, the seller can:

◆ Appeal the claim by providing proof that the claim is false (showing where in the listing he detailed whatever you're saying is wrong with the item).

◆ Send a replacement item (but you must return the original item first).

◆ Send you a refund (usually you will be required to return the original item first).

If your claim is because an item is a fake (and you have either a manufacturer's or law enforcement certificate showing that the item is counterfeit), you are not required to return the item. In some cases, eBay will require it is destroyed and will assume the cost for the item's destruction.

After seven days have passed since eBay contacted the seller, the eBay customer support agent will contact you (the buyer) to see if the situation was resolved. If you are satisfied, the case is closed. If you're still working with the seller, eBay will check back with you in a week to see how it's going then.

If you are not satisfied, the customer support agent will review the case. If he finds in your favor, eBay will refund you the purchase and shipping cost you paid to the seller.

eBay usually recovers the refund from the seller through his PayPal account, or if the payment method was not PayPal, through whatever method he uses to pay his eBay fees. Occasionally, eBay will just assume the cost of the refund rather than recover it from the seller.

If your claim was for **Not as Described,** you usually have to return the item to the seller to receive a refund through eBay.

All open claims display in the **Cases** section at the top of your My eBay **Summary** page, and also in the **Resolution Center** main page (which can be accessed via a link at the very bottom of the eBay home page, or from the drop-down list when you hover your mouse over the **Help** tab).

But remember, getting eBay involved is a last resort. You should make every effort to work with the seller directly first. If you don't tell the seller, she can't fix the problem. If her first knowledge of a problem is negative feedback or a claim filed with eBay, she will not exactly be inclined to help you.

If you assume that the seller did not deliberately do whatever caused the problem (she accidentally shipped the wrong item, she didn't see the flaw in the item, and so on), you should give her the opportunity to be politely apologetic and fix it for you. If you go in making accusations and being rude, you will get the bare minimum service she is required to give you.

Plus, you don't want lots of notes on your eBay account for filing claims if they could be resolved without involving eBay.

PayPal Buyer Protection

PayPal offers fraud coverage (called PayPal Buyer Protection) on most eBay items purchased using its service. The coverage and terms are the same as eBay's Resolution Center. Because of this, I think it is smarter to stick with eBay's Resolution Center for eBay purchases. You can talk to a customer service agent on the phone (not available through PayPal) and the service seems to be far more streamlined because they only deal with eBay purchases.

If you really prefer to use PayPal's Buyer Protection, you can file a claim through www.PayPal.com. However, once you file a claim with PayPal, you cannot later change your mind and use the eBay Resolution Center.

Tips

The default funding source for your PayPal payments is any balance currently in your account; the second is your bank account. You must use **More Funding Options** to select your credit card each time you make a high-ticket purchase to be able to file a chargeback request with your credit card company, if needed.

Card Chargeback and Insurance Programs

Most credit card companies (including Visa, Discover, MasterCard, and American Express) offer some level of fraud protection when you make a credit card purchase. Some of them also offer actual insurance that you can purchase or that they give you for free if you have a gold or platinum card.

I don't recommend filing a chargeback request without first trying eBay's Resolution Center. Usually it can be resolved at this level rather than involving your credit card company. However, if you have no other option, just call the customer service number on the back of the credit card; tell the operator the situation and say that you want to file a chargeback request. Each company has different procedures and may require copies of information such as sales receipts, copies of e-mails, transaction numbers, and so on.

If you use your credit card to fund your PayPal payment, you can still file a chargeback request, but it will automatically close any claim you currently have open with eBay or PayPal. You cannot get reimbursed by both your credit card company and PayPal (although it would be nice if you could!).

buySAFE

buySAFE (www.buysafe.com) is a third-party trust and safety company that bonds online shoppers' transactions for the full purchase price (up to $25,000 when you buy from a buySAFE Bonded Seller). Whenever you see the buySAFE Bonded Seller Seal in an auction (see Figure 11.1), you can click on it to confirm that the seller is bonded. Thousands of eBay sellers use buySAFE—especially those who sell expensive goods, but you'll see it available on some cheaper items, too.

Figure 11.1

Don't exclude a seller simply because he is not a buySAFE member—but if he is, it is one extra level of protection for you.

It isn't easy to become bonded through buySAFE, so if you see a seller who is, you know that she is reliable and trustworthy, follows good shipping practices, has a good financial record, and is experienced.

Shark in the Water

Because the buySAFE Bonded Seller Seal doesn't have an automatically updating current date on it, theoretically, a fraudulent seller could create a fake seal and point the link to a spoof site.

This is very easy to catch. Just check the address the link takes you to. Alternatively, you can go directly to www.buysafe.com and enter the seller's user ID and the item number to confirm that the item is bonded.

SquareTrade Warranty Services

SquareTrade has been in business since 1999 and has a long history with eBay. They offered a trust seal program and dispute-resolution process for many years, but it was discontinued after eBay changed its policies and there was no reason for it to continue. However, SquareTrade expanded into the warranty market.

Buying a used or refurbished item always involves some risk. You never quite know how well electronic items work or how long they will continue to work.

A few years ago, I bought a used Dell laptop for $500 from a seller on eBay. It worked for about six months before it started having major issues (stopped turning on, overheating, and so on). It would have cost me $400 to fix it. That was one time when the risk came back to bite me. But now you have another option.

SquareTrade has really revolutionized the way we look at warranty services. It is the only company I've ever seen that will warranty a used item. SquareTrade sells extended warranties for new, used, and refurbished items sold on eBay.

Most warranties (from major retailers) cost upward of 20 percent of the retail item cost (for new items). SquareTrade charges closer to 10 percent (depending on the item type and condition).

Now consider the other advantages:

♦ There are no difficult hoops to jump through to file a claim.

♦ There's no need to scour the house looking for receipts (the eBay item number you provided is your proof of purchase).

> **Did You Know?**
>
> SquareTrade doesn't offer warranties just for eBay purchases. If you buy an item at a major retailer (or even another online website), rather than paying 20 percent for the warranty, go to SquareTrade within 30 days and get a warranty that's much simpler to manage and lasts longer, for 40 to 70 percent less.

♦ If an item needs to be repaired, you can easily print a shipping label and overnight the item to SquareTrade; they will repair it, and you'll have it back in your hands within five days. If your item is large (50-inch plasma TV, desktop computer, and so on), they will schedule an in-home repair guy to contact you within the same time frame. (Compare that to some electronics retail warranties!)

♦ Claims are paid within five days of filing.

♦ If you sell the item, you can either transfer the warranty or cancel it and receive a prorated refund.

If you've ever dealt with a regular warranty, you now see why I used the term *revolutionary*.

SquareTrade currently offers warranties (Product Care Plans) for many items. The main item types include:

- Video games consoles

- Laptop and desktop computers

- TVs and associated peripherals (DVD, Blu-ray, TiVo, and so on)

- Audio systems

- Cell phones (including iPhone)

- Cameras and camcorders

- MP3 players (such as iPods)

- eBook readers (Kindle, Sony eReader, and so on)

- Car electronics

- Home and appliances (washer/dryer, home security, vacuum cleaner, and so on)

- Computer peripherals

- Watches and jewelry

If you are interested in purchasing a warranty for your item, go to www.squaretrade.com to get started. You may also see the option of buying a warranty, and the price, on the listing page for some large electronics sellers.

Accidental damage coverage is available for an additional cost. If you're comparing a retailer warranty to SquareTrade, ensure you are comparing the same total coverage and time frame.

The Least You Need to Know

- The eBay Resolution Center is not the first step if you have a problem. Always try to work it out with the seller directly first. Your claim cannot continue until you have attempted to work with the seller directly.

- Fraudsters will almost always find a reason for needing a banned payment method (check, money order, Western Union, and so on). Never send these types of payment, no matter what reason the seller gives you.

♦ If you paid with PayPal, you can choose to use PayPal's Buyer Protection coverage or eBay's Resolution Center. You can only pick one.

♦ Look for the buySAFE Bonded Seller Seal for an extra level of protection, but don't exclude a seller if he doesn't have it.

♦ SquareTrade offers warranty services for new, refurbished, and used items sold on eBay, as well as new items purchased anywhere (on- or offline).

♦ Change the funding source for your PayPal payment to your credit card if you are buying a high-ticket item so that you have fraud protection from your credit card company as well as from PayPal.

Part  3

Getting Ready to Sell on eBay

If you're anything like me, you'll find yourself getting addicted to buying on eBay. So to offset the cost, and clear some space in your house for your new treasures, this is where we look at selling on eBay.

All the information in Parts 3, 4, and 5 assumes that you are selling items you already own. Whether this is as far as you want to go, or you want to ultimately build an eBay business, you need to start with the basics. The best way to do that is to sell items you already have. The idea isn't so much to make a big profit, but to get some experience—and you probably will make more than you would get from a yard sale.

Once you have some selling experience, you can look at purchasing for resale and start looking at sell-through rates, profit margins, and the like. Right now, though, let's concentrate on learning the mechanics of smart selling.

Chapter 12

Getting Started as a Seller

In This Chapter

- ◆ Registering as a seller
- ◆ A quick look at how to list an auction
- ◆ What eBay expects of you as an eBay seller
- ◆ What you can't sell on eBay
- ◆ Making the most of PayPal's selling tools
- ◆ Refunding a buyer using PayPal

Selling on eBay is fun as well as profitable! Even though I have been doing it for a number of years, I still get excited when I watch the last few minutes of my auctions and see two or three people bidding and counterbidding to win my items.

This chapter takes you through the steps to register as an eBay seller and customize your PayPal selling tools. After you've done this once, you can forget about it and concentrate on selling your items.

We also talk a bit about what you can and can't do as a seller on eBay. Since eBay can cancel your auctions and sometimes even suspend your account for violating these rules, you need to have a good feel for them before you start.

Registering as a Seller

This is fairly mechanical, so I'm going to run through it as quickly as possible so we can get on to the fun stuff. You can't sell on eBay until you have registered as a seller, so make sure you don't skip any of the steps. Make sure you have your credit card handy, because you will need it in a moment. I am assuming you are already registered as a buyer and signed in to your eBay account before you start.

1. Go to the eBay home page and click on the **Sell** navigation tab.

2. Enter your credit card details and change the billing address if it is different from your eBay registered address. You can use MasterCard, Visa, Discover, or American Express. You can also use a debit card if it allows credit (that is, non–PIN number) purchases. Click **Continue** when you're done.

3. Now you need to agree to eBay's Credit Card Usage Agreement. eBay runs an authorization for $1 to check that the card is valid and in good standing. They won't actually charge it, though. It's more like the hold a gas station puts on your card when you pay at the pump—it's just making sure the card is valid, and then later they charge it for the actual amount you spent. eBay just doesn't come back and charge your card after the $1 hold is approved, so it just expires. Make sure you read the agreement before you click **Authorize Credit Card.**

 Tips _____

You can change your account from Individual to Business if you are starting an eBay business, but you are not required to do so. If you choose to make this change, it is done in the **Account** tab within **My eBay**.

4. Any eBay fees you incur as a seller will now be automatically charged to your credit card once a month. You can change this so that the fees are withdrawn from your bank account (called the DirectPay program) or PayPal, if you prefer. This change is made in the **Account** tab of My eBay (handily, where you have just been redirected to). Just click **Update Your Automatic Payment Method** and follow the prompts to link your PayPal account or add your bank account details.

That's it. Now you're a registered eBay seller.

The Abridged Version of How to List an Auction

Many people start off with great plans to sell things on eBay, but some never go any further, usually because they're afraid of "doing it wrong." Honestly, it's really not that scary. Just follow the simple steps and you will be selling in no time.

The following steps provide a quick overview. For a more detailed explanation, see the chapters noted in every step. Click the **Sell** tab on the home page and then the **Start Selling** button to get started.

1. Enter keywords about your item into the box and click **Search.**

2. Select your preferred category from those suggested by eBay, or click the **Browse Categories** tab and select your own category and subcategories. When you are done, click **Continue.** We talk about how to choose the best category in Chapter 16.

3. Enter your listing title. In Chapter 16, we show you how to write your title and decide whether you need a subtitle as well.

4. Use the menus to select the Item Specifics relevant to your item (color, brand, size, condition, and so on) if available for your item type. Be sure to fill in all the details, because your listing's visibility may depend on them.

5. Upload your pictures to your listing. Taking your pictures is covered in Chapter 15. How to upload them is in Chapter 16.

6. Enter your item description. In Chapter 17, we show you the best way to write a description and how to use the design options available in the HTML Editor.

7. Select a listing designer template (if you want to use one) and a visitor counter (to see how many people have actually clicked on your listing).

8. Choose a selling format (fixed-price, auction, auction with a Buy It Now option, and so on). We talk about these different options from a seller's perspective in Chapter 18.

9. Specify your starting price, quantity, and auction duration. (We talk about these in Chapter 19.)

10. Select your payment options and shipping methods/costs (also discussed in Chapter 19).

11. Set your Buyer Requirements to automatically limit the buyers (for example, no bidders from countries you don't ship to), and specify your returns policy. Again, this is covered in detail in Chapter 19.

12. Select any optional listing upgrades (such as Bold, Subtitle, Gallery Plus, and so on) that you want to use. Remember, eBay charges extra for upgrades. We go through these in Chapter 20 so you know what you are paying for.

13. Preview your listing to make sure it looks right and check the fees eBay will charge you. What you will see doesn't include your Final Value fee, which is the more expensive one. To see the current fees and what you get for each of them, go to Chapter 14. When you're happy with how your listing looks, click the **List your item** button.

You can add some other options, but these are the basics. See, it's not so scary. Throughout Part 4, we go through each section in detail, so don't panic if any of this seems complicated or a little intimidating right now.

eBay Rules for Sellers

eBay has a number of rules for sellers that are designed to protect all eBay users— buyers, sellers, and eBay itself. As issues arise, eBay develops a new policy on the subject. You can find eBay policies in the Help files.

I outline the major eBay rules for sellers here, but if you want to read about all of eBay's policies, go to http://pages.ebay.com/help/policies/overview.html.

Alternatively, you can click on the **Help** navigation tab and then click **Rules and Policies** under the **Membership and Account** heading.

If you do violate any of eBay's rules, eBay can do a number of things. The most common is to cancel your listing, but depending on the offense and how many warnings you have already had, you could face limits on your account privileges, demotion of item placement in the Best Match search results, loss of PowerSeller or Top-Rated Seller status, and even account suspension. eBay looks at each case individually and you can appeal most rulings, so don't get too worried about it. Having one listing cancelled isn't the end of the world, but you don't want to make a habit of it.

Selling Practices Policy

eBay holds sellers responsible for their listings and terms. Most of it is common sense, but by specifying it in a policy, eBay is given the authority to enforce it.

Here are the details of the Selling Practices Policy:

- ◆ Sellers are required to write an accurate and consistent description about the item. This includes Item Specifics. A seller who lists "New" for the Item Specifics but then says the item is refurbished in the description is in violation of this policy.

- Sellers are required to have available quantity of the item listed for the duration of the listing.

- Sellers may only charge reasonable shipping and handling fees.

- Sellers can only include relevant terms and conditions, and they must be consistent with what the seller writes in the item description. No conflicting information is allowed.

- Seller must specify a returns policy (even if it's just "No returns") and a handling time (from receiving payment to mailing the item).

- Sellers must use professional language and refrain from using language that undermines confidence in the eBay marketplace. You cannot say "negative feedback will be given to nonpaying bidders" because this is not something sellers can do. Nor could you say "Due to bad newbie bidders, if you have less than 10 feedback you must contact me before bidding."

These are not hard rules to follow, and you should be following them without being told to do so—it's just good business to give consistent information and good customer service.

The Short List of Banned Items

Okay, so the list isn't that short. In fact it's really quite long, so I cover only the major ones here. The following table shows a few of the major types of items that are banned or have specific restrictions. It would take way too much space to list all of them, so before you decide what you want to sell, browse the prohibited and banned items list at http://pages.ebay.com/help/policies/items-ov.html. You can find a link on the **Rules and Policies** page in the **Help** files if you don't want to type that whole link.

Items That Are Banned or Restricted on eBay

Item Category	eBay Policy
Alcohol	Restricted
Animals or wildlife products	Restricted
Bootleg recordings	Banned

continues

Items That Are Banned or Restricted on eBay (continued)

Item Category	eBay Policy
Drugs or drug paraphernalia	Banned
Electronic covert surveillance equipment	Banned
Firearms, weapons, and knives	Restricted
Gift cards	Restricted
Lock-picking devices	Banned
Manufacturers' coupons	Restricted
Medical devices	Restricted
Offensive material (such as Nazi memorabilia)	Banned
Plants and seeds	Restricted
Political memorabilia	Restricted
Police-related items	Restricted
Recalled items	Banned
Replica or counterfeit merchandise (even if identified as a fake— except replica coins provided they are identified as such)	Banned
Tobacco	Banned
Tobacco-related products	Restricted

In addition, eBay bans any item whose use or ownership would violate local or federal laws. For example, you can't sell a radar detector to someone who lives in a state where they are illegal to use.

Shill Bidding

I'm sure you've heard about shoddy in-person auctions where there is a stooge (or "shill") in the audience placing false bids to bump up the price of an item for the seller. It's illegal there, and it's illegal on eBay.

It may seem innocent enough—a friend offers to place the first bid on your auction to get the bidding started, or to increase the final selling price if it's going for way lower than you had hoped. But this is the same as having a stooge working for you in a live auction. It's not fair to the other bidders, and it completely undermines the foundation of eBay and what it stands for.

The worst shill bidders have multiple eBay accounts and bid on their own auctions using another eBay account. If they end up winning the item, they offer the item to the highest legitimate bidder through Second Chance Offer (if the bidding went high enough for them) or just claim that the high bidder decided to withdraw from the transaction and get their Final Value fees refunded.

The good news is that these shill bidders don't last very long on eBay. eBay has very sophisticated software that looks for patterns common in shill bidding and is extremely aggressive in locating and dealing with shill bidders, so don't even think about trying this.

Did You Know?

You may hear comments about how eBay's user ID masking (changing the User ID to e***r or w***l) means that shill bidders can't be caught. This is nonsense.

eBay has very sophisticated software that tracks which buyers are bidding on which seller's items and flags shill patterns for further investigation.

You can even see some of this tracking yourself. Go to the **listing** page and click on the **number of bid** to go to the **Bid History**. Now click on a bidder's masked ID. Among other things, this will show you the number and percentage of bids this buyer has made on this seller's listings during the last month.

Fee Avoidance

Fee avoidance is usually excessive shipping and handling. For example, Joe sold a $40 item for $10 and charged $35 in shipping when it actually only cost him $5 for the postage. This is fee avoidance because eBay charges sellers the Final Value fee on the selling price only, not the total price including shipping. Joe paid the Final Value fee on $10, not on the $40 he actually made (after you deduct the $5 actual shipping cost).

eBay is not very clear about what "excessive" means, but just use your common sense and you should be fine. It's okay to charge a little extra to cover your shipping materials or a small handling fee, but just don't make it a major profit center.

If you gouge on shipping, you won't get the bids and those you do get will give you low Detailed Seller Ratings for Shipping and Handling, which will eventually get you demoted in the search standings. It's not worth it.

Certain categories have maximum shipping charges that apply to specific items. Currently, these are all media items (books, DVDs, video games, and so on). You can offer faster services for a higher price, but you must also offer a shipping option that is priced at or below the maximum (in most cases, this is Media Mail). Go to http://pages.ebay.com/sell/August2008Update/MaxShipping/. Or click on the eBay **Site Map** (top-right corner of the home page), select **Shipping Center** from the **Selling Resources** section, and then click **Maximum Shipping Costs**.

Solicitation of an Off-eBay Sale

If a buyer finds your item on eBay and you offer to sell it to him off eBay, you are violating eBay's terms and conditions. This is also a type of fee avoidance because you aren't paying eBay its fees.

This is a little bit complicated because in some circumstances you can end a listing early to sell to one of your bidders.

Here are a few examples of what is *not* allowed:

◆ Ending a listing early to sell the item off eBay to a buyer who found the item on eBay.

◆ If an auction ends without meeting the reserve price, offering to sell the item to the highest bidder directly without sending a Second Chance Offer.

◆ Ending a listing early to sell the item to the highest bidder for a price *higher* than the current bid. (You can end it early and sell it for the *current* bid as long as you go through eBay's system, but there are very few circumstances when this is worthwhile for a seller.)

Tips

A good rule of thumb is to ask yourself, "Will I pay a Final Value fee on the total selling price?" If the answer is yes, then you're fine. If the answer is no, you are likely in violation of eBay's policy.

You can find the full policy on eBay at http://pages.ebay.com/help/policies/rfe-spam-non-ebay-sale.html. (It's in the **Rules and Policies—Rules for Everyone** section of the **Help** files.)

Now once you sell something to a buyer on eBay, that person becomes your customer. In your end-of-auction e-mail or when you follow up to confirm he got the item and ask him to leave feedback, you can invite him to visit your website, if you have one. Sales after the initial eBay purchase are fine to conduct directly between you and the buyer, but you don't get PayPal's Seller Protection if the sale is not conducted on eBay (more on this in Chapter 23).

Seller Nonperformance

You could be considered a nonperforming seller in three instances:

1. You accepted payment but didn't deliver the item.

2. The item delivered was significantly different from what you represented in the original listing. (For example, you didn't mention major flaws that affect the functionality, value, or appearance of the item.)

3. You didn't place a reserve on your auction, or the reserve was met, but at the end of the duration you refused to sell to the highest bidder, or you refused to accept a payment method you originally listed as acceptable in your auction description.

Having whatever item you are selling in your hand before you list it for sale on eBay is very important and can prevent many instances of seller nonperformance.

For example, John asks his neighbor Suzie to sell his power tools on eBay. Suzie lists the auction and gets a winning bidder. But John changes his mind and decides that the winning bid isn't high enough for him to want to sell the tools. Now Suzie has to explain to her high bidder why she can't deliver the item. Her feedback and Detailed Seller Ratings are on the line, and I can pretty much guarantee that she will receive negative feedback for this transaction.

Had Suzie required she take possession of the item, she would have made sure John really was prepared to part with it. That would also have opened a dialogue about the minimum price he was willing to sell it for (so Suzie could have set a reserve price).

The moral here is to never list an item under your user ID unless you have it in your possession.

Seller nonperformance is more prevalent with preorders around the holidays. eBay has very strict rules about listing hard-to-find items (like the newest toys or game consoles). These rules include showing a picture of the box and the original sales receipt showing the date of purchase so your buyers know you really do have the item in hand

and ready to ship. The value of a hard-to-find item goes down significantly if the buyer has to wait until three weeks after Christmas to get it.

Honestly, there's no reason you should be accused of seller nonperformance if you stay on top of things and deliver what you promise. It's important because you need to build excellent feedback. If you get comments like "shipped two weeks late" or "refunded after couldn't find item," you are not exactly instilling confidence in other potential buyers, and you may lose future sales. Plus, remember that every one of your Detailed Seller Ratings must average above 4.1 (out of 5) to continue selling.

PayPal for Sellers

In Chapter 2, I explained how to get your PayPal account verified (add a bank account), address confirmed (link your credit card), and the withdrawal limit removed (confirm your credit card). If you didn't complete all of these steps already, you need to go back and finish them all. Confirming the credit card you have linked to your PayPal account is usually the final step that gets forgotten because it's not necessary for buyers. Here's a reminder of how to do it:

1. Log in to your PayPal account and click **View limits** on your **My Account** page.

2. Click **Lift limits** next to **Withdrawal limit (monthly).**

3. Click **Link and confirm your debit or credit card.** If your card has already been linked, this automatically begins the confirmation process. If not, you are given the opportunity to link the credit card now.

4. When you click **Save and Continue,** PayPal charges your card $1.95. Look for this amount on your credit card statement with a four-digit code next to it (if you have online banking that shows pending transactions, you should see the charge immediately).

5. Return to PayPal and navigate to that same screen (see Figure 12.1).

6. Enter the four-digit code in the **PayPal code** box and click **Submit.** Assuming you already added your bank account to your PayPal account, your withdrawal limit is now removed and PayPal has refunded your $1.95 charge to your PayPal account.

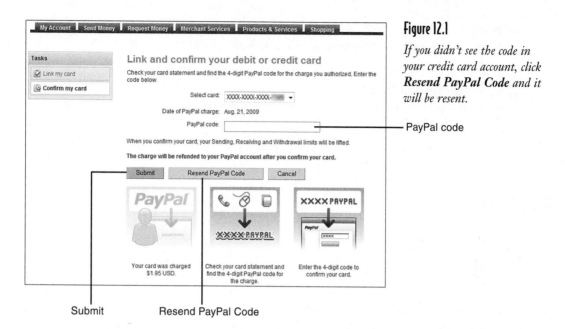

Figure 12.1

If you didn't see the code in your credit card account, click **Resend PayPal Code** *and it will be resent.*

Remove the Withdrawal Limit Using Your Social Security Number

If you need the withdrawal limit removed immediately, or you don't have a debit or credit card, you can remove the withdrawal limit by adding your Social Security number instead.

Follow the first two steps above, but then select **Confirm your Social Security Number** instead of **Link and Confirm Your Debit or Credit Card** in step three. Now just enter your Social Security Number in the box provided. It doesn't cost you anything, and your withdrawal limit will be immediately lifted. But this means your Social Security Number is now on file with PayPal.

Upgrade Your Account

You need to upgrade to a Premier PayPal account if you want to be an eBay seller. This is a requirement of the PayPal User Agreement, but it is worth doing for other reasons. The fees are the same whether you use a Personal account or Premier account, but you get better customer service options as a Premier account holder, and you don't have the $500 per month receiving limit Personal accounts have.

PayPal fees are based on the type of payment you receive: Personal or Purchase. If it comes through eBay Checkout (as all eBay payments will) it is automatically marked as a purchase.

The domestic fees for purchases are based on monthly transaction volume (how much you receive in purchase payments per month) as shown in the table.

U.S. Domestic PayPal Fees

Monthly Payments	Fee
Up to $3,000	2.9 percent plus 30¢ per transaction
$3,000–$10,000	2.5 percent plus 30¢ per transaction
$10,000–$100,000	2.2 percent plus 30¢ per transaction
Over $100,000	1.9 percent plus 30¢ per transaction

As an eBay seller, you will likely be either at the 2.9 or 2.5 percent levels. Throughout this book I have calculated PayPal fees in my examples using 2.9 percent plus 30¢.

The neat thing about PayPal's fee structure is that you can send and receive personal payments without paying fees.

So it doesn't matter if you upgrade to a Premier account so you can sell on eBay—you can still send cash to your kids at college or split a restaurant check with a friend using PayPal without it costing you anything. The only time fees apply to personal payments is when you use your credit card as the funding source. PayPal has to pay a fee to process a credit card, so they pass that on to you. The fee for a credit card funded personal payment is 2.9 percent plus 30¢, but the sender chooses who pays it (you or the recipient).

If you want to keep things totally separate, you can have one Personal and one Premier or Business PayPal account, but they have to have different bank accounts, credit cards, and e-mail addresses attached to them.

Customized PayPal Tools for eBay Sellers

PayPal offers some excellent selling tools that you can personalize. eBay and PayPal are well integrated, but you have to initially link the accounts yourself. I explained how to link the accounts in Chapter 4, so if you haven't already done so, refer back to that information and link your accounts.

Once your accounts are linked, you can customize your auction tools. Start by logging in to your PayPal account and go to your **My Account** page. Click on the **Profile** tab, and then click **Auctions** on the next page (see Figure 12.2). Figure 12.3 shows you the next page you will see (**eBay Accounts**) and the two options you can change: **PayPal Preferred** and **End of Auction Email.**

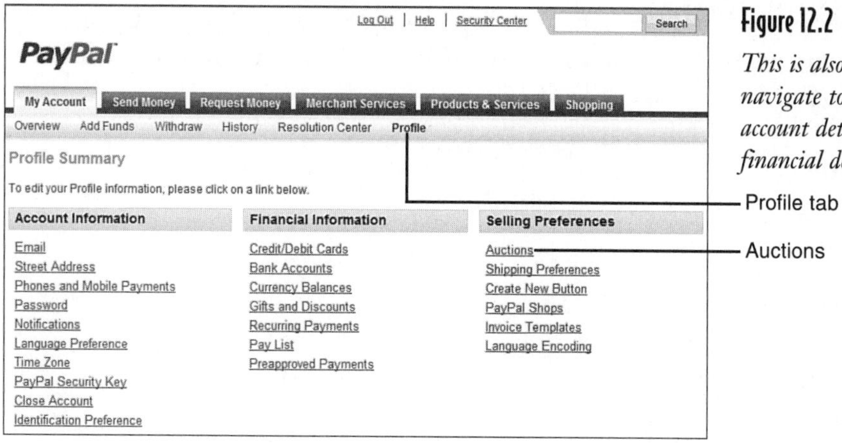

Figure 12.2

This is also the page you navigate to when changing account details, addresses, and financial details.

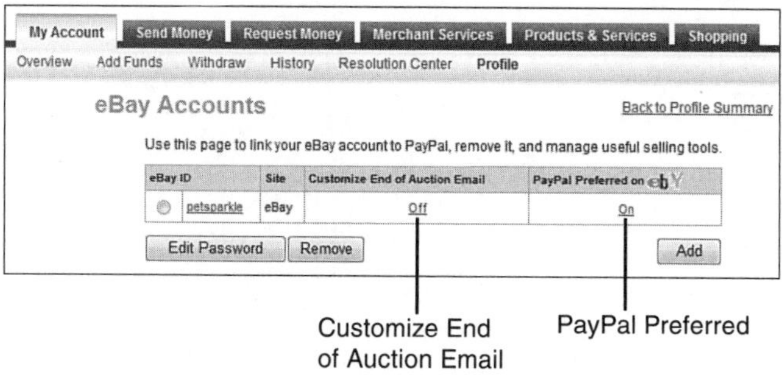

Profile tab

Auctions

Figure 12.3

You may link more than one eBay account to this PayPal account. If so, you will see both accounts listed on this page.

Customize End of Auction Email

PayPal Preferred

PayPal Preferred

You should be on the **eBay Accounts** page right now (see Figure 12.3). If not, go to your **My Account page,** click **Profile,** then click **Auctions** to get there.

Beneath **PayPal Preferred** it may say **On** or **Off.** If it says **Off,** click on that word and select **On** so that your auctions show that you prefer PayPal as your payment method. Some buyers look for this logo and tag line when they scan listings, so if it's missing, they may think you don't accept PayPal when you actually do.

End of Auction Email

Navigate to the **eBay Accounts** page shown in Figure 12.3 (from your **My Account** page, click **Profile** and then **Auctions**) and look for **Customize End of Auction Email.** Whether the word beneath this is **On** or **Off,** clicking it takes you to a page where you can modify the e-mail that is automatically sent to your buyers, and turn this feature on or off (see Figure 12.4).

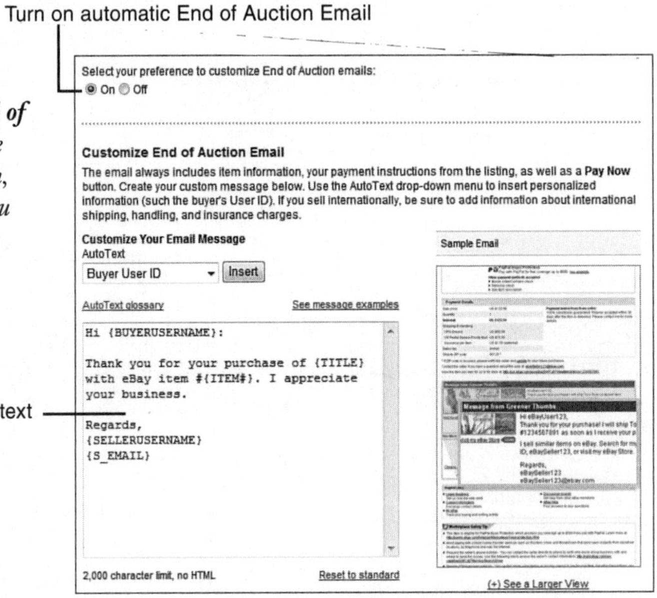

Turn on automatic End of Auction Email

Figure 12.4

*You can turn off the **End of Auction Email** the same way that you turned it on, if you decide later that you just want to send e-mails manually.*

End of Auction Email text

You can see the default e-mail in Figure 12.4. To modify it, just change the text in the box. The all-caps text within the braces { } inserts whatever text it specifies. So {BUYERUSERNAME} will insert the user ID of the buyer who will receive this particular End of Auction Email.

I highly recommend that you do change the default e-mail, because it is quite impersonal. I like to include a bit more specific information. This is my version:

Hi {BUYERUSERNAME},

Thank you for your purchase of {TITLE}, eBay item #{ITEM#}. I appreciate your business! Your item will be shipped within two business days from when I receive your cleared PayPal payment (please note that PayPal eChecks take up to four business days to clear PayPal's system).

You will receive an e-mail from PayPal when I print the shipping label. Your parcel will be mailed that same day or the following business day.

You will see the tracking number beneath this item in the "Won" section of My eBay (it is also on the e-mail PayPal sends you).

Please understand that delivery confirmation is not "tracking," it just confirms that you have received the item. If you require in-transit tracking for your item, please select either Express Mail or one of the UPS shipping options I offer when you use eBay Checkout.

Don't forget that I offer combined shipping, so check out my other items at http://search.ebay.com/_W0QQfgtpZ1QQfrppZ25QQsassZpetsparkle.

Please let me know ASAP if you want to bid on anything else so I can combine your shipping and save you some money!

If you have any questions, please don't hesitate to e-mail me.

Regards,

Lissa McGrath

{SELLERUSERNAME}

{S_EMAIL}

www.lissamcgrath.com

You have 2,000 characters, so that's plenty of space. My example is 1,123 characters.

If you have a business logo, you can upload that here as well, but don't worry about it if you don't have one. Most people don't.

When you're finished changing the e-mail text, make sure to click the **On** button before **Submit,** otherwise it will save your text but won't turn on the auto-sending feature.

Now whenever an auction ends, the winning bidder will receive this End of Auction Email automatically, without you having to do anything.

Refunds

Even with the best will in the world, some transactions don't end satisfactorily. You may have made an error in the listing, or the buyer may have returned the item. Either way, you may need to provide a refund of some kind.

Thankfully, this is remarkably easy as long as you have a balance in your PayPal account to cover the refund amount. If you don't, it's a little more complicated, but still not too bad.

1. Log in to your PayPal account and locate the transaction in the **History** tab.

2. Click on **Details** next to the payment to go to the **Transaction Details** page.

3. Click **Issue Refund** (see Figure 12.5) to go to the Issue Refund page.

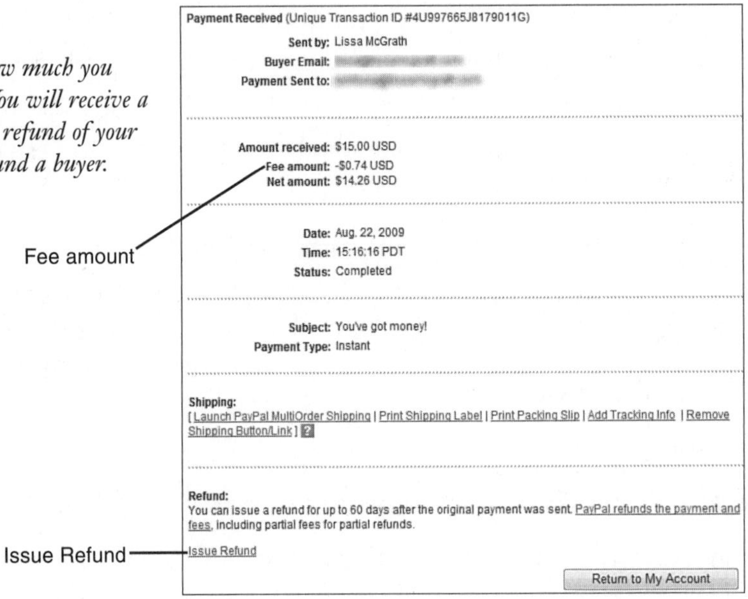

Figure 12.5

You can see how much you paid in fees. You will receive a full or partial refund of your fees if you refund a buyer.

Fee amount

Issue Refund

Payment Received (Unique Transaction ID #4U997665J8179011G)

Sent by: Lissa McGrath
Buyer Email:
Payment Sent to:

Amount received: $15.00 USD
Fee amount: -$0.74 USD
Net amount: $14.26 USD

Date: Aug. 22, 2009
Time: 15:16:16 PDT
Status: Completed

Subject: You've got money!
Payment Type: Instant

Shipping:
[Launch PayPal MultiOrder Shipping | Print Shipping Label | Print Packing Slip | Add Tracking Info | Remove Shipping Button/Link] ?

Refund:
You can issue a refund for up to 60 days after the original payment was sent. PayPal refunds the payment and fees, including partial fees for partial refunds.
Issue Refund

Return to My Account

4. Enter the amount of the refund in the **Refund amount** box (see Figure 12.6). This doesn't have to be 100 percent of the original payment. If you have arranged a partial refund, just enter the lower amount here.

5. If you want to write a note to the buyer, enter it in the **Note to buyer** box, then click **Continue.**

6. Review the refund details (see Figure 12.7) and then click **Issue Refund** to send the refund payment.

You'll notice in Figure 12.7 that the amount being refunded by the seller is not the total refund amount the buyer will receive. PayPal calculates the amount of fees they will be refunding to the seller and includes that in the refund amount. So if the seller refunds $10, and PayPal calculates the fee refund will be $0.29, PayPal will only actually debit the seller's account $9.71 ($10.00–$0.29) and sends the buyer $10.

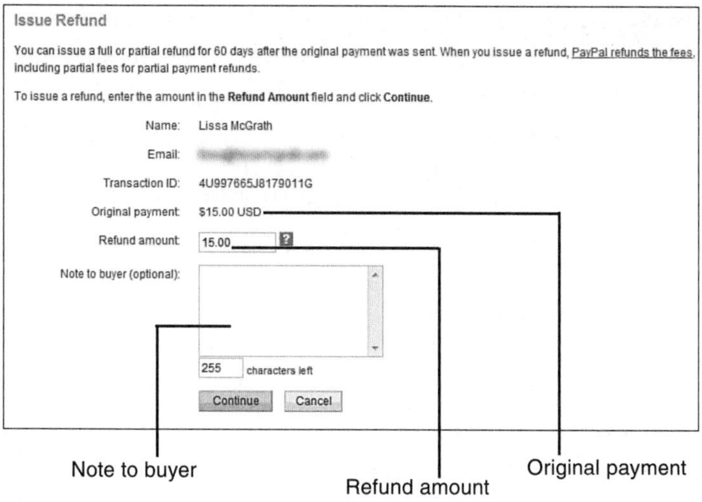

Issue Refund

You can issue a full or partial refund for 60 days after the original payment was sent. When you issue a refund, PayPal refunds the fees, including partial fees for partial payment refunds.

To issue a refund, enter the amount in the **Refund Amount** field and click **Continue**.

Name:	Lissa McGrath
Email:	
Transaction ID:	4U997665J8179011G
Original payment:	$15.00 USD
Refund amount:	15.00
Note to buyer (optional):	

255   characters left

Continue   Cancel

Note to buyer   Refund amount   Original payment

Figure 12.6

Sometimes buyers are willing to accept a partial refund rather than deal with returning an item to you (at their cost).

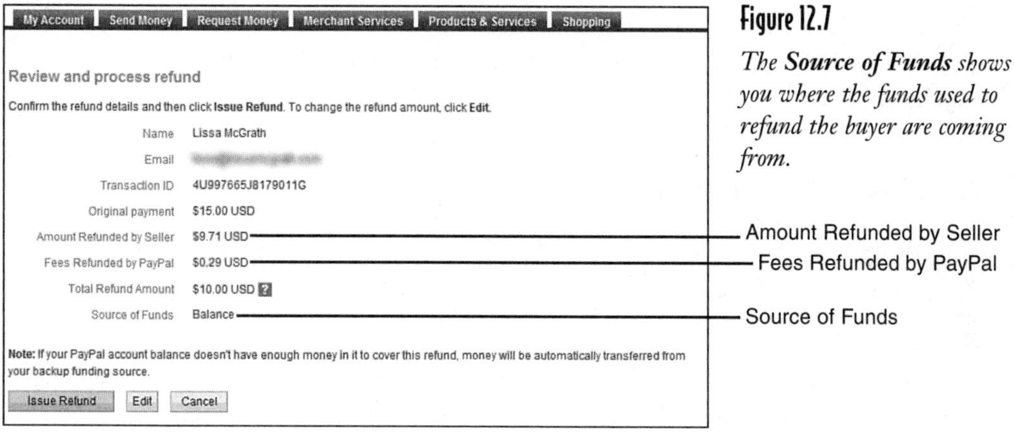

My Account   Send Money   Request Money   Merchant Services   Products & Services   Shopping

Review and process refund

Confirm the refund details and then click **Issue Refund**. To change the refund amount, click **Edit**.

Name	Lissa McGrath
Email	
Transaction ID	4U997665J8179011G
Original payment	$15.00 USD
Amount Refunded by Seller	$9.71 USD
Fees Refunded by PayPal	$0.29 USD
Total Refund Amount	$10.00 USD
Source of Funds	Balance

Note: If your PayPal account balance doesn't have enough money in it to cover this refund, money will be automatically transferred from your backup funding source.

Issue Refund   Edit   Cancel

Amount Refunded by Seller
Fees Refunded by PayPal

Source of Funds

Figure 12.7

*The **Source of Funds** shows you where the funds used to refund the buyer are coming from.*

The payment will come out of your PayPal balance if you have enough money in there. If not, it will come from your bank account.

Strict credit card regulations prohibit PayPal from funding a refund with your credit card. This is because it is technically a cash advance. So the payment must come either from your existing PayPal balance or from your bank account. Instant transfers are not an option, either (because if the bank account transfer doesn't clear, PayPal is not allowed to charge it to your credit card).

So if you send a refund when the funds are not already in your PayPal account, this will show up as "Pending" in the buyer's PayPal account until the bank account transfer clears (three to five days). This is not good for your feedback.

My way of getting around this is to have two PayPal accounts (which is completely legal). I have a Personal account and a Premier account. So if I need to refund a buyer from my Premier account and I don't have the funds available, I send a personal payment for that amount from my Personal account to my Premier account. It sends the payment as an instant transfer, so it clears immediately and I don't pay any fees on it. Now I have the funds available to refund my buyer from my Premier account.

This doesn't violate the rules because the refund is not being funded directly by the credit card, and doesn't take time to clear because it's an instant transfer. It's just like using a payment from another buyer to fund the refund.

You must always go through the Issue Refund process; otherwise, you won't get your PayPal fees refunded. If you're interested in more details about this topic, you can read my AuctionBytes article about PayPal refunds at www.auctionbytes.com/cab/abu/y206/m11/abu0178/s02.

The Least You Need to Know

♦ The **Profile** tab in PayPal links to all of the tools PayPal offers for eBay sellers.

♦ eBay deals with shill bidding very strictly; if you try it, you'll likely get suspended.

♦ eBay restricts or bans the sale of many items, so be sure to check that your item is allowed before you list it.

♦ You have to upgrade your PayPal account to a Premier account to sell on eBay.

♦ PayPal charges fees for all purchase payments, but not for personal payments.

♦ If you're selling for someone else, make sure that you have the item in your possession and that you set a reserve price if the seller wants to get a minimum amount for the item.

What Can I Sell on eBay and Where Do I Find It?

In This Chapter

◆ Is it worth the effort to sell your item on eBay?

◆ Items that sell well on eBay

◆ Where you can find items to sell

◆ When is a good time to sell?

◆ Using closeout stores when your item supply dries up

In Chapter 12, we talked a little bit about what you *can't* sell. In this chapter, we talk about what you *can* sell. We also talk about how to find those items.

Most new eBay sellers start out selling things they have around the house and then move on to items they can pick up at garage sales, thrift shops, flea markets, outlet malls, and even wholesale clubs like Costco and Sam's Club, and closeout stores like Big Lots.

Wholesale product sourcing is beyond the scope of this book, but one of the most reliable sources of real wholesale information is WorldWide Brands. This is the only company providing wholesale and drop-shipper information that is endorsed by eBay. You can read about a discount Skip has negotiated for you by going to the resources page www.skipmcgrath.com/cig.

Where to Find Items to Sell

I should reiterate that, in this book, we are not looking at this topic from a business perspective. I am assuming that you are wanting to sell items that you have or can get easily, without a state resale number, on a part-time basis.

If you are looking to start an actual eBay business selling quantities of the same item, first get some experience selling items you do have, and then look at some eBay business books (see the recommended reading section of Appendix B) to learn about starting a part-time or full-time eBay business. A good place to discover eBay trends and find reliable sources for products is www.whatdoIsell.com.

Items from Your Home

Is your house completely clutter free? If so, good for you! What about your storage locker?

The most likely sources for items to sell are the things in your attic, garage, closets, or storage locker. Remember that sweater Aunt Alice bought you for your birthday two years ago and you've never worn, or that bridesmaid's dress from a wedding five years ago? It might be just what someone else is looking for. Maybe your house is overrun with knick-knacks, your wife told you that you had to sell your old power tools before you could buy new ones, or you lost weight and have an entire wardrobe of clothes that are now too big. Or maybe, like my parents, you have a huge attic packed with boxes full of books. Everyone has stuff they no longer want or need, but your clutter might be exactly what someone else is looking for.

Some people use yard sales to get rid of clutter, but frankly, being ready to go at 6 A.M. never agreed with me, and it would take as long to inventory, price, and set out all of the items in the morning (not to mention advertising around the neighborhood) as it would to list the items on eBay! Wouldn't you rather sleep in on a Saturday morning and list your items to a worldwide market rather than just your neighborhood?

At yard sales, the temptation is to let items go for very little. Everyone bargains and no one wants items left at the end of the day. Except for the true junk, you will almost always get more for an item on eBay than you ever will at a yard sale.

On eBay, it is much less frantic and there's no chance of someone walking off with one of your expensive but small items while you're distracted with another customer. Because of that, you make more money.

Yes, you do have to ship the items, but you'll get into a routine with that. Your mail carrier will even pick up your packages from your home if you pay for the postage through PayPal and use Priority or Express Mail for at least one parcel.

Now to look for items .... Wander around your house with a notepad and write down items you would like to sell and what condition they are in (New, New in Box, Used, Used with Box, New with Tags clothing, New Without Tags clothing, Retired collectibles series, and so on). Even items that are broken can sell for decent money because people buy them for the parts.

> ### I Remember When ...
>
> My husband and I went on a cruise a few years back, and the baggage handlers broke the LCD screen of our laptop. It was an Apple Titanium PowerBook (very expensive at that time), so it would have cost a fortune to fix. We looked on eBay and discovered that we could strip it down and get over $700 by selling it for parts.

Items that you plan to sell should be clean (no dirt or dust), washed, or dry cleaned (if clothing). Electronic or electrical items should be tested to make sure all functions work; be sure to note any parts that don't work.

Personal electronics (iPod, CD player, digital camera) and their associated accessories are very popular on eBay. Baby clothes, gear, and toys are hot, but you must always check for recalls at www.cspc.gov before listing anything of this nature. Designer clothing, wedding items, sporting equipment, DVDs, video games and consoles, small kitchen appliances, computers and their accessories, art, antiques, and collectibles are also all hot items.

Yard Sales

If you happen to be an early bird on the weekends, you might consider a yard-sale crawl. Go early to get the best items, and don't forget to haggle. Yard-sale sellers are more interested in shifting items than getting the best price for them, so use that to your advantage when you're haggling.

You'd be amazed by how much stuff I have found at yard sales for a few bucks that I've been able to clean up, turn around, and sell on eBay for a nice profit. Some eBay sellers get their entire inventory this way.

At yard sales, you'll find items that you can sell individually but also some that you can use to pad a "lot" of items you are selling. This is particularly true in kids' clothing and toys. These "fillers" are very cheap, usually not fancy brands, but they should always be clean and free of stains, rips, and defects. (Never buy anything that is not in good used condition or better.)

Shark in the Water

There are many recalls related to children's products (particularly clothing and toys). Few yard-sale sellers check the recalls list before putting an item out in their yard. So if you purchase something, always check the recalls list at www.recalls.gov before listing it on eBay. You cannot list a recalled item on eBay, and safety is far more important than the few bucks you might have paid for something at a yard sale.

You may also find accessories that go with items you're selling (such as a tripod to go with a digital camera). If you can pick up a tripod for $3.50 and list it as a bonus with the digital camera you are selling, you will increase the value of your auction by far more than the price you paid for the tripod. This also makes you far more competitive with other sellers of the same item: "It's the same camera, but this one has a tripod as well, so I'll bid on this one."

Have an idea of what price certain items sell for on eBay before you go, and always carry small denominations of cash.

Making Sure Your Effort Is Worthwhile

Once you have your list of possible items from your home, mark down how much you would put on a yard-sale price tag for that item. Now run an eBay search for each item and use the **Preferences** to see only the **Completed Listings.** Look at the average selling price (you can refresh your memory on how to do this in Chapter 7). You might be surprised by how high or low the average selling price is.

You may have to look at the actual auctions to make sure the ones you are considering in your average price are, in fact, the same as your item. There's no point comparing an auction for a PlayStation 3 console with five games and two controllers, to an auction for just the console. Similarly, a new-in-box item almost always sells for more than a used item (particularly in the electronics categories), so consider that as well when looking at past auctions.

Tips

You will find items that you won't be able to sell on eBay. These may be books in poor condition, clothes that aren't in very good condition, stuffed toys that take up a lot of room in your house but may not sell well, and items that there is just no demand for on eBay. You could hold a yard sale just for these items, or donate them to your local thrift store (and books to your library). You can take a tax deduction for items you donate, so that's still better than giving them away or throwing them out.

Once you have an idea of the average selling price, use www.ebcalc.com to calculate the eBay and PayPal fees if the item sold for the average selling price on eBay. Subtract the fees from the average selling price. Is the net amount higher than your yard sale price? If so, put a check mark against it and move on to your next item. We talk about time-saving alternatives to Completed Listings in a moment.

www.ebcalc.com is a great resource for calculating fees for eBay and PayPal. You can adjust the numbers to see what a different starting price or selling price does to your fees.

Trading Assistant Consignment Program

You must wait to join the *Trading Assistant* program until you have some experience. This doesn't mean that you can't sell items for other people; it just means that you can't call yourself a Trading Assistant and can't get a listing in the Trading Assistant directory.

To be an official Trading Assistant, you must maintain …

♦ A feedback score of over 100 at 98 percent positive or higher.

♦ Sold 10 items during the preceding three months and maintain 10 sales per three month period.

def•i•ni•tion

Trading Assistants are experienced sellers who sell items on behalf of other people. It's a type of consignment program. The Trading Assistant charges a fee (usually a percentage of the final selling price) to sell the item for someone else.

Still, as I said, you don't have to be an official Trading Assistant to sell for other people. Let word-of-mouth work for you. Mention it at barbecues, ask your friends if they have anything they would like to sell, put up flyers in your neighborhood, do a mail drop, and put flyers under neighbors' doors.

You cannot use the eBay logo or the Trading Assistant logo in your flyers, but you can mention that you sell on eBay.

A few pieces of advice if you're selling for someone else:

- Make sure you have a simple agreement that specifies exactly what you are responsible for doing and who pays which fees (especially if you're selling an item for a friend).

- Find out what minimum price the owner will accept for the item, and set that as the starting price or reserve price.

- Always take possession of the item before you list it. People change their minds, decide that the highest bid isn't enough, lose it, break it, and so on. You still have a high bidder to satisfy, and it's your feedback on the line if you can't deliver.

Following these pieces of advice will help you preserve friendships and keep your reputation intact by preempting any issues that could arise.

Closeout Section of Outlet Stores

If you have a local Sam's Club or Costco, it's worth the $50 or so a year to be able to shop there. Cash-and-carry stores like these have all kinds of items, and as long as you do your research before you buy, these can be a great source of extra income once your supply of household items runs dry.

Another great source is local closeout stores such as Big Lots. A friend of mine bought a really nice high-quality outdoor chaise lounge chair from Big Lots during the summer. She paid $20 for it. I have yet to find one of the same quality selling on eBay for less than $100.

Another friend of mine bought six pressure washers at Big Lots for $92 each. He sold them all on eBay at an average price of $170 within a two-week period. Most of them sold using **Buy It Now.**

Thrift Stores

Depending on the type of thrift store (or secondhand store), you might find some high-quality items or you might find junk. You won't know until you go and check.

I recall one lady who found a very expensive genuine designer bag at a thrift store. The store obviously didn't know what it had (probably thought it was a fake). She bought it for $2.50 and resold it on eBay for nearly $200.

I don't have a problem with buying from a thrift store and reselling the item for a higher amount on eBay, particularly since thrift store purchases usually need some cleaning up before they are resale quality.

If I see an item that is obviously underpriced (like that designer bag), I usually offer to sell it for them on consignment, so I do the work for a percentage of the final selling price. That way the charity makes most of the money (and usually gets far more than they would have otherwise), and I still make something from the commission. If I'd sold that bag for them, the charity would have received $120 and I would have received $60 (the rest would be fees)—$120 is a whole lot better than the $2.50 they priced it at, and most charities would be very happy for you to do that. (I explain the eBay fee breakdown in Chapter 14.)

You can find some great bargains at thrift stores. Once you find a good store, get to know the volunteers who work there. I've gotten to the point where they call me when they get something in that they think I would be interested in. You might not get that far, but you could probably call them once a week and ask about specific types of items, to save yourself a trip. Again, the caveat about recalls applies. Many thrift stores do check the recalls websites, but some don't. You should always be in the habit of checking before listing any children's items.

How Do I Know What Will Sell?

This goes back to what we talked about in Chapter 7: research, research, research. You can't expect to list an item, place a starting price of what you think the item should sell for, and expect the item to sell without researching it.

Over five million items are listed on eBay every day. Not every one of them sells. Often it is because the listing is written poorly, the photograph is bad, the title has missing keywords, or something like that. But just as often it is because the seller didn't look to see whether that item is actually desirable to eBay buyers and what amount it is actually selling for. So how do you do that? The free way is using eBay's Completed Listings search, as I explained earlier, but what if you don't have time for that?

Tips

The **Sell** page has a **What It's Worth** box. However, this tells you only the range of what price items matching those keywords have sold for. You can't tell if the high-priced listings were bundled or the low-priced ones sold for parts. For this reason, I don't bother with it. I'd rather use **Completed Listings** and the tools in the next section.

Third-Party Research Tools

Busy sellers don't have time to trawl through Completed Listings to determine the average selling price, the best day to list the item, the starting price, and so on. They pay a third-party company to analyze the data for them.

Personally, I like Hammertap (www.hammertap.com), but Terapeak (www.terapeak. com) is also very good. These are paid services that will make your life easier, but they are not requirements for selling on eBay.

Research programs like Hammertap and Terapeak are very useful to sellers. They show you not only what items have sold for, but also the best day and time to list an item, which special features the most successful sellers used, whether reserve prices were used, the price range, average and highest prices, and what keywords the most successful sellers used to attract hits to their auctions. You can't find that level of detail in a Completed Listings search.

Did You Know?

Using a third-party research tool is really useful for buyers, too. It shows you the best and worst days/times to sell that particular item (based on final selling price). As a buyer, those are the days and times you want to buy so that you pay the lowest price.

If you're using eBay as a yard sale alternative, it's worth getting Hammertap for a month or two and then cancelling it when you no longer need it (there's no minimum subscription term). You get a two-week free trial, and then it's $17.95 a month. That may sound like a lot for an occasional seller, but it saves you a lot of research time and frustration, and it can help you get higher selling prices for your items.

Really, the question is, how much is your time worth? Before I started using Hammertap, I spent about 15 minutes per item on research (inexperienced sellers will take longer). I cut that to 5 minutes when I started using Hammertap, plus I got much more in-depth analysis. Using Hammertap saves me 10 minutes per item. Even if I list only 12 items per month, Hammertap saves me 2 hours of research time. If I list 50 items, I save over 8 hours on research. That's a full day's work! Plus, since the research part is the boring bit that can get tedious, Hammertap can keep you on focus and help you list more efficiently.

Most people starting out on eBay find they have a long list of items to sell. If you plan properly and have your list ready, you can run through the research for all of them during the 14-day free trial from Hammertap. As long as you plan to list the items within the next couple of weeks, the prices should hold true (unless you check them right before Christmas and then sell them after Christmas).

If you batch your work like this, it will save you a lot of time and money. You might also want to set up a photo station (see Chapter 15) and take all of your photos at once. This will also save you a lot of time later.

When Should I Sell?

This may sound obvious, but many sellers forget that items are often seasonal. A winter coat for sale in May will sell for much less than the same item in October. There are exceptions, such as selling the winter coat in July to a buyer in Australia or Alaska, where it is likely snowing; or selling swimwear in January to a buyer for a winter getaway. But the point is that the *majority* of buyers look for items appropriate to the season they are currently in, or approaching. You want to reach the majority of buyers because the more people who are looking, the more bids and the higher the final price you'll get.

I know, if you have kids, your instincts are to sell all of your kids' winter clothing as soon as spring peeps through the clouds, to make room for spring and summer clothing. But if you have space to store the items (Space Bags are a wonderful invention to help with this) and can wait just six months, you'll get more for the items than you ever will selling them off-season.

If you are selling items related to a specific day (such as Mother's Day or Valentine's Day), the selling season starts about 30 to 45 days before. For example, if you are selling a Valentine's Day item, you would want to start listing it around January 14. The exception is Christmas: the Christmas selling season starts on eBay at the end of October and runs right up until Christmas Eve.

Electronics and other highly desirable gift items sell for a lot more during the run-up to Christmas than at any other time of the year. I attribute this to experienced buyers really wanting the item and forgetting everything they know about waiting to buy, or new buyers who have come to eBay because they are looking for deals on Christmas presents and don't know what the item is actually worth.

> **I Remember When ...**
>
> When the Nintendo Wii came out, you could not find one in any major city in America—but Costco, Sam's Club, and Walmart in some rural areas had them in stock. Savvy eBay sellers in these areas were buying them at full retail and doubling their money selling them right before Christmas on eBay.

Of course, if you manage to get your hands on "the toy" or "the gadget" for that season, you'll probably make some serious cash.

It's not just Christmas. Jewelry sells better and for higher amounts around Valentine's Day; patriotic items sell better around Memorial Day, Independence Day, and so on.

And it's not just holidays, either. A good friend of mine made a lot of money selling official licensed Red Sox and White Sox Major League Baseball jerseys she purchased from an overstock store a couple of months before the 2005 baseball season began. She started selling the Red Sox jerseys right before the season started and then both types throughout the season. The Boston Red Sox were the 2004 winners, so their shirts were very popular right from the beginning of the season, and the Chicago White Sox ended up winning the 2005 World Series. She made $30 to $50 profit on each of the 120 shirts (she paid $10 per shirt, so that is 200 to 400 percent profit).

Statistically, July and August are the slowest months for eBay sales because people are on vacation, or have just come back from vacation, and they don't have a lot of disposable income left. Once the school year starts, sales begin to pick up again. Christmas sales start around the end of October and really explode right after Thanksgiving. Incidentally, that means July and August are great times to buy!

So sometimes the best thing you can do is hold on to an item and wait.

The Least You Need to Know

- ◆ Using Hammertap or Terapeak makes it a lot easier to determine how much to list your item for (and what day, time, and features will maximize your profit).

- ◆ You don't have to be an official Trading Assistant to sell things for your friends, but always have possession of the item before you list it.

- ◆ Many items are seasonal. Off-season items get lower bids and lower final prices.

Chapter 14

What It Will Cost You

In This Chapter

- ◆ How much it costs to sell on eBay.com
- ◆ What all the extras cost
- ◆ How much it costs to sell your car on eBay
- ◆ What it costs to set up and maintain your own store

eBay fees are different in every country. For the purposes of this chapter, I am assuming you are selling on eBay.com. If you are selling on one of the other sites, click on the **Help** tab from the home page and click **Seller fees.** If you don't see that option, just search for "eBay fees" in the **Help search** box, and it will be one of the top results. Currently, the direct link for eBay.com is http://pages.ebay.com/help/sell/fees.html. You'll notice if you go there that I am not covering every type of fee. I'm not covering real estate, ad format, or business and industrial category fees because they are very specific areas. No beginner should be selling in those categories. If you are interested in any of these areas, go to the **fees** page, where you can view all of the corresponding fees.

> **Shark in the Water** _____
>
> Be careful looking at these tables. Each type of listing has different fees for the same thing. So the Insertion fee for eBay Stores, fixed-price listings, eBay Motors, and auctions are all different. All of the fees have the same or similar names, so be sure to look at the heading before you find the fee you are looking for.

Some sellers think eBay's fees are high; others (usually those who have sold through other marketplaces) consider them quite reasonable. They are certainly competitive with other online selling venues.

Still, fees do add up, so be careful when you're looking at optional listing upgrades. We talk about fee-saving strategies in Chapter 19 and which optional upgrades you should use in which circumstances in Chapter 20. For now, though, here is an easy reference for all the fees.

eBay Auction Fees

Auctions are likely where you will start as a seller, so we deal with these fees first. I'm not discussing how to minimize your costs here; that comes in later chapters. Here you will find a general discussion of the different auction fees. You'll probably want to dog-ear this page so you can come back and check these fees when you start your actual listing.

Insertion and Final Value Fees

The Insertion fee (also commonly called the listing fee) is charged when you list an item. It is determined by the starting price (or reserve price, if you set one). There are lower fees for media items (books, DVDs and movies, music, and video games) in some fee brackets.

The first five auctions you list per month have no Insertion fee. But you must use the eBay Sell Your Item form to list them (we talk about this in Chapter 16). After those first five auctions, the following fees apply.

Auction Insertion Fees After First Five Per Month

Starting or Reserve Price	Insertion Fee All Other Items	Insertion Fee Media Items
1¢–99¢	15¢	10¢
$1–$9.99	35¢	25¢
$10–$24.99	55¢	35¢
$25–$49.99	$1	$1
$50–$199.99	$2	$2
$200–$499.99	$3	$3
$500 or more	$4	$4

In addition to the Insertion fee, you are charged a Final Value fee if the item sells (you are not charged if the item does not sell).

The Final Value fee is determined by the selling price. For the first five auctions per month, it is 8.75 percent of the selling price or $20, whichever is lower.

Tips

Be aware of where the price breaks fall: a starting price of $24.99 costs you 55¢, but if you go one penny higher to $25, you pay almost twice as much for the Insertion fee ($1).

When you list your sixth auction (and from then to the end of the month), you have to use the Final Value fee table that follows to calculate the fee. It's a bit more complicated, so look for the explanation and examples after the fee table.

Auction Final Value Fees After First Five Per Month

Closing Price	Final Value Fee
Item did not sell	No fee
1¢–$25	8.75 percent of the closing value
$25.01–$1,000	8.75 percent of the initial $25 ($2.19), plus 3.5 percent of the remaining balance between $25.01 and $1,000
$1,000.01 or higher	8.75 percent of the initial $25 ($2.19), plus 3.5 percent of the portion from $25.01 to $1,000 ($34.12), plus 1.5 percent of the value from $1000.01 up

I know I use this phrase a lot, but don't panic. The Final Value fee table looks confusing, but it's actually quite simple.

If your item sells for $25 or less, you pay 8.75 percent of the final price (before shipping). So if it sells for $17, your Final Value fee would be $1.49.

If your item sells for over $25 but under $1,000, there is a really easy way to calculate your fee. The trick is to remember that 8.75 percent of $25 is $2.19, so there's no point in calculating it every time if your item sold for over $25. All you need to do is calculate the next fee section:

1. Subtract $25 from the selling price.

2. Multiply the remainder by 3.5 percent.

3. Add $2.19.

4. The answer is your Final Value fee.

Let's explain it in a real-world example. Your item sells for $55. You subtract $25, which leaves you $30. Now, 3.5 percent of $30 is $1.05. Add $2.19 to $1.05 to get $3.24. That is your Final Value fee.

The same principle applies for items that sell for over $1,000:

1. Subtract $1,000 from the selling price.

2. Multiply the remainder by 1.5 percent.

3. Add $36.31 ($2.19 from the first fee level plus $34.12 from the second level).

4. The answer is your Final Value fee.

So here's your real-world example for an item over $1,000. Let's say your item sells for $1,450. Subtract $1,000 to get $450. Now multiply $450 by 1.5 percent to get $6.75. Add $36.31 and $6.75 to get your Final Value fee of $43.06.

If this is all a bit much for you, don't worry. www.ebcalc.com is a free online fee calculator that can do all the work for you. Just make sure you select the correct type of listing (auction, fixed-price, store inventory, and so on) to get the correct calculations.

Listing Upgrades

We talk about the benefits and strategies of using optional listing upgrades in Chapter 20, so I don't explain each of them here. Some of these you have heard me mention before. If you're unsure about a particular term, either look ahead to Chapter 20 or look in the glossary for the definition.

Auction Listing Upgrades Fees

Upgrade Option	Fee	Upgrade Option	Fee
Listing Designer	10¢	Bold	$2
Gallery Plus	35¢	Scheduled Listing	10¢
10-Day Listing	40¢	Subtitle	50¢
Value Pack (Gallery Plus, Subtitle, Listing Designer)	65¢		

There is also a List in Two Categories option, which allows you to have your item display in two categories simultaneously. I rarely use this option because you have to pay the Insertion fee twice, as well as any of the optional listing upgrades (except scheduled listing). If you are considering using this option, make sure to work out the difference in cost and see if you are really going to make that much or more by using two categories.

Most of these fees seem quite low, but believe me, they do add up. In Chapter 20, I explain which fees you need when others are useful but not essential, and which fees you can avoid completely.

International Site Visibility

If you want your listing to display on international eBay sites, you will need to pay for International Site Visibility. This has a tiered price structure as shown in the table.

International Site Visibility Fees

Starting Price	Fee
1¢–$9.99	10¢
$10–$49.99	20¢
$50 and up	40¢

It's worth looking at the tier breaks (as I suggested with the starting price) so that you pay the lowest fee feasible for your item.

Buy It Now

If you choose to have a Buy It Now option in your auction, eBay charges a small fee based on the Buy It Now price you set.

Buy It Now Fees

Buy It Now Price	Fee
1¢–$9.99	5¢
$10–$24.99	10¢
$25–$49.99	20¢
$50 or higher	25¢

Reserve-Price Auction

At one time, eBay refunded the Reserve fee if the item sold, but that is no longer the case; you now pay the fee whether or not the auction is successful.

Reserve-Price Auction Fee

Reserve Price	Fee
1¢–$199.99	$2
$200 or higher	1 percent of the reserve price (max $50)

There is one other auction optional listing fee called Featured First. This gives a change at the listing displaying in a special Featured Items section at the top of the first page of Best Match search results. Featured First can only be purchased by Top-Rated Sellers, so you won't be able to use it until you have some experience and a proven track record of excellent customer service. It costs $24.95.

Fixed-Price Listings

Fixed-price listings have no bids—only sales. You set the price the buyer must pay to purchase the item, and you can't receive lower than that amount. The other big advantage of fixed-price listings is that each listing can run for up to 30 days and have as many identical items in that one listing as you have available for sale. The Insertion fee is lower, but the Final Value fee is higher and is category specific (as you'll see shortly).

Fixed-Price Listing Insertion Fees

Unlike auctions, the Insertion fee for fixed-price listings is flat rate, based on whether they are media items (books, DVDs, movies, video games, music) or nonmedia items. There's no free Insertion fee for the first five per month, as you get with auctions—you pay the fee for every listing.

Fixed-Price Listing Insertion Fees

Category	Fee
Media items	15¢
All other items	35¢

Fixed-price listings must begin at $1 or higher.

Fixed-Price Listing Final Value Fees

The Final Value fee for fixed-price listings varies based on the category the item is listed in. Be aware of this if you're trying to decide between two categories for your item.

I'm showing you the "all other categories" table fully written out; the second table shows you the percentages for each tier for each category.

Final Value Fees for All Other Categories

Tier	Selling Price	Fee
N/A/	Item did not sell	No fee
1	$1–$50	12 percent of the closing value
2	$50.01–$1,000	12 percent of the initial $50 ($6), plus 6 percent of the remaining balance between $50.01 and $1,000
3	$1,000.01 or higher	12 percent of the initial $50 ($6), plus 6 percent of the portion from $50.01 to $1,000 ($57), plus 2 percent of the value from $1000.01 up

Final Value Fee Tiers for Specific Categories

| Category | Fees | | |
	Tier 1 ($1–$50)	Tier 2 (50.01–$1,000)	Tier 3 (over $1,000)
Books, Music, Video Games, DVDs & Movies	15%	5%	2%
Clothing, Shoes & Accessories	12%	9%	2%
Computers & Networking	6%	3.75%	1%
Consumer Electronics	8%	4.5%	1%
Video Game Systems	8%	4.5%	1%
Cameras & Photo	8%	4.5%	1%

Let's look at an example to make this a little easier. Judy sells a digital camera for $150. It was listed in the Cameras & Photo main category. Her Final Value fee is 8 percent of the first $50 ($4), and then 4.5 percent of the remaining $100 ($4.50). Judy's total Final Value fee is $8.50.

John sold a laptop (in the Computers & Networking category) for $1,200. His Final Value fee is 6 percent of the first tier ($1 to $50), which works out to $3; plus 3.75 percent of the second tier ($50.01 to $1,000), which is $35.63; and finally 1 percent of the remaining $200 ($2). So John's Final Value fee is $40.63. That may sound like a lot, but it is actually just over 3 percent of the $1,200 selling price.

Again, if this is all a bit much for you right now, go to www.ebcalc.com and let it calculate the fees for you.

You pay a Final Value fee for every item that sells from your fixed-price listing. So if your listing has five identical items available for sale and three sell, you pay three Final Value fees.

If you reach Top-Rated Seller status, you will receive a 20 percent discount on all of your Final Value fees. That's something worth working for!

Fixed-Price Listing Optional Listing Upgrades

This is where it gets a little complicated. Fixed-price listings can run for 3, 5, 7, 10, or 30 days. The Optional Listing Upgrade fees are split into two levels:

1. Those with the same duration as auctions (3, 5, 7, or 10 days)

2. Those listed for 30 days

The fees for durations of less than 30 days are the same as the auction fees (but the 10-day duration option is free); the 30-day duration fees are almost always higher. I've shown both in the following table, for easy comparison.

Fixed-Price Listing Optional Upgrades Fees

Upgrade Option	3-, 5-, 7-, 10-Day Duration Fee	30-Day Duration Fee
Gallery Plus	35¢	$1
Listing Designer	10¢	30¢
Subtitle	50¢	$1.50
Bold	$2	$4
Scheduled Listing	10¢	10¢

continues

Fixed-Price Listing Optional Upgrades Fees   (continued)

Upgrade Option	3-, 5-, 7-, 10-Day Duration Fee	30-Day Duration Fee
Value Pack (Gallery Plus, Subtitle, Listing Designer)	65¢	$2
10-Day Listing Free		
Featured First (Top-Rated Seller only)	$24.95	$74.95

International Site Visibility Fees

Starting Price	3-, 5-, 7-, 10-Day Duration Fee	30-Day Duration Fee
$1–$9.99	10¢	25¢
$10–$49.99	20¢	50¢
$50 and up	40¢	$1

Listings With Variations

Fixed-price and eBay Store listings can offer item variations. So if you have the same pair of new shoes in three different colors and different sizes, you could list them all in one fixed-price or eBay Store listing for an additional 35¢ per listing (not per item). But be aware that they must be identical new items except for the choice options you offer (color, size, and so on). That's a lot cheaper (and easier to manage) than separate listings for each item.

The big advantage of fixed-price listings over eBay Stores (which I cover next) is that fixed-price listings show up in the main results. Best Match pulls a mixture of fixed-price and auction-style listings, so you're not always stuck at the back of the results. Plus, there is no monthly subscription for fixed-price listings but you still get the option of 30-day listings. This makes it more feasible for occasional sellers who don't want to deal with the uncertainty of auctions.

I talk more about the different types of listings and when they're most appropriate in Chapter 18.

eBay Stores Fees

If you are planning to be a casual seller, I wouldn't bother with an eBay Store. But if your casual selling gets you hooked on eBay and you want to build a part-time or full-time business, you may eventually want to set up an eBay Store.

eBay Stores are primarily used by sellers who have a lot of similar merchandise, or have a very high number of listings and want to categorize them to make it easier for buyers to find other items from them. There are also fee breaks and extra tools available for a reduced rate (or free) to eBay Store sellers.

I don't go into great detail about eBay Stores because of the business aspect, and because most of the benefits of an eBay Store can be realized using fixed-price listings. Still I do want to show you the fee structure.

Monthly Subscription

There are three levels of subscription, and each level gives you different features and exposure on the eBay site. You can read more about the different levels by going to http://pages.ebay.com/storefronts/Subscriptions.html. Your subscription is on a month-to-month basis, so you can cancel at any time.

eBay Store Monthly Subscription

Store Level	Monthly Fee
Basic	$15.95
Premium	$49.95
Anchor	$299.95

Insertion and Final Value Fees

eBay Store Insertion fees are lower, and the listings run for 30 days, but they do not show up in a regular eBay search (using the main search box on the home page). They display in search results only if a buyer specifically searches in eBay Stores, selects the **Buy It Now only** tab at the top of the search results page, or checks the **Include Store Inventory** box in the search results page **Preferences.** Your eBay Store inventory also displays if a buyer clicks **See other items** in the **Seller info** box on one of your listings (whatever type of listing it is).

eBay Stores Insertion Fees

Starting Price	Insertion Fee (for a 30-Day Listing)
$1–$24.99	3¢
$25–$199.99	5¢
$200 and up	10¢

You can list an item for 30 days or select **Good 'Til Canceled** for your eBay Store listings. If you select **Good 'Til Canceled,** you will be charged the Insertion fee every 30 days until all of the items are gone or you cancel the listing.

As with auctions and fixed-price listings, Final Value fees are charged only on the items that sell. In most cases, the Final Value fee for eBay Stores is higher than the other listing formats.

eBay Stores Final Value Fees

Closing Price	Final Value Fee
Item did not sell	No fee
$1–$25	12 percent of the closing value.
$25.01–$100	12 percent of the initial $25 ($3), plus 8 percent of the remaining balance between $25.01 and $100.
$100.01–$1,000	12 percent of the initial $25 ($3), plus 8 percent of the portion from $25.01 to $100 ($6), plus 4 percent of the remaining value from $100.01 to $1,000.
$1,000.01 or higher	12 percent of the initial $25 ($3), plus 8 percent of the portion from $25.01 to $100 ($6), plus 4 percent of the remaining value from $100.01 to $1,000 ($36), plus 2 percent of the value from $1,000.01.

Let's say you sell a pair of sneakers for $60. The Final Value fee is $3 (12 percent of the first $25), plus $2.80 (8 percent of the remaining $35), which gives you a total Final Value fee of $5.80.

Optional Listing Upgrades for eBay Store Inventory

The Bold and Subtitle options are much cheaper for eBay Store sellers, but the other listing upgrades are the same as for auctions.

eBay Stores Listing Upgrades Fees

Upgrade Option	Fee
Gallery Plus	35¢
Listing Designer	10¢
Subtitle	2¢
Bold	$1
Item Variation Listing	35¢

Comparing the Fees for Auctions, Fixed-Price Listings, and eBay Store Inventory

You've probably noticed that the Final Value fee is significantly higher for eBay Store inventory and fixed-price listings versus auctions.

To make it a little easier to see, here is a fee comparison for a digital camera sold for $65. I'm assuming that the auction is listed at the same price it sells; for the fixed-price listing, I'm using the "All Other Categories" Final Value fee table.

The **First 5 Auctions** column refers to the fees for the first five auctions listed within the month. As I mentioned earlier, there is no Insertion fee for the first five auctions, and the Final Value fee is 8.75 percent of the final price (or $20, whichever is lower).

Insertion and Final Value Fees Comparison for Auctions, Fixed-Price Listings, and eBay Store Inventory

Fee Type	First 5 Auctions	6th + Auction	Fixed-Price Listing	eBay Store
Insertion fee	$0	$2	35¢	5¢
Final Value fee	$5.69	$3.59	$4.68	$6.20
Total fees	$5.69	$5.59	$5.03	$6.25

Remember, an auction usually has a starting price that is lower than the selling price. It makes no difference if it's one of your five auctions in the month, but if we start the sixth auction at $9.99 instead of $65, the Insertion fee would be much lower (35¢) and the total fees for the **6th + Auction** column would drop to $3.94.

So why would anyone use a fixed-price format? Well, first, auctions can be risky, particularly for business sellers. If you paid $50 for an item to resell, you don't want to risk selling it for less than that. Fixed-price listings and eBay Stores are fixed-price only, so you are guaranteed of what you will get for the item.

Also, fixed-price and eBay Stores listings usually run for 30 days, which makes them much more cost-effective if you're listing a lot of items. You can also have more than one quantity within the same listing. So you could sell 10 items to 10 different buyers with one fixed-price or Store listing, whereas if you'd listed the 10 items at auction, you'd have to list 10 separate auctions to get those 10 sales.

The option of listing item variations (color, size, and so on) is a big plus for fixed-price and eBay Store listings for sellers who purchase their inventory to resell. It saves a lot of money versus listing the same items at auction.

Fixed-price listings tend to be more popular than eBay Stores for occasional sellers because fixed-price listings are included in the main search results. eBay Store listings are not. Also, there is no monthly fee for fixed-price listings.

However, the different fixed-price listing Final Value fees for different categories often make eBay Store fees more competitive. For example, in the earlier fee comparison, I used a $65 digital camera (which would be listed in the Cameras & Photo category). The Final Value fee was $4.68 for a fixed-price listing. However, had I picked a $65 pair of sneakers (which would be in the Clothing, Shoes, & Accessories category), the Final Value fee would be $7.35. Or if it were a $65 TV series on DVD, the fee would be $8.25. eBay Store fees do not adjust based on the item's category, so it remains at $6.25 no matter what the actual item type is.

The biggest advantage of eBay Stores over fixed-price listings is that you can reduce your eBay Store Final Value fee using the Store Referral Credit. This is more advanced and you need a website or other way to drive traffic to a specific link, but it saves you 75 percent off your Final Value fee if the buyer enters your store through one of your custom links and buys something from your store.

I don't go into detail about the Store Referral Credit because it is not a tool for beginners or occasional sellers. You can read more at http://pages.ebay.com/storefronts/referral-credit-faq.html. Just so you have an idea of the savings, if our seller of the $65 digital camera had been eligible for the Store Referral Credit, the Final Value fee would have been $1.55 instead of $6.20. That would put his total eBay fees at $1.60, compared to $3.94 for the auction (with the reduced starting price), or $5.03 for the fixed-price listing.

Tips _____

eBay Stores are most cost-effective for people who have ways to drive traffic to the store from off-eBay. For most other people, fixed-price listings and auctions are the way to go, and that's what I recommend you stick to unless you decide to start purchasing for resale.

eBay Picture Hosting

eBay can host your photographs and even offers basic editing tools through eBay Picture Hosting. The first photograph is free, and each additional one costs 15¢. This applies to all categories except Art, Collectibles, Pottery and Glass, and Antiques. All listings within these four categories get free pictures.

You have some other options for picture services. Some of the prices, however, are different for online auctions and eBay Stores, so both are included in the following table.

eBay Picture Services Fees

Feature	Auction Fee	eBay Store Fee
First picture	Free	Free
Each additional picture	15¢	15¢
Picture Pack (6 pics)	75¢	N/A
Picture Pack (12 pics)	$1	76¢

Chapter 15 deals specifically with photography, so I talk there more about how many pictures you need and cost-saving techniques.

eBay Motors Fees

Selling on eBay Motors is quite different from selling on the rest of eBay. This is a very specific niche and not an area for brand-new sellers. The potential for problems is much greater when you're selling high-priced used items that the buyer has not physically examined.

Feedback is incredibly important to your success, so get some experience selling other items before tackling this area.

Pretty much everything is different with eBay Motors: taking vehicle photographs, writing your listing, determining fees, communicating with buyers, understanding legal responsibilities, and more. For this reason, it is beyond the scope of this book to cover it all. If you are looking to buy or sell a vehicle through eBay Motors, *The Pocket Idiot's Guide to eBay Motors* (Alpha, 2008) will help you.

The following fee structure is very different from the rest of eBay, so keep this in mind when you set your starting and reserve prices.

Insertion and Successful Listing Fees

On eBay Motors, the Successful Listing fee is similar to the Final Value fee. However, it is a flat rate based on the vehicle type and is charged as soon as you have your first bid on the vehicle above your reserve price (assuming there is a reserve). If there is no reserve price, it is charged when you receive your first bid. This is considered a "successful listing" even if you and the buyer don't actually follow through with the sale.

No Insertion fee is charged for the first four vehicles you list within a 12-month period. This covers the majority of individual sellers. On the fifth item within a 12-month period (and on all subsequent items), an Insertion fee is charged. The Successful Listing fee also changes at that fifth item mark.

Items relisted using eBay's **Relist Item** links do not count towards this total per year. So it doesn't matter how many times you have to relist an item, it only counts once towards this total.

Insertion and Successful Listing Fees for First Four Vehicle Listings Within 12 Months

Categories	Insertion Fee	Successful Listing Fee
Cars & Trucks, Boats, Other vehicles	Free	$125
Motorcycles	Free	$100
Powersports	Free	$100
Powersports (under 50cc)	Free	$10

Insertion and Successful Listing Fees for Fifth Vehicle Listing Within 12 Months

Categories	Insertion Fee	Successful Listing Fee
Cars & Trucks, Boats, Other vehicles	$20	$100
Motorcycles	$15	$80
Powersports	$15	$80
Powersports (under 50cc)	Free	$10

If you are selling a vehicle, I recommend that you always have a reserve price. The reserve fee is $7 for all vehicles except Powersport vehicles under 50cc, which is $2. This is the same however many vehicles you've listed in a 12-month period.

The optional listing upgrade fees vary based on the category within eBay Motors, so rather than listing them all here, you can go straight to them on eBay through this link: pages.ebay.com/help/sell/motorfees.html.

PayPal Seller Fees

You have to have a Premier account to sell on eBay, but this doesn't determine the fees you pay—that comes from the payment type. So upgrading your account (as I explained in Chapter 12) doesn't mean you will pay fees on money transfers you make to family or friends. You only pay fees when the sender marks the payment as a "purchase." This is automatic when the payment comes through eBay Checkout (as all your eBay payments will), so you will always pay a fee on payments for your eBay items.

As a small U.S. seller, you are most likely to pay 2.9 percent of the amount you receive plus 30¢ per transaction. This table shows the domestic fees (from U.S. buyers paying U.S. sellers in U.S. dollars).

U.S. Domestic PayPal Fees

Monthly Payments Received	PayPal Fee
Up to $3,000	2.9 percent plus 30¢ per transaction
$3,000.01–$10,000	2.5 percent plus 30¢ per transaction
$10,000.01–$100,000	2.2 percent plus 30¢ per transaction
$100,000.01 and up	1.9 percent plus 30¢ per transaction

If you are being paid in U.S. dollars by a buyer from another country, you need to add another 1 percent to all of the fees in the table. If you are receiving payment in a different currency, go to http://tinyurl.com/yobyqa to see the correct fees. I used TinyURL to make the link much smaller, but if you want to use the full link, it is https://www.paypal.com/us/cgi-bin/webscr?cmd=_display-xborder-fees-outside&countries=.

Use the drop-down menu on the right to select the currency the payment is in, to find the cross-border transaction fee (see Figure 14.1).

If you are not a U.S. seller, you can find the fees for your country by changing the country in the left box from **United States** to your own country. It will then display the cross-border fees for your country for whatever currency you select. If you want to see what the domestic fees are, just click **See Domestic Transaction Fees** (the link is in the same place as it shows in Figure 14.1).

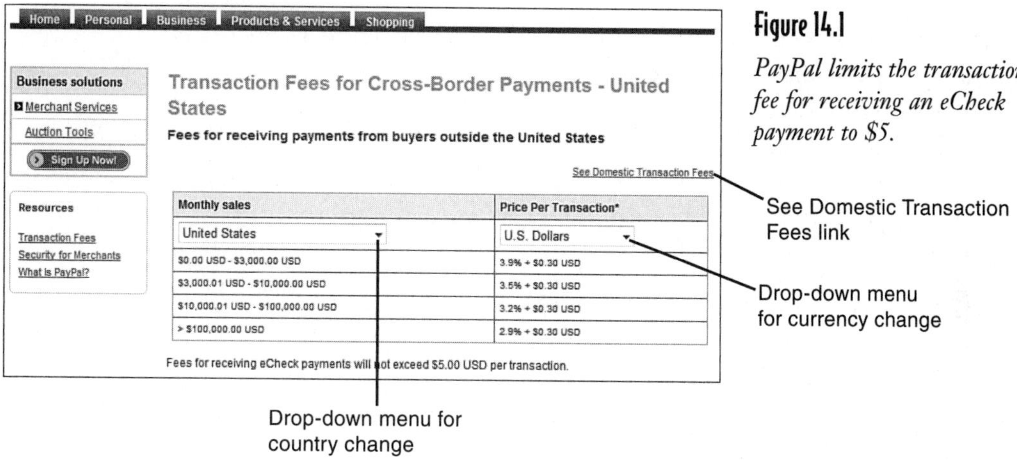

| Home | Personal | Business | Products & Services | Shopping |

Business solutions
▶ Merchant Services
Auction Tools
▶ Sign Up Now!

Resources
Transaction Fees
Security for Merchants
What is PayPal?

Transaction Fees for Cross-Border Payments - United States

Fees for receiving payments from buyers outside the United States

See Domestic Transaction Fees

Monthly sales		Price Per Transaction*
United States ▾		U.S. Dollars ▾
$0.00 USD - $3,000.00 USD		3.9% + $0.30 USD
$3,000.01 USD - $10,000.00 USD		3.5% + $0.30 USD
$10,000.01 USD - $100,000.00 USD		3.2% + $0.30 USD
> $100,000.00 USD		2.9% + $0.30 USD

Fees for receiving eCheck payments will not exceed $5.00 USD per transaction.

Drop-down menu for country change

Figure 14.1

PayPal limits the transaction fee for receiving an eCheck payment to $5.

See Domestic Transaction Fees link

Drop-down menu for currency change

The Least You Need to Know

◆ A Final Value fee is charged only if the item sells. However, eBay Motors' Successful Listing fee is charged as soon as there is a bid above your reserve.

◆ Final Value fees for fixed-price listings vary based on the category the item is listed in.

◆ Listing fees are charged based on the starting price, so you can save money by listing at the high end of the lower bracket instead of the low end of the higher bracket.

◆ PayPal charges fees for all payments received once you upgrade to a Premier account.

◆ Your first five auction listings per month have different fees if you use the Sell Your Item form.

◆ Cross-border PayPal transaction fees are higher, so make sure it is worthwhile before accepting buyers from other countries.

◆ eBay fees change periodically so go to http://pages.ebay.com/help/sell/questions/what-fees.html to check what the current fees are for each listing type.

Chapter 15

Pictures That Sell Products

In This Chapter

- Type of equipment you need to take photographs for your listing
- Three easy steps to taking better auction photos
- Photograph tips for different item types
- Common photography errors and how to fix them
- How you can avoid paying to put photos in your auction

Trying to sell without a photo is a rookie mistake. It's like waving a sign saying, "I'm a new seller and I don't know what I'm doing."

Having a *good* photograph is just as important. If you have a photo and it looks blurry or the color is off, or it's too low resolution, the buyer isn't going to bother reading your description. Poor photographs cost you nearly as much in low or no bids as no photographs at all.

You don't have to be a photography genius. In this chapter, we cover a few things you can do to vastly improve your photographs with very little time or effort (and no expense).

Camera Specifics

I assume you have a digital camera or can borrow one from a friend. It really is essential to have a digital camera when taking auction photographs. You can pick one up cheaply on eBay if you don't have one already.

Set your camera to 3 or 4 megapixels for your auction photography. This is your resolution setting. If necessary, eBay's picture services uploader will compress it to fit. However, if your picture is too low resolution, it will look choppy on the screen when it is enlarged (you can see an example of this later in the chapter).

Tips _____

If you have lost your camera manual, try going to the manufacturer's website and see whether you can download it. Most manufacturers offer free manuals via download for cameras built within the last 7 to 10 years.

You should be able to find the resolution option in your settings, but check your manual if you're not sure where it is.

I use some camera terms throughout this chapter. I explain them where possible, but if you're unclear, check the glossary in Appendix A for a full explanation.

How to Set Up Your Shots

I see poor photos from new sellers all the time. They place the object on their dining room table, open the flash, and take a shot. As you will see, this is the worst thing you can do. I know you want to take your pictures quickly so you can get the auctions listed, but taking a few minutes to set up a clean background and simple lighting will pay dividends in more bids and higher selling prices for your auctions. Once you've got your setup ready, you can photograph all of your items so they're ready for whenever you want to list them.

The first thing you need to do is create a clean, uncluttered background. You want to avoid distraction. There are professional studio tools you can buy to help you, but if you don't have much to sell, you'll want a cheap (or free) solution.

In all of the photographs shown in this chapter (except the one without a proper background), I used a piece of white poster board taped to the wall and curved so it rested on a folding table. It took five minutes to set up and take down. I set my camera on its tripod in front of it and took my pictures from there. That's about the easiest setup you can get.

If your item is big, you can use an ironed sheet tacked to the wall, or even outside draped over two ladders, to make your continuous background. This gives you a much bigger backdrop, perfect for furniture, or large items that won't fit on a table. Be careful about wrinkles in the fabric though. Those can be just as distracting as a poor background.

Lighting

Poor lighting is one of the biggest mistakes sellers make. They turn on the overhead light and take their photos with flash. Then they wonder why it looks washed out with too high contrast.

Tips

If you are selling jewelry, a dark background is useful to help contrast the item. I've seen excellent photos of silver watches with a midnight blue corduroy background. The texture complements the metallic watch perfectly and really draws your eye to it in the thumbnails images on the search results page.

The best lighting is indirect natural outdoor lighting (not direct sunlight). This includes shooting outdoors on a cloudy day, in the shade, or inside with natural light coming in through a window. If you happen to have a deck and live somewhere that is usually nice but cloudy, this is a great place for you to set up your studio. If not, you can set it up by a well-lit window.

I used to live in Florida and I couldn't shoot outside because the sun was too bright. Clouds diffuse the light and help prevent harsh shadows and reflections, but since we didn't usually have clouds, I had to shoot indoors. Now I'm in Washington State, where the cloudy conditions are perfect for outdoor auction photography. As long as it's not raining, I usually shoot outdoors and don't need any additional lighting.

If you have to shoot indoors, you need two lamps. I use inexpensive gooseneck lamps. You can also purchase inexpensive clamp-on lights from any hardware store (if your setup gives you places to clip them to). Basically any type of lamp that allows you to direct the light will work.

Think of your setup as a triangle. Your item is at the top point and the two lamps are positioned at the other two corners pointing at the item (see Figure 15.1). This helps fill shadows and gives you even lighting. Your tripod and camera should be an equal distance between the two lamps.

Figure 15.1

Basic lighting setup to fill shadows.

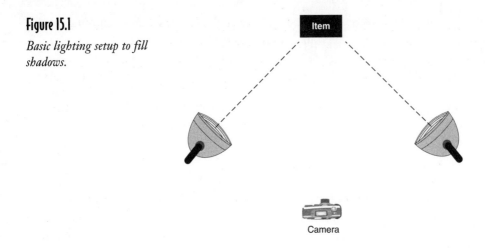

I'm sure you've seen daylight bulbs in the store, and you may even use them in your house. I don't like them for photography because they mess with the color balance. You're far better using regular bulbs in your lamps and adjusting the white balance settings on your camera.

White Balance

White balance is an adjustment for the type of lighting you are using. Some cameras have preset options on buttons on the camera; others show it in the settings, often as WB.

The following main settings appear on most cameras:

♦ Candlelight (for low lighting)

♦ Daylight (for outdoors)

♦ Fluorescent (for fluorescent bulbs)

♦ Incandescent or Tungsten (for regular household bulbs)

Tips

It is very important to use the correct white balance settings. This one adjustment will make your photographs look tons better, and more true to the color of the item, which means you're less likely to get Not As Described claims from buyers.

You will most likely use the Incandescent setting (usually the icon is a lightbulb shape). However, if you use compact fluorescent bulbs in your home, you might want to try both the Incandescent and Fluorescent settings to see which looks better.

On my camera, I have an option to set the white balance based on the current lighting. I set up my shot and take a picture, and it determines what setting it needs for that lighting. That is the best way I have found to get perfect color, but if you don't have that option, don't worry—the preset options are usually fine.

If you're not sure which of the white balance settings is right, just flick through them all. Whichever one makes the image look closest to the true color is the one to use.

Tripod

A tripod is important because it takes away the natural shake of a human hand. Some newer camera models have an image stabilization function. Mine has this, but I sometimes still get a bit of a shake when I take handheld pictures. Just the act of pushing the button can make the camera move, particularly when you're trying to hold it very still.

Tripods are also wonderful for keeping your photo setup constant. Once you have your lighting and white balance settings adjusted, do you really want to put down the camera to change items and then possibly have to go through all the adjustments again? Keeping your camera on the tripod leaves your hands free. Use the timer function so there is no human interference, and you're well on your way to great photos.

Tips

Set up your photography station for your largest item first. That way, you can always use your optical zoom to get closer for smaller items, but you won't have to adjust your lighting setup or move your tripod farther back to accommodate a larger item.

Now all you do is switch out the items and shoot again. This is the quickest way to get all of your photos taken ready for listing.

Optical Zoom vs. Digital Zoom

Zoom is zoom, right? Wrong. There are two types of zoom: digital zoom and optical zoom. Digital zoom is nothing more than cropping out the background around the subject. It's not really a "zoom" at all. You lose resolution when you use digital zoom, just as if you'd put the picture into a photo editor and cropped the background away after taking the shot. So if you absolutely have to use this feature, you need to use the highest resolution setting you have on your camera. Otherwise, you'll end up with a low-resolution image like Figure 15.8 and have no idea why.

The other type of zoom is optical zoom, and this actually moves the lens so you don't lose resolution when you zoom in. On almost every camera with optical zoom, you will see and/or hear the lens move closer to the subject when you zoom in.

Many cameras have both optical and digital zoom. For example, my Canon has 3x optical zoom and 10x digital zoom. I never go further than 3x magnification. If I need to get closer, I move my camera setup closer to the subject rather than use the digital zoom.

Remember, though, that you must use your Macro setting if you're getting close to the item. It's well worth locating this setting, particularly if you're selling items like jewelry or small collectibles.

Photograph Composition

I've talked about the mechanics of taking good photographs, but half the battle is knowing how to photograph the different items you will be selling. Here is a list of common items and the typical composition I use. Whenever you photograph an item, you should think about what would showcase it best. Perform a search for that item and display the results in the **Snapshot** view. This will show you just the thumbnails. Which pops out to you? Which did you just scan past? Try to emulate the ones that caught your attention.

Clothing: Always iron clothing before photographing. If you have a mannequin, that is the best way to showcase clothing. If not, lay the poster board on the floor and arrange the clothing flat. Fold arms at the elbow (as if the wearer had their hand on their hip) to show long sleeves without having a really wide scarecrow looking image. Stand on a small ladder or chair and photograph the item from above. If you're selling a lot of clothes, you might look for a body form of the type of clothes you have (men, women, or children) this can help your items look different from other people's items. Make sure that the perspective of your photograph is correct (straight on, not at an angle). Otherwise you could be making pants legs look shorter than they are.

Handbags: Use a contrasting background to showcase your bags and put the straps behind the bag for your main thumbnail shot. Show additional pictures that shows the drop of the strap/handles, the interior, and the sides (to show the bag depth). If you are selling a designer bag, showing the authenticity number (printed inside the bag) is always smart. It is often obvious from this number if an item is real or fake, so that is one step towards showing the buyer that your item is genuine (remember, fakes are not allowed on eBay even if identified as a fake).

Glass or ceramic: Anything that reflects is a challenge to photograph. Never use flash and always make sure your lighting is diffused. Make sure to photograph a picture in frame straight on so you don't distort the picture because of the perspective.

Crystal: A dark colored background is usually a good idea for glass or crystal items because it helps the glass sparkle. It also gives the shape some contrast which wouldn't be available in a white-background shot. Be careful of flash and harsh glare from your lights.

Vases: Be careful when shooting vases of what you put in it. Many people showcase a vase with flowers in it. This does make it pop from the other items in the search results, but ensure it makes the vase pop not the flowers. Don't have leaves hanging down over the vase, and ensure the proportion of your flowers works with the vase size. In most cases, it's better not to put anything in the vase and just use a contrasting background to make it pop.

Electronics: Most electronic items look best when placed at an angle rather than straight on. Having a second picture showing all the extras (cables, CD, case, etc.) with the item is also useful. Be careful of flash and light spots causing glare on the item. Always use the Macro feature to keep the close-up details in focus.

Small collectibles: Show multiple angles of small collectibles. Most people who purchase these items are used to holding the item and looking at it before making a purchase. You need to give them the same level of detail in your pictures or they won't buy. Make sure your white balance is absolutely right for collectibles. The color (and whether it is faded or not) is usually very important to the collector. Always turn on the Macro setting to show close-up detail and be careful about light spots causing glare. Diffuse your lights if needed to remove glare.

Jewelry and watches: This is one of the hardest items to photograph. Always use the Macro setting and get a close-up shot to show all of the detail. The biggest error I see in jewelry items is the photo is taken from too far away, or the image is enlarged but is blurry. In the next section, I show you how to fix issues if you see some, but getting close to the item and using your Macro setting will prevent most issues you'll find with photographing jewelry or watches. You can also purchase display boards for earrings, rings, and so on. If you have a lot to sell, these are worth getting. If not, use a piece of velvet or corduroy in a contrasting color to place the jewelry on. Always show a front and side view of jewelry items. Later I talk about the Cloud Dome and EZ Cube. These are perfect tools for jewelry sellers.

Common Photography Errors and How to Fix Them

Everyone makes mistakes. You're not a professional photographer (or at least, I'm assuming you aren't), and you're not expected to be. It can be very frustrating when your picture doesn't look right but you have no idea how to fix it. Let's take the guesswork out of it. Here are 11 common errors I see frequently in auction photos, what they make the photo look like, and how you can easily fix them. If you're having a problem with one of your pictures, compare it to the pictures here; you should be able to work out what went wrong and how to fix it.

All of these pictures were taken with a point-and-shoot digital camera (a Canon PowerShot SD1100IS). That model is already out-of-date, but you should be able to find something similar for under $200. This proves the point that you don't need a professional camera to get good pictures.

In fact, I had a really hard time getting the "bad" examples using my camera because it automates so many of the functions for you and compensates so well for user error. I had to use the manual setting and overemphasize the error to get these. Most modern cameras are the same, so chances are good that you'll be able to get good auction pictures with whatever digital camera you already own.

Figure 15.2 is our "good" picture. This is how it should look. You could use extra lights to fill the shadow under the camcorder, but I am trying to make it clear that this is not a stock photograph. Since so many sellers of electronic items don't take their own pictures, I want it to be obvious this is not a stock picture. A little extra shadow does this quite nicely. It is not the quality of a professional catalog photograph, but it does display the item very well, so that works for me.

Figure 15.2

Good photograph of a camcorder.

You'll also notice that I flipped the screen around. This shows one of the really neat features about this camcorder without actually saying a word. Most of the thumbnail images of similar items show the camcorder closed. This makes my image "pop" more.

Figure 15.3

Same camcorder with poor lighting.

There are too many shadows in this picture. To fix it, simply add two light sources, as explained in the previous section (see Figure 15.1), shoot near a well-lit window, or use a combination of both.

Figure 15.4

Same camcorder with incorrect use of flash.

Automatic flash washes out pictures and causes harsh glare on shiny objects. Adjust your lighting so it's not a spotlight on the item and turn off the flash on your camera. If this doesn't fix it, tape a piece of thin paper over the lights so you can't see the bulbs, and use this diffused lighting. You will need to get the lamps much closer—and don't forget to remove the paper immediately after shooting to prevent a fire hazard. Alternatively, shoot outside on a cloudy day without flash.

Figure 15.5

Poor focus.

If you zoom in or get very near to the item to get a close-up shot, you will likely also need to use your camera's Macro feature. Macro adjusts the focus so that even when you're very close to the subject, you will still see all the details clearly. Figure 15.5 shows a close-up shot of the back of the camera without Macro. Figure 15.6 shows the same shot with Macro. Note that you cannot easily read the text in Figure 15.5, but can in Figure 15.6. Imagine if this were enlarged to full-screen size. Figure 15.6 would appear much sharper and the details far clearer.

Figure 15.6

Sharp focus using Macro.

Lack of focus can also occur in longer shots. If you are using autofocus, hold down the shutter button halfway so it can get the item in focus. Wait for the beep or a nice sharp image before pressing it the final halfway. If this doesn't work, use the autotimer and let it do it for you.

Figure 15.7

Shaky.

This is caused by hand movement. To prevent it, use a tripod and the autotimer on your camera. A lot of modern cameras have an image stabilization or antishake feature. If you find that hand shakiness is a problem for you in photography, look for a model with one of these features next time you replace your camera.

Figure 15.8

Low-resolution photo.

Your resolution setting should be no lower than 2 megapixels (sometimes shown on a camera as 2M or 2MP)—3 megapixels is much better. If you expect to be cropping a lot of background out of the picture, you may need to go as high as 4 megapixels. This is exactly the same image as Figure 15.2. The only difference is the resolution. Low resolution can be minor and just display as jagged edges, but it will look like Figure 15.8 if buyers enlarge it on the screen (as buyers often do).

Figure 15.9 shows too much going on in the background. Use a plain backdrop so buyers are looking at your item, not the rest of your house.

Figure 15.9

Distracting background.

Although the photographer in Figure 15.10 (on the next page) means well by showing all of the accessories, they are just thrown together, so it looks messy and unappealing. Neatly coiling and tying the cables and showing the accessories in a separate photograph would be a better idea here.

Figure 15.11 on the next page has too much white space. Either crop out the excess space when you are editing your pictures or use the zoom on your camera to zoom in on the item to see the details. If you plan to crop the picture, make sure you shoot at a higher resolution so you can crop it down and then enlarge it without losing clarity. If you use zoom to get very close, turn on the Macro setting to keep the image in focus.

Figure 15.10

Cluttered composition.

Figure 15.11

Can't see details of the item.

Flash can cause overexposure (as shown in Figure 15.12), but sometimes just the lighting and location you're using affects over- and underexposure (as shown in Figure 15.13). If your white background is coming out gray or your image is too dark even with the correct lighting, you may want to adjust your exposure up a notch. If you can't see the details in the item (as shown in Figure 15.12) and the background is stark white, you likely need to adjust your exposure down one setting.

Figure 15.12

Overexposed.

Figure 15.13

Underexposed.

You may have to go into manual mode to find your exposure setting (I can access it from any mode on my Canon). This is usually a plus and minus setting in increments of ⅓ up and down. You usually need to adjust only one or two levels in either direction. Try this and see how the results look. You want the background to look as close to white as possible (assuming that you're using a white background), but you don't want to wash out any of the details of the item. It's better to have a very slightly gray background than have a washed out item.

Your lighting and white balance settings also affect this, so make sure you have those adjusted correctly, too.

Photography Tools That Make Your Life Easier

If you're selling a lot of small shiny objects, it may be worth buying a Cloud Dome (www.clouddome.com) or EZ Cube (www.ezauctiontools.com). Basically, you put your item inside the dome or box and shoot through the opening. Your light sources point directly at either side of the item through the plastic (or fabric), which diffuses the light but keeps it bright enough to illuminate the item. This is the best way to get a professional photograph.

Skip is a distributor for EZ Cube and currently offers the 20-inch version at www.ezauctiontools.com for $79 (retail is $119).

This is a great product for all of your small knick-knacks, vases, and so on. I don't go into any more detail here, but you can find out more at www.ezauctiontools.com if you are interested.

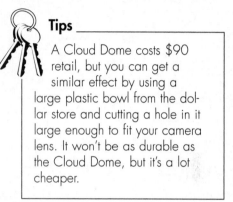

Tips

A Cloud Dome costs $90 retail, but you can get a similar effect by using a large plastic bowl from the dollar store and cutting a hole in it large enough to fit your camera lens. It won't be as durable as the Cloud Dome, but it's a lot cheaper.

Editing Your Photos

My husband, Chris, is an Adobe Photoshop wizard. He can take out things that are there, put in things that aren't, clean up items, add sparkle, remove shine, and more. In 20 years I'll be really happy about this, because he'll be able to keep me looking like I'm 30!

Using modern photo-editing programs, you can make your items look better than they really are. You must resist the temptation to do this for your auction photos because it is a misrepresentation of your item.

Here are a few things you can and can't do to your photos.

Do's and Don'ts for Editing Auction Photography

Do's	Don'ts
Crop to show just the item	Take out any flaws in the item
Fix the colors if they are not accurate	Add anything that would increase the value of the item that is not actually there

continues

Do's and Don'ts for Editing Auction Photography   (contineud)

Do's	Don'ts
Smooth out the background if it looks distracting	Make colors that are faded or dull on your item look brighter and fresher
Adjust the brightness and contrast	
Add minor sparkle to jewelry	
Remove glare	

You don't have to do any of these editing techniques, but you should avoid the don'ts list to keep from inadvertently misrepresenting your item.

In addition to changing the actual image, you might consider adding a border. As long as it is not distracting to the image, this can make your thumbnail image on the search results page pop. I've seen it look really bad (too thick a line) but also very good. Try it and see what you think.

File Sizes for Uploading to eBay

The maximum file size you can use for eBay Picture Services depends on the uploader you use. We cover the different options in Chapter 17, but for now, here are the file sizes:

◆ Basic Uploader, 4MB

◆ Standard Uploader, 4MB

◆ Enhanced Uploader, 8MB

The image will be compressed to fit the screen when using the Standard and Enhanced uploaders so your buyers don't have to scroll to the sides to view it.

eBay recommends that the longest edge of your image be 1,000 pixels or higher. If you're using Windows Picture Viewer (comes free with Windows Vista) to edit your pictures, click on **Edit Pictures** and then **Resize.** In the bottom-right corner, you'll see the pixel size for the image. You can use the Resize feature to get it smaller, if you need to. But as long as you set your camera to 3 megapixels (that is, 3,000 pixels), you should still be well over 1,000 pixels on the longest edge, even if you have to do some cropping. Adobe PhotoShop and other image-editing programs offer this feature, too.

Shark in the Water _____

Be careful if you're transferring photos from one computer to another via e-mail. Some e-mail programs automatically compress photographs when they are e-mailed, so you could end up with a much lower resolution image when it gets to the other computer. A better option is to use a USB thumb drive (you can pick up a 2GB thumb drive for about $10 brand new) and transfer your pictures that way. I picked up a 16GB thumb drive in the Thanksgiving sales last year for $17, so look for the bargains and don't pay full retail!

Stock Photography, Copyright, and VeRO

First let me explain what each of these terms means. Stock photography is an image provided by the manufacturer of the item. You will find it on the manufacturer's website and in its catalog.

Copyright tells you who the owner of the image is. In stock photography, this is the manufacturer. In auction photography, it is usually whoever took the photo.

VeRO stands for Verified Rights Owner, and this is eBay's policy on using other people's property. VeRO applies to more than just photographs, but that's all we talk about here.

It's okay to use a stock photograph in your auctions if you are an authorized distributor for that product and have permission from the manufacturer. But the likelihood is that you're not, so you cannot take a stock photograph from the manufacturer's website and use it in your auction.

If you use eBay's prefilled Product Details when you list your item (you'll be prompted if eBay has this available for your product), you may be offered a stock photograph. You may use that because eBay has arranged permission with the owner of the picture.

Copyright belongs to the photographer, so it's okay to take your own photo of the item, but it's not okay to take someone else's (including another eBay member's). Most buyers want to see a picture of the actual item they are buying anyway, so you should always take your own pictures.

VeRO basically protects the copyright of the photographer. Violating the copyright of the manufacturer or another eBay user violates eBay's VeRO policy and can get your listings cancelled and you suspended.

Minimizing the eBay Picture Hosting Fees

eBay Picture Hosting charges 15¢ for each photograph (after the first one, which is free) for all but four categories. You can get around this in a few ways. First, you could take all your photos and then create another image showing all the photos in one bigger photo. When you upload it, as far as eBay is concerned, you have only one image. However, to see the details of each item, the buyer would have to click on the enlarge link. Not everyone knows to do that, so you could put off some buyers because they can't see the details of each item.

Alternatively, you can host your own photographs on another site. eBay charges only to host your pictures, not upload them. Plenty of free sites offer image hosting. I like Photobucket (www.Photobucket.com) because it tells you which type of coding you need for eBay listings. www.Inkfrog.com is another favorite of eBay sellers. Ink Frog costs $6.95 a month but is very popular.

You could also look into using an auction-management program. If you use an auction-management program, you usually get image hosting for free as part of the package.

The Least You Need to Know

- Take a few minutes to set up a clean, uncluttered background.

- Changing your white balance settings and using correct lighting will really improve your photos.

- Use a tripod and timer function to prevent blurriness and shakiness in your photos.

- Don't forget to turn on the Macro feature when you're using optical zoom.

- Don't overedit your photos. If you make the item look better than it actually is, you are misrepresenting the item to your buyers.

- Copyright of a photograph belongs to the photographer, whether it is the manufacturer or another eBay seller.

- You can get around the eBay Picture Services fees by using either a free hosting service or making a photo montage so you only actually upload one image.

Part 4

Creating Your Listing

In this part, you'll learn exactly how to create a listing that will make buyers want to buy your item. We start at the beginning with the eBay Sell Your Item form and work through it, showing you what each choice means and what options you should use. Then we explain the optional listing upgrades in plain English and show you which you should always use, which are useful in certain circumstances, and which are almost never worth the cost.

We also look at a few third-party options that can make your life easier and your listings more profitable.

Chapter **16**

Describing Your Item

In This Chapter

- ◆ Adding and removing options in the Sell Your Item form
- ◆ Using Product Details to save time and effort
- ◆ How to write a winning listing title and subtitle
- ◆ Uploading your photos quickly and easily
- ◆ The difference between eBay's image-uploading tools

In this chapter, we start our listing with the Sell Your Item form. Although we take five chapters to go through the entire process, it won't take long for you to actually create your auction. As you get practiced at writing effective titles and descriptions, and become familiar with the options available, it will take less time for you to list items.

eBay's Sell Your Item Form

Most new eBay sellers start at the Sell Your Item form. This is the best option if you list only a few items at a time.

However, if you start listing a lot of auctions, you might find that Turbo Lister (eBay's free auction-management program) or Auctiva (www.auctiva.com) are better options, as they automate some of the repetitive tasks and help you manage your listings a little better.

We discuss both Turbo Lister and Auctiva in Chapter 20 and explain how to list an item using them. Turbo Lister isn't set up for a beginner and is not nearly as user-friendly as the Sell Your Item form. If you want, you can go straight into listing with Auctiva as a new seller, and there are some cost advantages to doing this if you have a lot of items. However, I still recommend that you list your first few items with the Sell Your Item form to get a feel for the eBay process. Then you can decide whether you prefer to use Auctiva (which is set up very similarly, but has a low monthly fee). The information you enter will be the same (and in the same order) for whichever form you use, so the explanations in the next few chapters apply to all listing forms.

Here we create an auction for the item photographed in Chapter 15: a used Sony Handycam DCR-SR100 HDD Camcorder. This is an older model, not the newest "hot" electronic item. That makes it more realistically something you would sell as an individual rather than as a business seller who would be looking for new or refurbished items.

Tips

Always have your photographs ready before you start the listing process. Stopping in the middle of creating your listing to go take the pictures will really throw off your focus and end up taking much more time.

I recommend that you create a new folder on your desktop for your auction photos so that you can find them quickly and easily when you get to that step and don't have to go searching in your **My Documents** or **My Pictures** folders.

Category Selection

Click the **Sell** navigation tab and then **Start Selling.** The first thing you are asked to do is type a few keywords about your item. This is not the title you will use—it is just a string of keywords to help eBay identify the most likely category. Three or four key-words work fine.

For this camcorder, we use "Sony HDD Camcorder."

Usually, the correct category is quite obvious from the selection eBay offers you. In our case, Cameras & Photo > Camcorders is clearly the right category. However, what if your item type doesn't have a specific subcategory or it could easily fit into two categories? Then you need to do your own research.

1. Open a new browser window and do a **Completed Listings** search for your item.

2. Click on the title of items with the highest selling prices and the most bids.

3. At the top of the listing page, you can see which category the auction was listed in. (See Figure 16.1.)

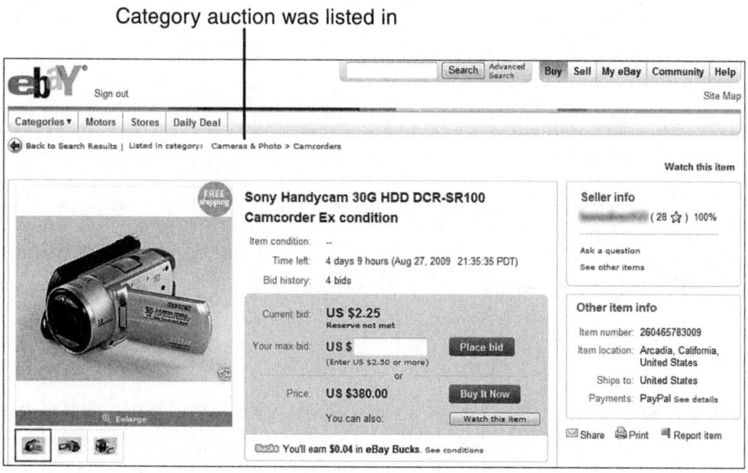

Category auction was listed in

Figure 16.1

This category line displays on active and completed listings, so if there aren't many completed auctions, it also takes a look at the active ones with the most bids and the highest price so far.

4. Repeat this process with the highest-priced items until you are comfortable that you know which category was the most successful for that item.

Now let's go back to the category options (see Figure 16.2).

Once you have selected your category, click **Continue.** If you accidentally click the wrong category, you can click **Remove** at the bottom to remove any category you previously selected. Here you can also click **See sample listings,** which shows you listings within that category that use similar keywords to the ones you entered.

If you want to use eBay's *List in Two Categories* feature, just select more than one category.

def•i•ni•tion

List in Two Categories displays your item in two different categories simultaneously.

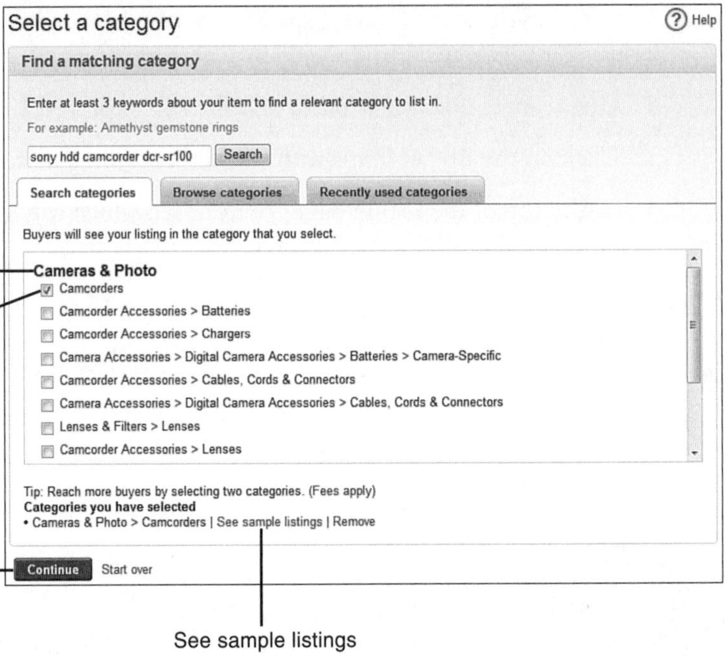

Figure 16.2

*If you don't see the category you want to sell in, click the **Browse categories** tab to select from the main categories and subcategories yourself.*

Main category ——

Select category ——

Continue ——

See sample listings

Select a category	⑦ Help

Find a matching category

Enter at least 3 keywords about your item to find a relevant category to list in.

For example: Amethyst gemstone rings

| sony hdd camcorder dcr-sr100 | Search |

| Search categories | Browse categories | Recently used categories |

Buyers will see your listing in the category that you select.

Cameras & Photo
- ☑ Camcorders
- ☐ Camcorder Accessories > Batteries
- ☐ Camcorder Accessories > Chargers
- ☐ Camera Accessories > Digital Camera Accessories > Batteries > Camera-Specific
- ☐ Camcorder Accessories > Cables, Cords & Connectors
- ☐ Camera Accessories > Digital Camera Accessories > Cables, Cords & Connectors
- ☐ Lenses & Filters > Lenses
- ☐ Camcorder Accessories > Lenses

Tip: Reach more buyers by selecting two categories. (Fees apply)
Categories you have selected
• Cameras & Photo > Camcorders | See sample listings | Remove

[Continue]   Start over

List in Two Categories sounds like a great option. Who wouldn't like to have twice as many people see their item? But there is a catch. If you use this option, eBay doubles all your listing fees. So double the Insertion fee and double all the listing upgrade fees. That's a lot of money going to fees. I try to keep my listing fees under 10 percent of my item's expected final selling price. If you're using List in Two Categories, that has to become 5 percent because of the doubling effect. So it's worth using this option only when you have an expensive item or when you will significantly lose out by having it in only one category.

Product Details

In certain categories, eBay offers Product Details from its catalog for you to use. This is product information (often including a stock photograph) about the item. You'll know if it is offered for your item because the **Find a product** page will appear (see Figure 16.3) after you click **Continue** from the **Category** selection page.

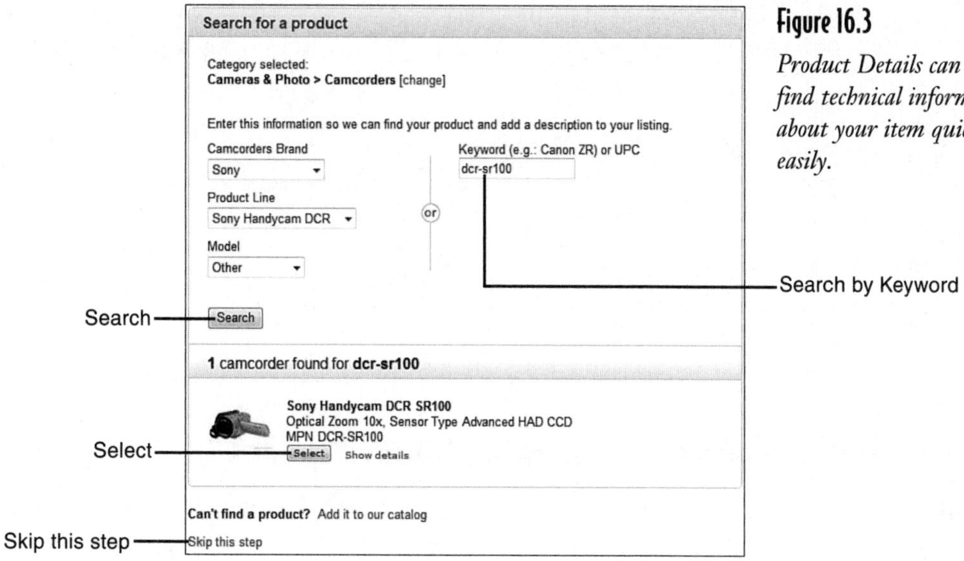

Search for a product

Category selected:
Cameras & Photo > Camcorders [change]

Enter this information so we can find your product and add a description to your listing.

Camcorders Brand
Sony ▼

Keyword (e.g.: Canon ZR) or UPC
dcr-sr100

Product Line
Sony Handycam DCR ▼   (or)

Model
Other ▼

Search—— [Search]

1 camcorder found for **dcr-sr100**

 Sony Handycam DCR SR100
Optical Zoom 10x, Sensor Type Advanced HAD CCD
MPN DCR-SR100

Select—— [Select]   Show details

Can't find a product? Add it to our catalog

Skip this step——Skip this step

Search by Keyword

Figure 16.3

Product Details can help you find technical information about your item quickly and easily.

You'll usually find Product Details for items in certain categories, including these:

- ◆ Books
- ◆ Cameras & Photo
- ◆ Cell Phones & PDAs
- ◆ Computers & Networking
- ◆ Consumer Electronics
- ◆ DVDs & Movies
- ◆ Video Games

Shark in the Water

Even if you use Product Details, you should write a description yourself. If an item is newly launched, be particularly careful to check that the information is correct because you are responsible for its accuracy, not eBay.

I tend to use the manufacturer part number (or ISBN) as a search keyword because it is the most accurate (and quickest) way of locating the item. But Figure 16.3 shows the drop-down menu selections, too, if you prefer that method. You'll usually find the most information for items that have been released six months to two years ago, but sometimes there is still catalog information for older models (as is the case for our camcorder).

Click **Select** once you have found your item (see Figure 16.3). Or if you don't find the correct item or don't want to use Product Details in your listing, click **Skip this step.**

Tips

Sellers with thousands of items tend to use Product Details exclusively because it is relatively automated. However, I like the personal detail of an actual written description. For used items, it's essential that you describe flaws, but a description is still worth adding for new items because it shows that you are a human being behind the computer screen. This suggests that you will provide better customer service than someone who has just mass-listed items.

Customizing the Sell Your Item Form to Show Other Options

Most of the listing is created here, on the main **Sell Your Item** page. At the top of the page, you'll see an option to **switch to simple form.** Don't ever click this—it takes away many of your options and fits you into a cookie-cutter listing. You can always ignore a section if you don't want to use it right now, but you should still have it available, just in case.

Many options are not included in the basic form you're currently looking at. Click **Add or remove options** at the top of each section to see the additional options that you can use if you want. For example, in the Shipping section, you won't automatically see international shipping options. To turn this on, click **Add or remove options** at the top of the section, and then check the **Show international services and options** box (see Figure 16.4). You can also uncheck boxes here. For example, if UPS doesn't service your area, uncheck the UPS box; then you won't be offered UPS shipping options when you create your listings in the future.

When you have finished adding or removing options for the section, click **Save** to go back to the **Sell Your Item** form. If you just close the window, eBay will not save your changes.

Show international services and options

Add or remove options

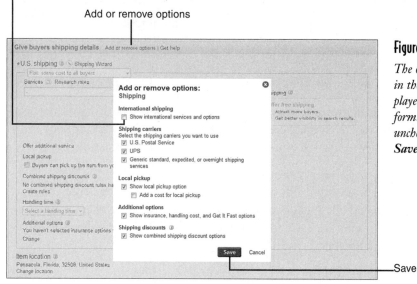

Figure 16.4

The options with checkmarks in the boxes are already displayed on the **Sell Your Item** *form. To turn them off, just uncheck the box and click* **Save.**

Save

Writing Your Listing Title

It doesn't sound hard, does it? Enter up to 55 characters about your item and you're done, right? You could do that. But there is a lot of competition on eBay, so if you want to get a lot of buyers clicking through to your listing, you need to consider a number of things before writing your title.

Almost all buyers include some level of search for their items, so you need to include as many keywords as possible. But at the same time, it has to make sense as a title for when the searchers are scanning the titles on the search results page. Just typing a row of disjointed keywords will get you onto that search results page, but it won't get buyers clicking through to your listing.

You need to include the keywords about the item and then add something the other listings don't have to make the buyer *want* to read your auction.

Start with the obvious keywords. The following list shows information you should include about your item. Obviously, a pair of jeans doesn't need the model number, nor does a camcorder need the size in the title. Look through the list and see which apply to your item type. Those are the keywords that buyers might search for and that you absolutely need to include in your title.

- Product name
- Brand name
- Size
- Color

- Style
- Model number
- Condition (only if it's new)

You should also include anything unique about the item, or features that will increase its value. Is it a signed rookie baseball card? Is it a first edition out-of-print book? Does it come bundled with more than just the main item? Is it a collectible in the original box?

There's not enough space to write "out of print" or "mint condition in original box" in the title. Over the years, eBay sellers have developed abbreviations that are fairly well understood to communicate extra information in a title. We listed these in Chapter 5, but here's a refresher:

BIN	Buy It Now
COA	Certificate of authenticity (used mainly for collectibles)
EUC	Excellent used condition
GU	Gently used
LTD	Limited edition (sometimes LE)
MIB	Mint in box (for collectibles)
NIB	New in box
NIP	New in packaging
NR	No reserve
NWOT	New without tags
NWT	New with tags
OEM	Original equipment manufacturer (you usually see this in relation to computer software, ink cartridges, and so on)
OOP	Out of print
PM	Priority Mail shipping
RET	Retired
S/O	Sold out

Remember that you have only 55 characters (including spaces) to convince your buyer that your item is better than all the others, so in addition to keywords, you should try to fit in some trigger words and phrases if you have space:

New	Authentic	Brand new
Beautiful	Boutique	Vintage
Awesome	Stunning	Rare
Unusual	One of a kind	Bonus
Unique	Handmade	Antique
Designer	Collectible	

Around the holidays, it's worth adding *Christmas, Xmas, Mother's Day, 4th of July,* or whatever holiday it is, along with the word *gift.*

Think about who your buyer is before you decide which trigger words to use. There's no point in using *vintage* if your target buyer is looking for something new, or in using *pretty* for a state-of-the-art technology item. Also, always ensure you have enough space for your item keywords before you use a lot of trigger words. It's much better to leave out a trigger word than a keyword.

 Shark in the Water

Be careful with words like *rare, antique, designer,* and *unique.* Use them only if this is actually true. Saying that a wooden bowl is antique and then in the description admitting that it was made in 1980 will only prejudice buyers against you and make them click away from your listing.

I collect watercolor prints by a wonderful English artist, Norma Nelson. They retail for between $70 and $200, but if I search eBay UK (www.eBay.co.uk), sometimes I can pick them up for much less. I recently bought three limited-edition prints (retail at around $180 each) for $30 for all three because the seller forgot to put the words *watercolor* (well, actually *watercolour,* since it was eBay UK) and *print* in her titles. I have a favorite search set up for the artist's name, so I found them, but I doubt anyone else did.

Here are a few examples of bad auction titles I have seen on eBay and how they could be improved. The first is the actual auction title for one of the Norma Nelson prints I bought.

Bad title:	**TRANQUILITY by Norma Nelson LIMITED EDITION**
Better title:	**FRAMED Watercolor Print ~SIGNED BY ARTIST~ Norma Nelson**
Bad title:	**PlayStation 3 in box with games**
Better title:	**BRAND NEW NIB 80GB 80 GB PlayStation 3 ~ BONUS 4 GAMES!**
Bad title:	**DKNY jeans size 8**
Better title:	**STUNNING designer * DKNY * blue bootcut jeans 8 PETITE**
Bad title:	**Nice Wooden Bowl**
Better title:	**Beautiful HANDMADE Rustic ** MAPLE WOOD ** large bowl**

You get the idea. In each of my improved examples, I used all 55 characters. Even if you have run out of things to say, use up the extra with symbols like ** or ~ to emphasize a particular word or phrase, and if you still have characters left, use extra spaces between words.

However, one word of caution when using these symbols: if you put a symbol such as ~ or * directly next to a word, the search engine sees that as a character and will not recognize that word in searches. For example, if you put *SONY* in the title and someone searches for SONY, your auction will not come up in the search. You need to put a space between the symbol and any words you want found in a search. For example, * SONY * is okay.

Tips

Using symbols is fine, but you shouldn't use them within a word like L@@K. Also, don't use capitals and lowercase alternatively in the same word LiKE tHIs. Both techniques are annoying, cheesy, and unprofessional. They may get buyers looking at your auction title, but they won't get buyers clicking through and buying.

In our previous example, I used **~signed by artist~**, but that's okay because I don't expect those terms to be searched for. I included the phrase to set it apart from the other items when the buyer is browsing the results. It's something that intrigues buyers but is not usually included in search keywords.

Take a look at the Completed Listings for your item. Look at the most successful auctions to get some ideas for trigger words and keywords for your particular item.

For our auction, we have a lot of keywords to use because it is a consumer electronics item. So let's look at the required keywords first:

Model number: DCR-SR100

Item type: HDD Camcorder

Brand: Sony

Model name: Handycam

Size: 30GB

Let's start with this:

Sony Handycam DCR-SR100 HDD Camcorder 30GB

That's already 42 characters (including spaces), so there's not much left to play with.

Tips _____

We are not adding the condition because it is not new. If it were, that would be an important one to add, as buyers often search for "new" as a keyword. However, very few buyers search for "used" as a keyword. Rather, they use the Refine Search options to select used items (which you identify in the Item Specifics section later in the Sell Your Item form).

We have a camera bag and cables included. There's not enough room to list both of those, so let's use the word "Bonus" instead and entice the buyer to look at the auction to find out what the bonuses are. Now we have used 51 characters for the text, and we can use up the extra four characters with extra characters and white space:

* Sony Handycam 30GB HDD Camcorder DCR-SR100 + BONUS! *

Incorrect Spellings Can Increase Sales

I know this sounds counterintuitive, but in some instances, using both the correct spelling and a common misspelling works to your advantage.

Take the shoe brand Skechers—or is it Sketchers? If you do a search for "Skechers Sandals," you will find hundreds of items. (I just did a search and got 827 listings.)

Now try "Sketchers Sandals." (Note the added *t* in *Sketchers*.) I still got 83 results. That's far fewer, but enough results for a buyer to not realize they've made a spelling mistake. Most will just think there are fewer items available and will pick from this selection. Because of that, there will be more competition driving the price up (particularly when the buyer refines the search to the correct size).

I found significantly higher selling prices in the misspelled auctions than in the ones with only correctly spelled keywords.

Think about it: you're not going to push your maximum bid to get an item if you know there are hundreds of other listings for the same thing available. But if there are only 5 or 10 of the item you want, you might be more tempted to bid it up.

This applies to international words and spellings, too, particularly if you're adding International Site Visibility as one of your optional listing upgrades (see Chapter 20). If you're selling sneakers, consider adding the British version, *trainers*, to your title. If you're using the word *jewelry*, consider adding *jewellery* as well. Of course, this is a little pointless if you're not offering international shipping, but you get my point.

If you are adding misspelled words, always remember to list the correct spelling for the word first in the title.

I recommend that you work on your title in a word-processing document where you can check the character count. In Microsoft Word (pre-2007 versions), the option is under the **Tools** menu. For Word 2007, click on **Words:** at the bottom of the window. This pops up a box showing the character count. Remember, you need to look at the total characters, including spaces.

Tips _____

If you are using a word processor, be careful of the spell checker. This is a good feature, but it can be a problem with brand names, so check directly on the brand website if you're not absolutely certain of the spelling.

For example, I think many of the incorrectly spelled listing titles with *Sketchers* instead of *Skechers* occur because a word-processing program will say that *Skechers* is the incorrect spelling (when it is actually correct) and try to correct it with *Sketchers*. This is because it assumes that you meant to use the word to describe a group of people who like to sketch, not the brand of shoes.

Write a few versions of your title with different trigger words and different orders of the keywords. When you find the one you like best, copy and paste (or retype) it into the **Title** box in the Sell Your Item form.

When and How to Use a Subtitle

A subtitle is an additional 55 characters that display below the listing title on the search results page (see Figure 16.5).

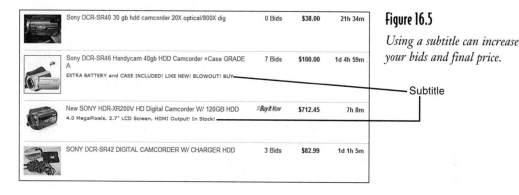

Figure 16.5

Using a subtitle can increase your bids and final price.

The subtitle is used for extra information, not searchable keywords. eBay's search engine searches only the main title unless the buyer checks the **Include title and description** box (which is rare).

Both subtitles in Figure 16.5 gave more information about the item's technical specifications and what was included in the auction, but you could also mention special deals like "Free Shipping with Buy It Now." If I'm selling a gift item around Valentine's Day, I usually add "Perfect Gift for that Someone Special" to my subtitle.

Some sellers put "Priority Mail Shipping" in the subtitle to indicate that the shipping cost covers the faster (and more expensive) Priority option. Others say "In Stock, Ships Next Day" to show that they are not waiting for the sale to order the item from their supplier.

The subtitle is also where you can use trigger words if there was no space in the auction title, or you can add extra item/listing features.

So let's look at our auction. We have a good title, but what else can we say to make it more enticing?

Well, we've said that it's an HDD camcorder, but some people might not know what that means. HDD means the camcorder has a built-in hard disc drive. So let's make it really clear with, "No tape/DVD needed." 30GB for the hard drive capacity is pretty decent, but it doesn't really explain how that translates to recording time. So let's also add "30GB/20 Hours" to show how it correlates. Let's also add another feature that is very important: optical zoom. Some modern models have far higher optical zoom (40x and up) but for the price this camcorder will go for, 10x is pretty good, so it's worth mentioning in the subtitle.

Here's our 55-character subtitle:

> 10x Optical Zoom ~ 30GB/20 Hours ~ NO TAPE/DVD NEEDED!

I like to use a combination of uppercase and lowercase words to emphasize certain sections. I also like to use the tilde (~) character between my sections. Some sellers prefer to use | instead. However, I find that doesn't give as much spacing for the same number of characters:

> 10x Optical Zoom | 30GB/20 Hours | NO TAPE/DVD NEEDED!

Use whatever character you prefer, but be sure to have some kind of separator if you have space to use one.

Let's take a look at how the subtitle displays with our auction title:

> *** Sony Handycam 30GB HDD Camcorder DCR-SR100 + BONUS! ***
>
> 10x Optical Zoom ~ 30GB/20 Hours ~ NO TAPE/DVD NEEDED!

The subtitle sets it apart from other camcorder auctions because it reminds the buyer of a major benefit of hard drive camcorders: they don't need tapes or DVDs. This increases the value of our item and makes it more desirable to buyers.

As with the title, write your subtitle in a word-processing program before transferring it to the Sell Your Item form. Look at it as we have with your auction title above it so you can see how it will end up looking and check that you are not repeating yourself unnecessarily.

Item Specifics

Beneath the **Subtitle** box on the Sell Your Item form, you may see a number of drop-down menus for specific details about the item (see Figure 16.6). This is called Item Specifics. You absolutely must complete these if the option is presented to you.

eBay's search engine doesn't just look at your listing title for searched keywords. It also looks at your Item Specifics responses. Let's say you're selling a red dress. You didn't put "red" in the title, but you did select red for the color in the Item Specifics menu. Your listing will still show up in the search results if the buyer uses "red" as one of her search keywords. If you hadn't completed the Item Specifics, your item would not have shown up because the word was not in the title or in the Item Specifics.

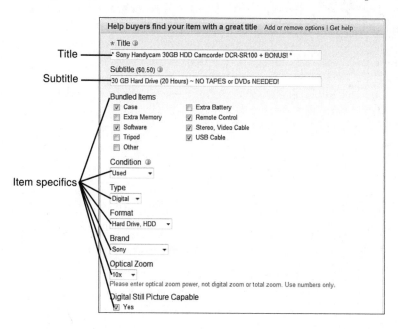

Figure 16.6

If you used Product Details, you will find some of these are already completed for you (usually brand and some of the technical specifications).

This goes a step further. In Chapter 5, I talked about Refine Search options from a buyer's perspective. This involves narrowing the categories and also the item attributes that correspond to the Item Specifics. If you don't complete the Item Specifics when you list the item, your listing will be in the Not Specified section for each of the Refine Search options. Very few people bother to select that option, so they won't see your item.

So if you don't complete the Item Specifics, you are potentially missing buyers who search for specific keywords that you may not have used in your title, as well as buyers who narrow their search results using Refine Search.

Uploading Pictures

Uploading photos is one of the major worries I hear from new sellers. Years ago, when eBay was starting out, you had to host your own photos and add HTML coding to the listing description yourself. If the idea of that makes you hyperventilate, don't worry. eBay is a teenager now, and as it has grown, so has its level of user-friendliness. Now uploading photographs is quick and easy using eBay Picture Services.

Click on **Add pictures** (see Figure 16.7) to get started. Earlier I said to make sure you had your photographs ready; now is when you need them easily accessible. If you used Product Details, a stock image may already be displayed in this section. You can delete it if you don't want to use it.

Figure 16.7

After you have added pictures, the thumbnail images appear in the center of this section.

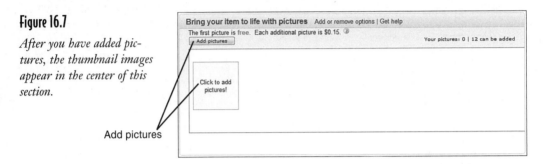

Add pictures

The picture uploading window displays in front of the Sell Your Item form (see Figure 16.8). The first time you use it, you may be prompted to download a small file to use the eBay Enhanced Uploader.

If you would rather not download anything, or if you're on a public computer, you can use the Basic or Standard Uploaders. We discuss these options in a moment.

Click **Add Pictures** in the top-left box. The photograph you put here will become your thumbnail picture on the search results page. An **Open file** box appears for you to navigate to your saved photographs. Having an eBay folder on your desktop (as I suggested earlier) makes this part easier. Click **Open** after you have selected your photograph, and it will display in the top-left box as well as in the main center box (see Figure 16.9).

Tips

You can edit your photos using the Enhanced Uploader, but I have had problems with making my changes stick in the past. I also find it to be incredibly slow, so I prefer to do any editing in a photo-editing program before I get to this stage. If you must, the most I would do using the Enhanced Uploader is rotate and crop the image.

The maximum file size you can use with the Enhanced Uploader is 8MB. This is the highest of the eBay uploaders. If the image is too large (in dimensions) for the template or screen size, eBay automatically shrinks it to fit. This is a big deal because you don't have to worry about the actual image size—just the file size. Frankly, you shouldn't be trying to upload an 8MB file for one photograph. If your file size is over 2MB, you likely had the camera on too high of a resolution setting. This can affect the picture's load time on your listing page, so don't go overboard just because you can.

Add Pictures

Basic tab   Self Hosting tab

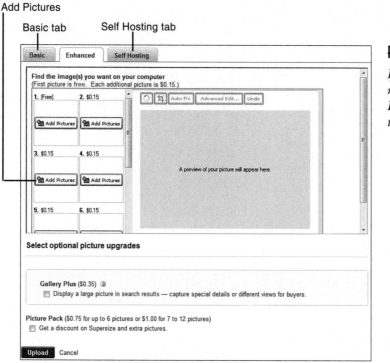

Figure 16.8

*If you already have an external picture host, click the **Self Hosting** tab to select the picture URL.*

Any pictures that you add other than the first one cost you 15¢ each. If you put a picture in the wrong box, select the picture so that it shows in the main box and then click **Remove Pictures** (you may have to scroll down to see that option beneath the main picture).

At the bottom of the box, you can select **Gallery Plus** or **Picture Pack** (see Figure 16.9).

Gallery Plus adds an **Enlarge** link to your listing in the search results. When the buyer clicks on this, your thumbnail image expands to fit the majority of the page. Some categories offer this for free, but most of the time, you'll pay a nominal fee (this varies based on listing type—see Chapter 14 for specifics). Personally, I like this for jewelry items, or other very small items with a lot of detail. But for most items, I don't see this as a necessary option. However, if it's free for your category or eBay is running a promotion, then go for it!

The other option, Picture Pack, is basically a bulk buy on picture-uploading services. You get six pictures for a lower price than paying for them á la carte.

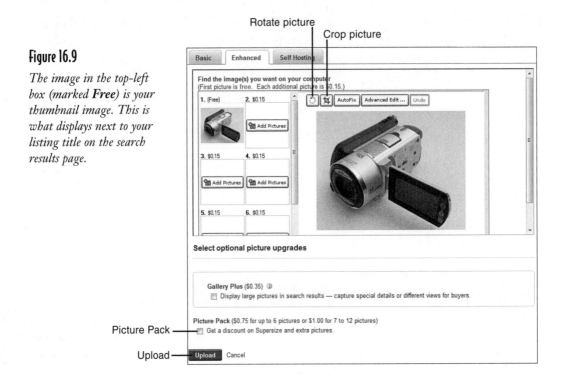

Figure 16.9

*The image in the top-left box (marked **Free**) is your thumbnail image. This is what displays next to your listing title on the search results page.*

Be sure to calculate the actual cost without the Picture Pack before deciding whether it's worth paying for.

When you've added all of your photos in the order you want them to display, and added any picture options you want to use, click **Upload.**

Depending on the size of your photographs, they may take a few minutes to upload. When uploading has finished, you are taken back to the Sell Your Item form; your uploaded photos now display in the center bar of this section.

Basic and Standard Uploaders

If you don't want to download the Enhanced Uploader file, click on the **Basic** tab (see Figure 16.9).

If you use the Basic Uploader as shown, you are limited to 4MB for the file size, and eBay will not compress the image if it is too large for the template or the screen. So your buyers may have to scroll side to side to see the whole image, or the image could take forever to load (in which case, your buyers will click away from your listing).

The alternative is the Standard Uploader. This is accessed from the **Basic Uploader** tab (the link is in the top-right corner). When you click **try the Standard Uploader,** you default to the **Standard Uploader** from that point on instead of the Basic Uploader, and the tab name changes to **Standard.** This is worth doing because the functionality of the uploader is the same and the file size limit is the same, but eBay compresses the image if it's too large.

You select the images the same way, whether you choose to use the Basic or Standard Uploader.

Click **Browse** to access the open file window and locate your photographs (see Figure 16.10). The file name displays in the box instead of a thumbnail (on the Basic Uploader, it is text only; on the Standard Uploader, you will see an icon, but it won't be a thumbnail of your actual picture).

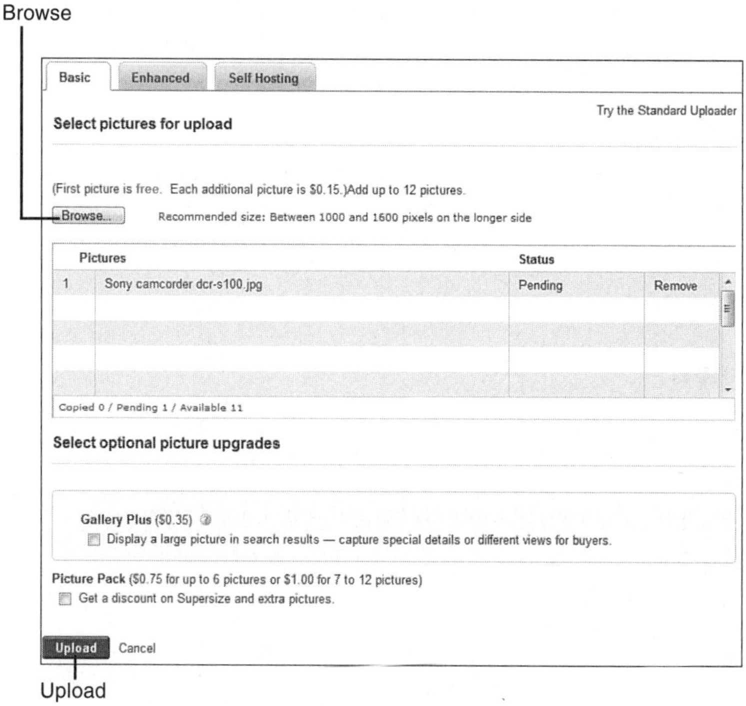

Browse

Figure 16.10

You cannot edit or preview your photos using the Basic or Standard Uploaders, so make sure they are labeled well so you know what order you are placing them in.

Upload

Click **Browse** again to add more pictures. The first picture will become your thumbnail image.

After you have added all of the photos, and Gallery Plus or Picture Pack, if you want to use either of these services, click **Upload.** Thumbnails of your images display in the center bar of the **Pictures** section of the Sell Your Item form, just as if you'd used the Enhanced Uploader (see Figure 16.11).

Figure 16.11

You can remove a photo by selecting it and clicking **Remove.**

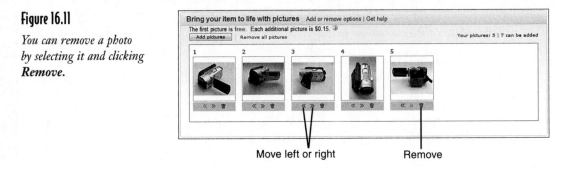

Move left or right   Remove

Look at the first thumbnail image critically. This is about the same size as the thumbnail will appear on the search results page. Is your item displayed clearly? Does it "pop"? If you were looking in the Snapshot view, where all you see is the first thumbnail image, would you honestly click through on yours? If not, you might want to retake the picture and try again.

If you decide that you want to change the thumbnail picture to one of the other pictures you uploaded, just use the left and right arrows (see Figure 16.11) to adjust the order. The first picture in the line is always your thumbnail image for the search results page.

The Least You Need to Know

◆ If an option you want is not displaying on the Sell Your Item form, click **Add or remove options** at the top of the section to see additional options.

◆ Make sure you have your photographs edited before you upload them.

◆ Use keywords and trigger words in your listing title to get buyers to click through.

◆ Use a subtitle to add extra noncritical information to entice the buyer to click through to your auction.

◆ Always complete the Item Specifics if they are offered to you.

◆ Make sure your thumbnail image is the best you have and clearly shows your item even in the smaller size.

Chapter 17

Writing Your Listing Description

In This Chapter

- Using the HTML editor to make your auction appealing
- How to grab your buyer's attention and keep it
- What exactly you should include in your description
- How to format your auction so it is easy to read

You've got the buyer's attention with your listing title and picture. Now it's time to close the deal. Your listing description determines whether the buyer clicks **Place bid** or clicks away from your auction.

Think about when you've made eBay purchases. Did the first impression from the description (even before you started reading it) make a difference to you? Of course it did.

If a listing is just a paragraph of unformatted text, you're going to assume that the seller doesn't really care about it. If he can't be bothered to write a good, appealing description, then he probably can't be bothered to take care of the item, ship the item securely, give good customer service, and so on. These are the things buyers look for, whether they realize it or not, and your first impression really counts. So instead of spending 5 minutes writing the description, spend 10 to 15 minutes writing it, make it look appealing, and sit back and watch the bids.

Writing the Description

In your description, you must include all of the relevant information about the item, as well as why your buyer should want it. But at the same time, if your auction is too long, the buyer won't read it or will skim it, and could miss vital details.

In time, you will develop your own layout preferences for your listing descriptions. For now, though, let's use mine. My order is as follows:

1. Product title

2. Retail cost

3. *One-line hook* about the item

4. Features and benefits of the item

5. Second one-line hook

6. Bulleted list of what is included in the auction

7. One-line special offer or one-line hook

8. Payment options

9. Shipping options

def•i•ni•tion

A **one-line hook** is a sentence about a benefit of this item that "hooks" buyers and makes them read on. I use this multiple times in the description to catch buyers who just scan the auction. If they read the hooks, they are more likely to stop and read the rest of the auction, and that's half the battle won.

Obviously, this varies based on your item. I can talk a lot about features and benefits of this particular camcorder, and it also has a lot of technical specifications and accessories that need mentioning.

However, if I'm selling a used party dress from my daughter's wardrobe, my description will be much more condensed and will likely have more photographs to show the detail. Here's the order I use for a single item listing (one with no accessories) that doesn't have any technical specifications:

1. Product title

2. Retail cost (only if it was expensive)

3. One-line hook

4. Specific details about the item (embroidery, size, design line, and so on)

5. Closing one-line hook

6. Payment options

7. Shipping options

In this second example, the features and benefits would be the one-line hooks. A kid's summer dress doesn't have that many features and benefits, so it doesn't warrant a whole section.

All About the HTML Editor

Think of the HTML editor as a word-processing program within the Sell Your Item form. It offers a number of formatting options, including color, font, size, alignment, bulleted lists, numbered lists, indent, spelling check, and inserts (see Figure 17.1).

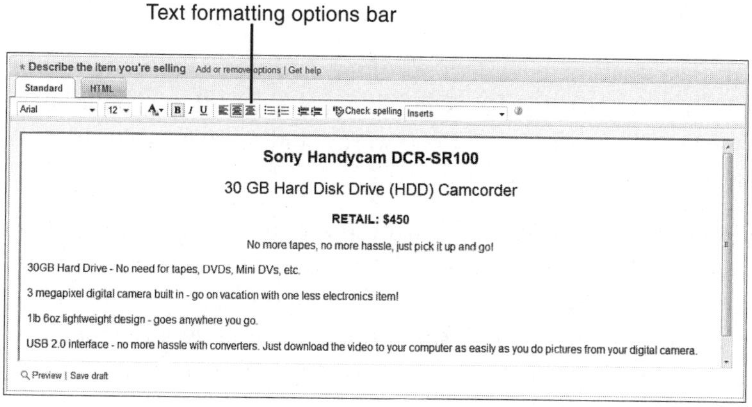

Text formatting options bar

* Describe the item you're selling   Add or remove options | Get help

| Standard | HTML |

Arial   ▼ 12 ▼   A ▾ B I U ☰ ☰ ☰ ☰ ☰ ☰ ☰ 🔤 Check spelling Inserts   ▼ ⓘ

Sony Handycam DCR-SR100

30 GB Hard Disk Drive (HDD) Camcorder

RETAIL: $450

No more tapes, no more hassle, just pick it up and go!

30GB Hard Drive - No need for tapes, DVDs, Mini DVs, etc.

3 megapixel digital camera built in - go on vacation with one less electronics item!

1lb 6oz lightweight design - goes anywhere you go.

USB 2.0 interface - no more hassle with converters. Just download the video to your computer as easily as you do pictures from your digital camera.

🔍 Preview | Save draft

Figure 17.1

If you happen to be fluent with HTML and you feel like showing off, you can click HTML and type the HTML yourself. But honestly, why do the legwork when there is an HTML editor to do it for you?

Shark in the Water

Be careful to choose colors that have contrast with the screen. If you're not using a template, then you're looking for contrast with a white background. However, if you do choose a template from the listing designer, you must make sure the text is easy to read with whatever background color the template uses.

I like to use the font size and color options to make certain parts of my auction stand out (like the one-line hooks and headings). I use 18-point text for my main headings, 14-point text for one-line hooks, and 12-point text for the rest of the auction.

The only time I change this is when I'm selling an item that has an obvious color scheme to it. For example, when I sell baby girl clothes, I usually use dark pink for the titles instead of red, and I use a brighter blue for the accenting text.

It's very easy to go over the top with the options available in the HTML editor. Resist the temptation to add multicolored type in the same word, strange fonts, changing fonts throughout the description, all caps for anything but the title, or symbols like "SAVE BIG $$$$." It may stand out, but it's not giving the impression you want to your buyers.

I only center align the first titles and the one-line hooks. All other headings and text are left aligned. This makes it more professional and easier to read.

Now let's get started writing the description for the camcorder.

But I'm No Shakespeare!

You don't have to be a professional writer to write professionally. Use full sentences and good grammar, spell check your work, be clear and concise, and think about how you would persuade someone to buy this item if you were standing in front of them. Now you're in the right frame of mind to start.

The first thing a buyer does when clicking on an auction is look at the pictures and details in the item summary at the top of the page. You need to convince buyers to look further down to see your description. I start at the top of the page with the name of the item, the retail cost, and a one-line hook about the item all in dark red, bold, 18-point text.

The first one-line hook has to be the single best thing about your item. This sounds like it should be obvious, but it depends on your target buyer. For this camcorder, it could be that there are no tapes to buy or lose, or it could be that it has a digital camera built in, or that it is cheaper than the top-of-the-line models but still has the relatively new technology features. It all depends on who you are selling to. So now is the time to think about your buyer. Answer questions like who he is, what he would use this item for, what he does for a living, how old he is, and so on.

Here are a few profiles for people who might be looking for a camcorder and why:

◆ A parent wants a durable (yet inexpensive) camcorder to film his kids, with an easy way to transfer the video files.

◆ A journalist wants a portable camcorder for interviews where there can't be a full camera crew but quality is important.

◆ A schoolteacher wants to document the classroom events and progress of her students.

◆ A techie "has" to have the newest gadget.

◆ A college student needs a camcorder to practice making speeches and presentations.

The price each is willing to pay really determines what we are focusing on. When this camcorder first came out, it was the newest technology (one of the first HDD camcorders) and it retailed at around $1,000. However, prices have since come down dramatically, and the brand-new models are selling for about $500. This model is selling on eBay for $200 to $350.

Of our potential buyers, the only one that I would exclude is the techie. This is too old of a model for him. This is not a new gadget, so he is not interested. However, all of the other buyers are still interested, perhaps more so because the price is much lower than for the newer models, without really sacrificing too much in features.

We have to try to appeal to all of them without excluding anyone. It shouldn't be too hard because all of them are looking for ease of use, good features, and a low price.

So now we know who we're looking for—let's reel them in. What phrases would entice these buyers to read more?

The biggest feature that sets this camcorder apart from the others on the market is its hard drive. This ties into the ease of use because there are no tapes to deal with. We've mentioned the size of the hard drive in the listing title and the benefit of it in the subtitle, but it doesn't hurt to reiterate it here. So our first one-line hook is this:

"No more tapes, no more hassle. Just pick it up and go!"

Features and Benefits

In this part of the description, you really need to think about your item, so it helps to have it in front of you. It doesn't matter what the item is—there are always some *features* and *benefits*.

def•i•ni•tion

A **feature** is a physical aspect of the item. A **benefit** describes what that feature does for you. "Built-in hard drive" is a feature. "No more tapes to lose" is a benefit.

Quite often you will see auctions that list only the features. That assumes that the buyer knows that he wants the item and needs no convincing. Your aim is to use the benefits to persuade the buyer to click **Place bid.**

In my auctions, I put the features in dark blue and bold so someone scanning to look for the features of the item can see them easily, and then I add the benefits next to the features in black.

Here are the features and benefits for the camcorder auction. In each sentence, the text in bold before the dash (–) is a feature. Everything after it is the benefit.

30GB hard drive – No tapes, DVDs, Mini DVs, etc.

3-megapixel digital still camera built in – Go on vacation with one less electronic item!

USB 2.0 interface – No more hassle with converters. Just download the video to your computer as easily as pictures from your digital camera.

1lb 6oz lightweight design – Goes anywhere you go.

2.7" swivel touch-screen LCD display – Compose and take family photos without dashing back and forth to the camera (remote control takes the picture for you, too).

One-touch burn to DVD – For when you need to make a copy immediately.

Dolby Digital surround sound recording – The high-quality sound you want to go with your videos.

10x optical zoom – Zoom in to get that real-life video of the kids without them playing up to the camera.

Steadyshot picture stabilizer – Even if your hand is a little shaky, your pictures won't be (great for taking video/photos from the car or chasing after the kids).

Congratulations. You've now written the bulk of the auction. That wasn't so painful, was it? You will need some more one-line hooks for between your sections, but most of the rest of it doesn't take much thought.

Before our next section (the bulleted list of included items), we need another one-line hook. I like to center align and make it bold:

The hottest camcorder technology for half the current retail price

These hooks appeal directly to the parent and teacher, who want a wise investment that will last a long time.

Okay, now on to the bulleted list. This is very easy because it is simply what is included in the auction. In our case, it is the following items:

- Camcorder
- AC adapter
- Rechargeable battery pack
- Remote control
- USB cable
- BONUS: AV connection cable
- BONUS: Samsonite camera bag

Your list may be longer or shorter, depending on your item. I marked the two extra items as bonuses to identify them as items that they won't get as standard from every seller of this item. Buyers love bonuses, so try to include one if you can.

If your item has any flaw, now is the time to explain it. Snags, stains, or pilling on clothes, scratches on metal or plastic, chips on china; whatever the flaw you must describe it fully. You should also show a photograph of the flaw. If the buyer files a Not As Described claim against you once they receive the item, showing eBay that you displayed a picture of the flaw in your item description goes a long way to helping you dispute the claim.

Next, let's close the sale. This time we'll ask for the bid and use a special-offer hook. You don't have to do this, but on an expensive item like a camcorder, it's worth it:

> **Don't lose out to a sniper. Use Buy It Now and get free Priority Mail shipping!**

We are asking for the bidder to take some action now, and giving him an incentive to do so. Make sure your Buy It Now price covers the priority shipping for you to make this worthwhile.

Now on to the final two sections: Payment Terms and Shipping Terms. There are separate sections for these in the Sell Your Item form, but I like to put them into the listing description, too. On the listing page, these are shown on a separate tab from the rest of the description, so it's worth including it in the description to get it onto both pages. I get fewer questions about payments and shipping by doing this.

Be sure to spell out your options and requirements very clearly so there's no ambiguity. I accept only PayPal because I don't feel the need to offer the alternative options eBay allows. Whatever policy you choose, spell it out clearly.

Here is the payment information for our auction. The heading would be in 18-point, bold, dark red text, like the other main titles.

PAYMENT TERMS

I only accept PayPal.

Payment must be received within three days of the auction ending.

I ship the next business day following cleared payment.

Next are the shipping terms. I list the actual rates in the Shipping box in the Sell Your Item form, but I spell out the terms in the item description.

SHIPPING TERMS

I combine shipping, so please check my <u>other items</u> to save some money on shipping. Insurance is included.

Your item will be shipped the next business day after your payment clears.

International Buyers—Please Note:

♦ Import duties, taxes, and charges are not included in the item price or shipping charges. These charges are the buyer's responsibility.

♦ Please check with your country's Customs office to determine what these additional costs will be prior to bidding/buying.

♦ I do not mark items as "gift" or understate the value, as this is illegal, so please don't ask me to.

The first two bullets in the International Buyers section come straight from eBay. If you allow international buyers, you must include these two bullets (or something very similar) in text no smaller than the main text of your listing description.

You do this for two reasons. First, it informs the buyer so there are no surprises. Second, if you receive a negative or neutral feedback from a buyer that mentions something like "extra shipping" or "had to pay Customs fees," eBay will remove that feedback comment and its impact on your Feedback Score and Rating.

In the first line of the shipping terms, the words "other items" are a link to my other items listed on eBay. To get this in your auction, go to the **Inserts** drop-down menu at the top of the HTML editor and select **Seller's Other Items.** This inserts a line in your auction that says "Check out my <u>other items</u>!" All you need to do is delete the words around the "other items" link and add your own text.

I always end my auctions with a line that says "Good luck and happy bidding!" You can use any sign-off you like, but it should be something short, polite, and encouraging.

Well, that's it! Congratulations, you've written your first auction description!

Listing Designer

For an additional 10¢ (30¢ for 30-day fixed-price listings), Listing Designer allows you to change the "theme" (background and border around the text) in your auction. Depending on your choice of theme, this can make your auction look catchy or cringe-worthy. There are some really gaudy borders, so make sure you preview your auction with the theme before you list it. (See Figure 17.2.)

Figure 17.2

Use the drop-down menu to change the theme.

If you can find a theme that works with the majority of your items, you'll find that helps you build your brand. We show you how to upsell and cross-sell in Chapter 22.

For this to be successful, you'll want to have the same look and feel in your auctions. Otherwise, buyers might think they are dealing with an entirely different seller.

If you do end up using an auction-management service, you will usually find a free listing designer as part of your subscription.

Tracking Your Traffic

It's really important to know how many people are looking at your listing. If you're not getting hits (visits) to your auction, then you know something is wrong with your title, thumbnail picture, and/or starting price. If you're getting hits but no bids, there's something wrong with your description, you need better additional pictures, or your shipping price is too high.

The only way you will know how many people visit your auction is by using a visitor counter. This is a free addition that displays at the very bottom of your auction. You can choose the basic style, the retro-computer style, or a hidden counter. The hidden counter is sometimes useful because it means only you can see the number of visitors; however, I usually find that it is more hassle than it's worth, so I stick with the basic counter.

The Least You Need to Know

◆ Use full, clear, and concise sentences. Always check your spelling and grammar.

◆ Think like your buyer. If you were the target audience, what information would you want included?

◆ Write about benefits, not just features.

◆ Use the HTML editor to make your auction description look appealing, but don't go crazy and make it look gaudy.

◆ Spell out your payment and shipping terms very clearly.

◆ Always link to your other items to help get cross-sales.

Chapter **18**

Choosing Your Listing Type

In This Chapter

- ◆ Types of listings and when to use them
- ◆ Additional options for auction-style listings
- ◆ Minimizing eBay fees using multiple-item fixed-price listings
- ◆ When choice is important

eBay offers a number of different listing options and styles. We've talked about them from a buyer's perspective, but each one has different advantages for the seller.

Types of Listing

If you have some idea of what an item is worth but you don't want to put a fixed price on it, you should use an auction-style listing.

This is the default when you use the Sell Your Item form and is particularly useful when you're selling art, antiques, or collectible items. Dealers and collectors often search eBay for valuable items that are underpriced. As long as you set a reserve for the minimum price you want to get for it, you might be surprised by how high the bidding goes.

> **I Remember When ...**
>
> I recall one lady who had a piece of art for sale. She didn't realize it was from a very famous artist. Her starting price was around $100. It sold for over $10,000 because two collectors got into a bidding war for it. If she had set it up as a fixed-price listing or an online auction with Buy It Now, the first of the collectors to see it would have snapped it up for a fraction of its worth and the seller would have been none the wiser.

The first five auctions you list per month have no Insertion fee and a flat-rate 8.75 percent Final Value fee. Although this sounds great, the flat-rate 8.75 percent Final Value fee means midpriced items ($25–$500) that you start at a low price may end up costing you more in fees.

Let's use the camcorder as an example. We list it at a starting price of $99 and it sells for $250. If it is one of our first five auctions of the month, there is no Insertion fee, and the Final Value fee is $20 (this is the maximum for the first five Final Value fee). So the eBay fees total $20.

Now let's say it's our sixth auction. The Insertion fee for a $99 start price is $2. But here's where it changes: the Final Value fee (using the tiered pricing shown in Chapter 14) is only $10.06. So, in this example, the eBay fees total $12.06. That's almost $8 different.

So the best items to list in your first five are items that will sell for under $25 or over $500, or that you don't know if will sell in two tries. The lack of Insertion fee means you're not paying to relist the item if it takes three or four tries to sell it.

You can easily see the price difference using www.ebcalc.com. Enter your starting and projected final prices and then look at the eBay fees with the Free Insertion Fees box checked (if it's a first five auction) and unchecked (if it's sixth or more).

This can help you decide what order to list your items to get the full benefit from the first five auction rule.

Lot Auction

Selling similar items in a group often gets you a higher average price for the items than selling them individually. It also means you pay eBay fees and upgrades on only one item, not on each item in the lot.

I find that children's clothing sell far better in lots than individually. It also gives me the opportunity to combine items that aren't quite as desirable in a lot with a really desirable item. Buyers will still pay more for the lot because there are more items, even if they wouldn't normally have bid on each item in the lot individually.

Let's say you have four two-piece Carter's outfits in the same size. You might expect to list them for $4 each. If you sold them individually (and the items sold for your starting bid), your eBay fees would be as follows:

Total selling price	$16
Total Insertion fees	$1.40
Total Final Value fees	$1.40
PayPal fees	$1.68
Total fees	$4.48
Profit	$11.52

The eBay fees eat up almost a third of the profit for the items when selling them individually. Plus, most buyers don't want to pay another $2 to $3 for shipping on an item that costs them only $4.

Yes, you could use these as part of your first five auctions of the month, and that would be a great use of your first five auctions if these items are desirable enough to sell individually. The total fees (if it were a first five auction) would be reduced by $1.40 because there would be no Insertion fee. The price is under $25, so the Final Value fee is no different (all items under $25 are charged a Final Value fee of 8.75 percent). So the total fees would be reduced to $3.08, giving you a profit of $12.92. Still, we can do better than that.

Let's look at it again, but this time let's sell the items as a lot. Statistically, lots get higher bids, but for the purposes of this example, assume that the lot sells for the same price as the individual items ($16) and that this was also the starting price.

Total selling price	$16
Total Insertion fees	55¢
Total Final Value fees	$1.40
PayPal fees	$0.76
Total fees	$2.71
Profit	$13.29

Tips

See all of the eBay fee tables in Chapter 14 or go to www. ebcalc.com if you need help calculating your fees.

Now if this were a first five auction, not only would it take up just one of your five auctions instead of four of them (if they were sold individually), the fee would be 55 cents less, so total profit would be $13.79. That's $2.27 more than selling the items individually. That doesn't sound like much, but it's almost 20 percent more than the individual sales, with far less effort in listing and shipping.

You could also increase the value by adding items that you wouldn't be able to sell individually (such as onesies) to increase the total value of the lot. If you added four onesies, your lot size just jumped to 12 items. Buyers will pay more for lots with more items.

Another reason for selling in a lot is the ability to use multiple keywords. Let's say the lot of clothing has items made by Oshkosh, Carter's, Gymboree, and Old Navy. Because the auction includes items made by each of these brands, you can use all of the brand names in your auction title. This means anyone searching for any of those individual brands will see your auction. That helps get your auction in front of more potential buyers.

You can sell pretty much anything in a lot: a set of Starbucks mugs, chinaware, toys, books, clothes, really anything you can think of. If you don't have much time to devote to selling on eBay, or individually your items may not be incredibly desirable, you will do much better by selling in lots, provided that the items complement each other.

Buy It Now

For a small fee, you can add a Buy It Now price to an auction. This must be at least 10 percent higher than the starting price. Don't confuse this with a fixed-price listing where there is only the Buy It Now price. (I cover those in a moment.)

Tips

Many sellers offer incentives to buyers who choose to use the Buy It Now option. That can be a discount on shipping, a shipping service upgrade, a free bonus, or something like that.

If the first bidder chooses to use the Buy It Now option, the auction ends immediately and that bidder wins the item. If the bidder chooses to place the starting bid instead, the Buy It Now option usually disappears and no future bidders will know it was ever there.

The Buy It Now option doesn't disappear upon receiving the first bid if you have a reserve price set on the auction. If so, the Buy It Now option remains active until bidding reaches the reserve price.

In some categories, the Buy It Now price may remain either until the bidding reaches a certain percentage of the Buy It Now or reserve price, or until only 12 hours remain on the auction. This is still a new feature that eBay is testing, so watch the Announcements board for updates.

Fixed-Price Listing

Fixed-price listings aren't auctions. They don't have a starting price; they have only a fixed selling price. That makes them far more similar to selling on a website or other nonauction venue. The listing ends when the item sells. Once someone buys the item, the buyer can pay immediately and you can ship the item. This is a good way to sell items near the holidays, when people want to get them quickly.

The fees for fixed-price listings are simple for Insertion fees and very complicated for Final Value fees (based on what category your item was listed in).

See Chapter 14 for more information on fixed-price listing fees.

The big difference between a fixed-price listing and an auction is that auctions can run for a maximum of 10 days (and you pay extra for that option). Fixed-price listings can run for the same durations as auctions, or for 30 days. This can make these listings a far more cost-effective option.

In addition, if a buyer sees a fixed-price listing with 25 days to go, but only one item available, she is more likely to purchase it over an auction for the same item with 6 days remaining on the auction. This is because the auction has a guaranteed 6 days remaining for her to think about it. Often during that time, she'll forget about it, or find something else that ends sooner. Even if there is a Buy It Now price, usually a buyer will "watch" the item rather than buy it immediately. That is because she has a chance of getting it for lower through the bidding option.

With fixed-price listings, there is no bidding. Therefore, anyone can swoop in and buy the item out from under her. She knows the price is not going to change, so if it's acceptable to her, she's more likely to go ahead and purchase, no matter how much time is remaining for the listing.

Best Offer

Best Offer is only available on fixed-price listings, and allows you to haggle with your buyers. This can be a lot of fun, but it can also be a little time-consuming if you don't use the automated options.

The buyer enters an offer lower than your fixed Buy It Now price. You can accept it, reject it, or counter it with an offer higher than the buyer's original offer but lower than your Buy It Now price. You go back and forth until either one of you accepts the offer or the offer expires.

Until you or the buyer accepts the offer, the buyer is under no obligation to purchase the item from you, so if he gets bored or sees it elsewhere, you could lose your buyer.

Reviewing, countering, accepting, and rejecting offers takes time. The good news is that eBay allows you to automate a lot of this. You can set your preferences to automatically accept an offer above a certain amount and automatically reject an offer below a certain amount. This protects you from low-ball offers.

Best Offer is a really good way to build a relationship with your buyer and prevent them from forgetting about your auction or looking elsewhere. It can help get repeat business, too.

If you are going to use Best Offer, you must be prepared to do a few things to be successful:

♦ Be near your computer and check your e-mail at least twice a day to see whether an offer has been placed on one of your items.

I Remember When …

I bought a sweater from a seller who said in her listings that she really liked to haggle. So I decided to give it a try. We went back and forth and settled on a price. It was a lot of fun, even though we were bartering only 50¢ up or down. I had so much fun that I added her to my favorite sellers immediately after the auction.

♦ Once you get an offer, expect to be at your computer until the haggling is done. Nothing is worse than making a counteroffer and having to wait until the following day to get a response from the seller.

♦ Make it fun! The more fun buyers have, the more likely they will buy from you again.

The listing page shows how many offers have been made on the item. This tells other potential buyers that if they want it, they'd better use Buy It Now quickly or the item will be gone.

If you're using Best Offer, you should set your Buy It Now price a bit higher than you expect to get for the item so you can plan for haggling down a bit. Buyers do not like it when they put an offer in and the seller counters only a couple of dollars below the Buy It Now price.

Multiple-Item Fixed-Price Listing

If you have more than one of the same item (maybe in a different size or color, but otherwise in identical condition), you can sell in a multiple-item fixed-price listing (yes, I know, that's a mouthful).

You simply select the quantity you have, and then each person who clicks Buy It Now is given the opportunity to select how many they want to purchase.

If it's a "choice" listing, in which they select size or color, the buyer uses the drop-down menus on the listing page to select color and size before clicking Buy It Now. If not, the buyer simply selects how many of the same item they want to purchase on the Buy It Now confirmation screen.

So if you have five items available in the same listing, you could potentially have five different buyers. As soon as a buyer clicks Buy It Now, he can pay and you can ship the item. The listing continues until either the duration ends or all of your items have sold.

Here's the great thing about multiple-item fixed-price listings: you pay only one Insertion fee. So it doesn't matter if you're selling 1 or 100 items within the listing— you pay the same amount.

You pay Final Value fees only on the items that sell, so it's in your best interest to list as many as you have so the listing stays active for as long as possible.

Final Value fees for fixed-price listings vary by category, so take that into account when you set your price. The difference can be quite significant.

eBay's Best Match search results order includes a variety of auctions and fixed-price listings, so you're not penalized for having a 30-day listing. In fact, you will be "raised" in the Best Match search order (that is, your listing will show up nearer the top) whenever your multiple-item fixed-price listing gets a sale.

The Least You Need to Know

◆ Selling items in lots can save you a significant amount of money in eBay fees.

◆ Best Offer is a fun way to build a relationship with buyers and get them to add you to their favorite sellers.

◆ You can sell the same item in different sizes, colors, and so on within the same multiple-item fixed-price listing.

◆ You pay only one Insertion fee for fixed-price listings, no matter how many items are for sale within it.

◆ Items in a multiple-item fixed-price listing sell for a fixed amount to all buyers. The listing ends when there are no more items for sale or the duration ends.

Chapter 19

Choosing the Listing Details

In This Chapter

- Setting a starting price, reserve price, and Buy It Now price
- The best (and worst) days and times to list your auction
- Flat-rate shipping versus calculated shipping
- How free shipping can actually make you money
- Automating the in-state sales tax calculations for your buyers
- Choosing your return policy details
- Automatically blocking buyers you don't want bidding

These little details can make or break your listing. You can write the best description in the world, but if the starting price is too high or you list it on a bad day, who's going to look at it? You must also learn how to balance your shipping fee so you don't lose money but, at the same time, make buyers feel they aren't being gouged. In this chapter, we walk through how to make good choices for each of these options.

Selling Format

In Chapter 18, we talked about the different types of listing. Here is where you select that choice. The default shows the **Online Auction** tab (see Figure 19.1). You'll see different price options: starting price, Buy It Now price, and an option to select a reserve price. The only required field is the starting price. The other two options incur fees (see Chapter 14 for specifics) but are often worth it.

If this would be one of your first five auctions of the month, you will see a line stating **Enjoy a $0.00 Insertion Fee when you list your item as an auction** at the top of this section. This lets you know that if you use an auction-format, you will be subject to the first five auction fees (no Insertion fee, but an 8.75 percent Final Value fee on the total selling amount). This is good for items expected to sell for under $25 or over $500, but not so great in the middle.

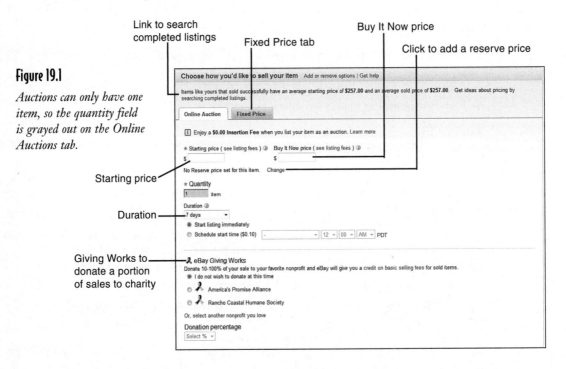

Figure 19.1

Auctions can only have one item, so the quantity field is grayed out on the Online Auctions tab.

First, let's look at the starting price. You should have an idea of the average selling price from your item research. However, it's always worth double-checking with the most recent Completed Listings before selling your item.

At the top of the section you'll see an average starting price and average selling price for items like yours. Don't use this. eBay only looks at items that have similar keywords to yours. For example, for the camcorder, it includes auctions for batteries, cases, and so on, not just the camcorder unit itself. That skews the results. At the top of this section there is also a link to **Get ideas about pricing by searching completed listings** (see Figure 19.1). This link will let you look at the completed listings yourself. So you can look for listings with an identical bundle of products to yours, or adjust your price accordingly. Buyers will always pay more when there are more accessories included.

This is where a service like Hammertap comes in handy. Instead of having to search through all of the auctions and write down the prices from comparable listings, Hammertap lets you filter the results by excluding any individual auction you want (see Figure 19.2). Just uncheck the box next to any auction that doesn't match your own item because of the condition, options, and so on. Then click **Filter This Report,** and you can look at the reports based on only the auctions you want.

You can also prevent lower-priced items (such as accessories for that product) from skewing the results by looking only for items within a certain price range. For example, if you set your price range at $50 minimum, you can get a better idea of what the camera you are selling actually sold for.

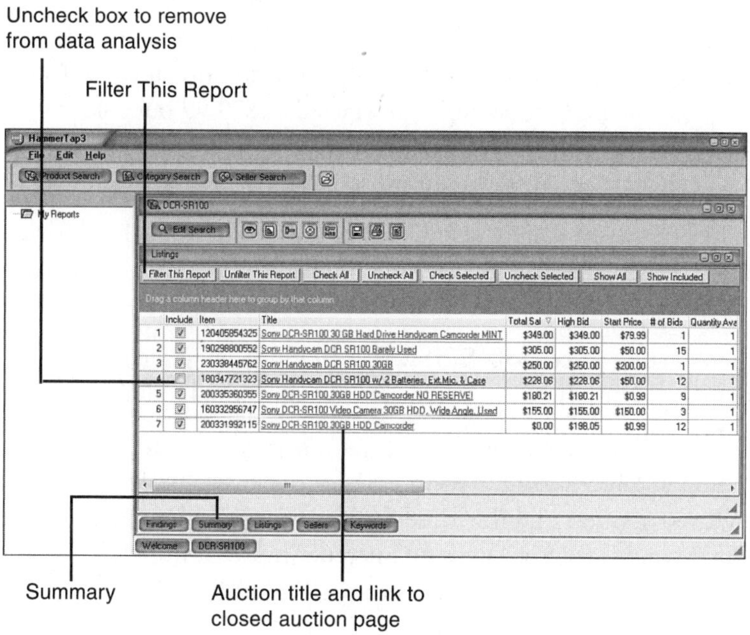

Uncheck box to remove
from data analysis

Filter This Report

Figure 19.2

Get a 10-day free trial of Hammertap and reduced monthly rate at www. hammertap.com/skip.

Summary

Auction title and link to
closed auction page

Now, again, you can find all of this information by looking at the successful auctions in Completed Listings if you don't want to spend the money for Hammertap, but if you have a number of items to list, this will save you hours of boring work. After filtering the report to exclude the irrelevant auctions, you are taken back to the **Summary** page. From here you can see the full results, but Hammertap makes it even easier for you. You can click on questions in the center, such as **What Day Should I End My Listing?** Clicking on this shows you each day, how many items sold on that day, and the average selling price. Using these links, I determined the following about our camcorder auction:

Average selling price	$247.84
Best starting price	$0.01–$99.99
Best start day	Saturday
Best end day	Tuesday
Best duration	3 days
Features that increased the price	Bold, Buy It Now

That's a lot of information for only five minutes' work!

For the starting price, the Hammertap summary shows you only a range. Go back to the actual **Listings** page (see Figure 19.1) and take a look at the additional columns to see the actual starting prices. The highest-selling item started at $79.99 but sold for $349 with the Buy It Now option. The second-highest started at $50. It had 15 bids and made it to $305. The third started at $200 and made it only to $250.

The seller who started the bidding at $200 not only realized a $50 lower selling price, with only 2 bids, but also paid an Insertion fee that was almost double what the other very successful sellers paid.

This tells me that a lower starting price ($50–$75) with a Buy It Now price and a reserve price (to ensure that the Buy It Now option remains until the bidding is over $200 or $250) is the best option.

I'm going to list the auction at $49.99 so I'll pay only $1 for my Insertion fee. Listing at $50 would double my Insertion fee, and if I listed for the average selling price ($257) suggested by eBay, I would pay $3. That's 300 percent more.

Reserve Price

There's one established fact on eBay: lower starting prices attract more (and earlier) bids. In general, a low starting bid will increase your chances of success. Because I am using a comparatively low starting price, I want to protect myself with a reserve. If the bidding doesn't reach the price I set, then I am not under any obligation to sell the item to the highest bidder. I can offer it to him if I want to (using a Second Chance Offer), but I don't have to.

 Tips

If you're selling a fairly cheap item, it's not worth paying the fees for a reserve price. But when it's an expensive item, like our camcorder, it is very important. Having a reserve price has the added bonus of keeping the Buy It Now price available for longer.

When setting your reserve price, consider both the average selling price and what you want to get for the item. Be realistic, though. At the end of the day, your objective is to sell the item, so don't list a ridiculously high reserve price. You won't end up with a bidding war at the end of your auction if the reserve has still not been met.

Buyers expect to see reserve prices on expensive items, but not on cheap ones. Most buyers prefer auctions with no reserve, but that is more risky for you. On expensive items, I recommend that you always use a reserve. On less expensive items, use your discretion to weigh the risk versus your expected selling price. The more popular an item is, the less risk you take by not using a reserve. Hot-selling items usually get enough bids to end up selling at their true value. Slower-selling items or obscure goods that have a limited market can be very risky to start at a low price without a reserve.

Most buyers bid in whole increments ($15, $50, $200, $325, and so on), so it's wise to list your reserve price just below one of those increments. If you want to set your reserve at $700, instead set it at $689; instead of $75, use $68. Once someone meets the reserve, the real bidding begins. For our auction, we know the average selling price is $247, so let's list our reserve at $199 (that way, we catch the $200 bidders as well).

To add a reserve, click **Change** next to **No Reserve price set for this item** and enter your reserve price. Remember: the fee for adding a reserve price is nonrefundable.

Buy It Now Price

You don't have to set a Buy It Now price. If you choose to, it will cost you between 5¢ and 25¢, depending on the price you set (see Chapter 14 for exact amounts).

If the first bidder chooses to place the starting bid instead of using the Buy It Now option, the auction usually reverts to a standard auction and the Buy It Now price disappears (unless there is a reserve price on the auction). Just like the reserve price fee, the fee to add a Buy It Now price is nonrefundable, whether or not the buyer uses it.

When you are setting your Buy It Now price, you should always set it significantly higher than your starting price; otherwise, there is really no point. eBay requires the Buy It Now price to be at least 10 percent higher than the starting price, but I recommend that you go higher and list it around the average selling price, or possibly a fraction higher.

Our average selling price is $247, but the most successful auctions were $300 to $350. Our Buy It Now price will be $297.70 because it's between the average and the top prices, and pricing it just below $300 makes it more desirable. It's also well below the retail cost for a newer model, so the buyer is assured that he is getting a good deal.

By pricing it a little lower, any buyer using Completed Listings to research prices will see our item as a good deal.

Tips

> Before you finalize your Buy It Now price, go to www.Amazon.com and see what the price is there. Marketplace sellers on Amazon are often very competitive with eBay. You don't want to be charging $10 more than a seller on Amazon, because a lot of buyers check both sites. Also take shipping into account on both sites—buyers certainly will.

Using $297.70 rather than $299.99 for the Buy It Now price may seem a little pointless, but there is a logic to it. Buyers will always see $299.99 as $300 because of retail store prices. $297.70 is only $2.19 lower, but it seems much lower because it's not a common price point. So you are more likely to get the buyer over another seller who priced his item at $299.99.

One tactic that can really attract sellers to use the Buy It Now price is offering free shipping. I simply add the shipping cost to my desired Buy It Now price, and I add another 50¢ to pay for the subtitle. Then I say "Free U.S. shipping with Buy It Now" in the subtitle. I started doing this about two years ago and saw a 20 percent increase in my Buy It Now sales. I talk a little more about free shipping in a moment.

Fixed-Price Listing

People are often confused about the difference between a Buy It Now auction and a fixed-price listing. Buyers can make an instant purchase on either listing type, but a fixed-price listing does not have an additional bidding option. The Buy It Now price is the only option. The buyer either buys it for that price or doesn't.

If you want to sell in a fixed-price format, click the **Fixed Price** tab (see Figure 19.3). The only amount you need to enter here is the Buy It Now price. Use the same reasoning as you do for a Buy It Now option in an auction to determine the price you set. You can also use the free shipping tactic to increase your fixed-price sales.

If you have easy access to your computer, consider using Best Offer. If you want to use this option, set your Buy It Now price a little higher to allow for haggling down with your buyer. That way, she feels like she got a deal and you don't actually lose any money.

If you select the **Best Offer** box, you will be given an opportunity to enter an amount that you want to be automatically accepted and an amount to automatically reject below. So I might set it to automatically accept an offer at $275 or higher, and automatically reject anything below $245. I will still receive notification of offers submitted with a Best Offer of $246 to $274 for my own review.

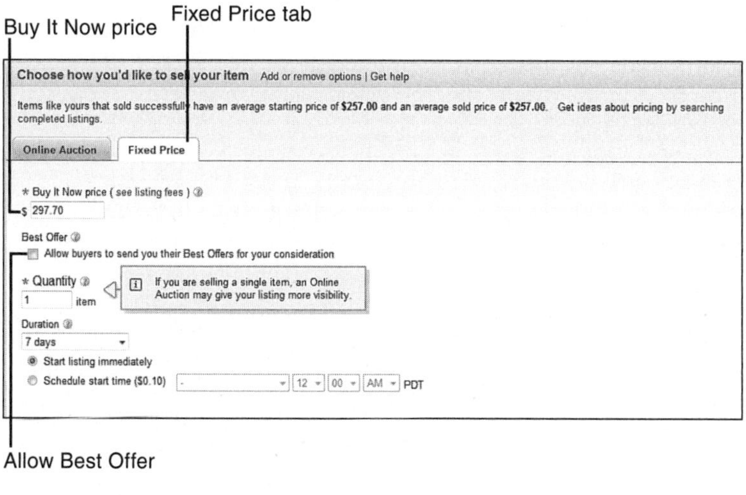

Buy It Now price   Fixed Price tab

Figure 19.3

Giving your buyer the option of Best Offer can get your item sold more quickly.

Allow Best Offer

More Selling Specifics

Whether you use an auction or fixed-price listing, the next options are the same. First up is the duration.

Duration

Your options are 1, 3, 5, 7, or 10 days for auctions, and 3, 5, 7, 10, or 30 days for fixed-price listings. You also have a Good 'Til Cancelled option for fixed-price listings. This automatically renews your listing every 30 days until all of the items are sold.

I usually stick to the five- or seven-day auctions unless my research clearly shows that a different duration is better. One-day auctions are too short unless it is time critical, such as tickets for an upcoming event, or a gift item in the last 10 days before Christmas. Three-day auctions are okay but don't always catch as many bidders. If you're selling a lot of items, three-day auctions will help you turn your inventory much quicker. But if you're not running a business, the five- or seven-day auctions work best. Ten days is usually too long for an auction, plus you pay extra for a 10-day auction, although this option is free for fixed-price listings.

If you're selling a single item at a fixed price, I recommend using a 7- or 10-day listing. If you're selling multiple quantities, use a 30-day duration. You will pay more in the listing upgrade fees for a 30-day listing, but once you've gotten your first sale, subsequent ones come a lot easier. You may as well get your money's worth and use the 30-day option.

We know from our research that the highest prices were realized by three-day auctions, but there were only a few results to base that on. I would rather play it safe and go with the standard seven-day auction, to make sure we reach all the business buyers and teachers who may be looking midweek as well as on the weekend.

Scheduled Start

This is one of those options that eBay charges for, but the charge is so little that it's worth it almost every time. For only 10¢, your auction will be listed for you at whatever day and time you set.

Think about it: your research shows that Thursday afternoon between 6 P.M. and 7 P.M. is the best time to launch your auction. But then you get stuck in rush-hour traffic and don't get back home until after 8:30 P.M. Do you list it anyway at a nonoptimal time or wait another week? Unless you are sitting at your computer all day every day and never forget any appointments, I strongly recommend you use this option.

We know from our research that Tuesday between 6 P.M. and 7 P.M. is the best time to end the auction. So we can schedule our auction for the next Tuesday at this time. Don't forget that the times are all "eBay time," which is Pacific time, not your local time.

Your end day is more critical than your start day. It's really easy to work out your start day if you're using a seven-day auction, but if it's a three- or five-day auction, sometimes it can get confusing. Does it include the day you list, or is the following day the first day of the duration?

Here's a table to show you exactly which day your auction will end for each start day of the week.

Day of the Week Your Auction Will End, Based on Start Day and Duration

List Day	Auction Duration (in Days)				
	1	3	5	7	10
Monday	Tues.	Thurs.	Sat.	Mon.	Thurs.
Tuesday	Wed.	Fri.	Sun.	Tues.	Fri.
Wednesday	Thurs.	Sat.	Mon.	Wed.	Sat.
Thursday	Fri.	Sun.	Tues.	Thurs.	Sun.
Friday	Sat.	Mon.	Wed.	Fri.	Mon.
Saturday	Sun.	Tues.	Thurs.	Sat.	Tues.
Sunday	Mon.	Wed.	Fri.	Sun.	Wed.

Best and Worst Days to End Your Auction

It is interesting that Tuesday is considered the best day for ending our camcorder auction. This is because Tuesday isn't generally considered one of the best days to end an auction. Traditionally, these are the best and worst days to end an auction:

Monday	Excellent
Tuesday	Good
Wednesday	Fair
Thursday	Good
Friday	Poor
Saturday	Fair
Sunday	Excellent

Sunday and Monday evening between the hours of 4 P.M. and 7 P.M. (again, these are Pacific time) are statistically the highest periods of activity on eBay and have the highest sell-through rate. Monday during lunch hour is also excellent.

These are general statistics, and all products are different, which is why I wouldn't argue with Hammertap's results for our camcorder. But in general, I seem to do best ending my listings on Monday. Buyers who were searching over the weekend don't forget about the auction by Monday. This also catches all the people who are surfing from work, and even business owners, depending on the item you're selling.

Savvy buyers avoid the high-traffic times like Sunday and Monday evenings. It's important to consider your buyer profile to determine when your target buyer will likely be on the computer. Think back to when you wrote your item description and the buyers you targeted. For us, the parent looking for a camcorder will most likely be searching during the evening after 7 P.M. (after the kids are in bed) or during the day at work. The teacher will likely be looking in the evening after work.

This item could also appeal to business owners, so a midweek end day could be a benefit. We're going to stick with Tuesday at 7:30 P.M., so we put that into the **Scheduled start time** box and move on.

 Shark in the Water _____

When your auction is submitted, it goes into a queue for uploading. Be aware of scheduled maintenance times (check the Announcements boards) and also peak times. If a lot of items are being uploaded, it may take longer for yours to become active. So if you are looking at a window of 6 P.M. to 8 P.M. as the optimal time on a Sunday (peak day), go earlier rather than later. I would list at 6:30 P.M. because if it does hit at that time, it is not detrimental to my sales, but if it takes an extra hour to post, it's still within my optimal listing time window. If eBay is in scheduled maintenance when I want to list, I always have it list earlier rather than later. That way, there is a two- or three-hour gap between my item's ending time and another seller's.

eBay Giving Works

Giving Works is an eBay program that allows you to donate all (or a portion of) your auction proceeds to a recognized charity. You can select any nonprofit from within eBay's system (there are hundreds) and choose to donate anywhere from 10 to 100 percent of the proceeds to that charity ($1 minimum if the item sells). eBay credits back a portion of your eBay fees equal to the percentage you donated. So if you donate 30 percent to Breast Cancer Awareness, you receive 30 percent of the Insertion and Final Value fees back on your next statement.

There are two reasons for using Giving Works. One is the satisfaction you get from helping others and supporting your favorite charity. The other is that it can sometimes increase your sales. Statistically, Giving Works listings appeal slightly more to women than men and to people over the age of 50. So if you are targeting this segment, it may actually help your auction. And remember, the portion that goes to charity is tax deductible.

Tips

You have to sign up for MissionFish, the Giving Works provider, the first time you use the program. It's quick and easy to do; when you first select a nonprofit, it prompts you to sign up for MissionFish.

This is really helpful when you are selling a used item. Let's say you have an old pasta machine gathering dust in your garage. If you sell it at a garage sale, you might get $10 for it. You list it on eBay with a 50 percent donation to your favorite charity, and it sells for $40. You end up netting $20 (before fees) and you get to take a $20 charitable donation deduction on your taxes at the end of the year.

Payment Methods

In Chapter 12, we showed you how to set up your PayPal account for selling so that PayPal will automatically show up as your preferred payment option, as in Figure 19.4.

PayPal already included   Add or remove options

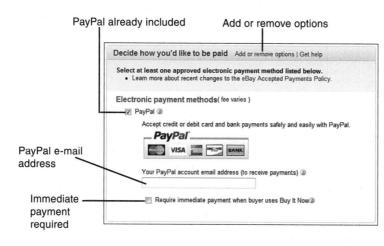

Figure 19.4

*Accept as many forms of payment as you can. If you want to accept another approved payment method, click **Add or remove options** and select the other methods.*

PayPal e-mail address

Immediate payment required

If you check the box below the e-mail address marked **Require immediate payment when buyer uses Buy It Now,** the buyer has to send a PayPal payment to you immediately after clicking Buy It Now. This prevents flaky buyers who click Buy It Now and then never pay. Most of the time it's not necessary, but if you're in a highly competitive category or you are on a time crunch to get the item shipped within a specific time frame, this might be worth using.

Shipping Information

eBay makes it very easy for you to calculate your shipping costs and add a handling fee, if you want.

Did You Know?
You can have up to three shipping options for domestic and three for international, but you don't have to use all three.

The default page shows only domestic shipping. As I mentioned at the beginning of the chapter, you have to click **Add or Remove Options** to get the international shipping options to display.

Make sure you are not undercharging if you use flat-rate shipping for all buyers. Use **Research rates** (see Figure 19.5) to decide what rates and services you want to offer.

Figure 19.5

Research Rates and the Shipping Wizard can help you determine your prices.

Select flat-rate or calculated shipping

Shipping Wizard

Research rates

Free shipping

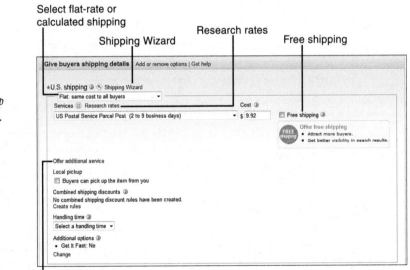

Offer additional service

Flat-Rate vs. Calculated Shipping

A flat-rate cost makes it easier for your buyers because they don't have to calculate anything. But calculated shipping is more accurate for you.

If the buyer is not signed in when they are looking at your auction, the calculated shipping to their zip code won't automatically display (on the search results page or in the listing). This can lose you a sale because there are plenty of other items with shipping costs that will display.

Flat-rate shipping rates display on the search results page right next to the current bid. I have tried it both ways, and I find I get more hits to my auction when I have a fixed shipping price.

Flat-Rate Shipping

Of course, the easiest way to do this is to use Priority Mail Flat-Rate boxes which are the same cost no matter where in the country you ship, and they are not weight specific, either. If it fits in the box, it ships for that rate.

The problem with this is that flat-rate boxes are often more expensive than regular Priority Mail. And some buyers would prefer the longer wait of Parcel Post for the lower price.

My advice is to use the **Research rates** link. Here you can get rates for a city far away from your location so you know you're not going to be charging too little. I'm in Washington State, so I calculate rates for New York City.

1. Click **Research rates.**

2. Select your **Estimated Weight** and **Package Size,** and click **Continue.**

3. Either add a destination zip code or use the **Sample rates** drop-down menu to select a major city. Click **Show Rates** when you've made your selection. This takes you to the rates page for both USPS and UPS (see Figure 19.6).

Make sure your zip code is correct. If not, click **Change** by **Seller's Zip Code** and change it.

You can add a handling fee by clicking **Change** beneath **Packaging and Handling Fee.** You can add a small amount, but don't make it obvious. This should be to cover your packaging and time taken for the post office run. A dollar or two is really the most I would use.

Figure 19.6

Both USPS and UPS rates display, but you don't have to offer services from both carriers.

Change destination zip code
for shipping cost calculation

Seller's Zip Code

Packaging and
Handling Fee

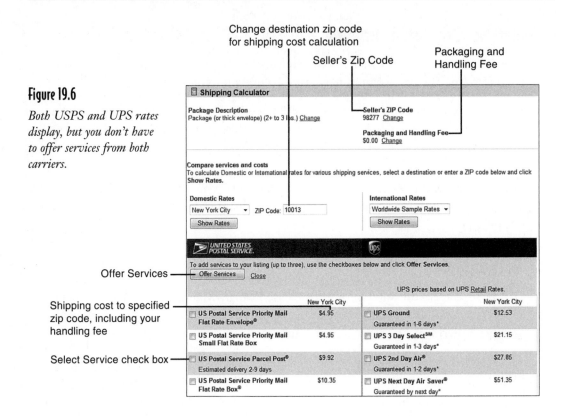

Offer Services

Shipping cost to specified
zip code, including your
handling fee

Select Service check box

If you are offering insurance, add the cost into your handling fee. You can't charge a buyer separately for insurance, so this is the only way you can include it in your fee to the buyer.

Tips

eBay sellers are responsible for packages until they reach the buyer—not just until they drop it off with the shipping carrier. Therefore, insurance is a good idea since you may have to refund a buyer if the shipping carrier loses the package.

Click **Show Rates** again after adding your handling fee, and the prices that display next to the service options will update to include your fee. Your buyers will not see the portion that is a handling fee—only the total cost.

Make your selections from UPS or the USPS or both, and click **Offer Services** when you're done. Remember, you can have only a total of three selections, so once you hit that maximum, all of the other options gray out.

I offer Parcel Post and Priority Mail as standard, and then around the holidays I also offer Express Mail (for those who have to get the item quickly).

Some categories have a restriction on shipping costs. For example, DVD listings must offer a shipping option at or under $3. If I'm selling in a media category that has this restriction (you will be prompted by eBay if you do), I also offer Media Mail. As long as you have one shipping option below $3, you can also offer additional options at higher costs.

Shark in the Water _____

Always list your cheapest shipping option first. This is the option that displays on the search results page and in the listing summary at the top of the listing page. If you enter your fastest (most expensive) option first, potential buyers will skip over your listing because they think you are gouging on shipping. They never see that you have cheaper options available.

Calculated Shipping

Calculated shipping requires the buyer to enter his zip code in the box provided on the **Shipping and Payments** tab. eBay then calculates the exact shipping cost to his location. If he is already signed in to eBay, it will show automatically.

To use calculated shipping, use the drop-down menu to select **Calculated: Cost varies by buyer location.** This changes the shipping section options (see Figure 19.7).

Select the package size and weight range, and then use the drop-down menus to select shipping services. You can use the Research Rates link to see what approximate costs will be.

Tips _____

You don't have to use the same option for both domestic and international shipping. You can choose to use flat-rate shipping on one and calculated shipping on the other, if you prefer.

Insurance and Tracking

You do not have to include insurance, but I recommend that you do. eBay holds sellers responsible for the item until it is received by the buyer. That means, if the carrier loses it in-transit or it gets damaged, you are responsible for replacing the item or refunding the buyer. For inexpensive items, it's not too much of a concern (items rarely get lost), but for more pricey items, it's worth including insurance in your handling fee and noting in your item description that the shipping cost includes insurance. You are not allowed to charge separately for insurance—it has to be included in the total cost shown to the buyer.

Figure 19.7

*Click **Change** to add a handling fee or any other options.*

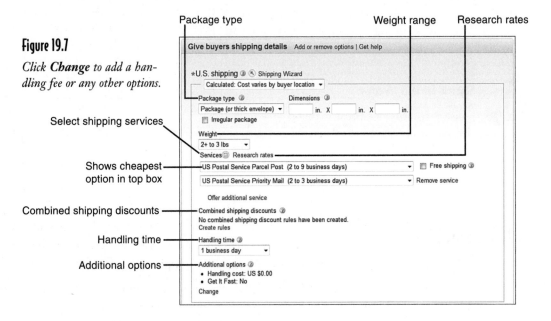

Package type   Weight range   Research rates

Select shipping services

Shows cheapest option in top box

Combined shipping discounts

Handling time

Additional options

Purchasing insurance from the USPS can be expensive, however there are some alternatives. If you use UPS to ship your items, $100 of insurance is automatically included. If you want to use the USPS, you can use a third-party insurer.

I use Shipsurance (www.shipsurance.com). This used to be called DSI (Discount Shipping Insurance)—they just changed the name. Here you can get a discounted rate for both USPS and UPS. The best deals are if you open an account with them and have a blanket policy to cover all of your items, but you can insure just one parcel at a time, if you prefer. The rates are significantly lower than you will find from the USPS.

There is a big difference between "tracking" and "delivery confirmation" and buyers get them confused all the time. Tracking means your parcel gets scanned throughout its journey to its destination. You can look online and see exactly where the item is while it is in-transit.

Delivery confirmation only confirms that the item has been delivered. It may be scanned when you drop it off with the USPS, and it may be scanned in-transit, but there is no guarantee that it will. The only time the USPS has to scan it is when the postal carrier delivers it.

Buyers get confused because eBay puts the "tracking number" in My eBay. This could be a tracking number or the delivery confirmation number. Buyers get worried when they don't see tracking information when they click the delivery confirmation number.

Delivery confirmation is free for Priority Mail and only a few cents for Parcel Post. Signature confirmation is more expensive, so make sure to include the cost for this option in your shipping and handling fee if you are selling an item over $250.

Shark in the Water

eBay requires delivery confirmation as proof that an item was actually received by your buyer in an Item Not Received claim. If the item sold for over $250, eBay requires signature confirmation. Make sure you include the required options to protect you in case of a buyer claim.

Free Shipping

There's a box next to the first shipment option for **Free Shipping.** If you offer a free service, always check this box. This ensures that it shows up if a buyer searches for auctions with free shipping (by checking the **Free Shipping** box in **Refine Search** on the search results page). It also flags your listing to eBay for Best Match promotion.

You don't currently have to specify the shipping service you use if you select flat-rate shipping. Most sellers who offer free shipping select **Standard Flat-Rate Shipping Service** as their shipping service. This could be anything. I prefer to specify what service I'm using. If I put Media Mail, the buyer knows it is going to take longer. You can offer a First Class or Parcel Post option for a fee, and many buyers will take that if they want the item quicker. This can prevent Item Not Received claims from being processed too early. eBay looks at your handling time and the projected delivery time based on the shipping carrier you used. If you put "Standard flat-rate shipping" they have nothing to go on.

You should include the cost of shipping in your starting or Buy It Now price if you're offering free shipping. I also find it useful to include a Priority Mail and sometimes Express Mail shipping option for those who want to get the item faster.

Tips

Listings that offer free shipping get a "raised" placement in the Best Match search order. Since most buyers don't realize they can change this default, it's important to do whatever you can to get higher in this sort order.

Free shipping also has the advantage of giving you good responses on your Detailed Seller Ratings. When the buyer leaves feedback for you, she is reminded that she got free shipping on this item. Usually that translates into a 5 star rating on the shipping and handling cost (at least it should!).

International Shipping and Customs

Filling out the international shipping rates involves the same process as with the domestic rates, except that you have to specify a country in addition to the service and cost. Make sure you research the rates for each country you ship to, because they are often wildly different.

Did You Know?

The USPS offers a flat-rate Priority Mail box service to international destinations. This is really useful if you're offering combined shipping. You can tell international buyers that they can buy more items from you and, as long as they all fit in the box (and do not total more than 20 lbs), the cost will not go up. This is a huge incentive for international buyers to buy more from you.

The current rates for a standard-size flat-rate box are $25.95 to Canada or Mexico, and $41.95 to all other countries.

Select **Choose custom location** from the **Ship to** drop-down menu to select country-specific rates. Just check the boxes next to the countries it applies to. If you're using calculated shipping, the rates will be calculated for your buyer.

If you're using flat-rate shipping, you will need to use the three options for the countries you're most likely to ship to (likely Canada, Australia, and United Kingdom). Select the other countries by checking the corresponding boxes in the **Additional ship to locations** section. If a buyer from one of these countries wants a shipping quote, he will need to contact you directly and you'll need to respond with the quote.

Did You Know?

eBay has announced (but not as of this writing implemented) an option to let you choose countries you do not want to ship to. So you could select Europe as a ship-to location, but exclude Italy. I anticipate this option will be with the ship-to locations.

Personally, I prefer flat-rate shipping for domestic parcels, and calculated shipping for international parcels. Remember, you can add a handling fee for international parcels if you want. I recommend that you do because you have to stand in line at the post office to hand over international parcels (which you don't have to do for domestic ones).

Again, Shipsurance offers international insurance options. I highly recommend insurance for all international shipments.

Combined Shipping Discounts

You can set up automatic shipping discounts for buyers who purchase more than one item from you, based on the item types and the shipping service. If you choose to automate this function, you set up one set of rules for flat-rate shipping and another set of rules for calculated shipping. For flat-rate listings, eBay charges the highest of the two costs and then adds an amount that you specify for each additional item, or deducts a specific amount from the subsequent items' shipping cost (depending on which option you set up). For calculated shipping, you can combine the item weights.

Once you set up a combined shipping rule, you get the option to add a hidden handling fee by item or by order.

This automation is useful for volume sellers, but when you're starting out, you only need to put it in your description that you offer combined shipping. That way, buyers can contact you to check the rate for two or more specific items. Rules tend to work better when you sell many items that are similar in size and weight.

Handling Time

You are required to set a handling time for your listing. This is the time from when you receive cleared payment from the buyer to when you actually mail the package.

In most cases, one or two business days is appropriate. Any more than that, and your Detailed Seller Ratings for Shipping Time will go down. The quicker you can get the item in the mail the better. If the buyer can see the tracking number in My eBay, he is less likely to e-mail you to ask if it has been shipped yet.

Item Location

The last part of the shipping section is your item location. The default shows your registered city, state, and zip code. You can change this to say something like "PowerSeller for seven years," but then your auction won't show up in a search by distance from the buyer's zip code. If you live in a small town, it's probably worth changing the location to the nearest large city. But if you're offering an item for pickup only, make sure your item location is exact so that buyers know where they will have to drive to.

If your item is located elsewhere, you need to list the *item's* location here, not your own. For example, if a friend asked you to list her collectible teapots but she's in Houston and you're in Chicago, you would list the item location as Houston. This is where the item will be shipped from.

Buyer Requirements and Return Policy

The last section on this page is titled **Other things you'd like buyers to know.**

First is your **Buyer requirements.** This automatically blocks bidders who have the characteristics you set up to block. You don't have to specify any buyer requirements, but I find that using them saves headaches.

Restricting bidders to only those in countries you ship to is a good idea because there's nothing worse than watching a bidding war between two buyers and then, after the auction ends, discovering that both live in countries you don't ship to. Now you have to make a decision to ship to that country, sell for the highest bid from a buyer within your ship-to countries, or relist the item.

Your buyer requirement options are to block buyers who have these characteristics (X refers to a drop-down menu numerical choice):

- Don't have a PayPal account.

- Have received X Unpaid item Strikes within X months.

- Are registered in countries to which I don't ship.

- Have X Policy violation reports in X months.

- Have a feedback score equal to or lower than X *(note that these options are all -1 or lower).*

- Have bid on or bought my items within the last 10 days and met my limit of X.

Click **Change buyer requirements** to select any blocks you want to use. These will apply to all future listings as well unless you change them again. In Chapter 21, I show you how to block individual buyers, and how to exempt an individual buyer from your Buyer Requirements, while keeping them in effect for all other bidders.

Return Policy

eBay requires all sellers to specify a returns policy. This can be as simple as "I do not accept returns," but you must include it.

Use the drop-down menu to select **Returns Accepted** or **Returns Not Accepted.** If you select **Returns Accepted,** you then get other options to complete. These include how long the buyer has to return the item (3, 7, 14, 30, or 60 days), who pays the return shipping (buyer or seller), and how the refund will be paid (money back, exchange, merchandise credit).

Allowing returns shows you have not intentionally misrepresented your item. You do have to be careful, though, because you can't guarantee the condition you will receive the returned item in.

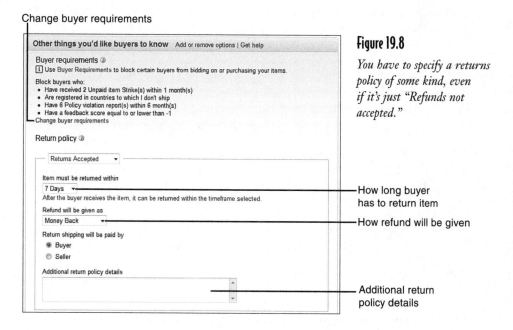

Figure 19.8

You have to specify a returns policy of some kind, even if it's just "Refunds not accepted."

It's up to you to decide who pays for the return shipping costs. My opinion is, if you sent the wrong item, or the listing misrepresented the item (accidentally or intentionally), you should pay the shipping both ways. However, if the buyer just didn't read the description, she should pay the shipping.

Shark in the Water _____

> Sometimes eBay will require you to accept a return if they find in favor of the buyer in an Item Not As Described claim. So just because you state no returns does not exempt you from this. A very clear description with photographs can usually prevent this from being a problem. If eBay does require a return, they determine who pays the shipping. Usually it is the buyer, though.

For my listings, I select **Buyer** from the **Return shipping will be paid by** options. But then I expand on this in the **Additional returns policy details** box and explain that if I made an error, I will pay the return shipping, but that all items must be received in the same condition they were sent for a refund to be issued. If the buyer is returning the item for any other reason, the buyer pays the return shipping, and the item must be received before a refund will be issued. That usually makes buyers pack it up properly.

Paying Taxes

If you sell to anyone within your state, you have to charge them sales tax at your local rate. If your state doesn't have sales tax, you can skip this section.

eBay doesn't make you specify a sales tax rate, but you are still required to charge (and pay) it for all in-state sales. You can have it automatically calculated as part of eBay Checkout, if you want. To do this, you need to add that option to the Sell Your Item form.

1. Go to the top of the **Other things you'd like buyers to know** section and click **Add or remove options** next to the section title.

2. Check the **Charge applicable sales tax to buyers** box and then click **Save.**

3. Now you'll see an option within this section that reads **Charge sales tax according to the sales tax table.** Check this box, and then click on the **View sales tax table** link beneath it (see Figure 19.9).

4. On the sales tax table, find your state and enter your local sales tax rate. You can also choose to charge sales tax on the shipping and handling as well as the purchase price. Some states require this, others don't. I buy my shipping supplies from out-of-state eBay sellers, so I don't pay sales tax on those, and my state doesn't require me to charge tax on shipping and handling so I don't.

5. Click **Save** once you've finished adding the sales tax rates. Now all of your list-ings will specify that sales tax is charged on purchases in the states you listed and the rate it is charged at for each state.

Charge sales tax according
to the sales tax table

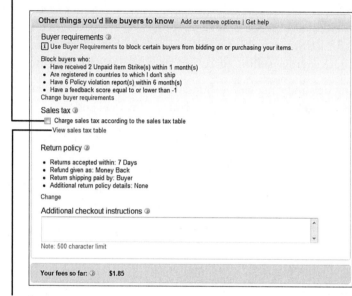

Figure 19.9

If you don't do this and you get an in-state sale, you still have to pay the sales tax even though you didn't charge it to the buyer.

View sales tax table

Did You Know?

The reason for a sales tax table is that many sellers have multiple locations. They may have warehouse locations in New York and California, as well as a retail location in Colorado. If this is the case, they have to charge sales tax to buyers located in any of these three states. The sales tax table allows the seller to specify all three rates and have it automatically calculated for their buyers. This saves the seller a lot of effort and also alerts buyers that they will pay tax on the purchase if they reside in one of these states, even if the item location on the listing page is not within their state.

At the end of each month/quarter, you cut the state a check for the total sales tax amount you collected. Any tax professional can show you how to do this for your state. You can often file it online and then mail the check.

There is a push towards an Internet sales tax in the works at the moment. If this becomes law, you will have to charge sales tax on all eBay sales.

That's it. You've finished completing the Sell Your Item form. So click **Continue** to look at the summary and upgrade options eBay recommends.

The Least You Need to Know

- ◆ Look at Completed Listings or a third-party research tool like Hammertap to determine an accurate average selling price and starting price for your item.

- ◆ Choose your ending day and time wisely. Sunday and Monday are good all-around ending days except for holidays and major sporting event weekends.

- ◆ Flat-rate shipping usually increases your bids.

- ◆ Free shipping gives you more promotion in the Best Match search results.

- ◆ Donate a portion of your sales to your favorite charity through eBay Giving Works. This helps increase bids and final selling prices, and it's tax-deductible.

- ◆ Set up the sales tax table to automatically calculate sales tax on in-state purchases.

- ◆ You have to specify a handling time and returns policy, so don't forget these steps.

20

Optional Listing Upgrades

In This Chapter

♦ To feature, or not to feature? That is the question

♦ Optional upgrades that are worth using

♦ Upgrades you can usually ignore

♦ Free alternatives to the Sell Your Item form

♦ Cross-promoting items in your listing

eBay has to make its money somewhere. Optional Listing Upgrades are one of its major profit centers. So when you come to this section, eBay will do everything it can to get you to upgrade your listing.

Honestly, very few options are critical to the success of your listing. A few others are useful in certain circumstances, but most of them you will never need. I show you how to determine whether an option is actually cost-effective. This is important. If you're not careful, you'll have the most promoted listing on eBay, but no profit left at the end. I show you how to avoid that.

This is the last page in the Sell Your Item form, so I think it is appropriate to talk a little bit about some alternatives to eBay's selling form. The two we cover later in this chapter are Turbo Lister and Auctiva. I have used both many times, and both have good and bad points, as we examine later. For now, let's look at the title upgrades.

Title Upgrades

When we talk about Optional Listing Upgrades, we are talking about how your listing displays on the search results page. Optional features don't change anything on the listing page itself. I am mentioning the fee each time, but for quick reference, Chapter 14 has a table of just the name of the upgrade and the fee for both auctions and fixed-price listings.

In each section title that follows, the first price covers auctions and up to 10-day duration fixed-price listings. The second price is for 30-day fixed-price listings only.

Gallery Plus (35¢/$1)

Gallery Plus enlarges the thumbnail picture on the search results page so the buyer can see more detail before clicking on your listing. This is really useful if you are selling something with very fine detail (like jewelry).

The thumbnail in Figure 20.1 doesn't look anything special, but when it is enlarged using Gallery Plus (see Figure 20.2), you can actually see the detail.

The other advantage to Gallery Plus is that your buyer can scroll through your additional photos right here on the search results page (as shown in Figure 20.2).

You should use Gallery Plus only when your pictures will really sell your item. You must ensure that your enlarged photographs are very sharp. If your pictures look fuzzy enlarged, you need to reshoot at a higher resolution. If it is a small item requiring you to use the optical zoom feature on your camera, make sure you also turn on the Macro feature. That changes the focal length to close focus and should help get your picture sharp. Also, always use a tripod and the timer when shooting zoomed in. For more photography tips, and to troubleshoot issues with photographs you have taken, refer back to Chapter 15.

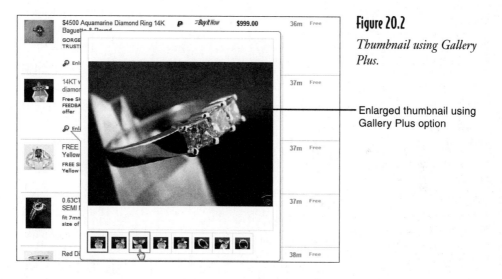

Figure 20.1

Thumbnail picture before enlargement.

Regular size thumbnail

Figure 20.2

Thumbnail using Gallery Plus.

Enlarged thumbnail using Gallery Plus option

Subtitle (50¢/$1.50)

A subtitle is an additional 55 characters that displays below the listing title on the search results page (see Figure 20.3). This is a way to call attention to extra information, like Free Shipping or extra technical specifications not included in the title.

CANON EOS REBEL XT DIGITAL SLR BODY CAMERA 8.0MP! 12 Bids $112.50 7h 43m +$30.00
CANON EOS REBEL XSi 12.2MP DIGITAL SLR CAMERA BUNDLE! 19 Bids $639.95 7h 59m Free
18-55mm LENS~~50-250mm LENS~~2GB SD CARD~FREE SHIPPING
Canon EOS rebel xs Digital Camera 10.1 MP NEW Black 33 Bids $350.00 8h +$10.00
EF-S 18-55 IS KIT LENS KIT
NEW CANON EOS REBEL XSI EF-S 18-55 IS CAMERA SYSTEM KIT 5 Bids $605.88 8h 16m +$8.95
Subtitle

Figure 20.3

Subtitle on search results page.

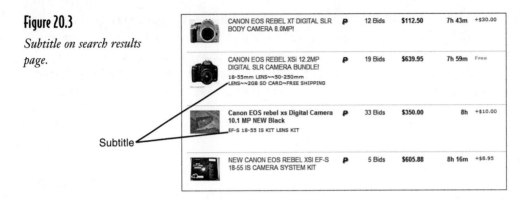

The eBay search engine does not look at the subtitle, so it is important for your searchable keywords to be in the main title. The subtitle is for extra, noncritical information that will entice the buyer to look at your listing.

Bold ($2/$4)

Bold is a very popular option, although it is more expensive. This can really make your auction title pop (see Figure 20.4).

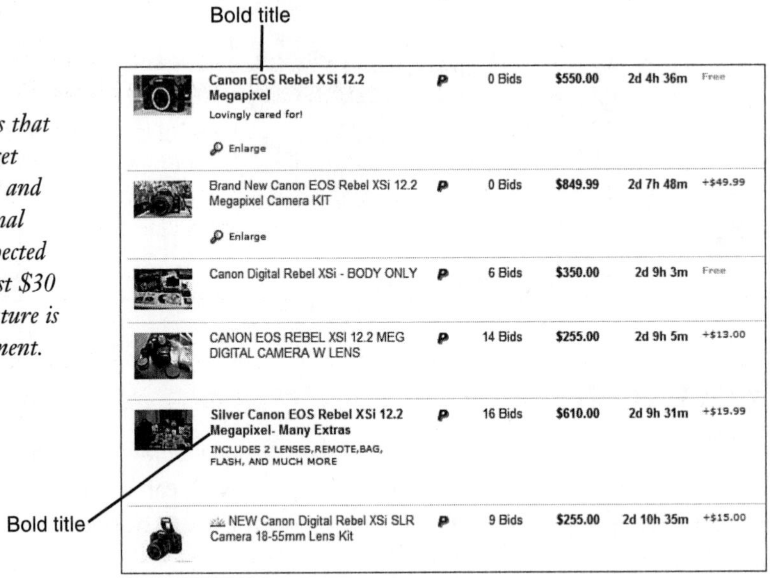

Bold title
Canon EOS Rebel XSi 12.2 Megapixel 0 Bids $550.00 2d 4h 36m Free
Lovingly cared for!
Enlarge
Brand New Canon EOS Rebel XSi 12.2 Megapixel Camera KIT 0 Bids $849.99 2d 7h 48m +$49.99
Enlarge
Canon Digital Rebel XSi - BODY ONLY 6 Bids $350.00 2d 9h 3m Free
CANON EOS REBEL XSI 12.2 MEG DIGITAL CAMERA W LENS 14 Bids $255.00 2d 9h 5m +$13.00
Silver Canon EOS Rebel XSi 12.2 Megapixel- Many Extras 16 Bids $610.00 2d 9h 31m +$19.99
INCLUDES 2 LENSES,REMOTE,BAG, FLASH, AND MUCH MORE
NEW Canon Digital Rebel XSi SLR Camera 18-55mm Lens Kit 9 Bids $255.00 2d 10h 35m +$15.00
Bold title

Figure 20.4

eBay's research shows that auctions using bold get 17 percent more hits and 11 percent higher final prices. So if your expected selling price is at least $30 or more, the bold feature is a pretty good investment.

In some situations, not using bold can be to your advantage. Before you decide on your options, take a look at the category where your item will be listed. If the majority of listings are using bold, paying for this feature won't make your auction stand out. In this case, not using bold will make the buyer notice it more because it looks out of place. As long as your thumbnail picture makes your item look as good as or better than the other items, you will likely get the hits (and, therefore, bids).

Featured First

This gives you a chance at your listing being displayed in a special Featured Items section at the top of the first page of search results in the Best Match order. You must be a Top-Rated Seller to use Featured First.

The fee is $24.95 for an auction or up to 7-day fixed-price listing. For a 30-day fixed-price listing, the fee is $74.95. That's pretty high considering it's only a "chance" of making it into the Featured Items section.

If you have a 30-day listing, you can choose to purchase Featured Plus for only 7 days. Using this at the beginning of a multiple-item fixed-price listing's duration can help you get that first sale. This will help raise your Best Match standings and help you get subsequent sales. As I've said before, it's that first sale that is always the hardest.

Did You Know?

eBay rates your seller performance and gives you a Best Match search standing as Raised, Standard, or Lowered. This is primarily based on your buyer satisfaction, feedback, Detailed Seller Ratings, and dispute-resolution reports filed with eBay. If you are raised, your items show up nearer the top of the Best Match results. If you're lowered, your listings show up on later pages.

You can see your current search standings on your *Seller Dashboard*. If you don't yet see the Seller Dashboard in My eBay, you can contact eBay's customer support and ask what your Seller Search Standing is.

def•i•ni•tion

Seller Dashboard is a part of My eBay for sellers. It helps you track how you are doing as a seller in terms of Detailed Seller Ratings, any discounts you're currently receiving, your search standings, how close you are to PowerSeller status, and more. It becomes active only after you've received 10 Detailed Seller Ratings within 12 months.

Upgrade Packages

Quite often the smartest move you can make is to combine the listing upgrades. Of course, eBay wants you to do that, too, so it has set up a package for you. Unfortunately, it doesn't include what I consider to be the best package.

In my opinion, if you want to spend a bit of money on listing upgrades, the best options are these, in order of importance:

1. Scheduled Listing

2. Subtitle

3. Gallery Plus

4. Bold

Figure 20.5 shows an auction with all of these options.

Figure 20.5

Combined optional listing upgrades using Gallery Plus, Bold, and Subtitle.

Value Pack (65¢/$2)

eBay offers a minor package deal that is worthwhile if you plan to use Subtitle as well as Gallery Plus. It offers both of these options as well as Listing Designer for 65¢. Gallery Plus and Subtitle alone cost 85¢ usually, so this would save you some money even if you don't use Listing Designer.

I used to wonder why eBay didn't offer a package that included Gallery Plus, Subtitle, and Bold, but I realized that many people will add Bold as well as the Value Pack, so eBay doesn't have to discount it.

If you're using pricier options, you need to spend extra time refining your listing title, description, and photographs. Remember the listing upgrades may get potential buyers to click on your auction, but it's your photographs and description that will keep them there.

Free Alternatives to the Sell Your Item Form

The Sell Your Item form is great if you're just selling a few items, but it's not really designed for more than that. eBay offers a bulk-listing service called Turbo Lister.

This is a bit less user-friendly than the Sell Your Item form, but it's much easier to manage with multiple items.

I have used Turbo Lister, and I find that it works fine, but it really isn't laid out for a beginner who might need prompting about available options (see Figure 20.6). For example, you have to find the **Edit** link next to **Item Specifics** to see the Item Specifics options. That's easy to miss, but it's a critical part of the listing. Likewise, you don't get category suggestions. You are expected to know what category you need to sell in and go straight to it. So get some experience with the Sell Your Item form first, and then move on to Turbo Lister after you know which options you will need.

Still, I like Turbo Lister. It integrates well with eBay, and I don't have to be connected to the Internet to use it. That's great if I am on the road and in a hotel that doesn't have Internet in the rooms. I can work on my listings on my laptop in my room and then just head down to the WiFi lobby to upload them. You can't do that with most other auction-management programs. And of course, it's free, which is always a plus.

Another huge advantage of Turbo Lister over the Sell Your Item form, is that Sell Your Item form listings disappear after 90 days. If you sell seasonal items you would have to recreate them each season. With Turbo Lister they are still there on your hard drive whenever you need them again.

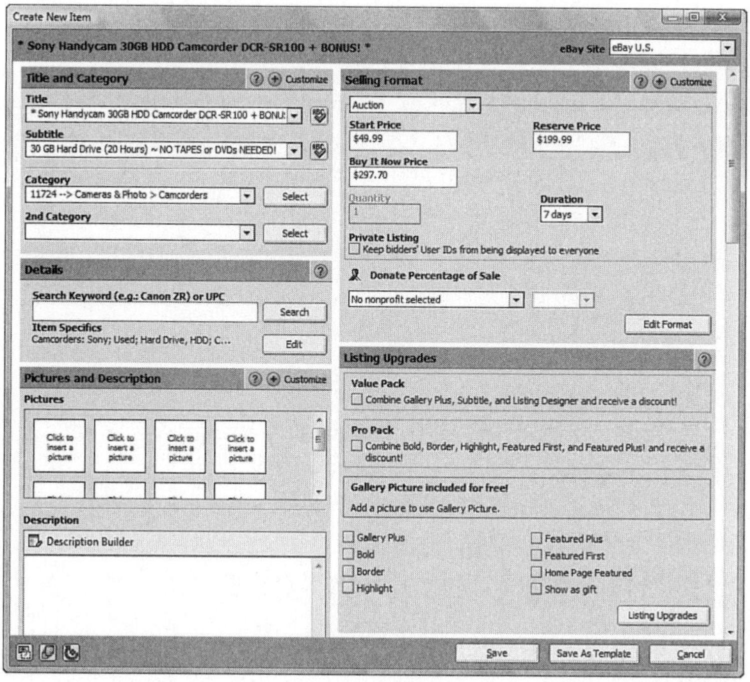

Figure 20.6

Turbo Lister does not give you as much prompting as you get with the Sell Your Item form.

Each auction-management program has its own niche of people who swear by it. If you find that Turbo Lister just isn't for you, you have other options. Most third-party (that is, non-eBay) auction-management programs are fee based, Auctiva is one of the lower-cost options.

Auctiva

For a long time, I stayed away from third-party listing tools. I was concerned that they wouldn't integrate properly or that the listing would look strange. Plus, I didn't like the idea of spending $20 or more per month when I didn't know how many items I would be listing. This all changed when I discovered Auctiva (see Figure 20.7).

When I started using Auctiva, it was free. They made their money through an eBay affiliate program that has since been discontinued. Auctiva's monthly fee is either $2.95 (for up to 15 listings per month) or $9.95 (for unlimited listings).

There are a number of things that come included in that fee (which eBay charges for):

Listing Upgrade	eBay Fee	Auctiva Fee
Image Hosting	15¢ each	Free
Scheduled Listing	10¢	Free
Listing Designer	10¢	Free

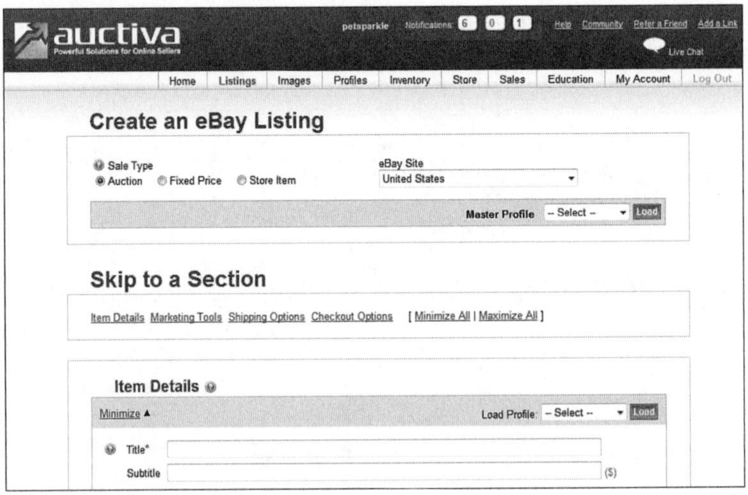

Figure 20.7

One thing I particularly like about Auctiva's Create a Listing page is that you just start at the top and work your way down. If you maximize every section, you can't miss anything as you go down the page. On Turbo Lister, it is a lot easier to miss options.

Using Auctiva to list my items means I use far more photographs. They're all free, so why not? Buyers would much rather see six pictures than one, and that helps my sales. I prefer the templates Auctiva offers, too.

But the number one feature I love most about Auctiva is the Scrolling Gallery. I'll talk about that in a moment because you can use this feature whether or not you choose to use Auctiva's listing tool.

Among the major differences between Auctiva and Turbo Lister are the types of programming. Auctiva is a web-based program (you log in to the site via the Internet and make changes to your listings there), whereas Turbo Lister is a program physically loaded onto your computer. A web-based program (like Auctiva) is infinitely easier for the programmers to make minor updates and adjust the appearance accordingly than a PC-based program (like Turbo Lister).

It's entirely up to you which type of program you prefer. To help you decide, consider these questions:

◆ Will you want to track and change your auctions on computers other than your own (at work, at the library, and so on)? If so, Auctiva is probably a better option.

◆ Do you have a slow Internet connection? If so, Turbo Lister is a better option.

◆ Do you know what options you want and have no problem looking for them if they are not right in front of you? If so, Turbo Lister will work fine for you, but if not, you might be happier with Auctiva.

◆ Is your volume high enough that $2.95 or $9.95 per month is worth it for the free photos, scheduled listing, and listing designer you receive on each item listing? If so, Auctiva may be your best option. If not, stick with the Sell Your Item form, or try Turbo Lister.

Using the Free Auctiva Scrolling Gallery to Increase Multiple Sales

Even if you choose not to use the management program part, I highly recommend that you use the Scrolling Gallery feature (see Figure 20.8). This is free and you don't have to subscribe to Auctiva's auction-management service to use it in your auctions.

Figure 20.8

Using Scrolling Gallery has really helped increase my cross-sales.

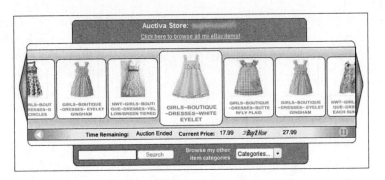

The Auctiva Scrolling Gallery is an interactive slideshow that displays all of your active items. If a buyer is interested in one of your other items, she can just click the picture to see the full auction. The images scroll so you can see seven items at once.

> **Did You Know?**
>
> eBay doesn't offer a feature like the Auctiva Scrolling Gallery to nonstore sellers. You will see some auctions with a static block or slideshow of the sellers' other items, but that option is available only to sellers who also have an eBay Store.

Using the Scrolling Gallery is particularly useful when you sell similar items. For example, if I'm selling my daughter's clothes, I know that a buyer of one dress may also be interested in a jacket-and-pants set in the same size. The Auctiva Scrolling Gallery puts those other items front and center so the buyer can see that I offer other similar items. I include a line in my description that says, "I offer combined shipping for multiple purchases. Take a look at the Scrolling Gallery below to see my other auctions for clothes in the same size."

This goes directly above the Scrolling Gallery. Since I started using this feature, I have found I get far more cross-sales than I do individual item sales. That works for me because it means fewer trips to the post office!

When you sign up with Auctiva, you get access to all of the listing options, if you want them. However, you can just ignore that, too, and never return to Auctiva again—and still benefit from the cross-sales coming from the Scrolling Gallery.

1. Start at www.auctiva.com and click **Sign Up** in the bar at the top left (see Figure 20.9).

2. Fill out the registration form (it requires only a username, password, and e-mail address). This is not your eBay registration information, so use a different username and password.

Sign Up

Figure 20.9

Signing up for Auctiva takes only a couple of minutes, and it's definitely worth it, even just for the Scrolling Gallery.

3. Click **Generate an eBay Token** on the next page. This gives Auctiva permission to add the Scrolling Gallery to your auctions without knowing your actual eBay user ID and password.

4. Log in with your eBay user ID and password to generate the eBay token for Auctiva.

5. Confirm that you want to set up an eBay token for Auctiva by clicking **Agree and Continue.** You are then transferred back to Auctiva.

6. If you are using Auctiva only for the Scrolling Gallery, you need to turn off the other features. Hover your mouse over the **My Account** tab to bring up the other options, and then click **Account** under the **Settings** heading.

7. Turn all of the options to **No** or **Off** except **Append Auctiva Scrolling Gallery to My Listings,** which should remain as **Yes.**

Now the default Scrolling Gallery will show in your listings. If you want to customize the look of it (color, shape, style, text, and so on), hover your mouse over the **Store** tab and then click **Customize** under the Scrolling Gallery heading.

Here you can change the color, placement, style of Scrolling Gallery, text, and so on. Once you've made your changes, you never have to deal with it again.

The Least You Need to Know

◆ Text in the subtitle is searchable only when the buyer checks the Include Title and Description box.

◆ Keep your optional upgrade fees below 10 percent of your expected selling price.

◆ Use Scheduled Listing to launch auctions when you can't be at your computer.

◆ Use the free Auctiva Scrolling Gallery to display all of your auctions in a slide-show at the bottom of all your listings.

◆ Both Turbo Lister and Auctiva are free/low-cost auction-management programs that help you manage multiple listings. Try them both and see which you prefer.

Part 5

During and After the Auction

Invariably, once you list your item, you'll notice a typo or something that needs changing. In this final part, you'll learn how to make changes to your listing once it's active, and the restrictions you have. You'll also learn how to manage your listings in My eBay both while they are active and after they end. We also cover the post-auction process, including using secure packaging techniques, using the Shipping Center to print your label from home, leaving feedback, and tracking your sold items. We'll even show you how to entice buyers to purchase more from you.

In the later chapters, we answer some of the common "what if?" questions I hear on a regular basis from new sellers. We teach you how to build and maintain your seller reputation, including how to qualify for eBay's PowerSeller and Top-Rated Seller programs. In the final chapter, we show you how to take your eBay hobby up a notch if you want to.

Chapter 21

Tracking and Revising Your Item

In This Chapter

- ◆ Tracking your items in My eBay
- ◆ Fixing mistakes in your auction
- ◆ Changing your starting or Buy It Now price
- ◆ When you can and cannot revise your description
- ◆ Canceling a bid or ending your listing early
- ◆ Blocking and unblocking buyers

Congratulations, you have listed your first auction. But it's not over yet. You have two choices: ignore your auction until it ends or track it through its duration. The second is far more fun, and it may well help you increase your bids if you notice something that has to be changed or you get questions from bidders.

Tracking your items is very easy to do in My eBay.

My eBay for Sellers

When you click on **My eBay,** your **Summary** page shows the selling sections where you have activity (such as **Scheduled, Active Selling,** and so on). You can also view all of your selling activity by clicking **All Selling** on the left-side bar.

Active Selling

At the top of the page, you will see your **Selling Reminders,** above your **Buying Reminders** box. This tells you if you have e-mails from bidders, items that need attention, ended items that are eligible for Second Chance Offers, and more. Next, you'll see an **Announcements** box, which shows the most recent three announcements from eBay. It's worth keeping an eye on these for promotions and changes to the site.

Beneath the Announcements is the **Scheduled** section, which shows all listings that you have created but are not yet active because you used Scheduled Listing to launch them at a later time. You can access the auction and make changes before it launches by clicking on the auction title. Note that if you use Auctiva or another third party to list your auctions, listings that are scheduled for later upload will not show up in this section because eBay doesn't yet know about them. You may not even see this section if that is the case.

On the left-side bar, you'll see your **Selling Totals,** which display how many active listings you have, how many items have sold over the last month, how much you have received in payments, and how much is still outstanding.

In the main part of the page, you'll see the **Active Selling** section (see Figure 21.1).

The Active Selling section is where you can track your active listings. The icon to the left of each listing title shows what type of listing it is. In Figure 21.1, there is a mix of auctions (denoted by the auctioneer's hammer symbol) and fixed-price listings (symbol looks like a bar code). Scroll down the page to see the icon legend for other types of listing (on the left of the page beneath the **Selling totals.** It is also shown later in this chapter as Figure 21.3).

From left to right, you'll see the icon for the type of listing, the listing title, the number of watchers, the number of bids, the current price (this is green and bold if the item will sell for that price or higher), the time remaining on the listing, and then a menu of options that initially reads **Sell similar,** to make it easy to sell another item with similar features.

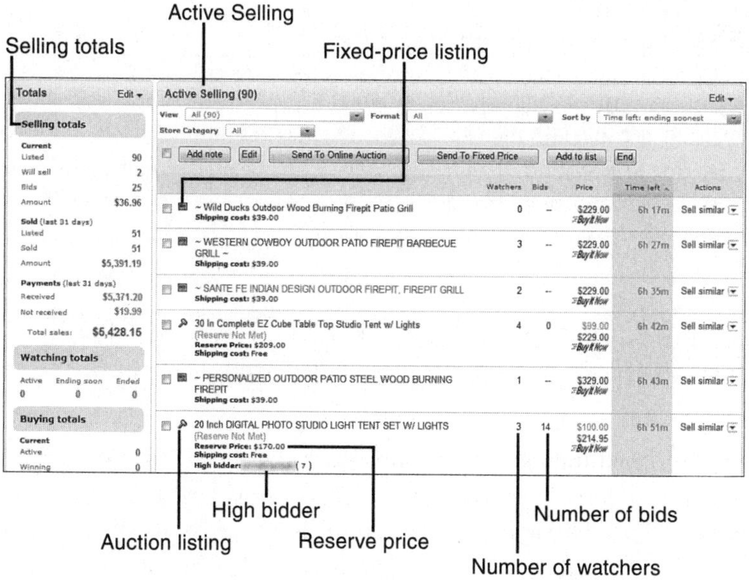

Figure 21.1

Even if you didn't list your auction using the Sell Your Item form, your active auctions appear in this section.

Beneath the listing title, you'll see the **Shipping cost.** If you placed a reserve on the auction that hasn't yet been met, you'll see **Reserve Not Met** and the **Reserve Price** between the listing title and the shipping cost.

If you have a bid on the listing, the high bidder's user ID and Feedback Score display at the bottom of the section (the user ID is blurred in Figure 21.1, but you can see where it is placed).

For multiple-item fixed-price listings, you'll see the **Initial quantity** and also the **Available quantity,** so you can clearly see how many you have sold and how many you have left.

I like to keep an eye on the number of watchers, the number of bidders, and the current price.

If your item doesn't have a lot of bids but has a lot of watchers, you might anticipate a bidding war near the end when buyers try to snipe each other. But it could just as easily mean that your auction description isn't closing the sale. You got buyers interested but didn't make them decide to bid.

As a buyer, how many times have you clicked **Watch this Item** and then forgotten about the auction until after it ended? A few changes in your listing description could make all the difference. You can still do that while the auction is active until you get your first bid (we explain how in a moment).

Tips _____

If you have a question from a potential buyer on one of your listings, you will see a bright red bar above that listing's title in your Active Selling section that reads "UNANSWERED QUESTION" (in all capital letters). The menu to the right also changes from **Sell Similar** to **Respond.** This makes it very easy to see when you have a question, and also to respond to it. The quicker you respond, the more likely you are to get a bid from that buyer.

The time to worry is when you don't have watchers or bids. Then you should really consider revising your item (we'll explain how once we've finished looking at My eBay for sellers).

You can see more detailed information about how many people have clicked on your listing, how often it has shown up on a search results page, and how well your listing is performing in comparison to similar listings using the **Search Visibility Tool,** which is accessed in the **Account** tab of **My eBay.** We cover this in detail in Chapter 24.

Items I've Sold

Figure 21.2 shows the Sold section. This is most comparable to the buyer's Won section.

Once your item sells, this is where you can keep track of your post-auction activity. You will see the listing title with the winning buyer's user ID beneath it, and the **Watch Count** (the number of watchers) beneath that. Next to the listing title, you'll see the sale price and the sale date. These details remain in your Sold section for 60 days or until you delete them (whichever comes first).

You'll also see five icons that are initially grayed out but become bold and colored once you complete each activity. Figure 21.3 shows the icons. You saw the Item Paid, Left Feedback, and Feedback Received icons when we looked at My eBay from a buyer's perspective. Now we're adding a couple more: Checkout Complete, Item Shipped, Request Total, and Relisted.

Checkout Complete simply means the buyer has used eBay Checkout and specified what payment method he intends to use (if there is an option). You will usually see the Checkout Complete and Paid icons illuminated at the same time.

You can select multiple listings and click **Print shipping labels** to create your label right from eBay and pay for it using PayPal. I talk more about this in Chapter 22. If you do this, the Item Shipped icon automatically illuminates once you print the label. Your buyer also is sent an automatic e-mail telling him that you have printed the label for his item shipment. Because of this, it's important to print your label only when you are ready to mail it. Printing it immediately but then mailing the item three days later only infuriates buyers.

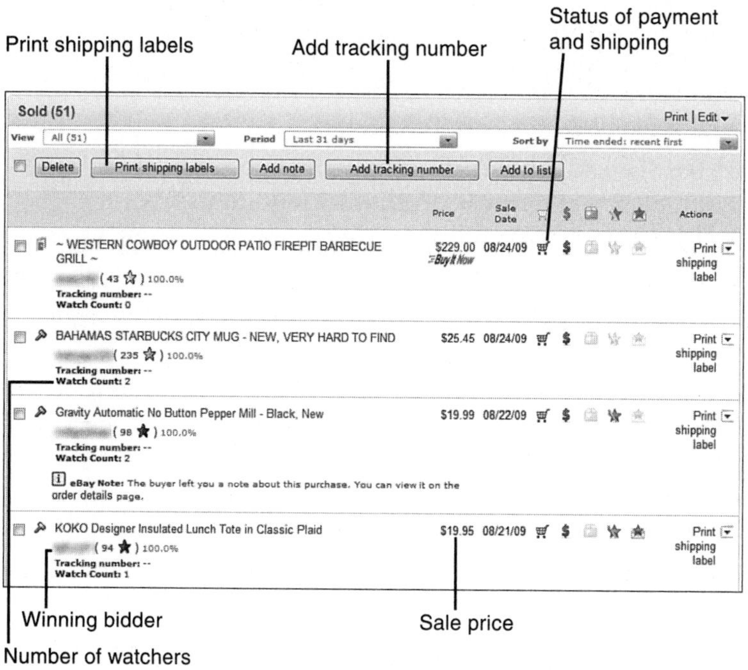

Print shipping labels   Add tracking number   Status of payment and shipping

Figure 21.2

User IDs of buyers have been blurred in this screenshot to protect their identity.

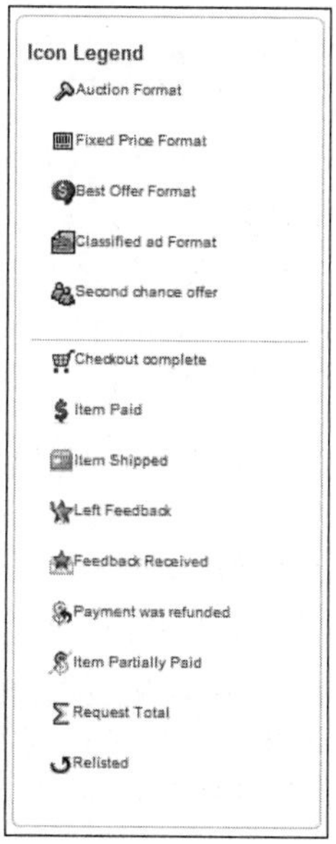

Winning bidder   Sale price

Number of watchers

Figure 21.3

eBay uses icons to help you track the status of payments.

If you print the label through eBay, the tracking number for the shipment automatically is added to the bottom of the listing section. It also displays in the Won section of My eBay for your buyer. This means he can track the item himself rather than bother you.

Remember: delivery confirmation is not true in-transit tracking. You may want to communicate this to your buyer so he doesn't get upset when he can't actually track his item from your door to his.

If you choose to pay for your postage a different way, you can select the particular listing using the check box to the left and then click **Add tracking number** at the top of the section (see Figure 21.2). Here you can manually enter the tracking number so your buyer can see it in his My eBay Won section, and you have easy access to it if the buyer contacts you regarding the delivery time or an item lost in the mail.

Unsold

The Unsold section shows you any items that didn't sell. You can see the same information as in the Active Selling section so you can see what went wrong. If you had bids but the reserve was not met, you have the option to send a Second Chance Offer to the highest bidder by clicking the link in the drop-down menu to the right.

To relist the item, use the **Relist** link in the drop-down menu. You must use this link to qualify for the Relist Credit (we talk about that more in Chapter 23).

Fixing Mistakes During the Auction

Always preview your item before you list it, but if you notice a mistake after the auction has been launched, or if another eBay member e-mails you pointing out a mistake you made, you can still make changes to certain sections.

Before the First Bid

If there are no bids on the auction (and there are still 12 hours remaining before the auction ends), you can change any of the auction details, including the title, start price, reserve price, Buy It Now price, listing description, listing upgrades, photographs, and more.

To revise an aspect of your listing, go to the active auction listing page and click **Revise Your Item** (see Figure 21.4).

Revise your item   Number of bids

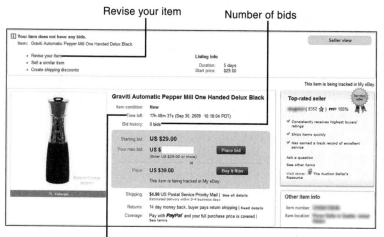

Time remaining

Figure 21.4

You can access the Revise Your Item page from either the listing page or the drop-down menu to the right of the listing in the Active Selling section of My eBay.

After you click **Revise your item,** you are taken to a page that looks identical to the Sell Your Item form, except that the title is **Revise Your Listing.**

Make your changes, and click **Continue.** Then select any additional upgrade features you want to add and click **Submit Revisions.** That's it. Your changes will be made to your listing.

Revising Your Item After the First Bid or Within 12 Hours of Auction End

If your item has no bids but is ending within 12 hours, or if your auction has any bids, you cannot revise certain aspects of the listing. These include the title, subtitle, starting price, reserve price, and Buy It Now price. You can add to your description, but you cannot change or delete anything in it. Any additions you make appear in a section below the original description box.

Raising or Lowering the Starting Price

If your item has no bids and isn't getting hits, look at your item title and your starting price. First, check that you haven't misspelled a critical keyword in your title and that your thumbnail picture is displaying correctly. If it's a spelling issue, just revise the title. If it's the picture, upload the photograph again.

If it's not a keyword or photograph issue, look at your listing in context. Look at your listing's placement in both the **Best Match** and **Time: ending soonest** search results orders. These are the two most commonly used by buyers. Do other items around yours have bids? Do they have more hits than your listing? Is their starting price lower than yours? Do they offer extra accessories or bonus items for the same price or a lower price? Do they offer free or cheaper shipping? If you are seeing Buy It Now prices lower than your starting price, you definitely need to adjust your pricing.

Follow the same process to raise your starting price if you notice that you have under-priced your item or accidentally started it at the wrong price ($10 instead of $100). Remember, you can't change any of the prices after the first bid is placed.

If you do accidentally list your starting bid way lower than you intended (or make a mistake in your reserve price) and someone gets the first bid in at that level, you can cancel the auction and relist it, but you don't get any of your listing fees refunded, so don't do it unless you have to. You can't just cancel the buyer's bid simply because you made an error in the starting price.

You can try contacting the bidder and explaining your mistake. You can ask whether she will allow you to cancel her bid so you can adjust the starting/reserve price rather than cancel the entire auction. Sometimes a buyer will be okay with that. Besides, if you cancel the auction, her bid will be cancelled anyway.

When a Buyer Asks for a Buy It Now Price

Sometimes a potential buyer will contact you and ask if you're willing to add a Buy It Now price to your listing. This is perfectly acceptable as long as there are no bids yet (or the only bid is from this person). You can revise the item just as if you were chang-ing any part of the listing's pricing and add the agreed Buy It Now price. You will pay a few cents to add this option, but for a guaranteed sale, I find that it tends to be worth it (as long as the price offered is acceptable to you).

Under no circumstances should you cancel the listing and sell directly to the buyer. This removes all fraud protection and is against eBay policies. Such actions could get your selling account limited or even suspended.

Cancelling a Bid

You cannot cancel a bid without a good reason. But in some circumstances it is appro-priate:

- ◆ The bidder has purchased from you in the past and has not paid.
- ◆ The bidder resides in a country you don't ship to.

◆ The bidder asks you to cancel her bid.

◆ You cannot verify the bidder's identity (the e-mail address and phone number on file are incorrect).

Cancelling a bid is a very simple process. Figure 21.5 shows the form you need to use, which can be found at http://offer.ebay.com/ws/eBayISAPI.dll?CancelBidShow.

You can navigate to this page by going to the **eBay Site Map** and clicking **Cancel Bids on Your Listing** under the **Sell** section heading.

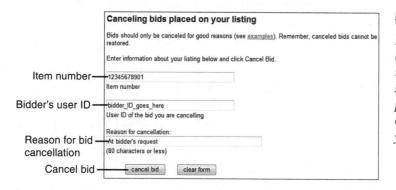

Figure 21.5

If you are cancelling your entire auction, you don't have to cancel the bids before you start the End My Listing process. One of the first options will take care of it for you if it is necessary.

Enter the item number, the bidder's user ID, and the reason you are cancelling the bid, and click **Cancel bid.** It's just that easy.

Cancelling an Auction

If you have to cancel your entire listing, you won't be charged a Final Value fee, but you won't get a refund on any of the listing or optional upgrade fees you paid, and you are not eligible for the Relist Credit (we talk about this in Chapter 23). You still need to have a valid reason, too.

If a buyer e-mails you and asks whether you will sell the item for his current high bid, it's completely up to you to decide yes or no. If you expect the item to go for a higher amount, I would generally say no (depending on the buyer's reason for the request). You will be charged the Final Value fee if you end a listing to sell to the current high bidder.

Whichever reason you have for cancelling the auction, the beginning of the process is the same. Go to the **Active Selling** section in My eBay and select **End item** in the drop-down menu next to the listing you need to cancel (see Figure 21.6).

Figure 21.6

This should be your last resort if you can't fix the auction by revising it.

End item

If there are bids on your auction, you will be presented with two choices:

- ◆ Cancel bids and end listing early
- ◆ Sell item to high bidder(s) and end listing early

If you are selling to the high bidder, select the second option. The auction will be cancelled and will show up in your Sold section.

If you're cancelling for any other reason, select the first option.

If you run out of inventory on a multiple-item fixed-price listing, you must cancel the listing before you get another sale. Use the first option to cancel a fixed-price listing. It doesn't affect previous sales you've received. Now you are presented with the four acceptable reasons for why you are ending your listing. Your bidders will be e-mailed and this reason will be given for the listing being cancelled. This will also display on the ended listing page.

The options are …

- ◆ The item is no longer available for sale.
- ◆ There was an error in the starting price or reserve amount.
- ◆ There was an error in the listing.
- ◆ The item was lost or broken.

> **Did You Know?**
>
> eBay investigates cancelled auctions to prevent sellers from just cancelling auctions that don't reach the price they want.

Select the option that applies to your situation and click **End my Listing.**

Managing Your Blocked Buyers

Sometimes you will want to block someone from bidding on your listings. If you've received negative feedback from her or she was particularly difficult to deal with, or if you got a crazy e-mail from her and think she might be a troublemaker, you'll likely want to add her to your Blocked Bidder/Buyer List.

Make a note of the buyer's user ID and then go to http://pages.ebay.com/services/buyandsell/biddermanagement.html. This page is easy to get to through the **eBay Site Map** using the **Block Bidder/Buyer List** link under the **Selling Activities** heading.

Click **Add an eBay user to my Blocked Bidder/Buyer List** and then enter the user ID in the box provided. Click **Submit** when you're done. That eBay user now will no longer be able to bid on your listings.

Sometimes your Buyer Requirements will automatically block a bidder that you actually want to be able to purchase from you. For example, I buy a lot on eBay UK and have the items shipped to my family who still live in England (then they parcel up a batch and send it on to me, which is much cheaper than sending individual items).

If an eBay UK seller had a Buyer Requirement set to block buyers in countries to which they don't ship, I would be automatically blocked. But since the item would be shipped to my family in England, that buyer block doesn't really apply to me.

If I am automatically blocked, I send an e-mail to the seller explaining the situation and ask to be put on his *Buyer Block Exemption List.*

If you want to exempt a particular eBay member from your Buyer Requirements, make a note of his user ID and then go to the same page as the **Block Buyer/Bidder List.** On the eBay Site Map, you'll see an additional link for **Buyer Block Exemption List** in the **Selling Activities** section, but it takes you to the same page.

Click **Add a buyer to my Buyer Block Exemption List** and enter the buyer's user ID, as before. Click **Submit.** That buyer will be unblocked, but your Buyer Requirements will remain in effect for all other buyers.

def•i•ni•tion

The **Buyer Block Exemption List** is simply a list of eBay users who you have manually set to be able to bid on your items even though your Buyer Requirements would otherwise block them.

The Least You Need to Know

♦ You can completely revise your listing until you get the first bid or only 12 hours are left until the auction ends.

♦ You can add to the description after your first bid or during the last 12 hours of the auction, but you cannot delete anything.

♦ You can cancel a bid, or even your entire listing, but you must have a valid reason.

♦ If you end your auction early, you do not get any of the listing fees refunded, but you don't pay a Final Value fee unless you ended the auction to sell the item to your current high bidder.

♦ You can block and unblock buyers at your discretion without it affecting your Buyer Requirements for other buyers.

Post-Sale Customer Service and Shipping Tips

In This Chapter

- ◆ How to increase multiple sales and repeat sales
- ◆ Why customer service is so important
- ◆ How to get free shipping boxes and get packing supplies tax free
- ◆ How to create a shipping label through eBay and pay for postage using PayPal
- ◆ What you need to do differently for international shipments

Making the sale is the first challenge you face on eBay, but what you do after the sale will determine your future as a seller. As you know by now, buyers depend on seeing a good feedback reputation before they will risk their hard-earned money. So building that reputation is essential to your future success as a seller.

Most negative feedback results from poor service or communications after the sale. The best way to grow your feedback and ensure a high rating is to communicate with customers and pay attention to the important details.

This process has an additional advantage: if you do it correctly, you will have the ability to *add-on sell* your customers or bring them back for more later.

def•i•ni•tion

Add-on selling is when you convince your buyer to purchase additional items from you which you can ship with the initial purchase.

Customer Service

Treat your buyers as you would want to be treated, and you can't go wrong. This starts with communication. Be nice. Write in complete sentences. If you encounter any problems or make a mistake, be honest and 'fess up early. Most people will be understanding if you are up front with them.

If you're abrupt or, worse, don't respond to questions, you won't get repeat sales from this buyer, and the feedback comment and Detailed Seller Ratings you'll receive won't inspire others to do business with you.

So how do you give great customer service? It could be as simple as sending the buyer an e-mail to let him know his item has shipped and to give him the delivery confirmation number (or explain how he can find it in My eBay). But if you take a moment to congratulate him on getting a good deal and thank him for his business, he will know that you really care and he'll be more likely to leave you glowing feedback. If you were about to buy from a seller, which feedback comment would impress you the most?

> Thanks. Nice item.

or

> Fantastic seller, Great item, good communications, Five *****

The key to getting feedback comments like the second example is to communicate with the customer and pack and ship your goods carefully and quickly.

The three most commonly asked questions by buyers after an auction has ended are ...

- ◆ Did you receive my payment?
- ◆ When did my item ship?
- ◆ How long does shipping take?

If the buyer uses the **Ask a question** link, he will be presented with some common questions and answers. For some of these, eBay can pull the answer from your listing or the My eBay status. All three of these items could be answered by eBay without your involvement. For example, eBay can see if you've received a PayPal payment. If you printed the label through eBay (I cover this in a moment), eBay acknowledges it in My eBay and provides the tracking number. If you specified the shipping carrier, eBay can tell the buyer the approximate shipping time (based on your handling time and the shipment method).

Still I like to send a few e-mails to my buyers to preempt these questions. I'd much rather answer a question before the buyer even thought to ask it. If you're still a low volume seller, this isn't much trouble. As you increase your sales volume, you'll want to look at some automated e-mail tools.

I use form letters that I customize for each buyer at each of these stages. I send the first one when they win the item (thanking them and reiterating the payment options and terms). This is the customized End of Auction Email that I showed you how to customize in Chapter 12. The second e-mail goes when the item has shipped (with the shipping time and the tracking number, and an explanation of how they can track it through My eBay). This preempts the three major questions so my buyers never wonder what is going on. It shows that you are ahead of the game and are anticipating your buyer's needs. Getting information from some sellers is like pulling teeth, so it is refreshing for a buyer to see a seller who is organized and considers buyers' needs.

Sometimes you will receive an eCheck payment rather than a cleared PayPal payment. If this is the case, you will need to send a couple of extra e-mails. Many buyers don't understand how eChecks work. They think they sent you the payment and you should ship the item immediately. They don't realize that it takes time to clear.

E-Mail Example for PayPal eCheck Payment

Dear <Buyer Name>,

Thank you for your eCheck payment of <$XX.XX> for <Item Name>! PayPal will e-mail both of us when it clears (usually 3–5 days); in the meantime, please don't hesitate to contact me with any questions.

Once your payment clears, I will be sending your item via USPS Priority Mail and I'll e-mail you the delivery confirmation number so you can track it. It usually takes 2–3 business days to get to you from then. You will be able to see the tracking number in your Won section of My eBay once I print the shipping label. Please note that I print shipping labels the night before I post the parcel.

Your complete satisfaction is my first priority. Please contact me if you have any questions.

Thanks again,

Lissa McGrath

www.lissamcgrath.com

E-Mail Example for When Payment Clears and Item Ships

Dear <Buyer Name>,

Your eCheck payment of <$XX.XX> for <Item Name> has cleared!

Your item will ship via USPS Priority Mail tomorrow morning. The delivery confirmation number is XXXX XXXX XXXX XXXX. It should take 2–3 business days for you to receive your item in <buyer's City and State>.

Thank you for a very pleasant transaction. I have left positive feedback for you, and I hope you will do the same once you receive your item. You can leave feedback through the Won section of My eBay, or go directly to the Feedback Forum at: http://feedback.ebay.com/ws/eBayISAPI.dll?LeaveFeedbackShow.

If for any reason you are not 100 percent satisfied, please let me know as soon as possible so I can work to rectify the situation.

Thank you again, and happy bidding!

Lissa McGrath

www.lissamcgrath.com

Make It Personal

The e-mail examples I used left areas where you can put personal information so it doesn't look like a form e-mail. I keep a copy saved in my e-mail drafts folder in Outlook, and I just copy and paste the text when I need it. That saves a lot of typing!

If possible, set up a rapport with buyers who contact you. It could be as simple as commenting on the weather in a particular area or mentioning that you have visited or lived near where they are located.

This sets up a connection between you and your buyer. Now the buyer can see a real person behind the sale. This helps get repeat business as well as really good, specific feedback.

Once a buyer trusts you and knows you will send what you promised, when you promised it, and in the condition you promised it, you are far more likely to get repeat sales from him.

Packing Your Item

Once you know that your item is going to sell, it's worth getting it packed up. You should always include a personal note and the invoice showing how much they paid, so you can't seal the box yet. Still, having it almost ready to go means you can get it to the post office or UPS store much quicker after the listing ends. It also means you don't have it cluttering up your home.

If you have multiple items, you can stack up the boxes ready to be mailed and just finish them up when the buyers pay. Just make sure you absolutely know what is in each box!

People do not want to receive their "treasure" in an old shoebox. Be careful with your packing materials. It is okay to reuse materials like bubble wrap and Styrofoam peanuts if they are clean and in good condition. The same goes for boxes. I often reuse a box that I received something in if it is in good condition. If not, it goes into my recycling bin. A word of warning about packing materials: studies have shown that people do not like to receive things wrapped in newspaper because the ink gets all over their hands. If you need something like this, you can buy plain newsprint very inexpensively from packing supply stores, or more cost effectively from eBay itself (search "newsprint" or "packing paper").

Shark in the Water

Never seal a box until you have a shipping label to attach to it. You risk sending the wrong item to the buyer, and that's an expensive mistake to make. It's much better to wait and seal the box at the same time you attach the label.

I have seen many sellers recently making a point to tell buyers that they recycle boxes. Most say something like this:

> "Please note that I reuse packing boxes wherever possible, as it is more environmentally friendly. However, I do have new boxes if you'd prefer. Just let me know when you send your payment if you'd prefer a new box."

Most of the time, this type of note in the item description prevents any concerns about used boxes. I still would use new packing paper if you need paper. Otherwise, reused bubble wrap (as long as it is still in functioning condition) or tissue paper works fine.

Tips _____

As you know by now, I buy a lot of girl's clothes on eBay. I love it when I receive a parcel where the item is wrapped up in tissue paper and a little sticker used to secure it. It feels like I'm opening a birthday present. If you sell clothing, this is a great way to leave a lasting impression on your buyer. It doesn't take much time to fold the clothing and wrap it up, but it can really pay dividends in your feedback, DSRs, and repeat sales. It also helps prevent the item from getting too wrinkled in the mail.

Shipping Supplies

The United States Postal Service (USPS) offers co-branded Priority Mail boxes for sellers who have sold at least one item in the last 30 days. Go to http://ebaysupplies. usps.com to place your order (see Figure 22.1). You can pick up the same boxes without the co-branding from your local post office or through www.usps.com until you can order the co-branded versions.

There are flat-rate boxes that cost the same no matter what the weight or destination within the United States, but they are not always more cost-effective. Always calculate the shipping for regular Priority Mail by weight before deciding if it is worth using the flat-rate option. Quite often the by-weight version is cheaper (particularly if the item isn't too heavy).

Figure 22.1

You must sign in so eBay can confirm that you have sold one item in the last month before you will get to this page.

There are three flat-rate box sizes: Small, Regular (Medium), and Large, each with different flat-rate prices. There is also a reduced-rate box for sending to military addresses overseas (APO or FPO addresses). The rates change frequently, and are different based on whether you purchase the postage online (through PayPal or USPS.com) or in-person at the post office. The table shows the current rates. You can see current rates at http://www.usps.com/prices/priority-mail-prices.htm.

USPS Flat-Rate Priority Mail Box Cost

Box Size	Online Price	In-Person Price
Small	$4.80	$4.95
Regular	$9.85	$10.35
Large	$13.50	$13.95

Safe Shipments

You have to understand that your item is not your treasure anymore. It now belongs to your buyer. So it's incredibly important to pack the item properly so it doesn't get damaged in transit. You are responsible for the item reaching the buyer in the condition you stated in the listing. If it doesn't, eBay will require you to replace the item or refund the buyer. So, following good shipping practices is as much to cover yourself as please your buyer.

Here are a few extra shipping tips:

♦ If you're sending a mug, wrap a strip of bubble wrap around the handle so it is completely covered before you wrap the rest of the mug. This will help prevent chips and handle breakage.

♦ Use packing peanuts or something similar to fill up any extra space in the box.

♦ Try to use water-resistant envelopes or mailing bags for clothing wherever possible. If that isn't an option, wrapping your item in plastic can prevent water damage en route.

♦ Remember, the last impression buyers have of you before leaving feedback is how their item arrives. Make it count.

Tips _____

You can buy shipping supplies on eBay far cheaper than in stores. Some sellers specialize in selling packing materials to other eBay sellers. Find one who offers all of the supplies you need at a good price, and combine the shipping. The category to look in is Business and Industrial > Packing and Shipping.

Extras to Include in the Package

Always include a copy of the invoice inside the box with both your address and the buyer's address on it, just in case something happens to the outside label.

You should also add a thank-you note to your buyer. This is approximately what I send, but I tailor it for each buyer so that each one is a little different:

> Dear <Buyer's Name>,
>
> Thank you for your purchase of <item name>!
>
> I hope you have found this a pleasant buying experience. If so, I would appreciate you leaving me positive feedback. I have already left positive feedback for you.
>
> I am listing a lot of new items over the next few weeks, so please come back and look at my auctions.
>
> I offer a 25 percent shipping discount for all repeat buyers!
>
> Just send me an e-mail before you check out, and I'll send you an adjusted invoice.
>
> Thank you again,
>
> Lissa McGrath

A little note like this reminds your buyer to leave feedback and acknowledges that you want them to contact you if there is a problem. That alone can save you from negative feedback if there is an issue.

Create a Shipping Label Through eBay

Go to the **Won** section in **My eBay.** You can create a shipping label for just one item by clicking **Print shipping label** on the drop-down menu next to the item.

Alternatively, if you have more than one to print, you can select multiple items using the checkboxes to the left and click **Print shipping labels** at the top of the section. You are prompted to sign in to PayPal and are then taken straight to the shipment page. You can sign in to PayPal directly and select the payment to print, but it's usually easier to reconcile if you start the process from My eBay.

Print shipping label

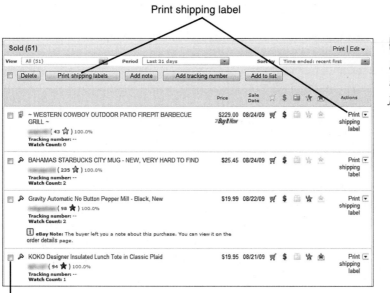

Figure 22.2

Save time by selecting all items you need to print labels for at once.

Checkbox

You are prompted to select USPS or UPS. These are currently the only two shipping carriers supported by PayPal. Figure 22.3 shows the shipment-creation page for a USPS shipment.

One of the advantages to creating your shipment online is that you get delivery confirmation for free if it's a Priority Mail parcel (70¢ if you pay at the post office) and 19¢ if it's a Parcel Post or First Class package (80¢ in store).

Tips

Hiding the price of postage can be important because if the buyer sees a price higher than they paid (even if it was justified for packing materials and insurance costs), you will not receive a 5 star rating in the Shipping and Handling Cost part of Detailed Seller Ratings.

Figure 22.3

Create a shipping label through PayPal to save time and money.

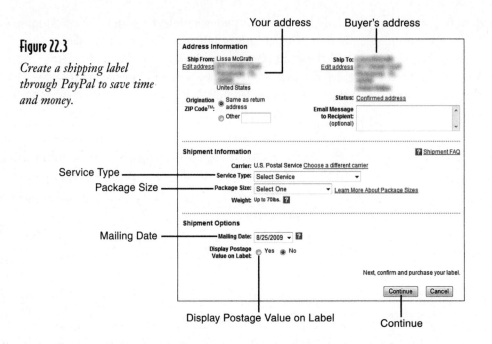

Your address   Buyer's address

Display Postage Value on Label   Continue

You can also choose whether you want to display or hide the postage on the package. Hiding it is a really good feature if you are adding a handling fee to cover insurance costs. It doesn't make a buyer feel good when she sees a package arrive with $4.05 worth of postage when she paid $8.95. Remember, and I can't reiterate this enough, this is the last impression you make on the buyer, and buyers do look at the postage cost.

It does work the other way, though. If you are offering free shipping, it's often worth putting the shipping cost on the label. That way, the buyer can see just how much he saved. Of course "saved" is a relative term because you should include your shipping cost in your starting price so you don't lose out. But the buyer has forgotten about that. He just knows that he got his item well packaged and a postage frank for $8.80 on it, yet he didn't pay a penny for shipping. That leaves the buyer feeling good about his purchase.

When you have finished completing the form and printed the label, you should attach it to the parcel immediately. As soon as you print the label, PayPal sends the buyer an e-mail with the details of the shipment. Most buyers think this means the parcel is in the mail. They don't realize that it just means you printed the label. So don't print labels on Friday night for posting on Monday morning. Even if you change the postage date, buyers will assume it's already in the mail. Always mail within 24 hours of printing your shipping label.

Insurance

I covered the importance of insurance in Chapter 19. If the item is damaged, it's your responsibility. So if you don't purchase insurance, you will have to refund the buyer out of your own pocket. In fact, you will likely have to do that anyway and then recover the cost from the insurance carrier.

I don't bother with insurance on inexpensive used items. If I lose out, it's minimal. But, if I purchased the item to resell, or it's more expensive, I always include insurance in my shipping fee. Remember: UPS includes $100 of insurance in its shipping cost.

The easiest way to deal with insurance is through a third-party insurer (such as www. shipsurance.com). You can insure just one parcel, or have a blanket policy to cover all of your items. The rates are far lower than the USPS or UPS and claims are paid far quicker. Shipsurance also offers international shipping insurance.

Shipping to International Destinations

Some specific rules apply when shipping to international addresses. You can create a shipping label for an international destination through PayPal. The options appear when you have an international ship-to address.

You must put a copy of the invoice inside the package showing the amount paid. You can print the **Transaction Details** from PayPal for this.

You must also fill out a Customs form for every overseas shipment (including those going to Canada or Mexico, or to military APO or FPO boxes). If the parcel weighs less than 1 lb., you can use the short form (the small green one); if it weighs more than a pound, you need to use the long form (the large white one). You can pick these up at your post office or order them online.

The Customs form is easy. It asks for the names of the items included in the parcel, the quantity, and the per-item value (what the buyer paid for it, excluding shipping). Then you enter your address and the buyer's address, sign it, and you're done. If you're worried about it, take your package to the post office and ask one of the clerks to check your form for you.

The buyer might be charged Customs duty on the import. If you receive a negative or neutral feedback from your international buyer mentioning additional shipping charges or Customs duty, eBay will remove the feedback. However, you must have the following text and first two bullets prominently displayed in your description. The second two are optional, but I highly recommend that you use them so there is no confusion for your buyers.

"International Buyers—Please Note:

- ◆ Import duties, taxes, and charges are not included in the item price or shipping charges. These charges are the buyer's responsibility.

- ◆ Please check with your country's Customs office to determine what these additional costs will be prior to bidding/buying.

- ◆ Customs duty is usually collected by the shipping carrier and should not be confused with an additional shipping charge.

- ◆ I do not mark international parcels as a "gift" or undervalue the merchandise. This would be a violation of U.S. and international regulations."

The text must be in the same font size as the rest of your description, not hidden away at the bottom of the page in tiny text.

Mentioning that I won't mark the parcel as a gift helps stop people from asking after the sale and putting me in a difficult position to have to say no and risk bad feedback. As long as they read the description, there is no problem. If they still ask, I can politely say no and remind them that it was in the Shipping Terms on the listing page, which they saw before they bid.

USPS International Services

The USPS does not offer a Parcel Post option for international shipments. The slowest (and cheapest) service offered for parcels is Priority Mail International. This uses the same boxes as the domestic Priority Mail (so you don't have to stock both types), but the fees are considerably higher.

There is a flat-rate option for international parcels, too. The fee is the same for Canada and Mexico ($25.95), and then higher for all other countries ($41.95). As with domestic shipments, check the by-weight price first to see if it is cheaper. For lightweight parcels, it usually is.

I like to offer free combined shipping for any other items the international buyer purchases that I can fit into the same flat-rate box. It costs me nothing more to offer this (and actually saves me some time), plus it increases the number of cross-sales to international buyers.

Free USPS Pickup from Your Door

If you ship using Priority Mail, Express Mail, or any USPS international service, your postal carrier will pick up your ready-to-mail parcels from your home. This is a huge time saver if you are organized enough to plan ahead and schedule it.

To schedule a pickup, go to www.usps.com and click **Request FREE Pickup.** Now select **Carrier Pickup** to get a free pickup. You can choose **Pickup On Demand Service** to get a pickup from your home that is time-specific, but you pay for this feature. Carrier Pickup is free because your carrier collects the parcels from you when he delivers your mail. Most people know the time frame for mail delivery, so planning around that shouldn't be too much trouble.

You can schedule a pickup for the following postal delivery day, or for a specific date up to three months in the future. Schedule pickup only for days you know you have parcels to send. Your parcel must be ready to go, with its shipping label and paid postage attached before the postal carrier arrives.

Yes, it does take a bit of organization to utilize this option fully, but if you print your labels the night before posting and schedule your pick up at the same time, you should be good to go. Just think about how much time you could save by not standing in line at the post office.

Leave Feedback

Some sellers choose to wait to leave feedback until the buyer does. If I have a difficult buyer, I tend to agree with that policy. But if everything went smoothly, I post feedback as soon as I ship the item. This has become part of my shipping routine so I don't forget it.

You can't really ask for feedback unless you give it. When you go to leave the comments, you can display all your items that need feedback at the same time so it doesn't take much to do it. You can copy and paste the response, if you want to.

When we talked about feedback from a buyer's perspective, I explained why it is important to be specific. The same is true from a seller's perspective. As a seller, it is your responsibility to show other sellers what they can expect from a transaction with this particular buyer. It's not fair to say "fast payment" if it took two weeks and four follow-up e-mails! So even if you have a standard feedback comment, tailor it when necessary.

Still, you have to be careful, since sellers cannot leave negatives but buyers can. You don't want to provoke your buyer.

Good seller feedback comments are ...

- Fast payment, great buyer, always welcome here!
- Very smooth transaction, great eBayer, thank you!
- Thank you for a super-fast payment and a great transaction!

Enticing Buyers to Purchase More

One sale is good, two (or more) sales are better. In this section, we look at a few simple ways to entice your buyer to click Place Bid on another one of your items.

Combined/Free Shipping

Even before the buyer receives his first item, you may be able to get an add-on sale if you offer shipping incentives for multiple purchases. There are so many ways you can do this. Here are a few examples:

- Fifty-percent-off shipping cost for second item
- Second item ships for 25 percent off, third item ships for 50 percent off
- Free shipping on any additional Buy It Now purchases
- Free shipping for any additional items that will fit in the same flat-rate Priority Mail box

You shouldn't have to absorb any of the shipping cost. The amount the buyer is paying for the second item should still cover the increase in cost of shipping the package with the weight/size increase. If you have added a handling fee, you may be able to cover the cost of shipping the second item free.

It's a lot less hassle for you, too. Think about it: you have to ship only one package, create only one shipping label, make only one trip to the post office, and so on, so it's a lot easier and less time-consuming.

Add-On Selling Strategies

In Chapter 20, I showed you how to get the Auctiva Scrolling Gallery of your other items to display in your listings. It's free, so you really should have this on all of your auctions and fixed-price listings.

If you sell a certain type of item (like I sell baby items), you will often find that buyers of one of your items are prequalified for another type. If you show them all of your other items at the bottom of your auction, they may well notice something they are interested in and click through. This technique costs you nothing, and is one of the easiest ways to increase your sales.

I Remember When ...

When I sell baby formula coupons, my sales of baby toys and clothing in the 0–12 month range jump. This is simply because a buyer of a formula coupon has to have a baby under 12 months, so there is a good chance her child will enjoy the toys I am offering or (if she has a girl) will fit into the clothing I have for sale.

Offers for Repeat Buyers

I sell enough items that it is worth giving special offers to my repeat buyers. In my printed thank-you note to my buyer, I usually offer 50 percent off the shipping for his next item. I have to assume a bit of the cost of the shipping for doing this, but it usually pays off because the buyer adds me to his Favorite Sellers. He gets the 50 percent off only once, so if he comes back again, I don't have to absorb any of the cost. But that means I got two new sales without worrying about promotion on eBay.

If you have a website, this is where you can really make some money. In your thank-you letter, offer the buyer a discount on the shipping from your website, rather than from eBay. This will get her looking at your site. Your prices have to be higher on your website than on eBay, but that's okay because now she is getting a discount from you. You should have additional items she won't have seen on eBay as well. The best part of this is, you don't pay any listing or selling fees to eBay for any purchase the buyer makes on your website. If you can get her to repeat-buy on your website, you stand to make a lot more money.

If you have an eBay Store, you can offer the discount on any purchases from your store. The link you give the buyer should have your Referral ID Code in it so you become eligible for the Final Value fee credit (75 percent) on all sales that buyer makes in your store. It stores a cookie (a small tracking file) on the buyer's computer, so you get this credit every time the buyer returns to your store (by any means) until he clears the cookies from his computer. Most people don't do that very often, so you could be looking at some good discounts if that buyer comes back to your store a few times.

I'm not covering the Store Referral Credit in detail because few new sellers have eBay Stores. However, if you're interested, click the **Help** tab and search "Store Referral Credit" (or go directly to http://pages.ebay.com/help/sell/referral-credit-faq.html).

Information Products

If you don't have items that complement each other, what about creating something? Information products are really hot sellers on eBay.

You could write an e-book about how to make wooden bird tables, how to choose a digital camera, a price guide for collectibles, a directory of where to find certain products, and so on. It doesn't matter what it is—it will interest someone. For example, Skip sells Starbucks collectibles on eBay and also sells an e-book called *Price Guide to Starbucks Collectibles.* Almost anyone who buys a Starbucks mug or Bearista bear from him is a potential customer for his e-book.

The trick is to make it affordable. Write it in Microsoft Word and use a free PDF creator (like www.primopdf.com) to turn it into a PDF document (Word 2007 has an integrated PDF creator, but earlier versions do not). Now you have an e-book. It has to be only a few pages long. If it is longer, charge more.

Shark in the Water

Add-on selling a digitally delivered information product is fine if it is not the initial eBay purchase. If you want to list information products on eBay you must burn the file to a CD or DVD and physically mail it to the buyer. Sellers may not list items on eBay that will be digitally delivered.

In your End of Auction Email, mention that you sell whatever product it is and, as a special offer for your buyers, you are offering it for $4.95 (or whatever price you want to set). If it's only a few pages, you might charge $3.95; if it's 15 pages, you could probably get $8.95 for it. It depends on the price of the item you just sold as well. If the item was $65, then $8.95 isn't much. However, if your average item sells for $12.95, then $8.95 is a lot. You are appealing to the impulse buy, the "why not?" Keep that in mind when you price the e-book.

You might ask, why bother for $3.95? Well, if you list 16 auctions a month and 50 percent of them buy your information product, you just made an additional $31.60 without doing any real work.

If you sell it for $8.95 and the same number of buyers purchase it, you made $71.60. After the buyer purchases the product, e-mail him with the PDF file and you're done. It's that easy. If you start using an auction-management service, it may have a feature that will deliver it automatically upon payment for you.

Remember though: this can only be an add-on product. If you sell information products on eBay itself, it must be a physical item (book, CD, DVD) that you ship to your buyer. Add-on sales that are conducted after-the-sale are not bound by this regulation.

The Least You Need to Know

♦ Sellers cannot leave negative feedback, but buyers can. So don't do anything that will provoke your buyer!

♦ Add-on sell your buyers with shipping incentives, other related products, and special offers to get repeat sales.

♦ Buy insurance from a third-party insurer rather than your shipping carrier to save money. If you're shipping a lot of items, a blanket policy to cover all of your items may be more cost-effective.

♦ Don't list an eBay purchase as a "gift" on a Customs form or undervalue the actual cost the buyer paid.

♦ Be careful when packaging your item. The last impression the buyer has of you before leaving feedback is how the item arrives.

♦ You can schedule pickup for Priority Mail, Express Mail, and international packages for free from your mail carrier.

Chapter 23

The What-Ifs

In This Chapter

- ◆ What to do if your item doesn't sell
- ◆ What to do if the buyer doesn't pay
- ◆ How to sell another similar (or identical) item
- ◆ How to get the Insertion Fee Credit and the Final Value Fee Credit
- ◆ When you can (and should) use Second Chance Offer

All wannabe eBay sellers have "what if" scenarios that prevent them from getting started on eBay. I was lucky that when I started selling, I had Skip around to reassure me that I really could do this. Then the "what if" scenarios weren't so scary. Now I'm doing the same for you with a few of the most common concerns I hear from new eBay sellers.

What If My Item Doesn't Sell?

Your item might not sell for many reasons. Some of them have nothing to do with your listing. Did you list it during a major sporting event? Did your auction end during the finals of *American Idol?* Was a major chain offering a sale on that same item? Was half the country snowed in or under tornado watches?

Other times, your listing simply has listings that you can fine-tune before relisting.

You could make guesses all day about why something didn't sell, or you can look at the facts. First, look at the **Completed Listings** for your item. Did other listings get bids and sales when yours didn't? If not, it was likely an outside influence, and relisting the auction as is should be fine (provided that your previous research showed that there is usually a demand for this item).

If other auctions got bids, look at their visitor counters and note how many hits they got. Now go to the ended listing page for your item. How many hits did you get? If yours are much lower than the other sellers', you need to adjust your title, category selection, or starting price.

> **Tips**
>
> Remember, eBay pulls the first listed shipping cost to display on the search results page, so if you listed the fastest option first (usually the most expensive), you will likely be missing out on bids. Buyers will assume that this is the lowest cost available and will skip over your auction thinking the shipping is overpriced.

Take a look at the other listings that did get bids or sales and see what they did differently. Were their prices lower, were there more photographs, or did they end on a different day or time?

Professional sellers expect to go through this process a couple of times before they find the best selling strategy, so this minor fine-tuning isn't a big deal. Of course, you don't have multiple quantities of the same item, so you're looking to get it right within two tries.

If you were getting the visits to your listing page but no bids, the problem is somewhere within your listing. Again, check that it's not just you by using the **Completed Listings.** Look at the successful auctions and see what their descriptions did differently from yours. Were they clearer? Did they have better shipping or return policies? Did they look less cluttered? Did the listings look more professional? Do the sellers have a lot more feedback than you?

If everything looks similar, except your feedback rating is lower, you might want to wait and sell some other items to build up your feedback rating a bit higher before relisting this item. This is particularly true for items over $50.

Relisting Options

The good news is, you haven't lost everything if your item didn't sell on the first try. Remember, you're a new seller and you're learning. This is why I always suggest you start with cheaper items first.

eBay gives you one opportunity to relist the item and get a credit for the Insertion fee, but you should never relist your item until you know why it didn't sell the first time around. It may be a combination of things, so don't assume that you have figured it out if you spot one obvious error (like a thumbnail picture not displaying properly).

Insertion Fee Credit

eBay credits you one Insertion fee if your item doesn't sell the first time but sells after you relist it the second time. You are eligible for the Insertion Fee Credit only once (so if your item doesn't sell the second time, you can't qualify for it again). The Insertion Fee Credit is available only for relisted *auctions*. If your first listing was a fixed-price listing and the item didn't sell, you do not qualify for the Insertion Fee Credit if you relist it. It doesn't matter if you relist it as an auction, it's the format of the initial listing that counts.

There has been some confusion on how the Insertion Fee Credit works. New sellers sometimes think this is a "free relist," which it is not. You pay the Insertion fee for the relisted auction, but then if it sells, this fee is credited back to you on your next eBay invoice. If the item doesn't sell the second time, you don't get the Insertion Fee Credit. Here's how it works:

1. You list the item the first time and it doesn't sell.

2. You determine why it didn't sell and then use the **Relist** link on the ended auction page or next to the listing in the Unsold section of My eBay to relist it. You pay the Insertion fee for the second auction.

3. The item sells and you receive a credit for the Insertion fee that you paid for the second auction. Or the item doesn't sell and you do not receive any fee credits.

Some restrictions apply for your relisted item to be eligible for the Insertion Fee Credit:

- ◆ You have 90 days to relist the item. If you go outside this time window, you do not get the credit.

◆ You must use the **Relist** link from the item's menu options in My eBay (see Figure 23.1) or from the ended auction page.

◆ You are eligible for the credit only once. If your item doesn't sell the second time, you do not receive a credit for either the first auction or the relisted auction.

◆ You cannot raise the starting price.

◆ If your first auction used a reserve price, your relisted auction cannot have a higher reserve amount.

◆ If your first auction didn't have a reserve price, your relisted auction cannot have a reserve.

◆ The auction must be in auction format only.

Figure 23.1

The options in the drop-down menu change depending on the status of the transaction and which section of My eBay you are in.

If your item qualifies, you automatically get the Insertion Fee Credit on your next eBay invoice, so you don't have to do anything else to get it.

What If the Buyer Doesn't Respond to My End of Auction Email?

The first step is to send a polite e-mail with an invoice. The buyer might have forgotten about it or had some emergency that made it slip her mind. Sending the invoice with the e-mail acts as a friendly reminder without being too forceful.

Sending an Invoice

The End of Auction Email has a **Pay Now** button in it, so the buyer is not usually waiting on an invoice to pay. I usually wait 48 hours before sending an invoice.

Click **Send Invoice** from the drop-down menu for the item in the **Sold** section of My eBay. Until the item is paid, this is usually the first displayed option.

Always look over the invoice before you send it. If the buyer asks about a shipping option that wasn't originally available on the auction, you can click **Add Another** to add that shipping option to the invoice in addition to the other options (see Figure 23.3).

If your auction was not set to automatically add sales tax and your buyer is within your state, you can add the sales tax to the invoice.

If you offered a special discount to your buyer (such as the 50 percent off shipping option we mentioned in Chapter 22), you can use the **Seller Discounts** or **Charges** box to automatically deduct a specific amount. This is better than changing the shipping cost, because then the buyer specifically sees the discount (it's a psychological thing).

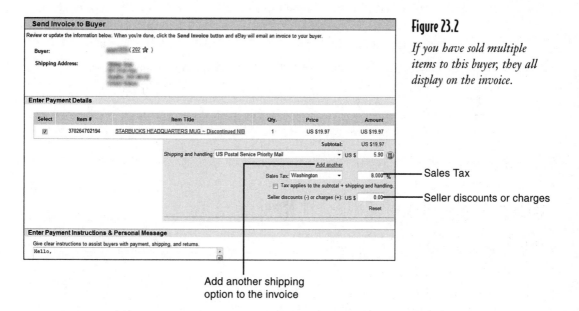

Figure 23.2

If you have sold multiple items to this buyer, they all display on the invoice.

Add another shipping
option to the invoice

You'll see a **Payment Instructions** box and a **Personal Message** box near the bottom of the invoice. This is where you need to be very specific about the payment options (particularly if you're sending the invoice as a reminder). If you're sending the invoice to discount the shipping for a combined shipping purchase, you should call attention to that with a personal message to the buyer here. Whatever you write, be very polite and friendly, never confrontational (even if they haven't paid within the time required).

Click **Send Invoice** once you are done. If you checked the box for **Copy me on this invoice,** you will receive a copy of the invoice in your **Messages** box (within My eBay) shortly.

Follow-Up E-Mails

If the invoice doesn't work, send a follow-up e-mail. You should still be very polite. Your buyer can leave feedback for you whether or not they paid, so if you are not polite, you risk negative feedback.

Dear <Buyer's Name>,

I know you are busy, but I wanted to check that you are still interested in the <item name> you won on <auction ending date>.

You can access eBay Checkout by going to the ended auction page and clicking Pay Now. You can get to the ended auction page by clicking on the auction title in your My eBay page in the Won section. The direct link to the auction is

http://cgi.ebay.com/ws/eBayISAPI.dll?ViewItem&ih=009&sspagename= STRK%3AMESO%3AIT&viewitem=&item=190062774706&rd=1&rd=1

If there is any issue with this, please let me know. I am willing to work with you, but if you no longer want the item, I would like to relist it as soon as possible.

Thanks and have a great week!

Lissa McGrath

You should always show the buyer how to access the page without clicking a link in the e-mail; otherwise, you risk the buyer thinking this is a phishing e-mail. That's another reason why it is important to give specifics like the auction title and ending date in the e-mail.

Giving the buyer an out is always a good idea. Sometimes buyers just forgot about it. Other times they change their mind and don't really want the item. It's better to give them the opportunity to say that they actually don't want it than it is to continue waiting and deal with the resolution process, or have them pay only to return the item as soon as they get it.

Tips

Always send the e-mail through eBay's Messages system. Many buyers don't monitor the e-mail address they registered with or notes from unknown senders that get automatically filtered into spam. Going through the Messages system means they are more likely to see the e-mail. Plus, eBay can see that you have attempted to contact the buyer.

If that e-mail doesn't work, it's time to look at other options.

Find the Buyer's Telephone Number

Your next step is to get the buyer's telephone number. Surprisingly, many sellers don't realize they can get this very easily.

1. Click **Advanced Search** (located to the right of the search box at the top of almost all eBay pages; see Figure 23.3).

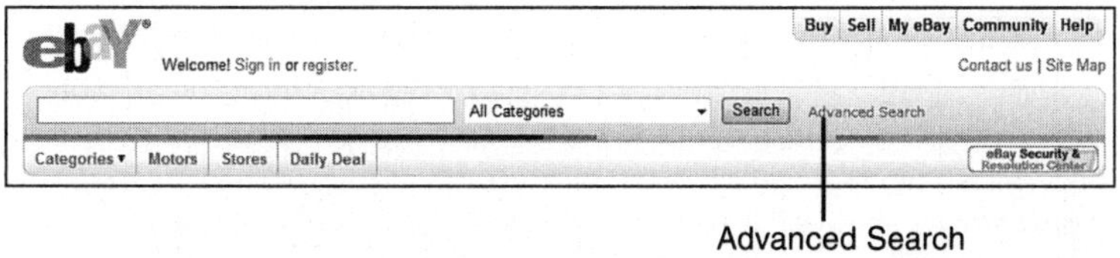

Figure 23.3

There's much more inside Advanced Search than just the search feature.

Advanced Search

Did You Know?

When you request a buyer's contact information, the buyer is sent your contact information at the same time.

2. Click **Find contact information** under the **Members** section on the left-side bar (see Figure 23.4). Make sure you have the item number for your transaction and the buyer's user ID, because you will need them now.

Complete the fields for the buyer's user ID and the item number, and click **Search.** eBay now e-mails you the buyer's contact information.

Figure 23.4

The process to get the other person's contact information is the same whether you are a buyer or a seller.

Enter buyer's user ID

Enter transaction item number

Search

Find contact information

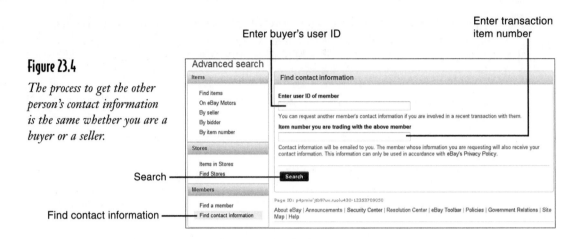

Part of the contact information shows the telephone number. If it's obvious that the number is fake, such as 123-456-7890, or if you call it and it is a disconnected number, you should report it to eBay, because that violates one of eBay's policies.

Tips

To report missing or false contact information, go to http://pages.ebay.com/help/policies/identity-false.html and click **Report** at the bottom of the page. This opens a page for you to send an e-mail to eBay's Customer Support with the correct subject title so that it goes to the right department.

If this happens, or if you call and leave messages that don't get returned, you should send one more e-mail before opening a claim with eBay:

Dear <Buyer's Name>,

I have tried contacting you via both e-mail and telephone regarding your purchase of <item> on <date>, but I haven't been able to reach you.

The original terms of the auction were for payment within 3 days. It has now been 10 days and I haven't heard from you.

If you no longer want the item, that is fine, but please let me know within three days and I will cancel the transaction with eBay so I can get my Final Value fees refunded and you will not be given an Unpaid Item strike.

Unfortunately, if I don't hear from you within that time, I will have to file a Non-Paying Bidder claim, which could result in an Unpaid Item strike for you. This is not my intention, but I will have no other choice to get my eBay fees refunded.

You can reach me via e-mail or at 360-123-4567.

Thank you,

Lissa McGrath

You have to get the buyer's permission to do a cancel transaction because she will be asked by eBay if this has been agreed upon. If she says no, you cannot then file an Unpaid Item claim, which means you cannot get the *Final Value Fee Credit* or the Insertion Fee Credit if it sells when you relist it.

In the last e-mail, I call the Unpaid Item claim a Non-Paying Bidder claim. That is the old name for it, and it evokes more of a personal emotion and explains exactly what you will be filing for. If the buyer is established on eBay, he would understand either term, but if he is a new buyer, using "Non-Paying Bidder" usually has a better impact than "Unpaid Item."

> **def•i•ni•tion**
>
> The **Final Value Fee Credit** refunds the fee you paid when the item sold. You are eligible for this credit only if the buyer didn't end up buying the item from you or returned the item for a refund. You must file for it through the Unpaid Item process either way.

What If the Buyer Still Doesn't Pay?

Well, you've given the buyer every possible chance. If she still doesn't pay or contact you, it's time to get eBay involved. Very few buyers would ignore all of your e-mails and calls, but unfortunately, some do. If you're unlucky enough to get one of those, you can often get the Final Value Fee Credit and also be eligible for the Insertion Fee Credit.

Report Unpaid Item

The Unpaid Item process begins the same way, whether you are cancelling the transaction or filing a full Unpaid Item dispute. You can cancel the transaction immediately after the auction ends (or the purchase is made if it's from a multiple-item fixed-price listing). However, if you are filing for an Unpaid Item, you have to wait four days, to give the buyer a chance to pay or respond to your e-mails.

You can start the process in multiple ways, but the easiest is to go to My eBay and find the transaction in the **Sold** section. Select **Resolve a problem** from the drop-down menu (see Figure 23.5).

Figure 23.5

You can cancel a transaction immediately, but you cannot open an Unpaid Item claim for four days.

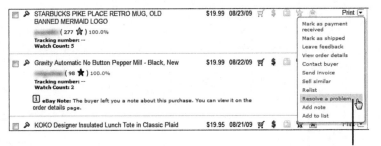

Resolve a problem

Using the link in My eBay is easier than the other options, because it automatically catches the listing details so you don't have to find the item number and type it yourself. All you need to do is select the issue and click **Continue** (see Figure 23.6). Your options are:

◆ I sold an item and haven't received my payment yet

◆ I sold an item and want to cancel the transaction

If four days have not elapsed from the end of the auction or the purchase date, you will not be able to select the first option. However, the second option is available as soon as the purchase is made.

Cancel Transaction

You must give the buyer a reason to cancel the transaction. The drop-down menu shows them all. They include: "The buyer did not want the item," "The buyer has returned the item," and "I ran out of stock." There are many other options here as well.

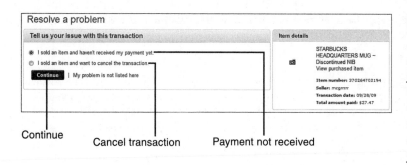

Continue   Cancel transaction   Payment not received

Figure 23.6

*If you have an issue with a buyer that is not listed here, you can click **My problem is not listed here** to see a list of alternate questions to ask eBay. The rest of the process differs based on which option you select here.*

Once you've selected your reason, you can add a message to the buyer in the box provided (see Figure 23.7). I highly recommend you do add some kind of message. Even if it's just a short note confirming that this will cancel the transaction without the buyer receiving an Unpaid Item strike. Click **Send request** when you're done.

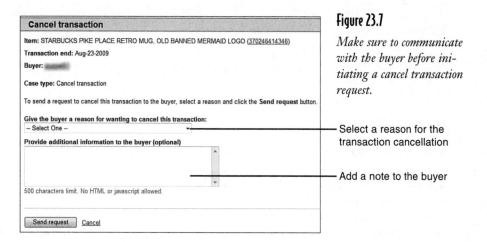

Select a reason for the transaction cancellation

Add a note to the buyer

Figure 23.7

Make sure to communicate with the buyer before initiating a cancel transaction request.

The buyer then has seven days to respond. As soon as he accepts the transaction cancellation (or if he doesn't respond at all within seven days), you can close the case and receive the Final Value Fee Credit and become eligible for the Insertion Fee Credit if the item sells the next time you list it.

If the buyer responds rejecting the transaction cancellation, you cannot then file an Unpaid Item claim. This is why it is imperative that you communicate with the buyer in advance and explain what you're doing. Most buyers will accept the transaction cancellation when eBay contacts them though.

Until the buyer accepts the cancellation or you close the case, it will display in the **Open Cases** section of My eBay.

Filing an Unpaid Item Claim

If your buyer doesn't pay and doesn't respond to your e-mails, even those offering to cancel the transaction, you will need to open an Unpaid Item claim to recover your fees. You must wait four days before you can begin this process.

Once four days have passed from the end of the auction or the purchase date, find the transaction in your **Sold** section of My eBay and click **Resolve a problem** from the drop-down menu next to the item. Click **I sold an item and have not received my payment yet.** This begins the Unpaid Item process.

Use the drop-down menu to select **What has happened so far?** and click **Continue.** This brings up the review page. Confirm all of the details are correct, and click **Continue.** Your Unpaid Item case is now open.

The buyer has four days to pay or respond before you can close the case and become eligible for your fee credits (and the buyer receives an Unpaid Item Strike).

Your case will display in the Open Cases section within My eBay until you close it.

You have three options for closing the case, and the consequences are different for each of them.

Options for Closing Unpaid Item Dispute

Reason to Close Dispute	Seller Gets Fee Credits?	Buyer Gets Unpaid Item Strike?
We've completed the transaction and we're both satisfied.	No	No
We've agreed not to complete the transaction.	Yes	No
I no longer wish to communicate with or wait for the buyer.	Yes	Yes

If you are choosing one of the first two options, you can close out the dispute at any time. If you want to use the third option, you have to wait four days after you initially opened the case before you can close it.

If you are eligible for the Final Value Fee Credit, it will automatically be posted to your account once your dispute is closed. Allow 7 to 10 days for the credit to show up on your account, but you can see in the Resolution Center when it has been approved because of the green checkmark next to the case (see Figure 23.8).

Your cases (20 cases over the last 18 months)					
No open cases	20 cases have been closed				
	✔ 17 cases closed - you received Final Value Fee credits				
View [All cases (20) ▼]				Item # or Member ID [Search]	
Item	Problem	Case opened on	Trading Partner	Status	
Closed cases					
AMAZON.COM SEATTLE... (370233215631)	The buyer hasn't paid for this item yet.	Aug 12, 2009		Case is closed.	See case details
DUBLIN, IRELAND... (370198974872)	You want to cancel this transaction.	May 11, 2009		✔ Case is closed. You received a Final Value Fee credit.	See case details
TEXAS COWBOY OUTDOOR... (370155407856)	The buyer hasn't paid for this item yet.	Feb 25, 2009		✔ Case is closed. You received a Final Value Fee credit.	See case details

Final Value Fee Credit granted

See case details

Figure 23.8

Access the Resolution Center from the link at the bottom of all eBay pages.

You can see in **Your cases** what type of case it was. If the case is closed but you don't see a green checkmark, that means you did not receive a Final Value Fee Credit. This is usually because you filed an Unpaid Item case and then the buyer paid. In which case, you shipped the item and the transaction was completed. To see the case details, click **See case details.** This is also where you can put notes to the buyer, and see any information the buyer has submitted.

Unpaid Item Assistant

If you sell more than a few items a week, it may be worth turning on the **Unpaid Item Assistant** (from the Site preferences in My eBay Account tab). This automates the process for unpaid items. You select how long after the end of listing you want to wait before it opens an Unpaid Item case (the minimum is four days). If the buyer doesn't then pay within four more days, the Unpaid Item Assistant automatically closes the case and you receive the Final Value Fee Credit. Here's the interesting part: if you use the Unpaid Item Assistant, the buyer is blocked from leaving feedback if the case is closed without him paying. If you open the case manually, the buyer is not blocked from leaving feedback. This can be a very good reason to use the Unpaid Item Assistant.

If you arrange with a buyer that he will have longer to pay, you can turn off the Unpaid Item Assistant for that specific transaction once the case has been opened. Go to the Resolution Center and click **Disable UPI Assistant** for that case. You can still close the case if the buyer doesn't pay, but you will have to do it manually.

Once a case is closed, you can relist the item or, you can choose to offer the item to another bidder for the highest bid they placed. This is a Second Chance Offer.

Second Chance Offer

You can send a Second Chance Offer to a nonwinning bidder in three situations:

- ◆ Your high bidder didn't complete the transaction.

- ◆ You have multiple items to sell but offered only a single item in the listing.

- ◆ Your item didn't sell because your reserve price was not met.

If you are sending it because the high bidder backed out, make sure the Unpaid Item case is closed before you offer a Second Chance Offer to someone else. Otherwise, you could end up getting payment from the original high bidder after you shipped the item to someone else. This isn't a problem if you had multiple quantities of the same item not yet listed, but if you had only that one item, you'd be in a sticky situation, since both can leave you feedback and one will not get the item he paid for.

If you have an auction in which the bids did not reach the reserve price, you can send a Second Chance Offer for the buyer's highest bid. If the high bidder's bid was $47.50 and your reserve was $54, you can only send a Second Chance Offer for $47.50 or lower.

> **Did You Know?**
>
> No fee applies when sending a Second Chance Offer, and you pay the Final Value fee only if the buyer accepts the offer.

The only exception to this rule is if you're selling a vehicle on eBay Motors. In that case, you can send a Second Chance Offer up to the reserve price you set, but no higher.

As with most of these options, you can start the process from several places. Figure 23.9 shows the Second Chance Offer link by the listing in the Sold section of My eBay.

This automatically puts the item number in the next page, so all you need to do is click **Continue**.

Now you need to select the bidders you want to send the Second Chance Offer to (see Figure 23.10).

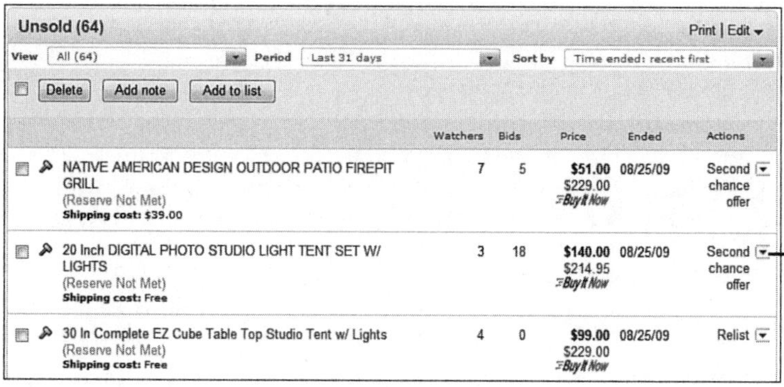

Unsold (64)						Print | Edit ▾
View All (64) ▾	Period Last 31 days ▾		Sort by Time ended: recent first ▾			
☐ Delete Add note Add to list						
		Watchers	Bids	Price	Ended	Actions
☐ 🔎 NATIVE AMERICAN DESIGN OUTDOOR PATIO FIREPIT GRILL (Reserve Not Met) Shipping cost: $39.00		7	5	$51.00 $229.00 ⚡Buy It Now	08/25/09	Second chance offer ▾
☐ 🔎 20 Inch DIGITAL PHOTO STUDIO LIGHT TENT SET W/ LIGHTS (Reserve Not Met) Shipping cost: Free		3	18	$140.00 $214.95 ⚡Buy It Now	08/25/09	Second chance offer ▾
☐ 🔎 30 In Complete EZ Cube Table Top Studio Tent w/ Lights (Reserve Not Met) Shipping cost: Free		4	0	$99.00 $229.00 ⚡Buy It Now	08/25/09	Relist ▾

Figure 23.9

The Second Chance Offer displays only if there were multiple bidders in the auction or if the item didn't meet the reserve price.

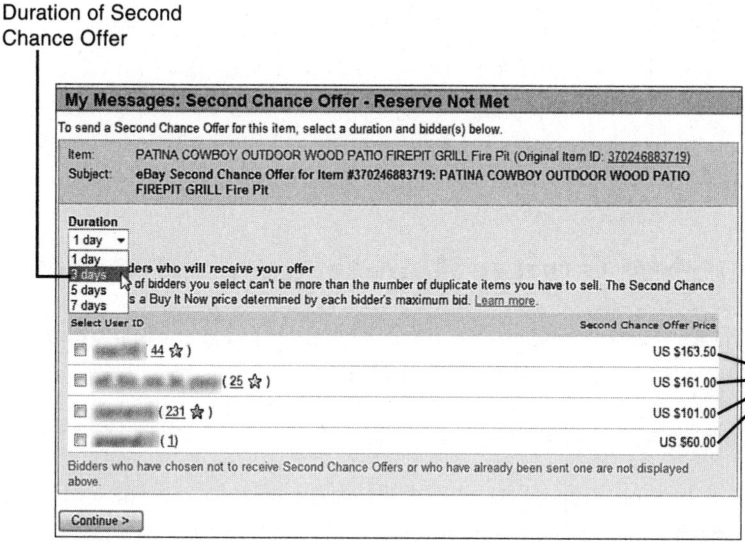

— Second Chance Offer

Duration of Second Chance Offer

My Messages: Second Chance Offer - Reserve Not Met

To send a Second Chance Offer for this item, select a duration and bidder(s) below.

Item: PATINA COWBOY OUTDOOR WOOD PATIO FIREPIT GRILL Fire Pit (Original Item ID: 370246883719)
Subject: eBay Second Chance Offer for Item #370246883719: PATINA COWBOY OUTDOOR WOOD PATIO FIREPIT GRILL Fire Pit

Duration
1 day ▾
1 day
3 days
5 days
7 days

...ders who will receive your offer
...of bidders you select can't be more than the number of duplicate items you have to sell. The Second Chance
...s a Buy It Now price determined by each bidder's maximum bid. Learn more.

Select User ID	Second Chance Offer Price
☐ ___ (44 ☆)	US $163.50
☐ ___ (25 ☆)	US $161.00
☐ ___ (231 ☆)	US $101.00
☐ ___ (1)	US $60.00

Bidders who have chosen not to receive Second Chance Offers or who have already been sent one are not displayed above.

Continue >

Figure 23.10

Buyers can set their preferences to never receive Second Chance Offers, so if you see fewer bidders than you were expecting in the list, that is why.

— Amount bidder would pay

Use the check boxes to select the bidders, and then use the drop-down menu to select the duration that the Second Chance Offer will be good for. Your options are one, three, five, or seven days. I recommend three days because most people check their e-mail within three days. Click **Continue** when you are done.

If the bidder accepts the item, you will get an e-mail from eBay just as if you had received a Buy It Now purchase from a buyer, and it shows up in your **Sold** section of My eBay. If he doesn't, it just expires at the end of the duration.

Shark in the Water _____

You can only have as many Second Chance Offers as you have identical items to sell. If you only have one item, and offer it to three nonwinning bidders, you risk getting three purchases with only one item to sell. If you offer it to more than one buyer, you must cancel the others (using the cancel transaction form) as soon as one of them accepts the offer.

Tips _____

The Second Chance Offer feature is a great way to sell multiple items without paying the Insertion fees for additional items. It can often get you higher prices, too.

If two buyers go head-to-head in a bidding war for a single item you have listed, at the end of the auction, only one bidder can win. But the other bidder was all fired up about it and is now likely feeling frustrated about losing the item.

If you immediately send a Second Chance Offer, the buyer is likely to accept it without looking at other active auctions that might end up being cheaper.

What If I Have Another Similar Item to Sell?

eBay makes it really easy for you to sell another item like one you have already listed. If you want to repeat the exact same auction, go to the listing in your **Sold** section of My eBay and select **Relist** from the drop-down menu (see Figure 23.11). If you want to sell a similar item, click **Sell similar.**

You are sent to the Sell Your Item form, but all of the information from your earlier listing will already be entered for you. All you need to do is change the information you want and finish the listing as if it were the first time you listed it.

Shark in the Water _____

If your item didn't sell the first time, you must use the **Relist** link from the ended auction page or in My eBay to get to the Sell Your Item form and relist it. If you use the **Sell Similar** link or copy and paste the text into a new listing, you are not eligible for the Insertion Fee Credit if the item sells the second time.

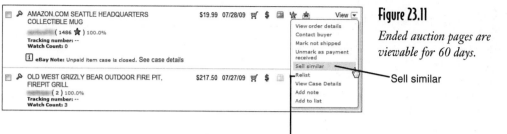

Relist

Figure 23.11

Ended auction pages are viewable for 60 days.

Sell similar

The Least You Need to Know

◆ If the item doesn't sell the first time, you may be eligible for the Insertion Fee Credit if it sells the second time.

◆ If you're relisting an item, be sure to use the official Relist link. Don't start a new listing (or use Sell Similar) because then you won't be eligible for the Insertion Fee Credit if it does sell the second time.

◆ The Insertion Fee Credit doesn't include optional listing fees (Bold, Listing Designer, Scheduled Listing, and so on).

◆ If your buyer doesn't pay, you may be eligible for the Final Value Fee Credit and (if you choose to relist the item and it sells again) the Insertion Fee Credit as well.

◆ You can send a Second Chance Offer to nonwinning bidders if your high bidder backs out of the transaction, or if you have multiple identical items available for sale (but not offered in the original listing).

◆ You don't have to offer a Second Chance Offer if the high bidder backs out of the transaction, nor does the nonwinning bidder have to accept it, but it is an option.

Chapter 24

Building and Monitoring Your Seller Reputation

In This Chapter

- ◆ Why you should get ID Verified
- ◆ About Me, My World, and other self-promotion pages
- ◆ Why you might get negative feedback and how to get it removed
- ◆ How to use the Seller Dashboard to monitor your seller performance
- ◆ The importance of Detailed Seller Ratings
- ◆ Why it's good to be a Top-Rated Seller

Everything in this chapter is optional. I highly recommend you use these tools to build and maintain your seller reputation, but you can sell on eBay without doing any of this. The part about negative feedback and how to get it removed is important, so make sure you read that part even if you have no intention of doing any of the self-promotion techniques. The Seller Dashboard is also important to all sellers and can really help you see how you're performing and where you can improve.

Self-Promotion Pages

Currently, you can create two pages to tell other eBay users about who you are. They are the About Me page and the My World page.

About Me

If you see the ME icon after an eBay member's ID, that means this member has created an About Me page.

About Me pages are really useful for new sellers because they give you a chance to tell potential buyers about you. Simply seeing the About Me icon after a new seller's user ID makes the buyer more confident buying from him.

You can set up your own About Me page by clicking on the **Community** tab from the home page and then clicking the **Create an About Me page** link in the **More Community Programs** box at the bottom of the page.

It's quick and easy to set up, and I highly recommend you do it.

1. On the main About Me page, click the **Create Your Page** button to get started.

2. Unless you are an HTML expert (which most of us aren't), make sure **Use our easy step-by-step process** is selected and click **Continue.**

3. Add a title for the page. It could be "All About Me," the name of your retail business, or really whatever you like.

4. Use the HTML editor to write your text just as you did with your listing description. You'll see that it is broken up into separate boxes for paragraph one and paragraph two. This is to help with the layout design.

5. eBay will host up to two photographs for free. Click **Browse** to find them on your computer, and add a caption in the left box if you want. The combined size of both pictures must be under 2MB.

6. If you want to show any of your recent feedback, use the **Show Feedback You've Received** drop-down menu to select how many comments to display. Your options range from no comments to 100 comments. I find 10 is about right.

7. If you want, you can use the **Show Your Current Listings** drop-down menu to select a number of current listings to display. You can select 10, 25, 50, 100, or 200. Here again, I recommend selecting 10 or a maximum of 25, as people are unlikely to scroll through all of your products.

8. Now you can add any links you want. This is the only place on eBay where you can link to your external website, if you have one. Or you can just use sites that interest you or that are related in some way to the items you sell. Click **Continue** when you are done.

9. When you're done writing, it's time to look at the layout. Figure 24.1 shows the three layout options. Now you see why you had two pictures and two paragraphs of text.

10. After you select your layout, preview what your page will look like. Click **Submit** when you're happy with it.

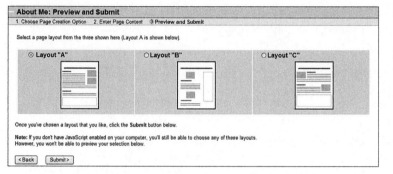

Figure 24.1

The empty box shows where your feedback comments/current items will display.

That's it, now you have an About Me page. You'll see the icon displaying after your user ID. You can edit your page at any time by going to your About Me page (click on the icon after your user ID) and then click **Edit Your Page.** You can delete it entirely by clicking **Delete Your Page,** but your page is irretrievable if you do delete it.

My World

My World is essentially your profile page. Whenever buyers click on your user ID, they are sent to your My World page.

Figure 24.2 shows Skip's My World page.

As you can see, Skip uses a picture of him and his wife, Karen, at *eBay Live!* for their profile photograph.

Treat My World like a MySpace page. Predators could look at these pages, so don't use a picture that might make you look like a target. Unlike MySpace, where you have to give your contact information to the other person, all a predator has to do is bid on one of your items, and he can then have your mailing address and easily get your phone number, too. He wouldn't even have to pay for the item. Please understand that I'm not trying to scare you—only raise your awareness to prevent any possible problems.

Figure 24.2

Your recent feedback and Detailed Seller Ratings show on this page, too.

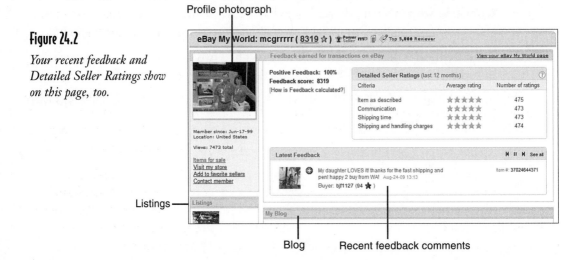

Profile photograph

Listings

Blog   Recent feedback comments

You can set up a blog to talk about pretty much anything. I would keep it related to eBay or the products you sell, but this is another way to get potential buyers to know you. Remember that people reading your blog are considering entering into a business transaction with you, so your writing should be clear. It can be informal, but it shouldn't be constant rants and raves. You need to show your positive side (at least until you become an established seller).

Reviews and Guides

You access Reviews and Guides at http://reviews.ebay.com or through the link in the **More Community Programs** box at the bottom of the **Community** page. Writing Reviews and Guides establishes you as an expert on a subject. Things that are second nature to you may be completely confusing for someone else.

> **Did You Know?**
>
> A review is about a product (camera, toy, and so on). A guide is about how to do something (spot a fake, take good photos, write a how-to book, and so on).

Your reviews and guides also show your profile and a couple of your current listings, so you are getting extra exposure for your items. They can also help build credibility for you.

One eBay seller, user ID BuyTommy, specializes in Tommy Bahama items. Quite a few cheap knock-offs of Tommy Bahama items have been sold on eBay, and it can sometimes be difficult to determine just from the picture which are real and which are fake. This seller is a licensed Tommy Bahama distributor and is an expert on their items. He wrote an excellent guide to spotting fake Tommy Bahama items, including very specific information about labels, colors, and more.

Not only does this really help buyers who are looking for Tommy Bahama items (I've used it!), but it positions him as one of the good guys. After all, if he were selling fakes, why would he tell you how to identify his items as fakes? He now has over 16,000 feedback comments at 100 percent positive. All combined, this makes it very easy to see that he is not selling fakes, and that only serves to increase his sales.

Even if you're not an expert about a specific topic, you can always write a review. There are so many products on the market that you're bound to find one that hasn't been written about (or the review might have been poorly written). Think about items you have used for a while: your digital camera, your kids' toys, your car, your computer, and more. Figure 24.3 shows the main Reviews and Guides page.

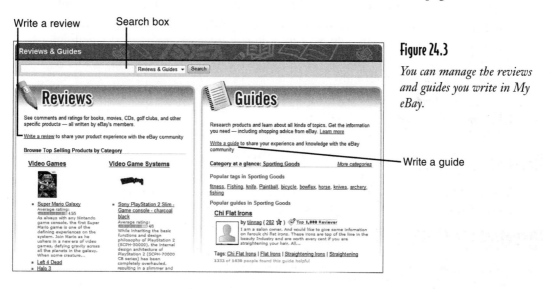

Write a review   Search box

Write a guide

Figure 24.3

You can manage the reviews and guides you write in My eBay.

Use the search box to see whether a review or guide has already been written about the product or subject. If it has, that's okay—you have a different opinion, so it's not a big deal if the subject has already been covered. Just try to look at it from a different perspective.

To write a review or guide, click the corresponding link and follow the instructions. The basic process is as follows:

1. Choose a title.

2. Enter a rating (for a product review).

3. Write your review or guide.

4. Preview and submit.

You do need to pay a little bit of attention to the style you write in. It should be clear and concise. If you're writing a criticism, don't get hot-headed. Lay out your argument logically and rationally. Saying "This product stinks" isn't appropriate. "I was not satisfied with this product because …" is far more acceptable.

You might find it easier to write your review or guide in a word-processing program, leave it alone for a while, look at it again later, and then copy and paste it into the review or guide box. I often do this with my item descriptions as well.

Don't forget, some of the items you have for sale will show on the Reviews and Guides page, so you need to sound like you know what you're talking about. Writing reviews about items you usually have for sale is a great way to boost the visibility of your listings to prequalified buyers. (If a buyer is reading a review, chances are, she is looking to purchase that item.)

Feedback Profile

We talked a lot about the Feedback Profile and how to read it in Chapter 7, so I won't repeat myself. Here we talk about the dreaded negative feedback, how to avoid it, and what to do if you do get one.

Negative Feedback

You might get a negative feedback comment for many reasons—the buyer left feedback for the wrong seller, your computer crashed and you couldn't communicate with your buyers, you had a family emergency, you took too long to send the item, you sent the wrong item, you made some rookie mistakes on shipping and handling, or maybe the buyer was just in a bad mood. Don't laugh at the last one—it happens!

Whatever the reason, you can do some things to fix it. But let's start by looking at ways you can prevent getting negative feedback in the first place.

1. Always give excellent customer service. Answer e-mails twice a day (minimum) so your buyers are never left hanging.

2. Never overcharge for shipping (if you're adding a handling fee, be sure to pay for your postage through PayPal and don't check the box to show the buyer the amount you actually paid).

3. Always deliver what you promise. If you say you will ship within two business days, don't wait five.

4. Ship items with some form of tracking so your buyer can see where the item is. This also doubles as proof of delivery, which can prevent problems of buyers claiming they never received an item.

5. Always describe your items fully, including flaws. You should take photos of any flaws so the buyer knows exactly what he is actually buying.

That said, there will come a time when you will get negative feedback. Getting your first negative feedback feels devastating. You feel like your feedback rating is ruined and no one will ever buy from you again.

Okay, once you've gotten that out of your system, it's time to do something about it.

Replying to Feedback Received

The first thing you should do is put a response on the feedback comment as soon as you have found out from the buyer what was wrong. You should specify the problem and how you are fixing it. This will reassure other potential buyers while you try to get it sorted out.

To leave a response to feedback you have received, click the **Community** navigation tab from the home page and click **Feedback Forum** (the top option).

In Figure 24.4, you can see the various options for managing your feedback. Click **Reply to Feedback received.**

The next page shows your feedback comments and a **Reply** link to the right of each link. You may not be able to look at the closed auction page, but you can leave a reply to feedback for as far back as you have been an eBay member.

 Tips _____

The response you leave for a buyer who left negative feedback tells potential buyers far more about you than the other buyer. Never use terms like "deadbeat buyer," because that just makes you look like you're avoiding your responsibility.

Figure 24.4

You can also learn a bit more about feedback on this page.

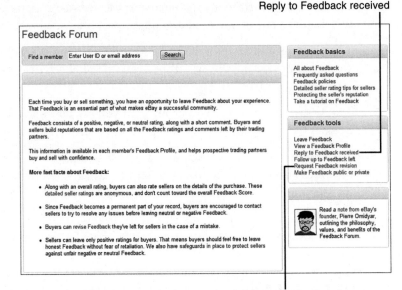

Reply to Feedback received

Request Feedback revision

You have 80 characters for your reply. You can reply to a feedback comment only once, so make it count.

Now that you've got your comment on there, let's look at revising the negative feedback rating.

Revising Negative Feedback

Unless the buyer leaves a comment that violates eBay's feedback policies, you're not going to get that negative feedback comment removed by eBay. Here are a few of the only circumstances when eBay will actually remove a comment:

♦ The buyer used profanity in his comment.

♦ The buyer was suspended indefinitely by eBay within 90 days of initially registering on eBay.

♦ The buyer doesn't pay for his item, you file an Unpaid Item dispute, and he doesn't respond.

♦ The buyer put your contact information in the feedback comment.

♦ The buyer gave you a negative feedback comment that included reference to Customs fees.

However, if you make good on the mistake or the buyer accidentally left you a negative instead of someone else, you can request that the buyer revise the feedback.

You are limited to five revisions per calendar year. If you sell over 1,000 items in that year, you are eligible for five more revised feedback requests per 1,000 feedback comments.

The first thing you should do when you get a negative feedback is contact your buyer. Be very polite. If you had no indication that she was upset, you should calmly ask what the problem was. The key to this is calm, professional behavior.

She has to agree to a feedback revision, and you want the new comment to be glowing, so be as accommodating as possible. If she left the wrong type of feedback for you by accident, you can skip straight to the feedback-revision process.

If it was something minor (the item was shipped a little late, there was a piece broken, and so on), you could offer a refund of part of the price, or something like that. It's worth it to get the feedback revised. Most buyers will consider a feedback revision if it means they will get a refund or something from you.

Requesting a Feedback Revision

You have 30 days from when the negative feedback was left, to request a feedback revision. From the Feedback Forum, click **Request Feedback revision** (see Figure 24.4). This displays all feedback comments that are eligible for feedback revision. The number of feedback revisions you still have remaining for that year displays at the top of the page.

Select the feedback comment you want to be revised, and then select the reason to give the buyer. You can add details for the buyer in the box before you click **Send.**

I highly recommend that you talk with your buyer before submitting this request. Be sure she will do it before you bother with the form.

eBay will send the buyer an e-mail and an alert (which displays on the home page whenever she signs in) with the revision request. She has 10 days to respond either by accepting and revising her original feedback comment, or by rejecting it and providing a reason for you why she won't do it. After 10 days, the revision request expires if the buyer does not do anything.

If your buyer does revise her feedback comment, you will see a tag line that says **This Feedback Has Been Removed,** indicating to other buyers that this feedback was a neutral (or, more likely, a negative) comment that was changed.

The –1 rating on your Feedback Score goes away, and you get a +1 score added. But the big thing is to have the comment changed.

It does display on your Feedback Profile how many feedback comments have been revised, but few people actually look at that.

buySAFE and ID Verify

As good as the feedback system and Resolution Center is, there are other, non-eBay services you can pay for that offer an extra level of trust for the buyer.

buySAFE (www.buysafe.com) bonds you for the full purchase price of each item you sell (up to $25,000). You pay 1 percent of the final selling price, which is very minimal, considering the increase in sales you should experience (the fee for a $50 item is only 50¢). There is no monthly fee for buySAFE, so if you take a vacation, you're not still paying for buySAFE while you have no active listings. You pay to bond only items you actually sell, so if your item doesn't sell, you don't owe anything. Also, you can choose which items you bond (you don't need to bond everything), which gives you more flexibility.

Covering buyers for the full price they paid is a big deal and pretty much gives you instant credibility. buySAFE's screening process for sellers is quite extensive, so it also shows that you adhere to their standards for reliability, trustworthiness, fast shipping, financial stability, and so on, which helps build trust in you as a seller.

You will likely not qualify for buySAFE immediately because you need a proven track record, but when you have some selling experience, this is a really good way to increase buyer confidence and boost your sell-through rate (that is, the amount of your listings that end successfully).

The second option is ID Verify. In my opinion, all new sellers should be ID Verified. This just tells the buyer that you have gone one extra step to make them more comfortable buying from you, and it confirms that you are who you say you are.

Becoming ID Verified

ID Verify costs $5. eBay keeps changing the location of the link to sign up. The easiest way to do this is to go to the **Help** tab and search "ID Verify." Click on **Use ID Verify** and you will be taken to the ID Verify page. Click **Signing Up For ID Verify,** and then click the **ID Verify** link in the box.

Click **Sign Up Now** to start the process. On the next page, you need to agree to the $5 charge by clicking **I Agree.** Then you have to sign in to eBay again.

On the next page, you are asked for your personal information, including your address, phone number, date of birth, driver's license number, and issuing state.

When you click **Continue,** eBay runs an inquiry on your credit history. Don't worry, this doesn't hit your credit like a credit check. All eBay is looking for are recurring payments you have and verifying the personal information you just entered.

On the next page, you are asked to select the correct answer from five options. Questions include the following:

- Who is the credit provider for your mortgage?

- On which of the following streets have you lived?

- What is your scheduled monthly payment for your mortgage?

- In which of the following cities have you lived?

Once you have answered the questions, click **Continue** to get the answers verified. If they cannot verify your answers, you are not charged the $5 fee. If they do verify it, the fee is added to your next month's eBay bill and you immediately see the ID Verified logo after your user ID.

ID verification lasts until you move or change phone numbers (whichever comes first). Once you update those in your eBay account, you lose your ID Verify status and have to complete the process again.

Tracking Your Performance with the Seller Dashboard

The Seller Dashboard shows you how you're performing as a seller. You access it through My eBay. Hover your mouse pointer over the **Account** tab and select **Seller Dashboard** (see Figure 24.6).

The Seller Dashboard shows you the following:

- Your PowerSeller and Top-Rated Seller status (if you have either) and the Final Value fee discount you're receiving

- Your 30-day, 3-month, and 12-month Detailed Seller Ratings averages plus your number of low DSRS (1s and 2s) for the last 3 or 12 months

- Your Policy Compliance (whether you have had any recent policy violations)

- Your Account status

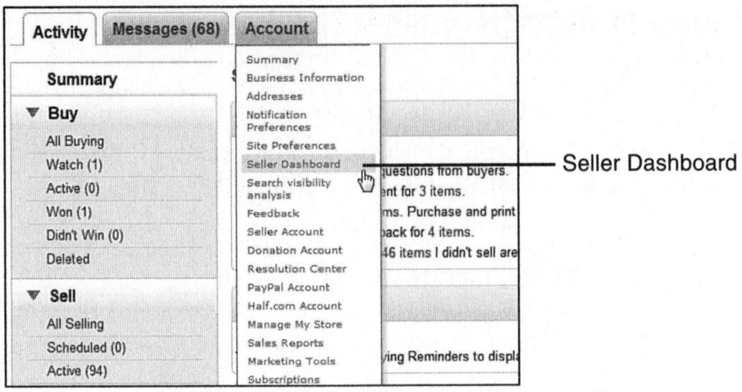

Figure 24.5

You get to see the Seller Dashboard only when you've received 10 Detailed Seller Ratings within the last 12 months.

Seller Dashboard

The **Performance** level (shown in the **Summary** box) affects the search placement for your items. There are many other factors that affect the placement of each individual listing (which I'll explain in a moment), but Seller Performance affects all of your listings. In Figure 24.6, you can see it listed as **Top-rated.** This is the highest you can get and is only for Top-Rated Sellers. You will likely see **Standard** or **Above Standard** until you reach Top-Rated Seller status. Above Standard and Top-Rated get a boost in visibility for listings in the Best Match sort order. If it says **Below Standard,** your items will be demoted in Best Match.

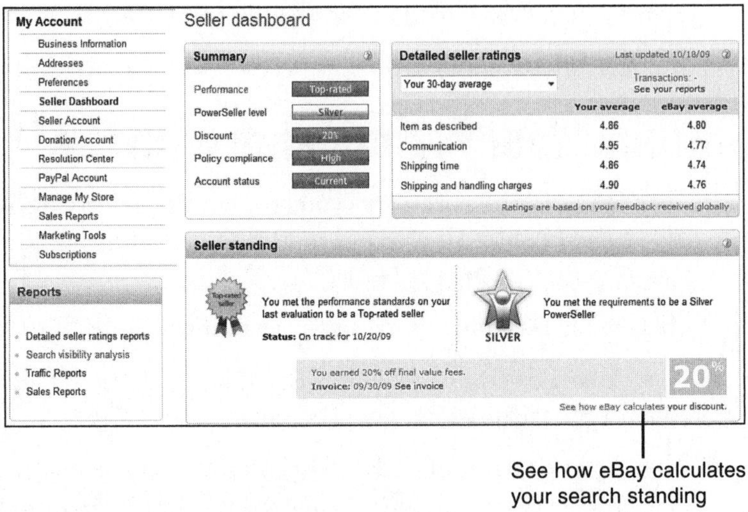

Figure 24.6

If you are not a Top-Rated Seller or PowerSeller, you won't see these specifics on the Seller Dashboard.

See how eBay calculates your search standing

How Important Are Detailed Seller Ratings?

Detailed Seller Ratings have an impact on everything.

eBay made some changes to the repercussions of low DSRs in late 2009. The focus shifted from average DSRs to specifically low ratings. That means that a 4 star rating isn't going to hurt you, whereas a 1 or 2 star rating will.

Sellers are demoted in the Best Match search results if they have too many low DSRs (1 or 2 stars). Sellers may have only 1 percent of overall DSRs at 1 or 2 rating, and no more than 2 percent of these low DSRs in the Communication, Shipping Time, or Shipping and Handling Charges categories.

The percentage of low DSRs is calculated over the previous three months for sellers with over 400 transactions in that time period. If you have fewer transactions, your percentage of low DSRs are based over 12 months.

The good news is that only U.S. buyers' DSRs count. So your DSRs may look lower, but for the purposes of Best Match ranking and the Top-Rated Seller qualification, only those from the United States will count.

> **Did You Know?**
>
> To protect new sellers, eBay doesn't demote your items until you've had four low DSRs (1 or 2 star ratings) in the same category.

DSRs are also instrumental in the Top-Rated Seller and PowerSeller qualifications. PowerSellers must maintain an average DSR of 4.6 in each of the four criteria. Four instances of a low DSR in the same criteria results in the loss of PowerSeller status.

Top-Rated Sellers must maintain the same 4.6 average as PowerSellers, but they may only have three instances of a low DSR in one criteria.

So if you see your ratings tanking, it's worth really kicking up the customer service, offering free shipping, or whatever it takes to get them up again.

PowerSeller Discounts

As of April 2010, PowerSellers are those who sell at least $3,000 a year (final value not including shipping) over 100 or more items. They have feedback and DSR requirements, but the financial one is the more difficult for new sellers. There are different levels, from Bronze to Diamond. If you are planning to make an income on eBay, you'll want to strive to become a PowerSeller.

One of the advantages of becoming a PowerSeller is that eBay rewards you with various discounts or promotions that are not available to other sellers. PowerSellers receive a 5 percent discount on their Final Value fees.

Occasionally, eBay runs additional promotions for PowerSellers. For example, right now eBay is offering double Final Value fee discounts for PowerSellers on items that have free shipping. Top-Rated Sellers are the elite of the PowerSellers and they receive a 20 percent discount on their Final Value fees. These sellers may have 1 or 2 star ratings on only 0.50 percent of their overall DSRs. Two instances are allowed in each DSR category before this 0.50 percent limit comes into effect.

Search Visibility Analysis Tool

This tool helps you determine how well your individual listings are performing. Go to **My eBay,** hover your mouse over the **Account** tab until the menu appears, and then select **Search visibility analysis.**

If you know the listing you're interested in, enter the item number and click **Run Report.** Alternatively, you can use the **Recently used categories** drop-down menu to select a category and then click **Search.** This displays all of the listings within that category beneath the Search visibility analysis box (see Figure 24.7).

Figure 24.7

Using the Search Visibility Analysis tool helps you see how well your listings are performing.

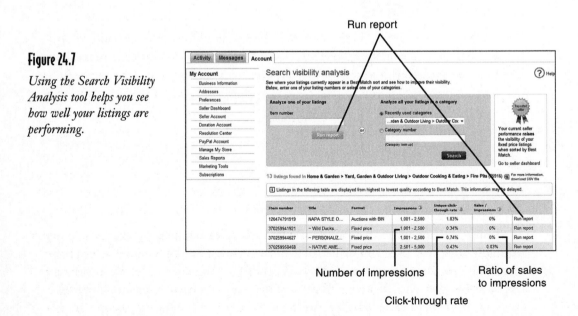

As you look at the table of listings, you can see the number of impressions (how many times your listing has appeared on a search results page), the unique click-through rate (the ratio of how many people clicked on your listing title in relation to the number of impressions your listing title received), and your sales to impressions ratio (how many sales you received in relation to the number of impressions).

To see a full report for a particular listing, click **Run report.** Figure 24.8 shows the **Search visibility report** for an auction listing.

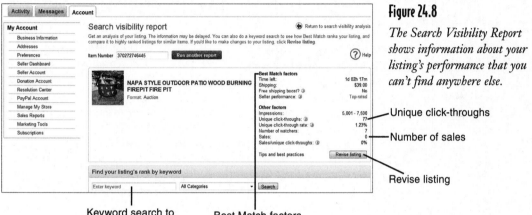

Figure 24.8

The Search Visibility Report shows information about your listing's performance that you can't find anywhere else.

You can see how many people have looked at your listing by looking at the **Unique click-throughs.** This number does not include multiple visits from the same person. This is a very important figure to know. If your listing is getting a lot of impressions but not click-throughs, your listing may be in the wrong category, have too general keywords, have too high a starting price or shipping price, or a picture that is not appealing from the search results page.

If you have a fixed-price listing with a lot of watchers but very few sales, your title is getting the buyers to click through to your listing, but something in your actual listing page is not closing the sale. You can make adjustments to your active listing by clicking **Revise listing** (see Chapter 21 for more information about revising a listing).

Another important section is the **Best Match factors.** This shows what is helping (or hindering) your Best Match placement. For auctions, the number one factor is how soon the item is ending. However, the shipping cost and your Seller performance rating are also factors. If you offer free shipping, you get a boost in the rankings. For fixed-price listings, the ratio of impressions to sales is a high factor in your listing's placement. A fixed-price listing with 50 impressions and 10 sales receives a higher placement than a listing with 100 impressions and 10 sales.

One of the most important features of the Search Visibility Report is the ability to check your listing's search ranking. Enter keywords from your title in the box towards the bottom of the page (see Figure 24.8) to see where your listing places amongst the search results for those terms.

We used a Sony camcorder as our listing example earlier. Here we could search "Sony camcorder" or "DCR-SR100" or "HDD camcorder." The more keywords that match from your title, the higher you place.

After you run a keyword search, you will see a list of statistics about the listings that are on page one of the search results for that keyword search. This helps you see what the top ranked listings are doing. If your listing's rank is low, look at this section as well as the Best Match factors at the top of the page to see what you need to adjust to improve your listing's ranking.

Keep an eye on your Seller Dashboard and Search Visibility Analysis Reports, so you know exactly how well you are performing. There's always room for improvement, and this can show you exactly where you need to improve to get better promotion or discounts from eBay.

The Least You Need to Know

- Creating an About Me page and My World profile tells potential buyers a bit about you and builds a relationship between you and your future customers.

- You can leave one follow-up comment in reply to a feedback comment you have received.

- Negative feedback can be removed under only very limited circumstances, but it can be more easily revised by the buyer if you initiate the request.

- ID Verify confirms your identity and is cheaper than other third-party services like buySAFE.

- The Seller Dashboard shows you how you are performing as a seller and displays any PowerSeller or Top-Rated Seller discounts you currently receive.

- Use the Search Visibility Analysis tool to see how well your individual listings are performing and where they rank in searches.

25

Taking the Next Step

In This Chapter

- ◆ Can I really make a steady income from eBay?
- ◆ What to sell
- ◆ Organizing your business
- ◆ Automating your auctions
- ◆ Wholesale product sourcing
- ◆ Consignment selling for others
- ◆ Beyond eBay: selling on other sites and your own website

By now, you should have some experience with the basics of selling and will have found that, in addition to being fun, it has made you some money. This is the point where people often wonder, "Could I make a steady income doing this?" The answer is probably yes.

In this chapter, we discuss how you can take your eBay hobby to the next level. We cannot possibly cover everything you need to know about setting up an eBay business (look in Appendix B for suggestions of books that can help you with that) but we show you the basics to help you decide whether you do want to go that route.

I should stress that many eBay sellers are content just selling odd things from their home or those that they come across in closeout stores. You do not have to go any further. But if you are thirsting for more, read on.

Can I Really Make a Steady Income from eBay?

The majority of sellers on eBay are part-time sellers who sell on a regular basis. However, over 1 million sellers (like Skip) make a large portion of their income from selling on eBay.

Before you decide to take the leap to a part-time or full-time eBay business, there are a few things you should consider:

- ◆ Do you have enough time? If you are a stay-at-home parent around the house most of the day, you can probably find time to list auctions, answer e-mails, and ship products when the kids are napping or otherwise occupied. But if you work a full-time job, you will have to find time in the evenings and on weekends to work on your business.

- ◆ Are you passionate about something, or do you have a hobby or interest in a certain type of product you want to sell? Trying to compete with full-time eBay sellers in the hot consumer goods area takes lots of time, money, and resources. The easiest path for the little guy is to start selling something you know about and can access a supply to sell.

- ◆ Are you patient and willing to work at this and stick to it? Not all ventures start out great. We all make mistakes and have setbacks. If selling on eBay was some-thing everyone could do with very little work, there would be 6 million full-time sellers instead of a fraction of that number. So this is something you have to work at, and be prepared to overcome your mistakes by learning from them and moving on.

What to Sell

A lot of buyers use eBay to get a bargain on the latest, hottest consumer product, whether it is a really hot toy, the coolest electronic gadget, or a name-brand pair of sneakers. They see thousands of these products sold every day and think to them-selves, "I can do that."

Well, I am sure there are a few people out there who could—after all, many of them have. But selling the latest and greatest gadget is a highly competitive arena. Product categories like digital cameras, MP3 players, GPS devices, and hot consumer clothing brands are highly competitive, crowded with big-time sellers with very deep pockets. The large dealers on eBay are companies with warehouses, employees, sophisticated inventory control, and automatic auction-launching software. Unless you have a lot of money to invest, your chances of success in these product areas are pretty slim. But that doesn't mean you can't succeed somewhere else.

So how does the little guy or gal make money on eBay? The secret is niche marketing. The dictionary definition of a *niche* is "a specialized but profitable corner of the market." The key word in that definition is *specialized.* The secret to niche marketing is to find a product that has enough demand to support a business, but not so much that it attracts lots of competitors. It would be very difficult to find a niche on eBay where there was no competition at all, but as long as the field is not too crowded, there is usually room for another seller.

> **I Remember When ...**
>
> One guy makes thousands of dollars selling plans and kits for the annual Cub Scout Pinewood Derby car races. Another seller collects and sells vintage Hollywood photographs. He sells thousands of dollars' worth each month.

You can find hundreds, if not thousands, of small interesting and profitable niches on eBay. It would take too much room to list them here, but they include people who sell their own handmade arts and crafts, sellers who specialize in old fountain pens or vintage fishing lures, people who sell coupons, specialized tour and travel operators, and people who sell information (such as how to build an espresso stand or start a knife-sharpening business).

Virtually any type of hobby, special interest, or collectible area is ripe for developing a niche market.

The only limit to finding a niche is your imagination. If you can think it up, you can try it out. If there is a market for what you are selling, people will find it. If not, you will know pretty soon, and you can just move on to something else.

Organizing Your Business

Once you make the decision to start an eBay business, you will need to treat it like a business if you want to succeed. This means you need to have enough time to devote to it. You will want to set up a regular schedule and make time to find products, take photographs, list auctions, ship sold products, and answer questions and e-mails from bidders and buyers.

You may want to give some thought to your user ID and the name of your business. If your user ID is already related to what you are going to sell, such as Pencollector or Doll_miniatures, it already reflects your interest. But if you originally set up a user ID such as Suzy888 or Ibidoften, you may want to think about changing it to a user ID that reflects your interest, specialty, or business.

You keep your old feedback when you change your user ID, but you will have a **changed user ID** icon next to your user ID for the next 30 days.

Tips

If you are going to be purchasing a product from wholesale companies for resale, you may want to come up with a business name, create a letterhead, and even print business cards. These will make you look more professional when dealing with businesses.

You can change your user ID in the **Account** tab within My eBay. Click **Edit** on the far right of the user ID line, sign in to eBay again, then select a new user ID.

There is also the issue of a business address. Most people who are buying and selling occasionally on eBay tend to just use their home address. However, once you start listing a lot of auctions, you might consider getting a post office box or renting space in a mailbox service location such as the UPS Store. This way, you are not giving out your home address to everyone and you have a place that can receive packages for you even if you are not at home.

A mailbox service can often pay for itself simply because it is a business address. If you are buying merchandise for resale, you will be paying for those items to be shipped to you. You will also pay for the mailing supplies (boxes and packing materials) that you buy to be shipped to you. Most suppliers ship via a service like UPS or FedEx Ground that charges less for shipping to a commercial address than to a residence. The difference can be as much as 20 percent. So depending on how much you receive, the savings could offset the cost of renting a box.

Tips _____

FedEx and UPS cannot ship to a post office box (rented from the U.S. Postal Service), so if you are doing business with companies who ship using these commercial services, it is probably worth looking into a box at the UPS Store or a similar company. These places can receive USPS mail as well as FedEx, UPS, and similar companies, so you get the best of both worlds.

Business Licensing, Taxes, and Insurance

You need to concern yourself with several types of business licenses and two types of taxes. Most cities and towns in the United States have some type of licensing requirement for businesses. However, these are rarely required for a business that you run out of your home, unless you have customers actually coming to your premises. Since this is rare in an eBay business, you more than likely do not need a local business license unless you decide to rent commercial space. However, check with your city hall to see if you need any form of local license. Don't just assume you don't need one.

The other type of license is not really a license in the technical sense, although some states call it that. All states, with the exception of Alaska, Delaware, Montana, New Hampshire, and Oregon, have some type of sales tax. These states require you to collect sales tax on sales made to people in your same state.

For example, if you live in California and sell on eBay, you will be selling to people all over the United States. Whenever you sell something to someone else in California, the State of California requires you to collect sales tax from that person and remit it to the state. But when you sell to someone outside California, you are not required to do this unless your business takes in more than $4 million a year. (If you fall into this latter category, you won't need this chapter—you can hire a tax expert to advise you.)

Registering for a sales tax certificate (or getting a sales tax license or ID number, as some states call it) is fairly simple. It is usually a matter of filling out a form and paying a small fee. Some states also let you register a business name at the same time. If you go to the website for the state you live in, you can usually find the forms and instructions. Most states in the United States have a website address that consists of www.XX.gov. Just replace the XX with the abbreviation of your state, such as www. NY.gov or www.MI.gov. If this doesn't work, simply Google a term such as "Florida department of licensing," and you will probably find the correct page. (Florida's is www.myflorida.com.)

As you saw in Chapter 22, eBay and PayPal automatically calculate and collect sales tax as part of the payment process. However, you need to keep a record of the taxes you collect so you can pay them to your state (you can download this from PayPal provided that is your only payment method).

Most states allow very small businesses to pay their sales taxes quarterly, although a few states require you to file a statement and remit the taxes monthly. Don't stress out over this. This is very easy—usually a one-page form where you list the amount of taxable sales and how much tax you collected. You just write out a check and mail it with the form.

The other advantage to having a sales tax number is that companies that sell goods to you for resale will not charge you sales tax when you purchase the goods. When you are buying goods for resale, simply fax the company a copy of your sales tax certificate, and the company will sell to you without charging sales tax. This also works when you're buying at Sam's Club or Costco if you change your membership to a business account and give them a copy of your sales tax certificate.

The other tax you need to be aware of is federal income tax. You are required to declare any income you make and pay taxes on it. Most people don't declare yard sale income or other minor income, but they should. Technically, any income should be reported.

You are required to pay taxes only on your profits, but you will declare the gross amount you made and then list your deductions, such as what you paid for the goods, shipping, packing materials, eBay fees, and PayPal fees. After you deduct your expenses, the number you end up with is your gross profit.

Now the fun starts. Since you are now a business, you can also claim other expenses, such as a portion of the cost of your computers, digital cameras, Internet connection, paper, telephone, and office supplies; the IRS even allows you to deduct some costs for an office in the home if you have a dedicated room for your business. Once you subtract these additional expenses from your sales, the remainder is your net profit. This is the amount you pay taxes on.

I am not a tax expert, and this sort of tax advice is outside the scope of this book, so you may want to get some help from a local Certified Public Accountant (CPA) or a tax service such as H&R Block. Turbo Tax is also a good do-it-yourself tool for calculating your tax liability online. There are also a number of good books on the topic of eBay sellers and taxes. We have listed a couple of them in Appendix B.

You must keep good records. When tax season arrives, you can't guess at your expenses—you have to keep records so you know exactly how much you earned and how much you can deduct as expenses. You also need records in case you get audited.

Insurance

Once you are running a business, you should give some thought to insurance. Most people working out of their home don't realize that their standard homeowner's insurance doesn't cover their business equipment, inventory, and materials. The answer to this is actually quite simple. Most homeowner's insurance companies offer a business-in-the-home rider. Insurance agents charge an extra fee for this, but it is actually fairly low—and so is the coverage.

So while it's better than nothing, other options may be better, depending on how much inventory you're keeping on-site and whether you need business interruption coverage.

I wrote an article for WHY (Work Home You) Magazine detailing all the insurance options for home-based businesses. Rather than repeat it all here, if you want to see the insurance alternatives for work-at-homers, go to www.workhomeyou.com/backIssues/novDec08 to read the article.

Equipment and Software

If you are going to run an actual business, you will soon discover the truth in the old saying "Time is money." It is especially true if you also work a regular job and have only a few hours to work on your eBay business. This doesn't mean you have to rush out and buy the latest, fastest computer on the market, but you may want to give some thought to equipment, services, and software that can save you time and help you keep better records.

The first thing you absolutely need is a high-speed Internet connection, such as cable or DSL. You will be spending a fair amount of time online, and you don't want to spend a lot of it waiting for a slow Internet connection (remember, you can usually deduct a portion of this cost on your business taxes).

If you are shipping a lot of products, you will have to spend time packing your goods, creating shipping labels, and standing in line at the post office. There are some ways to save time and reduce or eliminate some of these tasks.

If you will be shipping more than 10 or 12 items a week, you may want to set up a small area in your home or garage as a shipping station. You will need a postage scale, a tape gun, and an area to store your shipping and packing supplies. Having everything organized and handy will save you time and allow you to do a better job.

If you ship via the post office or UPS, you can print your shipping label with postage through eBay and pay for it with PayPal. I covered this in more detail in Chapter 22.

Other services allow you to print directly from their websites, but then you have to manually enter the tracking number in My eBay for the buyer to see it.

If you open an account with UPS, a delivery driver will come to your home and pick up your packages. If you use USPS, you can either arrange to have your packages picked up (this is free if at least one is a Priority Mail parcel), or you can take your packages to the back door of the post office and drop them off without having to stand in line.

For small items under 7 pounds, I prefer USPS Priority Mail. Priority Mail is slightly cheaper and faster than UPS for small packages, and USPS provides free boxes. But UPS includes $100 of insurance on all parcels at no additional cost and provides in-transit tracking, so that is better when the item is expensive.

The other time-consuming process is taking photographs. Here again, it can take a lot of time to set up and take down your photo setup. So if you have the space, you should create a semipermanent small photo studio, consisting of a background and a couple of lights. If you start taking a lot of photos, you may even want to invest in an EZ Cube photo system. Skip sells them below retail at www.ezauctiontools.com. An investment of a hundred bucks or so can result in huge time savings coupled with higher-quality photographs that will help you realize greater sales and profits.

Automating Your Auctions

Anything you can do to save time will allow you to launch more auctions and, therefore, sell more goods in the time you have.

In Chapter 20, we introduced you to Turbo Lister. This is a way to save time listing your auctions. eBay has another service called eBay Seller Manager that works with Turbo Lister and can automate some additional services, including sending End of Auction Emails, posting feedback automatically, and allowing you to print shipping labels in bulk. Selling Manager is an online tool you can find in My eBay. It is free for all sellers.

If you want more services, eBay offers a more advanced solution called Selling Manager Pro, which enables you to do the following:

♦ Manage your inventory

♦ Automatically list and relist items

♦ Automatically send feedback

♦ Keep records on monthly profit-and-loss reporting

♦ Use the free listing designer

Selling Manager Pro also comes with a 30-day free trial and costs $15.99 a month after that. This service is free for Premium and Anchor eBay Store subscribers.

Several other third-party tools on the market can do everything that Turbo Lister and eBay's tools do, plus a lot more. Some of the more popular ones are Vendio (www. vendio.com), Auctiva (www.auctiva.com), and Channel Advisor (www.channeladvisor. com). These sites also offer integrated image hosting and scheduling without the extra fees eBay charges (even if you use Turbo Lister). We talked a bit about Auctiva in Chapter 20. Vendio and Channel Advisor are a couple of alternatives, but they charge you a monthly fee based on your usage. These fees are often offset by the savings in eBay photo and scheduling fees, depending on your monthly volume of listings.

Wholesale Product Sourcing

If you are selling used products, art, antiques, or collectibles, you probably already know something about your market and where to source products. They can (and do) come from a variety of sources, including yard sales, flea markets, thrift stores, estate auctions, and small-town auctions. If you are selling your own handcrafted products, you are the wholesale source. However, if your product niche is some type of new product, you need to find suppliers who will sell goods and merchandise to you at prices that allow you to resell them at a profit on eBay. This is not as hard as it sounds, and the growth of the Internet has made this easier.

One word of caution: not every website that calls itself a wholesaler really is. Plenty of websites claim to have wholesale prices when, in reality, they are just retailers who sell at a discount. It is not impossible, but it is very difficult to buy from those sources at a low enough cost to make money on eBay. Remember, most eBay sellers are looking for a bargain. So unless you can sell for less than retail, you won't make that many sales. This means you would have to purchase something at 40 to 50 percent below retail to sell it on eBay at 20 percent lower than retail to make a profit.

The advantage you have over the retail store when doing this is that you do not have rent, employees, advertising, and other expenses that a retail store must pay to cover its costs.

Drop-Shipping on eBay

A very popular eBay business model involves a practice called *drop-shipping*. Some product manufacturers and distributors will ship products direct to your customers for you. This way, you can sell products without paying for them first and stocking them until they sell.

def•i•ni•tion

In **drop-shipping,** a supplier sends the item directly to your buyer after she purchases it. You do not have to hold inventory to use drop-shipping.

This is potentially highly profitable. There is no monetary risk, because you do not order the product until you receive payment from your customer. You launch the auctions and sell the product for more than the drop-shipper charges you. When your customer pays, you then turn around and pay the drop-shipper the lower (wholesale) cost, and he ships it direct to your customer for you.

Unfortunately, because drop-shipping is a potential profit maker for eBay sellers, the practice has attracted a lot of scam artists and other services that, although not an out-and-out scam, offer drop-shipping services that simply don't work. These companies are not real distributors—they are simply middlemen who create virtual warehouses with listings of products for sale and photos that you can copy to create your eBay listings. Some of them also offer premade websites loaded with these products. The problem is that their pricing is rarely low enough to actually sell the products on eBay. They suck you in with a monthly or annual membership fee, which is the real source of their income.

One of the tip-offs to this sort of site is that they will make claims that you can purchase famous name brands such as Gucci, Panasonic, Rolex, Armani, Apple iPods, and so on. In reality, the real distributors of those products will rarely work with small eBay sellers. In addition, many of the suppliers who list those products on these so-called drop-ship wholesale sites traffic in fake or counterfeit merchandise, which can get you kicked off eBay.

Some large authentic distributors drop-ship. They do not charge fees and usually insist on seeing your business letterhead and your sales tax certificate. If they don't, you may want to be wary of them.

You can find companies that will drop-ship their products in a lot of ways, but it can be a very time-consuming process. You have to research the products to find the manufacturers and then contact each one to see if they will drop-ship.

One legitimate service will do this for you. WorldWide Brands (www.worldwidebrands. com) is the only product-sourcing company endorsed by eBay. Chris Malta, the founder of the company, is the Product Sourcing Editor for eBay Radio and a frequent exhibitor at *eBay Live!*.

WorldWide Brands offers a Product Sourcing Membership. This service helps you locate light bulk wholesalers (those who sell in low quantities), regular wholesale distributors, and manufacturers and distributors who will drop-ship. This is more than a simple online directory. All of the companies have been contacted in advance to ensure that they will agree to work with small eBay sellers.

WorldWide Brands includes a free research tool that shows you how much competition a product has and the average prices that a product will sell for on eBay. The thing I like best about WorldWide Brands is that you pay only a one-time fee for lifetime access; there are no ongoing membership fees or other expenses.

Trade Shows and Gift/Merchandise Marts

Almost every industry has at least one trade show. These are annual events held in major cities around the United States where manufacturers and wholesale distributors show off their goods to retail stores and online store owners. Until recently, these companies shunned eBay sellers. But this changed after eBay really took off and they learned that over $52 billion worth of merchandise is sold on eBay each year. In my last few visits to trade shows, I have found many more suppliers willing to work with eBay sellers.

The other source for wholesale-priced items is gift and merchandise marts. These are huge buildings that contain shops where manufacturers and distributors display their products for sale year-round.

The general public is not admitted, so to get in, you have to show your letterhead, your business card, and a copy of your sales tax license or certificate. Once inside, you just go shopping.

Unless they are having a sample sale, which they sometimes do to clear out floor samples, you don't actually take possession of the merchandise you buy there and then. Instead, you place an order and pay for the items, and they are shipped to you.

Some merchandise marts are fairly small, with only about 50 to 60 dealers. Others, like the AmericasMart in Atlanta, have over 500 dealers. It can take several days to go through one that size. Fortunately, they all offer catalogs and guides, so you can go straight to the stores you are interested in.

Consignment Selling for Others

If you are struggling to find something to sell, or if you can't afford to buy inventory right now, you may want to look into consignment selling. We mentioned this briefly in Chapter 12. In consignment selling, you sell goods for other people and take a percentage of the sale as a commission. Thousands of eBay sellers do this, and eBay even has a formal program called eBay Trading Assistant to help you market your services.

Most consignment sellers charge a commission of between 20 and 40 percent based on the final price of the auction. So if you sold something for someone for $75 and took a 30 percent commission, you would earn $22.50 before paying your eBay and PayPal fees. Many consignment sellers pass on the eBay and PayPal fees to the consignor so they can't end up out of pocket.

If you want to be successful selling goods on consignment for others, remember four things:

◆ Learn how to say "no."

◆ Don't accept low-value items.

◆ Always take possession of the item before you list it.

◆ Always have a written agreement detailing your fees, who will pay the eBay and PayPal fees, the agreed upon starting, reserve, and Buy It Now prices, and so on.

The first rule, learn how to say "no," is very important. You don't want to waste your time selling goods that won't sell, that are heavy and difficult to ship, that are broken or damaged, or that have suspicious ownership.

Shark in the Water

Once word gets around that you sell merchandise for others, you may be approached by someone trying to sell misappropriated or even stolen merchandise. If a stranger approaches me to sell something that I think is suspicious, I tell them that I will take a photocopy of their driver's license and mail a check only to the address on the license. If someone is legitimate, they will not mind this. But if someone is being dishonest, they will usually refuse, for obvious reasons.

If in doubt, call your local police department and ask if that item has been reported stolen. If the item has a serial number, that's pretty easy to check. You have the consignor's driver's license details, so you can provide that to the police if it is indeed stolen.

The second rule, accept only high-value items, prevents you from wasting time doing a lot of work and making only a few dollars. Personally, I accept only items that I think will sell for over $100; many consignment sellers have higher limits. Remember the work involved. You have to collect and inspect the item, photograph it, write a description, list the auction, and then ship the item if it sells. You don't want to do all this work and earn only $5 or $10 after eBay and PayPal fees.

If you are going to offer consignment services on a regular basis, I highly recommend that you purchase a subscription to Hammertap. Using Hammertap can give you a quick snapshot of the average selling price and sell-through rate in less than a minute. You can do this while on the phone with the consignor so you immediately know whether it is worth your while accepting the item on consignment. You can also give the seller an indication of average price immediately so he can decide whether it's what he was expecting to sell it for. That is worth the monthly fee because it can save you a lot of wasted time dealing with consignors when the item isn't going to sell, or when the average price isn't what the consignor is hoping for.

The third rule, always take possession of the item before you list it, is critical. Even if you are selling an item for a good friend, you must always insist on this policy. What if the item got lost or broken? Or if the owner decided after the auction that she didn't really want to sell it, or that the highest bid wasn't high enough? Often people who have others sell on eBay for them have no idea about how it works. Remember, it's your feedback and reputation on the line.

The fourth rule is easy to forget, but having a written agreement (whether it's your neighbor, or a stranger you're selling for) is very important. If it's in writing, the consignor can't dispute who pays the PayPal fees, or that the selling price is too low. Include any details you and the consignor speak about.

We explained the requirements for the Trading Assistant program in Chapter 12, but you can still sell on consignment even if you are not part of that program.

Once you do qualify as a Trading Assistant, you can list your name in eBay's online TA directory (see Figure 25.1) and you can download flyers, advertisements, and business cards with the Trading Assistant logo.

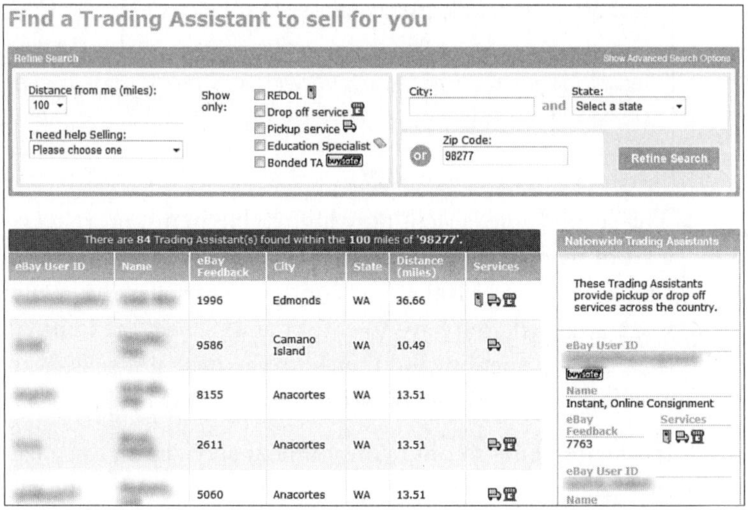

Figure 25.1

Buyers search by their location, and the closest Trading Assistants display first.

eBay offers educational materials, online seminars, and live seminars at *eBay Live!*. You can also download complete press kits and other publicity materials once you qualify for and join the Trading Assistant program.

To learn more about the Trading Assistant program, just go to www.ebaytradingassistant. com, or select **Trading Assistant Program** from the eBay Site Map under **Selling Resources.**

Beyond eBay

I have always felt very strongly that eBay offers the lowest barrier of entry to an individual wanting to make money selling online. But once you master eBay, you will want to expand your business.

Getting Your Own Website

In the beginning of this chapter, we talked about niche marketing. One benefit of niche marketing is that you can build a customer list of people who are likely to buy additional products from you.

Once you have a website where you list other products, you can direct your previous eBay buyers there for future purchases. This means you won't pay eBay fees on their subsequent purchases from you. You can't send new bidders to your website—this is against eBay rules. But once they buy from you on eBay, they become your customer and you can direct them to any other site you sell on, if you prefer.

It used to be that setting up a website was very difficult and expensive, but today dozens of services offer premade, template-based websites. If you can type, point, and click, you can set up a website with just a few hours' work.

Selling Up River

As eBay has made changes, some sellers have jumped ship and gone "up river," as they put it on the eBay Message Boards. This refers to changing platforms to selling on Amazon.com.

Personally, I think the two sites complement each other quite well. Amazon is a great venue for products that can be categorized and have specific item numbers or manufacturers. It is not a good venue for selling unique custom products and collectibles.

Many sellers sell on both Amazon and eBay, and I think this is a good idea. The fees are comparable, and you are then exposing your items to two different buying groups. Many savvy buyers check both sites to find the lowest prices, but some do not. Some people do not like the idea of shopping on eBay but will happily purchase a used item from a seller on Amazon.

The only trick to this is that you must have excellent inventory management. You do not want to be in the position of selling the same item on both locations and having only one available in stock to ship.

Etsy

Amazon may not be good for custom items, but Etsy is. www.Etsy.com is specifically for sellers of handmade gifts, crafts, clothing, and so on. Again, I would sell on this site in addition to eBay. The more platforms you sell on, the more sales you are likely to get.

The Least You Need to Know

◆ Millions of people make extra money or even a full-time living on eBay, but it is a business and you have to treat it like one.

◆ It is much easier for a small individual seller to make money in a specialized niche market than to try to compete against large sellers with popular consumer products.

◆ If you are going to run even a part-time eBay business, it pays to automate your processes and invest in auction-management tools to save you time and money.

◆ When looking for wholesale products, get a sales tax number and be wary of companies that charge a monthly membership fee to access their sources.

◆ If you want to sell on consignment, take the time to qualify for the eBay Trading Assistant program and access the training and promotional resources.

◆ Once you master your eBay business, you can expand to include your own website. Then you can market to your previous buyers directly and save some eBay fees.

◆ Selling on multiple platforms (such as eBay, Amazon, and Etsy) exposes your items to more buyers and gets you more sales.

Glossary

About Me page   Page where you can write information about yourself to share with other eBay users. This is the only place on eBay where you can put a link to your website.

auction-management program   Software program for automating and managing auction listings. Usually fee based and used mainly by professional sellers.

AuctionBytes (www.AuctionBytes.com)   The leading source for online-auction industry information and news.

Auctiva Scrolling Gallery   A free feature available at www.auctiva.com that automatically inserts a slideshow of your current auctions into each of your current listings.

bidder   An eBay member who places a bid on an auction. See also *buyer*.

Buy It Now   An instant purchase option that can be added to an auction. Listings can also only have a Buy It Now price. These are called fixed-price listings.

buyer   Member who purchases an item on eBay. See also *bidder*.

cloud dome   A professional photography tool that looks like a dome on a table, to help get even lighting for smaller items.

Completed Listings   A page of search results that display only listings that have ended (usually within the last two weeks).

Condition Guarantee by Seller   Fraud protection for eBay Motors buyers. This covers minor discrepancies. See also *Vehicle Protection Program* and *Vehicle Purchase Protection.*

copyright   Protects the ownership of photographs and text for the creator or legal owner. See also *VeRO.*

crop (photograph)   Remove extra space around the item that is not needed for the photograph.

Detailed Seller Ratings   A section of the Feedback Profile that shows the average rating of the seller from previous buyers in four key areas (shipping time, communication, item as described, and shipping and handling cost).

drop-shipper   Supplier who ships items directly to your customers after they purchase from you.

eBay Live!   Yearly convention of eBay users and eBay and third-party company staff. Locations have included Orlando, New Orleans, San Jose, Las Vegas, Boston, and Chicago.

eBay Motors   Part of eBay devoted to vehicles and vehicle accessories.

eBay Stores   Web page within eBay's site where eBay Store owners can list items for longer durations and lower Insertion fees, and showcase all their items together.

eBay Toolbar   Toolbar for web browser with shortcuts to various places on eBay. Also has account-guard feature to help protect you from fake websites.

eBayer   A person who buys or sells on eBay.

EZ Cube   A professional photography tool used to filter lighting and provide a blank background for items. This product comes in various sizes to accommodate different-sized items.

Featured First   Listings that display at the top of the search results or category page. Sellers pay between $24.95 and $74.95 for this option. It is only available to Top-Rated Sellers.

feedback   eBay's system of checks and balances. All buyers can leave positive, neutral, or negative feedback for sellers. Sellers may leave only a positive Feedback Score for buyers (or not leave feedback at all).

Feedback Profile   The page that shows a particular eBay member's feedback information.

Final Value fee   A fee eBay charges based on the selling price of your item. Sometimes called a selling fee.

fixed-price auction   A listing that doesn't have a starting bid. Each "bid" is a purchase for the item at the price specified.

Gallery   Section of eBay that displays the search results with larger pictures and in a different layout view.

Gallery Plus   Puts an Enlarge link below the thumbnail image on the search results page, which enlarges the picture when the link is activated. The seller pays 35¢ to $1 for this feature.

Hammertap   A third-party data-analysis program to help you choose the day, time, keywords, and starting price for your items.

HTML editor   Feature of the Sell Your Item form, which converts the text and formatting you type into HTML (a different computer/web language).

Insertion Fee Credit   If your item does not sell the first time, you can relist it; if it sells the second time, eBay will credit you one of the Insertion fees.

Insertion fee   Fee eBay charges to list an item on eBay. The fee is based on the starting price you select.

Item Specifics   A list of questions about the item that eBay asks sellers when they list an item using the Sell Your Item form. The Finder box on the category results page or search results page uses this information to narrow the results based on the buyer's selections.

Item variation listing   A fixed-price listing where otherwise identical items are available in different sizes, colors, and so on. Currently these are only available in the Clothing, Shoes, and Accessories, or Home and Garden categories.

listing   Page used to post an item for sale. Types of listing on eBay include auctions, fixed-price listings, and store inventory.

Listing Designer   An option in the Sell Your Item form to add a theme or border to the listing page.

lot auction   An auction of multiple items that will all be sold to the same person.

megapixel   Setting for your camera. The higher the megapixel, the higher quality the printed images.

multiple-quantity fixed-price listing   A fixed-price listing with more than one identical item for sale. Buyers specify the quantity they wish to purchase, from one to the total quantity available. The price is the fixed-price multiplied by the quantity selected.

My eBay   The hub of all your eBay activity. It shows all the items you have bid on, bought, listed, and sold.

My Messages   eBay's e-mail system, to keep e-mail addresses secure. It is accessed through the Messages tab in My eBay.

My World   A page like MySpace where you can put pictures and text about you.

negative feedback   A type of feedback comment used when the buyer was dissatisfied with your transaction. It removes one point from your Feedback Score and also affects your feedback rating percentage and buyer satisfaction rating.

newbie   New eBay buyer or seller.

Non-Paying bidder   A bidder who wins an item (or clicks Buy It Now) and then does not pay for it.

optional listing upgrades   Options that can be added to your listing for a fee.

PayPal   The preferred payment processing system on eBay.

PayPal Buyer Protection Policy   Protects the buyer from seller fraud, up to the value of the transaction including shipping. This is the same as the coverage available through the eBay Resolution Center.

PayPal Confirmed Address   The address most sellers require you to give as your shipping address. This is the billing address attached to the credit card you registered with PayPal.

PayPal Seller Protection Policy   Protects the seller in the same way as the buyer. See *PayPal Buyer Protection Policy*.

PayPal Verified   Confirms your identity through your bank account details. PayPal deposits two small amounts into your bank account, which you locate on your statement and then enter into the boxes provided in PayPal. Once you have done this, you are PayPal Verified.

phishing e-mail   E-mail that appears to come from eBay but is actually a fake.

Picture Services   eBay's image hosting uploader tool.

PowerSeller   Seller who has achieved $3,000 or more in sales over 100 or more transactions within the last 12 months, maintains a 98 percent positive feedback percentage, and a 4.6 Detailed Seller Ratings average in all rating areas. Four low DSRs (1 or 2 star ratings) in one DSR area results in the loss of PowerSeller status. PowerSellers receive a 5 percent discount on their Final Value fees.

proxy bid   Placing your maximum bid rather than the next bidding increment.

Refine Search   A box on the search results page that shows (and offers links to) the most popular categories/subcategories the items are listed in and other options to narrow down the results.

reserve-price auction (RPA)   Minimal price the seller is willing to sell the item for. If the bidding doesn't reach this amount, the seller doesn't have to sell the item.

Resolution Center   Place where you can report an unpaid item, an item not as described, or an item not received. Accessed through My eBay.

Reviews & Guides   Place where eBayers can read or write about a product (review) or specific technique (guide).

Second Chance Offer   Option for seller to offer an identical item to bidders in his auction other than the high bidder. This is also used when the high bidder doesn't complete the transaction.

Sell Your Item form   The form eBay devised to create your eBay auction listing.

sell-through rate (STR)   The percentage of listed items that actually sell.

Seller Dashboard   Area of My eBay (accessed through the Account tab) that shows the seller's current standings for Top-Rated Seller status, PowerSeller status, Best Match search standings, and more.

sniping   Waiting until the last few seconds of an auction to place your bid so that no other buyers have time to bid (and outbid you) before the auction ends.

spoof site   A fake eBay or PayPal website that is trying to get your user ID and password. See also *phishing e-mail*.

stock photography   Photograph from the catalog or website.

Terapeak   Another third-party research tool of eBay data.

third-party tool/program   Not managed or owned by eBay.

Top-Rated Seller   PowerSeller who has 0.50 percent of all Detailed Seller Ratings at 1 or 2 stars. Three instances of a low DSR rating in one area results in the loss of Top-Rated Seller status. Top-Rated Sellers receive a 20 percent discount on Final Value fees.

Trading Assistant   Seller who sells items for other people on a commission basis.

user ID   The name all other eBay users will know you by.

username   See *user ID*.

Vehicle Protection Program   The fraud program for eBay Motors. It includes *Condition Guarantee by Seller* and *Vehicle Purchase Protection*, and offers different levels of fraud protection for different vehicles.

Vehicle Purchase Protection   The portion of fraud protection on eBay Motors that deals with major fraud and misrepresentation. See also *Condition Guarantee by Seller* and *Vehicle Protection Program*.

VeRO (Verified Rights Owner)   Copyright program to ensure that the ownership of text and photographs is not exploited.

Want It Now   An area of eBay where buyers can post "wanted" ads for items they cannot find on eBay. Sellers search the Want It Now posts and respond with matching auctions they have listed.

Watch This Item   A button on the auction listing page that will add that particular listing to your Items I'm Watching section of My eBay.

white balance   A camera adjustment to make the image colors more true to life.

Where Do I Go from Here?

That all depends. If you just want to buy and sell a few things on eBay, you probably have everything you need in this book. But if you want to expand your eBay adventure, there's always more to learn. eBay and the wider Internet are always changing and evolving, so it helps to have additional resources. Here are some in the form of books and websites that will help you ramp your eBaying up a notch.

Resources Website

Skip and I have created a resources page on his website specifically for you, our readers. On this page, you will find links to important eBay pages, links to other important resources mentioned in this book, a link to Skip's 77 Tips for eBay Sellers, and much more. I can't list everything here because it evolves as eBay makes changes and as we find new resources that may be of interest to you. Skip tries to update the page frequently as things change.

The website is www.skipmcgrath.com/cig. Make sure you add the /cig, or it won't take you to the right page. (CIG stands for *Complete Idiot's Guide*, if you were wondering.)

If you decide to learn to sell on eBay, Skip's website contains tons of free articles and information for sellers. You can also subscribe to his monthly newsletter for professional eBay sellers, *The eBay Seller's News*.

AuctionBytes

AuctionBytes (www.auctionbytes.com) is the leading news and information site for the online auction industry.

AuctionBytes is a fantastic resource for any auction buyer or seller. Ina Steiner, the editor, is very sharp, and little happens in the online selling world that she doesn't catch and report.

AuctionBytes TV is a series of streaming video interviews and short information programs that Ina and her husband, David (who used to be a TV producer), create. If you want to know what's going on in the auction community, go to AuctionBytes for completely impartial coverage (and sign up for their free newsletter to keep up on everything right from your e-mail).

eBay Live!

eBay Live! is eBay's convention and the ultimate eBay geek experience. *eBay Live!* is usually held in June but moves around the country. You can typically register anytime after March 30 (there's a link on the home page once registration opens). The convention consists of seminars, panel discussions, over 100 exhibitors who offer goods and services to eBay members, and several social events, including a gala party with live entertainment.

In 2010, *eBay Live!* will be on the road. Rather than one static convention, eBay will be visiting many cities around the country. No details have been released regarding 2011 at the time of this writing.

Recommended Reading

Here are some books I recommend. Bear in mind that new ones may have been published since this one, so you should check the resources page (www.skipmcgrath. com/cig); I'll let you know about any new books I think are really worth a read.

The Complete Idiot's Guide to Starting an eBay Business, Second Edition, by Barbara Weltman (Alpha, 2008). Barbara Weltman is a business and tax expert, and her husband is an eBay fanatic. Although her book published before mine, this is somewhat of a prequel to hers. When I wrote this book, I made sure not to cover the same things Barbara had already written (unless it was absolutely necessary), so you won't find the same material in both books. As an eBay professional, I found her book informative and very easy to use. If you liked this book, you will like hers.

Titanium eBay: A Tactical Guide to Becoming a Millionaire PowerSeller, by Skip McGrath (Alpha, 2009). If you are really looking to kick up your existing eBay business, *Titanium eBay* is for you. It is written by our very own Skip McGrath and is considered the most advanced of the three eBay books published by Alpha. Beginners should start with *The Complete Idiot's Guide to eBay,* then read *The Complete Idiot's Guide to Starting an eBay Business,* and then if they still want to go further, read *Titanium eBay.* You won't find any basic information in *Titanium eBay;* it is advanced material written for the pros who want to kick up their sales.

The Pocket Idiot's Guide to eBay Motors, by Lissa McGrath (Alpha, 2008). If you're interested in buying or selling vehicles on eBay, this pocket-sized book walks you through it step by step. Whether you're looking to buy or sell, you'll learn tips from the pros who teach dealerships how to sell on eBay.

Turn eBay Data into Dollars, by Ina Steiner (McGraw-Hill, 2006). Ina Steiner, editor of AuctionBytes (mentioned earlier), shows eBay sellers how to use eBay and third-party research tools to analyze their current sales and change their strategy to get better sales. It's a great book, and certainly a must-read for all sellers.

Quick Reference Tips

These are my most important tips. You've seen these throughout the book, so this appendix gives you a quick and handy summary.

Buyers' Tips

1. Always read the auction carefully so you know what you are bidding on. Look for what is not said as well as what is. If an important accessory, cable, or piece that you need isn't mentioned in the auction, check with the seller to see if it is included before bidding.

2. Use the Refine Search and Preferences to narrow search results to a manageable size. Why waste your time sorting through irrelevant listings when you can make your results far more specific?

3. Use Completed Listings to see what similar items have been selling for on eBay during the previous two weeks.

4. Check local prices and other major online retailers' prices before deciding on your maximum bid. Remember to include the shipping cost for each item you are bidding on when you calculate what your actual maximum bid should be.

5. Bid within the last few minutes to get a better deal, or use sniping software to do it for you. Make sure you know how long it takes for your page to load before sniping so you don't cut it too close and miss the end of the auction!

6. On the search results page, look past the Featured Items to find the bargains hidden within the nonfeatured listings, but remember that only Top-Rated Sellers can feature their listings, so featured items are all from sellers with a proven track record of excellent customer service.

7. Use My eBay to track everything you are bidding on, have bought, are watching, have made an offer on, didn't win, and more. Don't forget that your My Messages box is in there, too!

8. Be aware of fraud and protect yourself by using the eBay Toolbar, checking that e-mails are really from eBay, using PayPal for payments, and using your general common sense. Never send a payment via Western Union, MoneyGram, or other similar services. Even money orders and checks are no longer allowed on eBay.

9. Try to work out any issues with your seller directly before using the Resolution Center. Negative feedback is your last resort, not your first step in a dispute.

10. If you get lost, use the Site Map, which is far easier than the Help files.

11. Check for hidden bargains lurking behind misspellings and alternative spellings in listing titles.

12. Always check the Shipping and Payments tab on the listing page. Often there's a cheaper shipping option than the one eBay shows at the top of the page and on the search results page.

13. Always read a seller's feedback; look at the Detailed Seller Ratings as well as the Feedback Score and positive percentage rating. Be a little more wary of sellers who are new to eBay or who are overseas selling on the eBay U.S. site (or both).

14. Consider buying on eBay International sites for items that originate in those countries. You may find you can get the item much cheaper, even after you add shipping. Start with eBay.co.uk (United Kingdom) or eBay.com.au (Australia), as both are English speaking and have similar trade regulations to those in the United States.

15. You can get the seller's phone number through Advanced Search if you are having trouble locating him.

16. When leaving feedback, be as specific as you can. This will likely get you more positive feedback in return. It also helps other potential buyers decide whether they want to do business with this particular seller. Remember, what you write reflects as much on you as it does on the seller.

17. For an extra level of fraud protection, change the funding source for your PayPal account to your credit card if you are buying an expensive item. That way, you can file a claim through your credit card company if you really have to.

Sellers' Tips

1. Do a Completed Listings search to see what comparable items are selling for on eBay, to help determine your starting price. Also make sure no major retailers are offering a sale on that product when your listing will be active.

2. Make sure your listing title contains the keywords buyers actually search for. Be sure to include brand names, important model names or numbers, and sizes or colors.

3. Check the price breaks on Insertion fees, and try to be at the top of the lower band instead of at the bottom of the higher one (for example, $24.99 instead of $25).

4. Know your buyer. Make sure you have an idea of who would want your item. Writing your listing title and description will be much easier if you have a target person in mind.

5. Know your item. Research it online if you don't know much about it. Seeing what others say about an item can help you cover all the important information in your own item description. Remember, the buyers have probably done their research—you should always know more about your items than your potential buyers.

6. Remember, you are trying to sell something. Write persuasively. List the features, but explain how the product and the features will benefit buyers. Don't be afraid to get personal. Tell them how you use the product and how it has benefited you. Once you make it personal, you usually have them hooked.

7. Always identify any flaws. The easiest way to get negative feedback, low Item As Described star ratings, and eBay or PayPal disputes is to "forget" to mention dings, chips, scratches, stains, holes, and other flaws.

8. Use the HTML editor features (bold, italic, underline, color, size, and font changes) to make your item description stand out.

9. Check misspellings for your item keywords. Sometimes the misspelling is so common that buyers don't realize they misspelled the word and pay more because fewer items show in the results. If this is the case, use both the correct spelling and the misspelling for that keyword in your title.

10. Review your photos. Are they sharp? Did you show the product from all angles? Are there enough photos to fully represent what you are selling? If your pictures don't grab them, bidders will often click away without ever reading your item description.

11. Look at your photos at thumbnail size, because this is what a buyer will see on the search results page. If it doesn't look good in thumbnail size as well as regular size, you may want to rethink your photograph composition, background, or whatever else is distracting in the picture.

12. Don't just use stock photographs (and certainly not for your thumbnail picture). Buyers want to see the actual item they are buying. Many stock photos (such as those on the manufacturer's website) are protected by copyright, so your listing could be cancelled if you are caught.

13. Choose the best day and time to list your specific item. Make sure you aren't going away for the weekend, or if you are, be sure that you have access to your e-mail to answer questions. Be careful to avoid listing items to end on holiday weekends or during major events like the Super Bowl, the World Series, or election night.

14. Don't forget to select what regions of the world you are willing to ship the item to, and countries you specifically want to exclude. You will probably change this for different items based on weight and size.

15. Don't use more listing upgrades than you need. Bold and Subtitle are useful but are rarely profitable on cheaper items (under $15).

16. Spell out your shipping policies very clearly and ship within one to two business days from payment. Always list your cheapest shipping option first, because that is the one eBay displays on the search results page.

17. Accept PayPal and make sure your account is Verified.

18. Preview your listing carefully before you click Submit so you can see exactly what your listing will look like to buyers.

19. Spell-check, and then spell-check again. This goes for your title as well as your description. You *will* lose bidders if your title keywords are misspelled, and you lose credibility if your description has spelling errors.

Index

A

abbreviations, common, 65
About Me page icon (Seller info box), 79
About Me pages, 101
   self-promotion, 344-345
Account Guard, 18
Account tab (My eBay), 50-53
   Addresses option, 52
   Feedback option, 53
   Notification Preferences option, 52
   PayPal Account option, 53
   Personal Information option, 51-52
   Site Preferences option, 53
accounts
   buyers, registering, 7-8
   credit cards, PayPal, 25-26
   logons, 12-13
   passwords
      creating, 9-10
      recovering, 13-14
      secret questions, 10-12
   PayPal
      bank accounts, 23-25
      Personal, 27
      Premier, 27
      seller accounts, 160-161
      setting up, 20-23
   security, 14
      Account Guard, 18
   setting up, 6-7
   takeover, 137-138
   user IDs, recovering, 13-14
acronyms, common, 65
Active Selling section (Summary page), 297-298

Activity tab (My eBay), 38-48
add-on selling, 308, 321
Addresses option (Account tab), 52
Adobe Photoshop, photographs, editing, 213-214
alternate endings, searches, 68
Amazon.com, 373
Announcements, 33
Answer Center, 33
auction titles, 32
auctions, 249-250.
   See also listings
   automating, 366-367
   Best Offer, 84-85, 254-255
   bidding, 103-104
      losing, 111-112
      maximum bids, 111
      Place bid option, 106-108
      retractions, 115-118
      rules, 113-115
   Buy It Now, 82-83, 252-253
   buyer requirements, 276
   cancelling, 303-304
   counterfeit merchandise, 138-139
   creating, 152-154
   descriptions, 219
      benefits, 244-247
      categories, 220-222
      features, 244-247
      HTML editor, 241-242
      inaccurate descriptions, 138
      Item Specifics, 232-233
      Listing Designer, 247-248
      one-line hooks, 240
      Sell Your Item form, 219-225
      uploading pictures, 233-238
      writing, 239-248
   duration, setting, 264

ending, 265-266
fees, 179-180, 191-193
    Buy It Now option, 184
    eBay Motors, 194-196
    Insertion fees, 180-182
    International Site Visibility, 183-184
    Picture Hosting, 193-194
    Reserve-Price Auction, 184-185
    upgrades, 183
fixed-price auctions, 83-84
Giving Works, 266-267
lot, 250-252
monitoring, 38-40
nonexistent products, 139-140
payment methods, 267
photographs, inaccurate photographs, 138
queues, 266
reserve prices, 83
reserve-price
    bidding, 105-106
    Second Chance Offers, 106
restricted access auctions, 86
returns policies, 277-278
revising, 300
    after first bid, 301
    Buy It Now requests, 302
    cancelling bids, 302-303
    prior to first bid, 300-301
    starting prices, 301-302
scheduled starts, 264-265
Second Chance Offers, 38
Sell Your Item form, alternatives, 286-291
selling formats, 258-260
    Buy It Now prices, 262
    fixed-price listings, 263
    reserve prices, 261
    starting prices, 258-260
shipping
    calculated shipping, 269-272
    combined shipping discounts, 275
    flat-rate shipping, 269-271
    free shipping, 273-274
    handling time, 275
    insurance, 271-273

international shipping, 274
    item location, 275-276
    tracking, 271-273
shipping information, 268
sniping, 109-111
subtitles, 231-232
taxes, 278-280
titles
    misspellings, 229-230
    writing, 225-230
tracking, 295-300
unsold items, 325-326
    hits, 326
    relisting, 327-328
upgrades, 281-282
    bold text, 284-285
    Featured First, 285
    Gallery Plus, 282-283
    packages, 286
    subtitles, 283-284
    titles, 282
violations, reporting, 118-120
visitor counters, 248
Auctiva, 220, 288
    Create a Listing page, 288
    fees, 288
    Scrolling Gallery, 289-291
    Turbo Lister, compared, 289
automating auctions, 366-367

B

backgrounds, photographs, 200-201
bank accounts, PayPal
    adding, 23-25
    instant transfers, 26
banned items, 155-156
Basic Uploader, 237
Best Offer auctions, 84-85, 254-255
Bid history option (listings), 76
bidding, 103-104
    cancelling, 302-303
    losing, 111-112
    maximum bids, 111

Place bid option, 106-108
reserve-price auctions, 105-106
    Second Chance Offers, 106
retractions, 115-118
rules, 113-115
shill bidding, 156-158
sniping, 109-111
Bidding section (My eBay), 41
blocked buyers, managing, 305
bold text, 284-285
browsing listings, pictures, 63-64
businesses
    Amazon.com, 373
    auctions, automating, 366-367
    considerations, 360
    consignment selling, 370-372
    equipment, 365-366
    Etsy.com, 373
    insurance, 363-365
    licensing, 363-365
    organizing, 362-363
    products, 360-361
    software, 365-366
    taxes, 363-365
    websites, creating, 373
    wholesale product sourcing, 367-368
        drop-shipping, 368-369
        merchandise marts, 369-370
        trade shows, 369-370
Buy It Now auctions, 4, 76, 82-83, 252-253
    fees, 184
    prices, setting, 262
    requests, 302
Buy tab, 31-32
Buyer Block Exemption List, 305
Buyer Protection (PayPal), 144
buyer requirements, auctions, 276
buyers
    blocked buyers, managing, 305
    feedback
        extortion, 114
        leaving, 319-320

    malicious, 115
    receiving, 128-133
    removing, 132
    replying, 133
    revising, 132-133
nonpayment, 333
    cancelling transaction, 334-336
    filing claim, 336-337
    reporting, 333-335
    Second Chance Offers, 338-340
    Unpaid Item Assistant, 337-338
registration, 7-8
rules, 113-115
unresponsive, 328
    calling, 331-333
    follow-up e-mails, 330-331
    invoicing, 329-330
buying, international transactions, 26-27
buySAFE, 145, 352

C

calculated shipping, 269-272
calling unresponsive buyers, 331-333
cameras, 200
cancelling
    auctions, 303-304
    bids, 302-303
    transactions, 334-336
Captchas, 7
cashier's checks, 19-20, 28
categories, descriptions, selecting, 220-222
Category sort option (search results page), 59
ceramic, photographing, 204
Changed User ID icon (Seller info box), 79
checkout, 124-126
    international transactions, 128
    PayPal, 125-128
claims
    Resolution Center, filing, 142-144
    unpaid items, filing, 336-337

closeout section, outlet stores, items, 174
clothing, photographing, 204
Cloud Domes, 213
collecting sales tax, 364
combined/free shipping, 275, 320
community pages, 33
    Announcements, 33
    Answer Center, 33
    Discussion Boards, 33
    Feedback Forum, 33
    Resolution Center, 34
    Workshops, 34
Community tab, 7
Compare feature, 91-92
Completed Listings page, 88-90
composition, photographs, 204-205
configuring searches, 71-72
Confirmed addresses, PayPal, 23-26
consignment selling, 370-372
contact information
    publishing, 115
    unresponsive buyers, obtaining, 331-333
contacting sellers, 121-124
copyrighted photographs, using, 215
Costco, items, purchasing, 174
Create a Listing page (Auctiva), 288
credit cards
    fraud protection, 144-145
    PayPal
        adding, 25-26
        instant transfers, 26
crystal, photographing, 205
customer service
    e-mail messages, 309-311
    feedback, leaving, 319-320
    packing items, 311-312
        extras, 314
    providing, 308-309
    repeat buyers, offers, 321-322
    shipping, 312-313
        combined/free shipping, 320
Customs, international shipping, 274

D

debit cards, PayPal
    adding, 25-26
    instant transfers, 26
delivery confirmations, USPS, 44
Description tab (listings), 80-81
descriptions, 219
    benefits, 244-247
    categories, selecting, 220-222
    inaccurate descriptions, 138
    one-line hooks, 240
    photographs, inaccurate photographs, 138
    pictures, uploading, 233-238
    Sell Your Item form, 219-225
        Item Specifics, 232-233
    writing, 239-248
        benefits, 244-247
        features, 244-247
        HTML editor, 241-242
        Listing Designer, 247-248
Detailed Seller Ratings (Seller Dashboard), 5, 99, 130, 354-358
Didn't Win section (My eBay), 45
digital cameras, 200
digital photographs, editing, 205-212
digital zoom, cameras, 203-204
Discussion Boards, 33
display order, search results page, changing, 59
distributors, wholesale product sourcing, 367-368
    drop-shipping, 368-369
    merchandise marts, 369-370
    trade shows, 369-370
drop-shipping, 368-369
DSI (Discount Shipping Insurance), 272
DSRs (Detailed Seller Ratings), 5, 99, 130, 354-358
duration, auctions, setting, 264

E

e-mail accounts, phishing, 15-17
e-mail messages, customer service, 309-311
eBay, 3-4
  home page, 29
    navigation tabs, 30-35
    signing in, 30
  security, 14
eBay Bucks, 48
eBay Motors
  fees, 194-196
  sellers, researching, 101-102
eBay Store icon (Seller info box), 79
eBay Stores
  fees, 189-193
  inventory items, 85
eBay Toolbar, 17-18
editing
  listings, 300
    after first bid, 301
    Buy It Now requests, 302
    cancelling bids, 302-303
    prior to first bid, 300-301
    starting prices, 301-302
  photographs, 205-214
either/or words, searches, 67
electronics, photographing, 205
End of Auction Email messages
  unresponsive buyers, 328
    calling, 331-333
    follow-up e-mails, 330-331
    invoicing, 329-330
  PayPal, 164-165
ending auctions, 265-266
Enhanced Uploader, 236
Enlarge link (listings), 76
equipment, businesses, 365-366
errors, photography, 205-212
escrow, 28
  fraud, 140-141
  services, 140
Etsy.com, 373

exact phrases, searches, 67
excessive shipping costs, reporting, 119
excluding words, searches, 67
extortion, feedback, 114
EZ Cubes, 213

F

fake merchandise, 138-139
Featured First, 285
Featured Items section, search results page, 62
features, descriptions, 244-247
feedback, 5, 53
  DSRs (Detailed Seller Ratings), 130
  extortion, 114
  leaving, 319-320
  malicious feedback, 115
  negative feedback, 307
    avoiding, 348-349
    revising, 350-352
  received feedback, replying, 349-350
  Recent Feedback Ratings box, 97-98
  removing, 132
  replying, 133
  revising, 132-133
  sellers
    DSRs (Detailed Seller Ratings), 99-100
    researching, 96-100
  self-promotion, 348-352
Feedback Forum, 33, 131
Feedback Profile page, 96-97
Feedback Score icon (Seller info box), 78
Feedback star icon (Seller info box), 78
fees, 179-180, 191-193
  auctions, 180
    Buy It Now option, 184
    Insertion fees, 180-182
    International Site Visibility, 183-184
    Reserve-Price Auction, 184-185
    upgrades, 183
  Auctiva, 288
  eBay Motors, 194-196

eBay Stores, 189-191
fixed-price listings, 185-189
Insertion fees, relistings, 327-328
PayPal, 196-197
Picture Hosting, 193-194
filing claims, Resolution Center, 142-144
filing unpaid item claims, 336-337
Final Value fees
    credit, 333
    fixed-price listings, 185-187
Find A Member, 7
finding items, 57
    search results page, 58-62
fixed-price auctions, 83-84
fixed-price listings, 77, 85, 253
    fees, 185-193
    multiple-item fixed-price listings, 255
    prices, setting, 263
flat-rate shipping, 269-271
follow-up e-mails, sending, unresponsive
  buyers, 330-331
forgotten passwords and user IDs, retrieving,
  13-14
fraud, 135-136
    account takeover, 137-138
    avoiding, 136-141
    buySAFE, 145
    counterfeit merchandise, 138-139
    credit card fraud protection, 144-145
    escrow fraud, 140-141
    inaccurate descriptions, 138
    inaccurate photographs, 138
    insurance programs, 144-145
    nonexistent products, 139-140
    PayPal Buyer Protection, 144
    seller impersonation, 136-137
    SquareTrade warranty service, 146-147
fraud protection, 28
free shipping, 273-274
    listings, 61
full-time businesses
    Amazon.com, 373
    auctions, automating, 366-367
    considerations, 360
    consignment selling, 370-372

equipment, 365-366
Etsy.com, 373
insurance, 363-365
licensing, 363-365
organizing, 362-363
products, 360-361
software, 365-366
taxes, 363-365
websites, creating, 373
wholesale product sourcing, 367-368
    drop-shipping, 368-369
    merchandise marts, 369-370
    trade shows, 369-370

G

Gallery Plus, 62-63, 282-283
Gallery view (search results page, 63-64
Giving Works, 266-267
glass, photographing, 204
goods. *See* items

H

Hammertap, 259-260
    consignment selling, 371
handbags, photographing, 204
handling time, shipping, 275
Help pages, 34-35
hits, unsold items, 326
home page (eBay), 29
    navigation tabs, 30-35
    signing in, 30
homes, items, selecting, 170-171
HTML editor, descriptions, writing, 241-242

I

icons, user ID icons, Seller info box, 78-80
ID Verify, 79, 352-353
images, 199
    cameras, 200
    Gallery Plus, 282-283
    inaccurate images, 138

listings, browsing, 63-64
Picture Hosting, fees, 193-194. *See also*
    photographs, 200
stock images, using, 215
uploading, 214-215, 233-238
incorrect spellings, titles, 229-230
information products, 322-323
Insertion fees
    credit, relistings, 327-328
    fixed-price listings, 185
Insertion fees, auctions, 180-182
insurance
    businesses, 363-365
    fraud protection, 144-145
    shipping, 271-273, 317
international sellers, researching, 94-96
international shipping, 274, 317-318
    Customs, 274
International Site Visibility, fees, 183-184
international transactions, PayPal, 26-27
Internet fraud, 135-136
    account takeover, 137-138
    avoiding, 136-141
    buySAFE, 145
    counterfeit merchandise, 138-139
    credit card fraud protection, 144-145
    escrow fraud, 140-141
    inaccurate descriptions, 138
    inaccurate photographs, 138
    insurance programs, 144-145
    nonexistent products, 139-140
    PayPal Buyer Protection, 144
    seller impersonation, 136-137
    SquareTrade warranty service, 146-147
invoices
    sellers, requesting, 122-123
    sending, unresponsive buyers, 329-330
Item condition option (listings), 76
item location, shipping, 275-276
Item Specifics (Sell Your Item form), 57-58,
    71, 232-233
items
    banned, 155-156
    bidding, 103-104

losing, 111-112
maximum bids, 111
Place bid option, 106-108
reserve-price auctions, 105-106
businesses, 360-361
consignment selling, 370-372
counterfeit merchandise, 138-139
descriptions, 219
    benefits, 244-247
    categories, 220-222
    features, 244-247
    HTML editor, 241-242
    Item Specifics, 232-233
    Listing Designer, 247-248
    one-line hooks, 240
    Sell Your Item form, 219-225
    uploading pictures, 233-238
    writing, 239-248
donating, 173
eBay Store inventory items, 85
finding, 57, 68-72
    Advanced Search, 68
    alternate endings, 68
    either/or words, 67
    exact phrases, 67
    excluding words, 67
    keyword searches, 64-66
    product pages, 72-74
    refined searches, 69-71
    search results page, 58-62
    symbols, 66-67
information products, 322-323
Item Specifics, 57-58, 71
listing violations, reporting, 118-120
listings
    subtitles, 231-232
    titles, 225-230
monitoring, 38-40
nonexistent items, 139-140
packing, 311-312
photographing, 200-201
    backgrounds, 200-201
    common errors, 205-212
    composition, 204-205

digital zoom, 203-204
lighting, 201-203
optical zoom, 203-204
tools, 213
tripods, 203
purchasing around eBay, 133
receiving unwanted, 141
researching, 175
    About Me page, 101
    comparisons, 91-92
    Completed Listings page, 88-90
    eBay Motors, 101-102
    overseas sellers, 94-96
    seller feedback, 96-100
    shipping costs, 92-94
    third-party research tools, 176-177
restricted, 155-156
selecting, 170-177
    homes, 170-171
    outlet stores, 174
    thrift stores, 174-175
    Trading Assistants, 173-174
    yard sales, 171-172
selling
    fees, 179-180
    timing, 177-178
shipping
    combined/free shipping, 320
    insurance, 317
    international shipping, 317-318
    labels, 314-316
    packing, 313-314
    pickups, 319
    supplies, 312-313
similar items, relisting, 340-341
tracking, 295-300
unpaid items, 333
    cancelling transaction, 334-336
    filing claim, 336-337
    reporting, 333-335
    Second Chance Offers, 338-340
    Unpaid Item Assistant, 337-338

unsold items, 325-326
    hits, 326
    relisting, 327-328
wholesale product sourcing, 367-368
    drop-shipping, 368-369
    merchandise marts, 369-370
    trade shows, 369-370

J–K

jewelry, photographing, 201, 205

keywords
    auction titles, 32
    searches, 64-66
        acronyms, 65
        misspellings, 66

L

labels (shipping), 314-316
leaving feedback, 128-133
licensing businesses, 363-365
lighting, photographs, 201-202
    white balance, 202-203
List in Two Categories option (Sell Your
  Item form), 221
Listing Designer, 247-248
listing types, search results page, adjusting, 61
listings, 75-77, 249-250
    automating, 366-367
    Best Offer listings, 84-85, 254-255
    Bid history option, 76
    bidding, 103-104
        losing, 111-112
        maximum bids, 111
        Place bid option, 106-108
        retractions, 115-118
        rules, 113-115
    Buy It Now auctions, 76, 82-83, 252-253
    buyer requirements, 276

cancelling, 303-304
counterfeit merchandise, 138-139
creating, 152-154
Description tab, 80-81
descriptions, 219
    benefits, 244-247
    categories, 220-222
    features, 244-247
    HTML editor, 241-242
    inaccurate descriptions, 138
    Item Specifics, 232-233
    Listing Designer, 247-248
    one-line hooks, 240
    Sell Your Item form, 219-225
    uploading pictures, 233-238
    writing, 239-248
duration, setting, 264
ending, 265-266
Enlarge link, 76
fees, 179-180, 191-193
    Buy It Now option, 184
    eBay Motors, 194-196
    eBay Stores, 189-191
    fixed-price listings, 185-189
    Insertion fees, 180-182
    International Site Visibility, 183-184
    PayPal, 196-197
    Picture Hosting, 193-194
    Reserve-Price Auction, 184-185
    upgrades, 183
finding, search results page, 58-62
fixed-price auctions, 83-84
fixed-price listings, 77, 253
    fees, 185-189
    multiple-item fixed-price listings, 255
free shipping, 61
Gallery Plus, 62-63
Giving Works, 266-267
Item condition option, 76
keyword searches, 64-66
    acronyms, 65
    misspellings, 66
lot auctions, 250-252

nonexistent products, 139-140
payment methods, 267
photographs, inaccurate photographs, 138
Place bid button, 76
queues, 266
Related Items and Services tab, 81
researching
    About Me page, 101
    comparisons, 91-92
    Completed Listings page, 88-90
    eBay Motors, 101-102
    seller feedback, 96-100
    shipping costs, 92-96
reserve prices, 83
reserve-price listings
    bidding, 105-106
    Second Chance Offers, 106
restricted access listings, 86
returns policies, 277-278
Returns policy, 76
revising, 300
    after first bid, 301
    Buy It Now requests, 302
    cancelling bids, 302-303
    prior to first bid, 300-301
    starting prices, 301-302
scheduled starts, 264-265
searches, 57
Sell Your Item form, alternatives, 286-291
seller information, 78
selling formats, 258-260
    Buy It Now prices, 262
    fixed-price listings, 263
    reserve prices, 261
    starting prices, 258-260
shipping
    calculated shipping, 269-272
    combined shipping discounts, 275
    flat-rate shipping, 269-271
    free shipping, 273-274
    handling time, 275
    insurance, 271-273
    international shipping, 274

item location, 275-276
tracking, 271-273
Shipping and Payments tab, 81
Shipping details option, 76
shipping information, 268
similar listings, relisting, 340-341
sniping, 109-111
Starting bid option, 76
subtitles, 231-232
taxes, 278-280
Time left option, 76
titles
appearance, 62
misspellings, 229-230
writing, 225-230
tracking, 295-300
unsold listings, 325-326
hits, 326
relisting, 327-328
upgrades, 281-282
bold text, 284-285
Featured First, 285
Gallery Plus, 282-283
packages, 286
subtitles, 283-284
titles, 282
user ID icons, 78-80
violations, reporting, 118-120
visitor counters, 248
Watch this item link, 76
logons, 12-13
lot auctions, 250-252
lowering starting prices, 301-302

M

malicious feedback, 115
managing blocked buyers, 305
marketing, 343
About Me pages, 344-345
Feedback profile, 348-352
negative feedback, 348-349
My World page, 345-346
Reviews and Guide page, 346-348
maximum bids, 111
merchandise marts, wholesale product
sourcing, 369-370
Messages tab (My eBay), 49-50
MissionFish, 267
misspellings
keyword searches, 66
titles, 229-230
money orders, 19-20, 28
MoneyBookers, 28
MoneyGram, 20, 28
monitoring
auctions, 38-40
listings, 295-300
seller reputation, Seller Dashboard,
353-358
multiple-item fixed-price listings, 255
My eBay, 5, 32, 37
Account tab, 50-53
Addresses option, 52
Feedback option, 53
Notification Preferences option, 52
PayPal Account option, 53
Personal Information option, 51-52
Site Preferences option, 53
Activity tab, 38-48
entering, 37
Messages tab, 49-50
Summary page, 296-298
Active Selling section, 296-298
Bidding section, 41
customizing, 46-47
Didn't Win section, 45
Scheduled section, 296
Sold section, 298-300
Summary links, 47-48
Unsold section, 300
Watching section, 38-40
Won section, 41-44
My Messages, 5
My World page, self-promotion, 345-346

N

navigation tabs, 30-35
negative feedback, 307
  avoiding, 348-349
  extortion, 114
  malicious feedback, 115
  replying, 349-350
  revising, 350-352
New Member icon (Seller info box), 79
nonexistent products, 139-140
nonperformance, sellers, 159-160
nonwinning bidders, Second Chance Offers, 338-340
notes, monitored items, 40
Notification Preferences option (Account tab), 52

O

off-eBay sales, 158-159
offers, repeat buyers, 321-322
one-line hooks, descriptions, 240
optical zoom, cameras, 203-204
organization, businesses, 362-363
outlet stores, closeout section, items, 174
overexposed photographs, 212
overseas sellers, researching, 94-96
overseas transactions, PayPal, 26-27

P

packages, upgrades, 286
packing items, 311-314
  extras, 314
part-time businesses
  Amazon.com, 373
  auctions, automating, 366-367
  considerations, 360
  consignment selling, 370-372
  equipment, 365-366
  Etsy.com, 373
  insurance, 363-365
  licensing, 363-365
  organizing, 362-363
  products, 360-361
  software, 365-366
  taxes, 363-365
  websites, creating, 373
  wholesale product sourcing, 367-368
    drop-shipping, 368-369
    merchandise marts, 369-370
    trade shows, 369-370
passwords
  creating, 9-10
  recovering, 13-14
  secret question, 10-12
  security, 14
PayMate, 28
payment methods, 267
PayPal, 5, 19-20, 53
  accounts
    Personal, 27
    Premier, 27
    setting up, 20-23
  bank accounts, adding, 23-25
  Buyer Protection, 144
  checkout, 125-128
    international transactions, 128
  Confirmed addresses, 23-26
  credit cards, adding, 25-26
  instant transfers, 26
  international transactions, 26-27
  PayPal Preferred, 163
  PayPal Verified, 23-25
  popularity, 20
  Premier PayPal accounts, creating, 161-162
  seller accounts, 160-161
    customizing, 162-163
    End of Auction Emails, 164-165
    PayPal Preferred, 163
    refunds, 165-168
    upgrading, 161-162
    withdrawal limits, 161
seller fees, 196-197
shipping labels, creating, 315-316

PDF creators, 322
personal checks, 28
Personal Information option (Account tab), 51-52
Personal PayPal accounts, 27
phishing e-mails, 15-17
photographs, 199
    cameras, 200
    common errors, 205-212
    editing, 213-214
    Gallery Plus, 282-283
    inaccurate photographs, 138
    listings, browsing, 63-64
    Picture Hosting, fees, 193-194
    stock photographs, using, 215
    taking, 200-201
        backgrounds, 200-201
        composition, 204-205
        digital zoom, 203-204
        lighting, 201-203
        optical zoom, 203-204
        tripods, 203
    tools, 213
    uploading, 214-215, 233-238
    VeRO (Verified Rights Owner)
        photographs, using, 215
Photoshop, photographs, editing, 213-214
pickups, shipping, 319
Picture Hosting, fees, 193-194
    minimizing, 216
Place bid button (listings), 76
PowerSellers, 5, 355, 358
preferences, searches, setting, 71-72
Premier PayPal
    creating, 161-162
    customizing, 162-163
Premier PayPal accounts, 27
Price + Shipping sort orders, 59, 89
Price Guide to Starbucks Collectibles, 322
prices
    Buy It Now prices, setting, 262
    fixed-price listings, setting, 263
    reserve prices, setting, 261
    starting prices, setting, 258-260

Product Details (Sell Your Item form), 222-224
product pages, 72-74
products. *See* items
ProPay, 28
purchases
    checkout, 124-126
        international transactions, 128
        PayPal, 125-128
    international, 26-27

Q-R

questions, passwords, 10-12
queues, auctions, 266
quotation marks, searches, 67

raising starting prices, 301-302
received feedback, replying, 349-350
Recent Feedback Ratings box, 97-98
recovering passwords and user IDs, 13-14
refined searches, 69-71
refunds, PayPal, 165-168
registration
    buyers, 7-8
    sales tax certification, 363
    sellers, 152
Related Items and Services tab (listings), 81
relisting
    similar items, 340-341
    unsold items, 327-328
reminders, items, 40
repeat buyers, offers, 321-322
replying, feedback, 133
reporting unpaid items, 333-335
requesting invoices, 122-123
researching items
    About Me page, 101
    Compare feature, 91-92
    Completed Listings page, 88-90
    eBay Motors, 101-102
    overseas sellers, 94-96

seller feedback, 96-100
    DSRs (Detailed Seller Ratings), 99-100
shipping costs, 92-94
third-party research tools, 175-177
Reserve-Price Auctions, fees, 184-185
reserve prices, setting, 261
reserve prices, auctions, 83
Resolution Center, 34, 53
    filing claims, 142-144
    Unpaid Item claims, filing, 336-337
restricted access auctions, 86
restricted items, 155-156
retracting bids, 115-118
returns policies, auctions, 277-278
Returns policy (listings), 76
Reviewer icon (Seller info box), 79
Reviews and Guide page, self-promotion, 346-348
revising
    feedback, 132-133
    negative feedback, 350-352
rules
    buyers, 113-115
    sellers, 154
        banned items, 155-156
        off-eBay sales, 158-159
        seller nonperformance, 159-160
        Selling Practices Policy, 154-155
        shill bidding, 156-158

S

sales tax
    certification, registration, 363
    collecting, 364
sales taxes, auctions, 278-280
Sam's Club, items, 174
saving searches, 68-69
scams. See fraud
Scheduled section (Summary page), 296
    Active Selling section, 296-297
scheduled starts, auctions, 264-265
Scrolling Gallery (Auctiva), 289-291

search results page, 58
    customizing, 60-61
    display order, changing, 59
    Featured Items section, 62
    Gallery view, 63-64
    listing types, adjusting, 61
    pictures, browsing, 63-64
    Snapshot view, 63-64
searches, 68
    Advanced Search, 68
    alternate endings, 68
    configuring, 71-72
    either/or words, 67
    exact phrases, 67
    excluding words, 67
    items, 57
        search results page, 58-62
    keyword searches, 64-66
        acronyms, 65
        misspellings, 66
    product pages, 72-74
    refined searches, 69-71
    saving, 68-69
    symbols, 66-67
Second Chance Offer, 38, 338-340
    reserve-price auctions, 105-106
secret questions, passwords, 10-12
security, 14
    Account Guard, 18
    e-mail, phishing, 15-17
    eBay Toolbar, 17-18
    fraud, 135-136
        account takeover, 137-138
        avoiding, 136-141
        buySAFE, 145
        counterfeit merchandise, 138-139
        credit card fraud protection, 144-145
        escrow fraud, 140-141
        inaccurate descriptions, 138
        inaccurate photographs, 138
        insurance programs, 144-145
        nonexistent products, 139-140
        PayPal Buyer Protection, 144

seller impersonation, 136-137
SquareTrade warranty service, 146-147
passwords, 9-10
self-promotion, 343
About Me pages, 344-345
Feedback profile, 348-352
negative feedback, 348-349
My World page, 345-346
Reviews and Guide page, 346-348
Sell tab, 32
Sell Your Item form, 219-225
alternatives, 286-291
categories, selecting, 220-222
Item Specifics, 232-233
List in Two Categories, 221
pictures, uploading, 233-238
Product Details, 222-224
Show Other Options, 224-225
Seller Dashboard, 285
DSRs (Detailed Seller Ratings), 354-358
seller impersonation, 136-137
seller information, listings, 78
seller nonperformance, 159-160
seller reputation, 343
About Me pages, 344-345
buySAFE, 352
Feedback profile, 348-352
negative feedback, 348-349
ID Verify, 352-353
My World page, 345-346
Reviews and Guide page, 346-348
tracking, Seller Dashboard, 353-358
sellers, 151
About Me page, 101
auctions, 152-154
contacting, 121-124
DSRs (Detailed Seller Ratings), 130
eBay Motors, researching, 101-102
feedback
DSRs (Detailed Seller Ratings), 99-100
extortion, 114
giving, 128-133
giving and receiving, 128-133
leaving, 319-320

malicious, 115
Recent Feedback Ratings box, 97-98
removing, 132
replying, 133
researching, 96-100
revising, 132-133
Feedback Profile, 96-97
invoices, requesting, 122-123
items, selecting, 170-177
overseas sellers, researching, 94-96
PayPal accounts, 160-161
customizing, 162-163
End of Auction Emails, 164-165
fees, 196-197
PayPal Preferred, 163
refunds, 165-168
upgrading, 161-162
withdrawal limits, 161
PowerSellers, 355-358
registration, 152
rules, 154
banned items, 155-156
off-eBay sales, 158-159
seller nonperformance, 159-160
Selling Practices Policy, 154-155
shill bidding, 156-158
Top-Rated Sellers, 62
selling formats (listings), 258-260
Buy It Now prices, 262
fixed-price listings, 263
reserve prices, 261
starting prices, 258-260
selling items
add-on selling, 321
fees, 179-180, 191-193
auctions, 180-182
Buy It Now option, 184
eBay Motors, 194-196
eBay Stores, 189-191
fixed-price listings, 185-189
International Site Visibility, 183-184
PayPal, 196-197
Reserve-Price Auction, 184-185
upgrades, 183

homes, 170-171
outlet stores, 174
Picture Hosting, 193-194
researching, 175
    third-party research tools, 176-177
thrift stores, 174-175
timing, 177-178
Trade Assistants, 173-174
yard sales, 171-173
Selling Practices Policy, 154-155
shill bidding, 156-158
shipping
    calculated shipping, 269-272
    combined/free shipping, 320
    combined shipping discounts, 275
    drop-shipping, 368-369
    flat-rate shipping, 269-271
    free shipping, 273-274
    handling time, 275
    insurance, 271-273, 317
    international shipping, 274, 317-318
    item location, 275-276
    labels, creating, 314-316
    listings, free shipping, 61
    packing, 311-314
    pickups, 319
    supplies, 312-313
    tracking, 271-273
Shipping and Payments tab (listings), 81
shipping costs
    excessive shipping, reporting, 119
    researching, 92-94
shipping details (listings), 76, 268
Shipping Wizard, 268
Shipsurance, 272
Shooting star icon (Seller info box), 78
Show Other Options (Sell Your Item form),
  224-225
similar items, relisting, 340-341
Site Map, 35-36
Site Preferences option (Account tab), 53
small collectibles, photographing, 205
Snapshot view (search results page), 63-64
sniping auctions, 109-111
software, businesses, 365-366

Sold section (Summary page), 298-300
spamming users, 115
SquareTrade warranty service, 146-147
Standard Uploader, 237
Starting bid option (listings), 76
starting prices
    listings, 258-260
    lowering, 301-302
    raising, 301-302
Stealing First Base scams, 136
stock photographs, using, 215
Stores (eBay), fees, 189-191
subtitles, 283-284
    listings, writing, 231-232
Summary links (My eBay), 47-48
Summary page (My eBay), 296-298
    Active Selling section, 296-298
    Bidding section, 41
    customizing, 46-47
    Didn't Win section, 45
    Scheduled section, 296
    Sold section, 298-300
    Summary links, 47-48
    Unsold section, 300
    Watching section, 38-40
    Won section, 41-44
suppliers, wholesale product sourcing,
    367-368
    drop-shipping, 368-369
    merchandise marts, 369-370
    trade shows, 369-370
supplies, shipping, 312-313
symbols, searches, 66-67

T

taking photographs, 200-201
    backgrounds, 200-201
    composition, 204-205
    digital zoom, 203-204
    lighting, 201-202
        white balance, 202-203
    optical zoom, 203-204
    tripods, 203

taxes
  businesses, 363-365
  sales tax, collecting, 364
taxes, auctions, 278-280
telephone numbers, unresponsive buyers, obtaining, 331-333
third-party research tools, items, 176-177
thrift stores, items, 174-175
Time left option (listings), 76
timing, selling items, 177-178
titles
  listings
    appearance, 62
    writing, 225-230
  upgrades, 282
Toolbar (eBay), 17-18
tools, photography, 213
Top Reviewer icon (Seller info box), 79
Top-Rated Sellers, 5, 62, 79
tracking
  listings, 295-300
    traffic, 248
  seller reputation, Seller Dashboard, 353-358
  shipping, 271-273
trade shows, wholesale, 369-370
Trading Assistants, 173-174
  consignment selling, 372
traffic, listings, tracking, 248
transactions
  cancelling, 334-336
  fraud protection, 28
  international, 26-27
    checkout, 128
  unpaid items
    filing claim, 336-337
    reporting, 333-335
    Second Chance Offers, 338-340
    Unpaid Item Assistant, 337-338
tripods, photographs, taking, 203
Turbo Lister, 220, 286-288
  auctions, automating, 366-367
  Auctiva, compared, 289

U

underexposed photographs, 212
Unpaid Item Assistant, 337-338
unpaid items, 333
  cancelling transaction, 334-336
  filing claim, 336-337
  reporting, 333-335
  Second Chance Offers, 338-340
  Unpaid Item Assistant, 337-338
unresponsive buyers, 328
  calling, 331-333
  follow-up e-mails, 330-331
  invoices, sending, 329-330
unsold items, 325-326
  hits, 326
  relisting, 327-328
Unsold section (Summary page), 300
upgrades
  fixed-price listings, fees, 187
  listings, 281-282
    bold text, 284-285
    fees, 183
    Featured First, 285
    Gallery Plus, 282-283
    packages, 286
    subtitles, 283-284
    titles, 282
upgrading PayPal accounts, 161-162
uploaders, 236-238
uploading
  files, 214-215
  photographs, 233-238
user IDs, 78-80
  creating, 6-7
  full names, 6
  recovering, 13-14
  rules, 6-7
  searches, 7
  security, 14
users, spamming, 115
USPS
  delivery confirmations, 44
  pickups, 319

V

value packs, listings, 286
vases, photographing, 205
verification, PayPal, 23-25
VeRO (Verified Rights Owner) photographs,
    using, 215
violations, listings, reporting, 118-120
visitor counters, 248
    unsold items, hits, 326

W–X–Y–Z

Watch this item link (listings), 76
Watching section (My eBay), 38-40
websites, businesses, creating, 373
Western Union, 20, 28
white balance, photographs, 202-203
wholesale product sourcing, 169, 367-368
    drop-shipping, 368-369
    merchandise marts, 369-370
    trade shows, 369-370
winning bids, sellers, contacting, 121-124
withdrawal limits, PayPal accounts, remov-
    ing, 161
Won section (My eBay), 41-44
Workshops, 34
WorldWide Brands, 169
wristwatches, photographing, 205
writing
    descriptions, 239-248
        benefits, 244-247
        features, 244-247
        HTML editor, 241-242
        Listing Designer, 247-248
    subtitles, 231-232
    titles, 225-230
        misspellings, 229-230

yard sales, items, selling, 171-172

zooming, cameras, 203-204